Studies in Regional and Local History

General Editor Nigel Goose

Cambridge and its economic region, 1450–1560

John S. Lee

University of Hertfordshire Press
Studies in Regional and Local History

Volume 3

First published in Great Britain in 2005 by
University of Hertfordshire Press
Learning and Information Services
University of Hertfordshire
College Lane
Hatfield
Hertfordshire AL10 9AB

The right of John S. Lee to be identified as author of this work has been asserted by him in accordance with the Copyright, Designs and Patents Act 1988.

© Copyright John S. Lee 2005

All rights reserved. No part of this book may be reproduced or utilised in any form or by any means, electronic or mechanical, including photocopying, recording or by any information storage and retrieval system, without permission in writing from the author.

British Library Cataloguing in Publication Data
A catalogue record for this book is available from the British Library

ISBN 1-902806-47-6 hardback
ISBN 1-902806-52-2 paperback

Design by Geoff Green Book Design, CB4 5RA
Cover design by John Robertshaw, AL5 2JB
Printed in Great Britain by Antony Rowe Ltd, SN14 6LH

For my Mother and in memory of my Father

Publication grants

Publication has been made possible by generous grants from the Marc Fitch Fund
and the Scouloudi Foundation in association with
the Institute of Historical Research, University of London.

Contents

List of figures	ix
List of tables	xi
General Editor's preface	xiii
Acknowledgements	xvi
Abbreviations	xvii

1 Introduction — 1
- Medieval English towns — 1
- Modelling urban regions — 2
- Medieval towns and their regions — 4
- The role of towns within transition and modernisation — 8
- The significance of the fifteenth and sixteenth centuries — 11
- The pattern of economic change, 1450–1560 — 13
- The debate over urban fortunes — 17
- Cambridge in the fifteenth and sixteenth centuries — 18
- Historiography and sources — 20

2 Population and wealth — 24
- Using sources to identify changes in population and wealth — 25
- Population of Cambridge — 28
- Comparing urban centres — 30
- Comparing counties — 35
- Comparing sub-regions and parishes — 36
- Additional evidence of areas of contracting population and wealth — 42
- Distributions of taxable wealth — 44
- Fertility and mortality — 46
- Conclusion — 50

3 Cambridge and its society — 52
- Occupational structure — 55
- Burgesses — 58
- University — 63
- Privileged persons — 67
- Parish churches and guilds — 69
- Religious houses — 72
- Aliens — 76
- Disputes — 81
- Conclusion — 83

4 Markets and trade — 85
- Grants of markets in the Cambridge region — 86
- Cambridge market — 89

	Rural marketing in Linton, Foxton and Whittlesford	93
	Debt cases in local courts	98
	Debt cases in London courts	100
	Regional trade: malt barley and saffron	103
	Conclusion	112
5	**Fairs**	**114**
	Late medieval fairs	114
	Fairs of Cambridge and its region	116
	Traders	120
	Consumers	130
	Regulation and ownership of the fairs	137
	Conclusion	139
6	**College consumption**	**142**
	Demand for goods and services	143
	Food and fuel supplies	152
	Suppliers of corn and fuel	162
	Wheat prices and shortages	165
	Conclusion	172
7	**Property and building projects**	**174**
	Urban land market	174
	Building projects	182
	Building materials	186
	Building craftsmen	190
	Wage rates	195
	Conclusion	198
8	**Conclusion**	**199**
	Bibliography	205
	Index	226

Figures

1.1	Conceptual model of Cambridge and its region	7
2.1	Cambridgeshire, from Christopher Saxton's map of 1576 (Cambridgeshire Collection)	36
2.2	Cambridgeshire parishes grouped by sub-region	37
2.3	Changes in the ranking of parishes by wealth, 1334–1524	40
2.4	Changes in the ranking of parishes by number of taxpayers, 1377–1524	41
3.1	Richard Lyne's map of Cambridge, 1574 (Cambridgeshire Collection)	53
3.2	Central section of John Hamond's map of Cambridge, 1592 (Cambridgeshire Collection)	54
3.3	Sketch of Cambridge market place, mid-fifteenth century (by permission of the Master and Fellows of Corpus Christi College, Cambridge)	57
3.4	Arms and statue of Lady Margaret Beaufort on the great gate of Christ's College	64
3.5	Memorial brass of Richard de Billingford, D.D., Master of Corpus Christi College, 1398–1432	70
3.6	Jesus College from David Loggan's *Cantabrigia Illustrata* of 1690 (Cambridgeshire Collection)	73
4.1	Markets of Cambridge and its region	87
4.2	Inspection of weights and measures, c.1587 (U.A. Hare A.1, fol. 276v: by permission of the Syndics of Cambridge University Library)	90
4.3	Linton guildhall (Cambridgeshire Collection)	93
4.4	Cambridge town pleas, 1389–90	99
4.5	Saffron cultivation in Cambridgeshire parishes	107
4.6a	Saffron crocus in the church of St Mary the Virgin, Saffron Walden (Saffron Walden Museum)	110
4.6b	Saffron "walled-in" from the borough seal of 1549 (Saffron Walden Museum)	111
4.7	Detail from Henry VIII's charter of 1514 to establish the guild of Holy Trinity, Saffron Walden (by permission of Saffron Walden Town Council; with thanks to Saffron Walden Museum)	112
5.1	Stourbridge Chapel, Newmarket Road, Cambridge	118
5.2	Plan of Stourbridge Fair, 1725, showing the 'streets' or rows of booths (Nichols, *History*, p. 71: by permission of the County Record Office, Cambridge)	120
5.3	Transfers of booths in Stourbridge Fair held by Cambridge burgesses	122
5.4	Income from treasurers' booths in Stourbridge Fair (adjusted for inflation)	123
5.5	Indenture for the lease of a booth at Stourbridge Fair, 1550 (CCA, III/10A, part 1: by permission of the County Record Office, Cambridge)	126
6.1	Trinity College, Great Court	146
6.2	Corpus Christi College, Old Court	147
6.3	King's Hall suppliers, 1451–1500	156
6.4	King's Hall suppliers, 1501–44	157

6.5	King's College purchases, 1450–80	158
6.6	King's College purchases, 1545–58	159
6.7	Trinity College fuel supplies, 1547–63	160
6.8	King's Hall wheat prices, 1450–1544	164
6.9	Average of King's Hall wheat prices, 1450–1544	165
7.1	Cambridge borough treasurers' accounts of 1488/9, showing list of property rents (CCA, X/71/5: by permission of the County Record Office, Cambridge)	177
7.2	Cambridge Corporation's property income	178
7.3	Decays of rent from Cambridge Corporation's property	179
7.4	King's College Chapel, looking south-west	183
7.5	Queens' College gatehouse, looking east	188
7.6	Bond sealed by carpenters of Cressing, Essex for the mayor and bailiffs of Cambridge, 1509 (CCA, VI/4: by permission of the County Record Office, Cambridge)	191
7.7	Craftsmen employed building King's College Chapel (*RCHMC*, p. 102: Crown copyright, National Monuments Record)	195

Tables

2.1	Estimates of the town and university populations, 1377–1587	29
2.2	Taxpaying populations of major towns and regional centres within 50 miles of Cambridge, 1377 and 1524–5	31
2.3	Taxable wealth of major towns and regional centres within 50 miles of Cambridge, 1334 and 1524–5	32
2.4	Taxable wealth of small towns around Cambridge, 1334 and 1524–5	33
2.5	Comparative county lay wealth in £,000 per acre, 1334 and 1515	35
2.6	Taxable wealth per acre, by sub-region	38
2.7	Taxpayers per acre, by sub-region	39
2.8	Distribution of taxpayers by wealth in Cambridge, 1524–5	44
2.9	Contributors to 1522 loan, by sub-region	45
2.10	Distribution of taxpayers by wealth in Cambridgeshire sub-regions, 1524	45
2.11	Net surplus or deficit in baptisms compared to burials in Cambridge parishes, 1540–70	47
2.12	Net surplus or deficit in baptisms compared to burials in Cambridgeshire sub-regions, 1540–70	48
3.1	Occupations recorded in wills in Cambridge, 1500–79	56
3.2	Burgesses admitted to freedom of Cambridge, 1422/3–1560	61
3.3	Geographical origins of known scholars of the University of Cambridge during the fifteenth century	65
3.4	Nationalities of aliens in Cambridgeshire, 1440	77
3.5	Occupations of aliens in Cambridge, 1440	78
3.6	Occupations of aliens in Cambridgeshire, 1463	79
4.1	Bakers, brewers and butchers amerced at Foxton, Linton and Whittlesford	94
4.2	Most common residence of creditors, by county, making loans to Cambridgeshire men, 1450–1509	101
4.3	Most common residence of Cambridgeshire debtors, 1450–1509	101
5.1	Dates of fairs of Cambridge and its region	117
6.1	Wealth and size of Cambridge colleges, 1546	144
6.2	King's College wheat prices, 1536–62	167
6.3	Cambridge wheat and barley prices, 1556–7	168
6.4	Wheat supplied to King's College in corn rents and other purchases, 1557–62	171
7.1	Property income of the Cambridge colleges, 1546	175
7.2	Cambridge rents of Corpus Christi College, 1536/7–1551	180
7.3	Distribution of reductions by parish in the Cambridge rents of Corpus Christi College, 1536/7–1551	181
7.4	College building projects, 1450–1560	184
7.5	Cambridge wage rates (accounts of Cambridge Corporation and churchwardens of Holy Trinity)	197

Studies in Regional and Local History

General Editor's preface

'Regional history', 'local history' or 'community history'? While this is not an appropriate place to enter the ongoing discussion about the similarities and differences between these approaches to historical study, it is perhaps worth taking notice of their existence, and in particular of the arguments that are being offered for a genre called 'community history' that is 'to some degree at least' different from local history more generally.[1] For the very fact that these debates are taking place testifies clearly to the vitality of the approach that privileges place as the appropriate focus for historical enquiry, whether that place be described as a community, a local society or is simply defined by its administrative boundaries. Of course place and community are not necessarily coterminous, even if a close relationship between the two might commonly exist: physical juxtaposition is ever likely to lead to the structures, associations, antagonisms, normative values and rhetoric that shape and define something that we might identify as a community. For practical purposes, moreover, the perspective of the local historian, although fully aware of the fact that parish or borough boundaries may have only limited significance, will inevitably be shaped to some degree by the nature of the historical documentation that survives, determined as it so often is by the administrative structures of the past – parish, borough, county, archdeaconry, and so forth. But this does not mean that the local historian's hands are tied, for it is perfectly possible to peer over the fence, and even distinctly local records often make it possible to do so. No historian who has worked on towns, from the medieval period into the nineteenth century, will be unaware of how towns shaded into the countryside, how distinctly agrarian pursuits could take place within borough boundaries, how inter-connected a town could be with its hinterland – economically, demographically and socially – and it is often borough documentation that reveals these relationships. But while many urban studies recognise these realities, and some even make an attempt to delineate various aspects of what is often called the 'urban region', few have taken these inter-connections as their primary focus. Herein lies the novelty of the third volume in the series *Studies in Regional and Local History*.

Cambridge and its economic region, 1450–1560, which arises from the author's Cambridge University PhD dissertation, takes advantage of documentation generated by the city's two primary communities – borough and university – to explore its economic development and regional impact during a key period of economic and demographic transition. In 1450 England was characterised by demographic depression, recession in trade, industry and agriculture, monetary scarcity and labour

---

1   D. Mills, 'Defining community: a critical review of "community" in *Family and Community History*', *Family and Community History*, 7 (2004), 5–12; B. Deacon and M. Donald, 'In search of community history', *Family and Community History*, 7 (2004), 13–18. For a particularly interesting discussion see P. Withington and A. Shepard, 'Introduction: communities in early modern England', in A. Shepard and P. Withington, eds., *Communities in early modern England* (Manchester, 2000), pp. 1–15.

shortage; by 1560 population was growing strongly, prices and rents were rising, exports had risen to new heights, internal trade was increasing to the benefit of towns large and small and the agricultural sector was entering a new period of prosperity – a prosperity shared by large landowners and yeoman farmers alike.[2] The particular fortunes of English provincial towns during these years are also of interest and have been subject to particular debate, most scholars now accepting that towns generally shared the economic depression of the fifteenth century, but some arguing that these difficulties continued deep into the sixteenth century while others detect clear signs of demographic and economic recovery, if somewhat faltering, from the early sixteenth century forwards.[3] The period encompassed by this study, therefore, forms a key period of economic transition and has given rise to significant historical debate. Cambridge was not a leading provincial town across these years, but was prominent amongst that group that has been characterised as towns of the 'second rank', or as the 'middle tier' of the English urban hierarchy.[4] Analysis of the Exchequer Lay Subsidies of 1524–5 suggests that it stood in fifteenth place in the urban rankings in terms of the size of its taxpaying population (London included), and in thirtieth position in terms of its taxable wealth.[5] It was, of course, different from all other English provincial towns with the exception of Oxford, for the presence of the university had particular significance for both its internal economy and for the manner in which it interacted with its hinterland, both near and far. But the town was far from being a mere appendage to the colleges, for it also constituted a centre of internal trade (and an inland port) of some significance, epitomised by the manner in which Stourbridge Fair, already with its designated 'streets' specialising in particular commodities in the early sixteenth century, was able to attract merchants and tradesmen from considerable distances.

This study presents a sophisticated analysis of the economy and society of Cambridge in this period, elucidating the ways in which Cambridge might be seen as representing a particular type of town as well as highlighting the respects in which it was exceptional or different. Using a rich and varied range of sources, John Lee examines the town's population and wealth, the various components of its society, its markets, trade and fairs, the impact of college consumption, the urban land market and its physical development. In doing so he sheds new light upon the town as an

---

2   J. Hatcher, 'The great slump of the mid-fifteenth century', in R. Britnell and J. Hatcher, eds., *Progress and problems in medieval England: essays in honour of Edward Miller* (Cambridge, 1996); K. Wrightson, *Earthly necessities: economic lives in early modern Britain* (New Haven and London, 2000), pp. 115–45.

3   C. Phythian-Adams, 'Urban decay in late medieval England', in P. Abrams and E.A. Wrigley, eds., *Towns in societies* (Cambridge, 1978), pp. 159–69; A. Dyer, 'Growth and decay in English towns 1500-1700', *Urban History Yearbook 1979*, 60–72; N.R. Goose, 'In search of the urban variable: towns and the English economy, 1500–1650, *Economic History Review*, 2nd ser., 39 (1986), 165–85.

4   P. Clark and P. Slack, 'Introduction', to Clark and Slack, eds., *Crisis and order in English towns 1500–1700* (London, 1972), pp. 4–5.

5   N. Goose, 'Economic and social aspects of provincial towns: a comparative study of Cambridge, Colchester and Reading, c. 1500–1700' (unpublished PhD thesis, University of Cambridge, 1984), tables 1.1 and 1.2, pp. 35, 37.

economic entity, as a community (or a collection of overlapping communities), and as a component of a wider economic framework that is characterised in terms of inter-related spatial areas. This study, therefore, makes a significant contribution to our understanding of the role that the middle tier of the urban hierarchy played in the wider economy during a key period of economic transition, as well as enriching our understanding of the city in its own right.

Nigel Goose
University of Hertfordshire
March 2005

Acknowledgements

This book is based on my PhD thesis and I am very grateful to my supervisor, Professor John Hatcher, for patiently supervising my research and for his continuing support and expertise. My examiners, Professors Barrie Dobson and Richard Britnell, have also offered a great deal of advice and encouragement. During my time at the University of Cambridge I was privileged to be funded by the Economic and Social Research Council, and to be accommodated by Corpus Christi College with fellow postgraduates in the beautiful surroundings of Leckhampton House.

I have relied on a number of archivists, librarians and staff to guide me through their collections. I would particularly like to thank Dr Philip Saunders, Sue Neville, and Gill Shapland at Cambridge County Record Office; Chris Jakes, Cambridgeshire Collection; Jacky Cox, Cambridge University Library; Gill Cannell and Catherine Hall, Corpus Christi College; Andrew Johnson, Downing College; Dr Rosalind Moad, King's College; Dr Roger Lovatt, Peterhouse; Malcolm Underwood, St John's College, and Jonathan Smith, Trinity College.

Many historians have kindly provided opportunities for me to share aspects of this work at seminars, and I have been particularly fortunate to be able to discuss ideas with Drs James Davis, Martin Heale and Chris Briggs and many others. Dr Mark Bailey gave many useful suggestions in the early stages of my research, and Drs Tessa Webber, Stephen Alford and Neil Wright provided helpful classes in palaeography and Latin. I am also grateful for the ideas and questions that I received while teaching a course on Late Medieval and Tudor Cambridge for the University's Board of Continuing Education.

Several members of the Department of History at the University of Durham first stimulated my interest in medieval and economic history while an undergraduate at St John's College. More recently, the Centre for Medieval Studies at the University of York has kindly provided the opportunity for me to retain my links as a Research Associate, while pursuing a career outside higher education.

I am very grateful to Professor Nigel Goose for his detailed advice in preparing the thesis for publication, and for permission to quote freely from his unpublished thesis, also to Bill Forster, Jane Housham, and Kerry Gilliland at the University of Hertfordshire Press. The Marc Fitch Fund and the Scouloudi Foundation in association with the Institute of Historical Research have assisted towards the costs of publication.

Lastly, but by no means least, thanks to my mother and brother for all their support.

Abbreviations

Annals	*Annals of Cambridge*, ed. C.H. Cooper, 5 vols. (Cambridge, 1842–1908)
BARSEH	British Academy, Records of Social and Economic History
CASLMS	Cambridge Antiquarian Society Luard Memorial Series
CASOS	Cambridge Antiquarian Society Octavo Series
CBD	*Cambridge Borough Documents*, ed. W.M. Palmer (Cambridge, 1931)
CCA	Cambridge Corporation Archives, Cambridge County Record Office
CCC	Corpus Christi College, Cambridge
CCR	*Calendar of Close Rolls*, HMSO, 46 vols. (London, 1892–1963)
CCRO	Cambridge County Record Office
CCTA	Downing College Cambridge, Bowtell MS 1–2, 'Liber Rationalis', Cambridge Corporation Treasurers' accounts, vol. i, 1515/16–1560/1, vol. ii, 1561/2–1588/9
Charters	*Charters of the borough of Cambridge*, ed. F.W. Maitland and M. Bateson (Cambridge, 1901)
Collection	*A collection of charters, letters and other documents from the MS library of Corpus Christi College*, ed. J. Lamb (London, 1838)
CPR	*Calendar of Patent Rolls*, HMSO, 54 vols. (London, 1891–1916)
CUHB	*The Cambridge Urban History of Britain*, i: *600–1540*, ed. D.M. Palliser, and ii: *1540–1840*, ed. P. Clark (Cambridge, 2000)
Documents	*Documents relating to the university and colleges of Cambridge*, HMSO, 3 vols. (London, 1852)
EcHR	*Economic History Review*
KC	King's College, Cambridge
KCMB	King's College, Mundum Books (where the books are foliated, references are given to folios, otherwise to the relevant year's account)
KH a/c	Trinity College, Cambridge, King's Hall accounts
LP	*Letters and papers, foreign and domestic, of the reign of Henry VIII*, ed. J.S. Brewer, J. Gairdner and R.H. Brodie, 23 vols. (London, 2nd edn., 1862–1932)
OED	*The Oxford English Dictionary*, 20 vols. (Oxford, 2nd edn., 1989)
PCAS	*Proceedings of the Cambridge Antiquarian Society*
PL	*Paston letters and papers of the fifteenth century*, ed. N. Davis, 2 vols. (Oxford, 1971)
QC	Queens' College archives, Cambridge University Library
RCHMC	Royal Commission on Historical Monuments, *An inventory of the historical monuments in the city of Cambridge,* 2 vols. (London, 1959)
RCHMNE	Royal Commission on Historical Monuments, *An inventory of the historical monuments in the county of Cambridge*, ii: *North-East Cambridgeshire* (London, 1972)
RCHMW	Royal Commission on Historical Monuments, *An inventory of the historical monuments in the county of Cambridge*, i: *West Cambridgeshire* (London, 1968)
St Radegund	*The priory of St Radegund Cambridge*, ed. A. Gray, CASOS, XXXI (Cambridge, 1898)
SJC	St John's College, Cambridge

SR	*Statutes of the Realm (1101–1713)*, Record Commission, 11 vols. (London, 1808–28)
TCJB a/c	Trinity College, Junior Bursars' accounts, i, 1550/1–1563/4
TCSB a/c	Trinity College, Senior Bursars' accounts, i, 1547/8–1563/4
Thetford	*The register of Thetford Priory*, ed. D. Dymond, BARSEH, new ser., XXIV–XXV (Oxford, 1995)
UA	University Archives, Cambridge University Library
VCH	*The Victoria history of the counties of England* (London, 1900 – in progress)
VCH Cambs.	*The Victoria history of Cambridgeshire,* 10 vols. (London, 1938–2002)

Chapter 1

Introduction

This study of the economy and society of Cambridge and its region between 1450 and 1560 has two main objectives. Firstly, it examines the relationship between a medieval town and its hinterland, by analysing aspects of the population, wealth, society, markets, trade and workforce of Cambridge and its region. Secondly, it explores the nature and extent of any changes that took place in these links between Cambridge and its region. The fifteenth and sixteenth centuries have traditionally been seen as a time of economic and social transition, while urban historians have debated whether English towns faced decay and crisis in this period, and the surviving sources permit a detailed examination of the Cambridge region over the 1450–1560 period.

Medieval English towns

Historians have often found difficulty in defining exactly what constituted a town in medieval England. English towns were small by both modern standards, and in comparison with those of medieval Flanders or the Italian peninsula. Many urban settlements in England had developed as boroughs where land was held by burgage tenure, with tenants who paid fixed rents, possessed the freedom to sell or bequeath their plots at will, and were able to participate in the privileges and responsibilities of the town. The members of some boroughs corporately received grants of customs and liberties, bestowing varying degrees of independent jurisdiction and trading privileges. Although many of these chartered boroughs formed the core of the urban sector, they were not completely synonymous with medieval towns. Many large and thriving industrial centres never obtained these privileges, while some boroughs never developed far beyond their agricultural base. The definition of a town adopted here is that of a dense and permanent concentration of people engaged in a variety of activities, many of which were not agricultural.[1] Cambridge was a borough by the time of the Domesday Book and developed a range of administrative, financial and judicial privileges during the twelfth and thirteenth centuries. Evidence of a variety of non-agricultural occupations is found among its inhabitants, and from the evidence of street-names like the Butchery and Cordwainer Row.[2]

By 1300 an urban network had developed in England, stretching from the capital, through major cities and provincial centres, to small market towns: a network which still forms the core of the marketing and urban structure today. This urban growth reflected the high degree of market orientation that had developed in English society

---

1   R. Holt and G. Rosser, 'Introduction: the English town in the Middle Ages', in R. Holt and G. Rosser, eds., *The medieval town: a reader in English urban history 1200–1540* (Harlow, 1990), pp. 1–4.

2   VCH Cambs., iii, pp. 31–3, 89–90; P.H. Reaney, ed., *The place-names of Cambridgeshire and the Isle of Ely*, English Place-Name Soc., XIX (Cambridge, 1943), pp. 44–50.

during the twelfth and thirteenth centuries, with substantial levels of market production and commercial activity, although often small-scale, among all social groups. This was aided by the growth of population, the foundation of new towns and the expansion of existing centres, the proliferation of new markets and fairs, the growth of market-dependent occupations, the development of record-keeping and official routine, and the increasingly sophisticated pattern of trade.[3]

Many areas lost about half their inhabitants during the Black Death of 1348–9, and never regained their former size during the medieval period. Despite the drastic reduction in population in most towns, the urban system that had been created by 1300 remained largely intact. Indeed there was no significant reduction in the importance of market transactions in the wider economy, as between 1300 and 1500 the currency in circulation per head increased, and there was a growth in regional specialisation, particularly in agriculture.[4] Around 1500, the towns of England could be classified into four main groups, on the basis of their size. London, with a population of around 60,000, stood apart by virtue of its size and range of functions. Major towns and cities, such as Norwich, Bristol and York followed, with populations of 5,000 to 10,000. Cambridge was one of the second rank of regional centres, whose towns contained between 1,500 and 5,000 inhabitants. Finally, there were several hundred small towns, with populations of between 500 and 1,500, that served as local market centres. While many urban centres had smaller populations at the beginning of the sixteenth century than two centuries before, the composition of the four groups had not remained static, with some towns growing in relative size and wealth, and others contracting.[5] These changes in the relative fortunes of different towns during the later middle ages have formed the basis of a long-running debate among urban historians, outlined below. Chapter 2 examines how the population and wealth of Cambridge and its region changed over the period, both in absolute terms and in relation to other parts of the country.

Modelling urban regions

Geographers often rank towns into urban hierarchies, according to population size and wealth, assuming that larger and wealthier towns support wider ranges of goods, services and administrative functions than smaller urban centres, and will therefore serve larger areas. The English urban system around 1500 formed such a hierarchy: there was a general relationship between the size of a town and the diversity of its crafts and occupations, although some towns, both large and small, specialised in particular trades.[6] The twenty largest towns, for example, shared a number of characteristics

---

3   R.H. Britnell, *The commercialisation of English society, 1000–1500* (Manchester, 2nd edn., 1996), pp. 79–127.

4   Ibid., pp. 228–34.

5   P.T.H. Unwin, 'Towns and trade 1066–1500', in R.A. Dodgshon and R.A. Butlin, eds., *An historical geography of England and Wales* (London, 2nd edn., 1990), p. 139.

6   W.G. Hoskins, 'English provincial towns in the early sixteenth century', *Trans. of the Royal Hist. Soc.*, 5th ser., 6 (1956), 13; N. Goose, 'English pre-industrial urban economies', in J. Barry, ed., *The Tudor and Stuart town: a reader in English urban history, 1530–1688* (Harlow, 1990), pp. 63–73.

that emphasised their regional importance and internal sophistication, and made them stand apart from smaller centres. These ranged from the possession of trading privileges like Statute Merchant seals to greater levels of educational provision reflected in the presence of schools.[7] Such hierarchies were also apparent on a regional scale. Both documentary and archaeological evidence has been used to construct a regional hierarchy of urban centres in the East Midlands during the later middle ages. Even among the small towns and industrial villages of sixteenth-century Suffolk, there was a distinct correlation between population size and the diversity of occupations.[8]

Every town has an area over which it provides markets, employment and professional services, and over which the area serves the town, by providing food, raw materials and labour. Urban centres act like magnets, both attracting and repelling people and institutions, and the fields of these spatial forces are described interchangeably as their hinterlands, regions, spheres of influence, catchment areas or urban fields. The range and complexity of functions that constitute an urban hinterland make its extent difficult to measure. In an attempt to do this, geographers studying modern towns usually select a number of indices which reflect both the town's level of specialisation and its various functions as a centre of marketing, employment, and administration. Measurements might include the delivery area of shops, the distance of journeys to work, the availability of public transport, and the circulation area of newspapers.[9] However, when mapped, these boundaries usually vary, and in part this reflects the different levels of specialisation for different functions within the same town.[10]

Geographers have also devised theoretical models to describe and measure urban hinterlands. Christaller proposed that larger towns, with their wider fields of influence, encompass the fields of neighbouring smaller towns, for which the larger centres provide more specialised functions. His central place theory modelled different spatial layouts of settlements and their regions on an idealised landscape where marketing, transportation, or administration, was the dominant factor.[11] The ring of smaller market towns around the larger marketing centre of Cambridge in the 1970s was described as 'an almost perfect example of central place theory'.[12] Applying the premises of central place theory to medieval England, Masschaele has proposed that by 1300, rural markets were integrated into regional systems that supplied the fifty

---

7   J. Kermode, 'The greater towns 1300–1540', in *CUHB*, i, pp. 442–5.

8   J. Laughton, E. Jones and C. Dyer, 'The urban hierarchy in the later middle ages: a study of the East Midlands', *Urban History*, 28 (2001), 331–57; J. Patten, 'Village and town: an occupational study', *Agricultural History Review*, 20 (1972), 1–16.

9   For an example pertaining to Cambridge, see R. Hamid, 'A service centre hierarchy in Cambridgeshire' (unpublished dissertation, Department of Geography, University of Durham, 1965).

10 R. Knowles and J. Wareing, *Economic and social geography made simple* (London, 4th edn., 1981), pp. 249–50; A. Smailes, *The geography of towns* (London, 1953), pp. 129–49; R.E. Dickinson, *City and region: a geographical interpretation* (London, 1964), p. 19.

11 W. Christaller, *Central places in southern Germany*, trans. C.W. Baskin (Englewood Cliffs, N.J., 1966); Dickinson, *City*, pp. 51–67.

12 J.P. Lewis, *A study of the Cambridge sub-region* (London, 1974), part 1, p. 19.

largest towns. Britnell, however, has argued that the primary function of rural markets was to allow local inhabitants to dispose of surplus produce and obtain money to pay seigneurial dues and taxes.[13] As Chapter 4 will show, the rural markets in Cambridgeshire predominantly supplied the needs of local consumers and suppliers, rather than those of larger towns like Cambridge.

Von Thünen modelled the pattern of agriculture around an urban centre, arguing that distance from the market determines the choice of crop and intensity of land use. He postulated that concentric zones of specialised production would develop around a large central market, such as a city. Intensive horticultural crops would be located closest to the city, while at progressively greater distances from the city would lay zones of forestry, intensive and extensive commercial grain production, and stock rearing. Similar zones of specialised agricultural production have been identified around London in 1300: horticultural produce came from city gardens and allotments, firewood from an area of between 10 and 25 miles from the city, and grain from up to 20 miles away when only land transport was available, and about 60 miles if water transport could be used.[14] Yet as Von Thünen acknowledged, local geographical conditions could frequently distort patterns of land use. The shortage of woodland in Cambridgeshire, for example, meant that contrary to Von Thünen's model, firewood and timber were transported to Cambridge over longer distances than grain supplies.[15]

In practice, these models have significant drawbacks. Both Christaller and Von Thünen placed their towns on an isotropic surface: a totally uniform, featureless plain with perfect ease of access to all points and uniform distribution of resources. In reality, the regions of individual towns will be modified by a variety of local geographical factors and may overlap where neighbouring towns compete for trade. Individuals rarely conduct their business in the rational and logical manner that these models suggest, and often possess incomplete information and make distorted evaluations. The precise demarcation of an urban hinterland is rarely possible, and is perhaps best conceived as a series of zones of declining urban influence.[16] While the models assume static conditions, urban hinterlands may change in response to economic and social developments from within or outside their region, as studies of medieval towns can demonstrate.

Medieval towns and their regions

Recent research has begun to illuminate the size of urban regions and the interaction

---

13   J. Masschaele, *Peasants, merchants and markets: inland trade in medieval England, 1150–1350* (Basingstoke, 1997); R.H. Britnell, 'Urban demand in the English economy, 1300–1600', in J.A. Galloway, ed., *Trade, urban hinterlands and market integration, c.1300–1600* (London, 2000), pp. 2–9.

14   P. Hall, ed., *Von Thünen's isolated state* (London, 1966); B.M.S. Campbell, J.A. Galloway, D. Keene and M. Murphy, *A medieval capital and its grain supply: agrarian production and distribution in the London region c.1300*, Historical Geography Research Ser., XXX (London, 1993), pp. 141–4.

15   J.S. Lee, 'Feeding the colleges: Cambridge's food and fuel supplies, 1450–1560', *EcHR*, 56 (2003), 243–64.

16   Knowles and Wareing, *Geography*, pp. 226–30, 252–3.

between towns and their hinterlands in the medieval and early modern periods, and this helps to place the study of Cambridge and its region in a broader context. London, at the apex of the English urban hierarchy, had the largest sphere of influence. Around 1300, when London's population numbered 80,000 or more, the city's demand influenced land use and agricultural development in much of south-east England. London acted as 'an engine of growth' in the late sixteenth century, when its phenomenal expansion stimulated, through the demands of trade and consumption, new methods of production and changes in the wider economy.[17] London was unable to exert the same scale of influence in the later middle ages, as its population fell substantially after 1300 and did not recover to its former size until around 1550. Yet the capital continued to increase its ascendancy over other English towns: in 1334 it was five times as wealthy as the leading provincial town, but by 1524–5 it had become ten times as wealthy. The capital's share of English cloth exports rose from 50 per cent in 1450 to almost 90 per cent by 1550, while London merchants were increasingly dominating many distributive trades.[18] Chapter 4 details the important trading links between London and Cambridge, and how the capital's growing economic ascendancy impacted on the Cambridge region.

The six or seven leading provincial towns and cities of England experienced mixed fortunes over the later middle ages. Some, like York, lost significant amounts of overseas trade to London merchants, and cloth manufacturing to smaller centres of production from the mid-fifteenth century onwards; other centres, like Exeter, benefited from the expansion of cloth production within their town and hinterland, and the growth of fishing and trade at nearby ports over the same period.[19] Of this group, Norwich was the closest centre to Cambridge. The city's population appears to have doubled between 1377 and 1524 to 10,000. The city may have benefited from the production of worsted cloth in north-east Norfolk, while the city's merchants were prominent in local trade along the rivers Yare and Wensum, and overseas trade from Yarmouth.[20] Norwich was also the administrative centre of a diocese that stretched into south-eastern Cambridgeshire. Yet trading links between Cambridge and Norwich were relatively limited, with Cambridge more closely tied to London.

---

17 Campbell et al., *Medieval capital*; F.J. Fisher, 'The development of London as a centre of conspicuous consumption in the sixteenth and seventeenth centuries' and 'London as an "engine of economic growth"' in P.J. Corfield and N.B. Harte, eds., *London and the English economy 1500–1700* (London, 1990), pp. 105–18, 185–98; E.A. Wrigley, 'A simple model of London's importance in changing English society and economy, 1650–1750', in P. Abrams and E.A. Wrigley, eds., *Towns in societies* (Cambridge, 1978), pp. 215–43.

18 D. Keene, 'Medieval London and its region', *London Journal*, 14 (1989), 99–111; E.M. Carus-Wilson and O. Coleman, *England's export trade, 1275–1547* (Oxford, 1963), pp. 97–119.

19 J. N. Bartlett, 'The expansion and decline of York in the later middle ages', *EcHR*, 2nd ser., 12 (1959–60), 17–33; J. Kermode, *Medieval merchants: York, Beverley and Hull in the later middle ages* (Cambridge, 1998), pp. 7–9, 188–9; M. Kowaleski, *Local markets and regional trade in medieval Exeter* (Cambridge, 1995).

20 B. Brodt, 'East Anglia', in *CUHB*, i, pp. 639–56; J. Whittle, *The development of agrarian capitalism: land and labour in Norfolk, 1440–1580* (Oxford, 2000), pp. 247–52; T.R. Adams, 'Aliens, agriculturalists and entrepreneurs: identifying the market-markers in a Norfolk port from the water-bailiffs' accounts, 1400–60', in D.J. Clayton, R.G. Davies and P. McNiven, eds., *Trade, devotion and governance: papers in later medieval history* (Stroud, 1994), pp. 140–57.

Medium-sized towns of similar size to Cambridge seem to have had varying impacts on their hinterlands. Colchester, for example, made little impact on its surrounding region, despite the substantial growth of its cloth industry in the later fourteenth century. Colchester had around 6,000 inhabitants in the 1370s, rising to 8,000 in the 1410s. The stimulus of the Colchester market was too small to prevent depopulation in surrounding villages and a contraction of arable cultivation, although urban development stimulated some demand for barley malt, meat and dairy products.[21] However, Yates found evidence of an urban-rural symbiosis at the smaller cloth-producing town of Newbury, Berkshire, in the late fifteenth century. The 2,600 inhabitants of this town provided investment for mills and chalk pits, a market for produce, and additional employment prospects for residents of the manor of Shaw, less than two miles distant.[22]

Small towns, with populations of up to 1,500 people, acted like larger urban settlements, as centres of exchange for adjoining agricultural regions. Cambridge was surrounded by a belt of around eleven small towns, which are examined in Chapter 2. Smaller towns generally lacked long-distance and large-scale trade, and their residents had to turn to larger market towns for higher-value goods and services. A few small market towns, however, developed specialist products that were distributed beyond their regular hinterland. In the later middle ages, Thaxted knives were distributed by London merchants, and Droitwich salt was sold in Derby,[23] while in the Cambridge region, the cultivation of saffron gave a new identity to the small town of Walden which developed as the centre for this trade.[24]

Cambridge's region, like that of any town, can be variously defined. Figure 1.1 represents diagrammatically the principal links between Cambridge and its region in the later middle ages. For many economic purposes, the town was served by its local region of about 10 to 15 miles in radius, running approximately along the county border, comprising a range of different sub-regions for which Cambridge was a marketing centre. Agriculture predominated along the river valleys and chalk and clay uplands to the south-east and west of Cambridge, with a growing emphasis on barley cultivation and sheep farming.[25] In the Fenland to the north, agriculture was supplemented by the products of the marsh (fish, reeds, birds, and turf), and in the Suffolk Breckland to the east by rabbit breeding, preparation of skins, flint mining and cloth manufacture.[26] Further south-east along the Suffolk/Essex border, a flourishing textile industry developed. By the early sixteenth century, the communities of

---

21 R.H. Britnell, *Growth and decline in Colchester, 1300–1525* (Cambridge, 1986), pp. 95, 141–60.

22 M. Yates, 'Change and continuities in rural society from the later middle ages to the sixteenth century: the contribution of west Berkshire', *EcHR*, 52 (1999), 627–36.

23 C. Dyer, 'Market towns and the countryside in late medieval England', *Canadian Journal of History*, 31 (1996), 17–35.

24 See Chapter 4, below.

25 A more detailed examination of the regions around Cambridge is provided in J.S. Lee, 'Cambridge and its economic region, 1450–1560' (unpublished PhD thesis, University of Cambridge, 2001), pp. 53–9.

26 H.C. Darby, *The medieval Fenland* (Newton Abbot, 2nd edn., 1974), pp. 23–84; M. Bailey, *A marginal economy? East Anglian Breckland in the later Middle Ages* (Cambridge, 1989), pp. 158–86.

Introduction

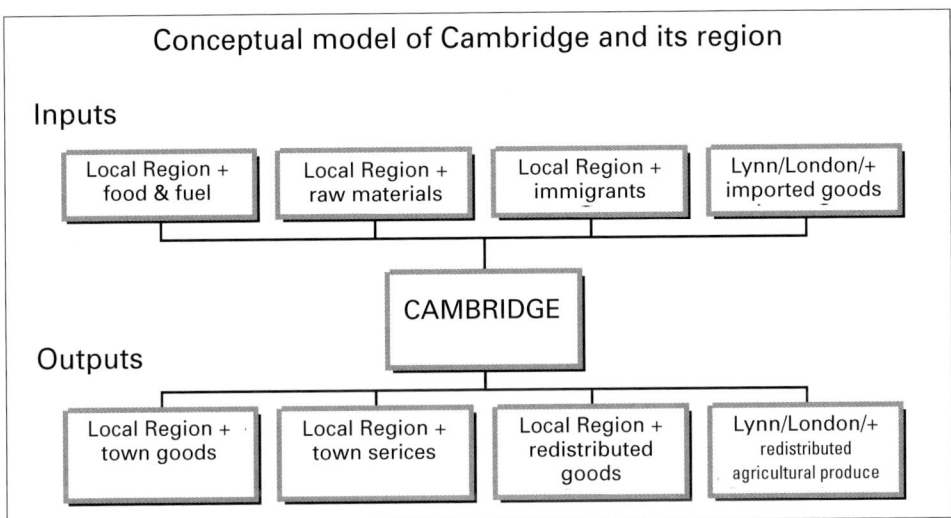

Figure 1.1 Conceptual model of Cambridge and its region

Lavenham, Hadleigh and Long Melford had become as wealthy as many larger towns.[27] Unlike many other towns that have been studied, the economy of Cambridge itself was unusual in not being dominated by cloth-making. It was essentially service-based, supplying the townspeople, surrounding countryside, and the particular demands of the university.

There were four principal flows into the town. Cambridge, like all urban centres, relied on supplies of food and fuel from the surrounding area. As will be shown in subsequent chapters, most food and fuel came from the immediate area of 10 to 15 miles around the town. Only a few items, including salt-water fish, imported spices, and coal, came from greater distances. Raw materials too generally came from the same local region as food and fuel, for processing by various urban industries such as mills, breweries and the leather trades. Some raw materials, though, particularly those used by the various building craftsmen in the town, came from adjoining counties or further afield. The town also drew immigrants, largely from the local region, but some from greater distances. Finally, trade with other urban centres brought goods into the town from other agricultural areas and towns, and from overseas. King's Lynn and London were Cambridge's two most prominent trading partners, although there were also important links with parts of Suffolk and the Midlands.[28]

Outputs from the town can also be grouped into four categories. They included goods produced from raw materials by the town's crafts and industries, and a range of administrative, legal and religious services provided by the town's inhabitants. With the exception of the university, none of the town's goods or services appear to have enjoyed a national or international reputation in this period, and most were supplied to

---

27 A. Dyer, *Decline and growth in English towns 1400–1640* (Cambridge, 2nd edn., 1995), pp. 62–3.
28 J.S. Lee, 'The trade of fifteenth-century Cambridge and its region', in M. Hicks, ed., *The fifteenth century*, ii: *Revolution and consumption in late medieval England* (Woodbridge, 2001), pp. 127–39.

customers within the local region. Cambridge, like most towns, also acted as an entrepôt. Some of the goods brought from Lynn, London, and elsewhere to Cambridge, were redistributed to traders and customers in the locality. Agricultural produce from the surrounding region was collected, marketed and distributed through the town's markets and fairs and by the town's merchants to other centres of demand, particularly to London.

The university enlarged the spatial impact of these processes. The colleges required foodstuffs, fuel, and a wide range of basic and luxury goods. The building projects of the colleges necessitated large quantities of materials and highly skilled craftsmen that could not be obtained in the immediate area. Scholars migrated to the university from across the country, and some from overseas. The specialist academic trades that developed to serve the university, as well as the catchment area of the university, meant that Cambridge's region for services was more extensive than that of other towns of comparable size. The university grew significantly during the fifteenth and sixteenth centuries creating new demand for the town and its hinterland.

The role of towns within transition and modernisation

While geographers use concepts of urban hierarchy and urban hinterlands, and models of central place and land use around an urban centre, historians have also devised theories in which towns influence and respond to wider economic developments. Towns have been characterised as alien to feudal society, playing an active role in the transformation into a capitalist economy. Alternatively, towns have been viewed as an integral part of the feudal system, playing no significant role in its demise. Towns have also been perceived as agents of modernisation, bringing the benefits of their specialisation and concentrated demand to the wider economy.

The majority of the medieval population was socially and legally subordinated to a lordly class through the feudal system. Some historians have portrayed towns as standing apart from this system, as 'non-feudal islands in feudal seas',[29] and even acting as a solvent on the bonds of feudal society. The dynamism of the town has been contrasted with the inertia of peasant society in the countryside, characterised by production for subsistence and limited development.[30] For Pirenne, the development of towns and trade released western Europe from 'the traditional immobility' of a social organisation based solely on 'the relations of man to the soil'. Peasants could now profit by marketing their surpluses, and were encouraged to increase their production. Towns caused the breakdown of serfdom and introduced a new social order – the middle class.[31] Sweezy similarly argued that feudalism, founded on a 'system of production for use', was debilitated by the expansion of commerce and towns, based on a 'system of production for exchange'. Towns and

---

29 M.M. Postan, 'The trade of medieval Europe: the North', in M.M. Postan and E. Miller, eds., *Cambridge economic history of Europe* (Cambridge, 2nd edn., 1987), p. 221, quoted in *CUHB*, i, p. 743.

30 J. Langton and G. Hoppe, *Town and country in the development of early modern western Europe*, Historical Geography Research Ser., XI (Norwich, 1983), pp. 4–16.

31 H. Pirenne, *Medieval cities: their origins and the revival of trade* (Princeton, N.J., 1952), pp. 101–3, 213–34.

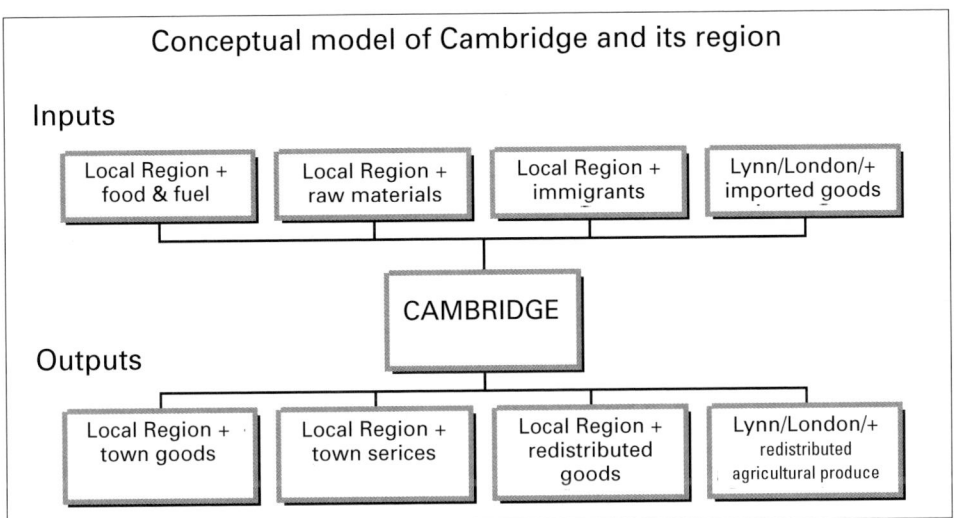

trade offered attractive new goods to lords, but the inefficiency of the manorial system and the unsuitability of its production for sale could not provide the revenue to meet the lords' growing consumption demands. So lords were encouraged to innovate by dismantling the manorial and servile system and develop new types of productive relations, leading to more rationalised specialisation and the division of labour.[32]

An alternative explanation, however, would claim that towns were an integral part of the feudal system rather than inimical to it, and towns could not, therefore, have brought about the collapse of this system. For Brenner, building heavily on the work of Dobb, the primary factors in the decline of serfdom were property relations and class struggle, and the key changes occurred in the countryside rather than within the town. The decline of serfdom was attributed to the imbalance within medieval society, centred on the heavy surplus extracted by lords from the peasantry. The expansion of towns and trade merely increased the consumption demands of the ruling classes, which were met, not through dismantling the productive system, but by pushing it to its limits, as lords made increasing exactions from their peasants. By the fourteenth century, the pressures inherent in the feudal system had led to the intensification of class conflict, resulting in the decline of serfdom, and preparing the way in England for the development of agrarian capitalism.[33]

Hilton also saw towns not as a development alien to feudalism, but as 'one of its essential constitutive components', and pointed to the considerable number of market towns founded by lords, the large amount of urban property owned by the nobility, and the extensive urban rights held by ecclesiastical institutions, which provided a strong feudal presence in medieval towns.[34] Feudal ties were particularly pronounced in the Anglo-Norman boroughs created in northern England, Scotland, Wales and Ireland. These boroughs were founded by the crown and lay and ecclesiastical magnates as a means of extending their control, increasing their revenue through profits of trade and rent, and providing markets where peasant produce could be exchanged for cash to pay seigneurial rents and dues.[35]

Other writers have looked at the role of towns not within the transition from feudalism to capitalism, but as agents of modernisation. The eighteenth-century political economist Adam Smith outlined the benefits of the specialisation of production and the growing division of labour through which specialised producers, like his famous pin-makers, become more dextrous in performing their tasks, reducing

---

32 P. Sweezy, 'A critique', in R. Hilton, ed., *The transition from feudalism to capitalism* (London, 1976), pp. 33–56.

33 M. Dobb, *Studies in the development of capitalism* (London, 1946), pp. 33–122; R. Brenner, 'Agrarian class structure and economic development in pre-industrial Europe', and 'Agrarian roots of European capitalism', in T.H. Aston and C.H.E. Philpin, eds., *The Brenner debate: agrarian class structure and economic development in pre-industrial Europe* (Cambridge, 1985), pp. 10–63, 213–328.

34 R.H. Hilton, *English and French towns in feudal society: a comparative study* (Cambridge, 1992), p. 18; R.H. Hilton, 'Towns in English medieval society', in Holt and Rosser, eds., *Medieval town*, pp. 19–28.

35 H. Swanson, *Medieval British towns* (Basingstoke, 1999), pp. 11–14; R.H. Britnell, *Britain and Ireland 1050–1530: economy and society* (Oxford, 2004), pp. 138–49.

the times taken to complete them. Towns provide groups of specialists, which are more attractive to consumers and more convenient to suppliers than if the same specialists are dispersed throughout the countryside. The gains to both town and country are reciprocal. The country supplies the town with food and raw materials, and the town sends part of its manufactured produce back to the country.[36]

Building on the benefits of specialisation, division of labour and concentrated demand in urban centres, Wrigley has outlined how early modern towns, by providing a substantial and dependable market, and acting as a focus for the transport network, encouraged the specialisation of production in the countryside. The 'Feeding the City' project has shown that London was generating this sort of impact by 1300.[37] Farmers in regions surrounding the largest urban centres of London and Norwich specialised in the production of particular crops and livestock. Under the stimulus of this urban demand, certain estates in Norfolk and Sussex achieved high and constant yields by using large amounts of labour. Campbell and Grantham argue that urbanisation can act as a forcing-house, generating technological improvements and innovations denied to other areas lying beyond the hinterland of major markets.[38]

Townspeople depended on the countryside for food and raw materials, but country dwellers only required towns for some services, being otherwise largely self-sufficient. So towns needed to stimulate rural interest in urban products to create an exchange of goods and generate growth.[39] Many urban centres, therefore, had a distinctive role in consumer behaviour: they were the places where new ideas were first introduced, and urban life and culture focused on display. Probate inventories of the late sixteenth and early seventeenth centuries show that decorative goods were commonly found first in towns, before appearing in the countryside. Towns were centres from which ideas and fashions were diffused. Medieval London redistributed ideas and innovations from outside the city, and imposed a uniformity of style.[40]

Towns, as centres of concentrated demand, also played a significant role in shaping the transport infrastructure of their regions. The larger towns of medieval England lay at nodes on the road network, which consisted of a cluster of routes radiating from major centres such as York, Lincoln, Salisbury, and above all, London.

---

36 A. Smith, *An inquiry into the nature and causes of the wealth of nations*, ed. R.H. Campbell, A.S. Skinner and W.B. Todd, 2 vols. (Oxford, 1976), i, pp. 13–20, 142–5, 376–8, 411; J. Hatcher and M. Bailey, *Modelling the middle ages: the history and theory of England's economic development* (Oxford, 2001), pp. 123–30.

37 E.A. Wrigley, 'Parasite or stimulus: the town in a pre-industrial economy', in Abrams and Wrigley, eds., *Towns in societies*, pp. 295–309; Campbell et al., *Medieval capital*.

38 B.M.S. Campbell and M. Overton, 'A new perspective of medieval and early modern agriculture: six centuries of Norfolk farming c.1250–c.1850', *Past and Present*, 141 (1993), 99–105; G. Grantham, 'Agricultural supply during the industrial revolution: French evidence and European implications', *Journal of Economic History*, 49 (1989), 43–72; G. Grantham, 'Privileged spaces: agricultural productivity and urban provisioning zones in pre-industrial Europe' (English summary), *Annales*, 52 (1997), 729.

39 E.A. Wrigley, 'City and country in the past: a sharp divide or a continuum?', *Historical Research*, 64 (1991), 115–17.

40 L. Weatherill, *Consumer behaviour and material culture in Britain, 1660–1760* (London, 1988); Keene, 'Medieval London', 106.

Residents of towns large and small made frequent bequests for the repair of highways, and built and maintained expensive bridge structures. Towns sited along navigable rivers or the coastline also provided port facilities such as quays, jetties, beacons, cranes and weigh beams, through a combination of individual efforts and civic investment.[41]

Yet the scale of urban demand in the middle ages can easily be overstated. Substantial variations in grain prices between regions show that markets for basic foodstuffs remained local and poorly integrated. Many towns were too small to have a significant impact on agricultural production in their region. The medium-sized town of Colchester did not dominate the supplies of marketed grain even within a radius of 8 to 10 miles. Even within the hinterlands of large towns, many lords used their lands held in demesne – lands that the lord could dispose of as he wished – to supply their own households instead of producing for the market. Without the stimulus of a major urban market, farmers still had the incentive to work their land profitably. This could mean responding to conditions in local markets and changes in prices and yields of different produce. At the demesne manor of Hinderclay in Suffolk in the early fourteenth century, despite lying in a land-locked area outside the range of a major urban market, the farm was managed with a remarkable responsiveness to market prices.[42]

The validity of an urban/rural dichotomy, and the consideration of towns as self-contained units of analysis, can also be questioned. The divide between town and countryside was particularly blurred in medieval England. Local trade and agricultural-based activities dominated many smaller towns, and were apparent even in larger urban centres. Towns had important structural analogies with rural society: the urban workshop was a small, family-run enterprise, like the peasant agricultural holding.[43] There has also been a reaction in sociological work against regarding towns as separate variables, and a move towards examining them within the wider environment. Writers often found that it was not the town itself that created change, but larger systems of social relations, frequently concentrated and intensified within urban areas. It has been suggested that towns should be examined in their historical context rather than as special entities, and that the integrated study of urban and rural change is more clearly illuminated at a regional level.[44]

The significance of the fifteenth and sixteenth centuries

Several of the models outlined above have identified the fifteenth and sixteenth centuries as a transitional phase of economic development, either as part of a movement from feudalism to capitalism or as an era of economic modernisation. Dobb and Sweezy suggested that feudalism was in decline but capitalism had yet to

---

41 Unwin, 'Towns and trade', pp. 144–5; D.F. Harrison, 'Bridges and economic development 1300–1800', *EcHR*, 45 (1992), 245; M. Kowaleski, 'Port towns: England and Wales 1300–1540', in *CUHB*, i, p. 470.
42 Hatcher and Bailey, *Modelling*, pp. 166–7.
43 Ibid., p. 153; Hilton, 'Towns', p. 24.
44 P. Abrams, 'Towns and economic growth: some theories and problems', in Abrams and Wrigley, eds., *Towns in societies*, pp. 9–33; Langton and Hoppe, *Town and country*, pp. 40–1.

emerge: strong vestiges of serfdom remained, the beginnings of wage labour were apparent, and many small producers faced an unstable position when attempting to produce for the market. Sweezy described the period as one of 'pre-capitalist commodity production'.[45] For Brenner, this was the period in which agrarian capitalism began to emerge in England. Although by the mid-fifteenth century peasants were breaking feudal checks, landlords were able to prevent land being lost to peasant freehold by appropriating vacant holdings and charging entry fines. Through these mechanisms, landlords were 'able to engross, consolidate and enclose, to create large farms and lease them to capitalist tenants who could afford to make capital investments', thereby creating a system of capitalist class relations in the countryside. The first stage of this, the build-up of larger holdings at the expense of smaller ones, occurred in many areas from the second half of the fifteenth century.[46] Karl Marx described the last third of the fifteenth century and the greater part of the sixteenth century as an 'agricultural revolution' in which rising agricultural prices and lagging rents 'enriched the farmer as rapidly as it impoverished the mass of the rural population'.[47] For Tawney too, this was an age of enclosure, land speculation, and rack rents, aggravated by the dissolution of the monasteries and chantries.[48] From a different perspective, Cunningham, writing in the tradition of Adam Smith, regarded the fifteenth century and first half of the sixteenth century as 'a period of transition from medieval to modern society': a natural economy was superseded with the common use of money, and prices, wages and rents were calculated according to market demand, rather than using customary rates. Other writers, from contemporaries up to the early twentieth century, have suggested that the fifteenth and sixteenth centuries were a period of transition in which modern society emerged.[49]

Recent research of the medieval economy has challenged many theories that emphasise change in the fifteenth and sixteenth centuries, by showing that similar developments arose much earlier. The commercialisation of the economy, regarded as an important feature in the emergence of capitalism, was more rapid between 1000 and 1300 than between 1300 and 1500, and many developments such as increased market orientation, the growth of larger units of production, and dependence on wage labour, were more characteristic of the pre-Black Death period rather than the years that followed. During the later middle ages there were only two significant moves towards capitalism: rents and wages became more contractual, and some parts of the cloth industry became increasingly dependent on organisation by merchant clothiers.[50]

---

45 Sweezy, 'Critique', pp. 50–1.
46 Brenner, 'Agrarian class structure', pp. 46–52; Brenner, 'Agrarian roots', pp. 305–6.
47 K. Marx, *Capital*, trans. E. and C. Paul, 2 vols. (London, 1930), ii, pp. 796–9, 812–13, 823–4.
48 R.H. Tawney, *The agrarian problem in the sixteenth century* (London, 1912); R.H. Tawney, *Religion and the rise of capitalism* (London, 1922).
49 W. Cunningham, *The growth of English industry and commerce during the early and middle ages* (Cambridge, 5th edn., 1915), pp. 457–72; K. Wrightson, *Earthly necessities: economic lives in early modern Britain* (New Haven, 2000), pp. 2–23.
50 Britnell, *Commercialisation*, pp. 233–5; R.H. Britnell, 'Commerce and capitalism in late medieval England: problems of description and theory', *Journal of Historical Sociology*, 6 (1993), pp. 359–69.

Many of the generalisations that have been used to build theories of transition from feudalism to capitalism have also been questioned. Recent empirical studies have stressed the continuities, rather than the changes, within the land market. Contrary to Brenner's claims, it is suggested that there was no precise relationship between landlord power, tenure, ownership, farm size and capitalist farming. Landlords were often unable to exercise arbitrary power over tenants, who were protected by their tenancies and the courts, and landlords showed little interest in agricultural innovation. The consolidation of land and the appearance of capitalist forms of agriculture could occur as a result of differentiation within the peasantry themselves, independent of lordly action.[51]

The assumptions of economic modernisation that have dominated the historiography of this period form part of a wider tradition of viewing the end of the fifteenth century as a turning point. The significance of two other principal events in this perspective, the Renaissance, and in England, the 'New Monarchy' of the Tudor dynasty, have been challenged, and the continuities highlighted.[52] As Bridbury has stated, 'the idea of a caesura in the succession of events, a breach of continuity marking the rapid emergence of a world which was modern instead of medieval', makes no more sense in economic history than in the history of political institutions, and as a recent survey of the medieval economy has suggested, there is no 'grand narrative' that can describe all the changes that took place within the economy and society.[53]

The pattern of economic change, 1450–1560

While the historians noted above have not generally singled out the years 1450–1560 as a key century of change, the chronological pattern of surviving evidence from Cambridge makes it sensible to concentrate on this particular period. The years between 1450 and 1560 seem to have been ones of very gradual, hesitant and interrupted economic development. It is helpful to briefly sketch the main economic developments of the period in order to illustrate this, and to enable developments within Cambridge and its region to be viewed within the national context.

The limits of this period were years of very different economic conditions. Population depression, static prices, monetary scarcity, an abundance of land, and a shortage of labour marked the English economy in the period around 1450. By 1560

---

51   R.W. Hoyle, 'Tenure and the land market in early modern England: or a late contribution to the Brenner debate', *EcHR*, 2nd ser., 43 (1990), 1–20; P. Glennie, 'In search of agrarian capitalism: manorial land markets and the acquisition of land in the Lea Valley c.1450–c.1560', *Continuity and Change*, 3 (1988), 11–40; M. Mate, 'The East Sussex land market and agrarian class structure in the late middle ages', *Past and Present*, 139 (1993), 46–65; Whittle, *Agrarian capitalism*, pp. 305–15.

52   J.L. Watts, 'Introduction: history, the fifteenth century and the Renaissance' and R.H. Britnell, 'The English economy and the government, 1450–1550', in J.L. Watts, ed., *The end of the middle ages? England in the fifteenth and sixteenth centuries* (Stroud, 1998), pp. 1–22, 113–15.

53   A.R. Bridbury, 'Sixteenth-century farming', *EcHR*, 2nd ser., 27 (1974), 555; C. Dyer, *Making a living in the Middle Ages: the people of Britain 850–1520* (London, 2002), pp. 363–5.

the country was experiencing population growth and rising prices, which were beginning to drive up the price of land and drag down real wages. But the transition between these two dates was slow and varied between different sectors of the economy.

England's population, substantially reduced by the Black Death and subsequent outbreaks of plague and epidemic disease, probably reached its lowest point of 2 to 2.5 million in the mid-fifteenth century. The population may have recovered to between 2.25 and 2.75 million by 1522–5 and 3 million by the early 1560s, although another estimate places the English population at only 1.8 million in 1524, suggesting an even larger or more prolonged decline during the previous century.[54] Whether the prolonged demographic recession of the fifteenth century was driven by continued high mortality from plague and epidemic disease, or by lower fertility, as labour shortages drew women into employment, is still debated. The date at which population began to grow again is also disputed, although any growth up to the 1520s was probably small-scale and localised.[55] Population growth from 1541 to 1556 was rapid, at 0.87 per cent per annum, and there may have been a similar rate of increase from the mid-1520s. Until the 1560s, when population growth increased to almost 1 per cent per annum, widespread outbreaks of epidemic disease continued to check the increase, with two particularly severe mortality crises in 1557–8 and 1558–9.[56] In summary, sustained population growth did not begin until the sixteenth century, possibly during the 1520s, and intensified further in the 1560s.

Agricultural commodity prices generally fell in the fifteenth century, although livestock and dairy prices showed greater resilience as consumption of these products increased with higher living standards. Prices were influenced not solely by the reduction in population: an important factor was a severe and widespread recession affecting trade, industry, and agriculture, and which doubtless owed something to the shortage of coinage in circulation during the mid-fifteenth century. Output of coins from almost all European mints fell, the total stock of coinage declined, and credit appears to have contracted.[57] Prices began to rise substantially in the second decade of the sixteenth century. The general explanation seems to lie in the growing imbalance between population and agricultural output, although other factors were influential. The initial rise can be at least partially attributed to temporary climatic conditions, interruptions of grain supplies from abroad, and market conditions elsewhere in Europe. The most severe period of inflation was between 1540 and

---

54 J. Hatcher, *Plague, population and the English economy, 1348–1530* (London, 1977), pp. 68–9; E.A. Wrigley and R.S. Schofield, *The population history of England, 1541–1871: a reconstruction* (London, 1981), p. 531; J. Cornwall, 'English population in the early sixteenth century', *EcHR*, 2nd ser., 23 (1970), 32–44; B.M.S. Campbell, 'The population of early Tudor England: a re-evaluation of the 1522 muster returns and 1524 and 1525 lay subsidies', *Journal of Historical Geography*, 7 (1981), 145–54.

55 M. Bailey, 'Demographic decline in late medieval England: some thoughts on recent research', *EcHR*, 49 (1996), 1–19; R.H. Britnell, *The closing of the middle ages? England, 1471–1529* (Oxford, 1997), pp. 242–7.

56 Wrigley and Schofield, *Population*, pp. 333, 566–9.

57 J. Hatcher, 'The great slump of the mid-fifteenth century', in R. Britnell and J. Hatcher, eds., *Progress and problems in medieval England: essays in honour of Edward Miller* (Cambridge, 1996), p. 244.

1560, when inflation rates were 3.6 per cent per annum and prices for agricultural and industrial products more than doubled over the twenty-year period. This was fuelled by the government's debasement of the currency.[58]

Wage rates rose as population fell in the fifteenth century, indicating a shortage of labour that was also reflected in official statutes and the complaints of individual employers. Day and piece rates for agricultural and building workers peaked between 1430 and 1460. As prices were low, real wages had risen considerably by the mid-fifteenth century, indicating a general rise in living standards: the period has been described as 'the golden age of the English labourer'. As the population grew again in the sixteenth century, wages rose, but these increases lagged behind price rises, causing real wage rates to fall. But as many families depended on wages for only part of their income, their standard of living may not have fallen as considerably as the decline in real wages would suggest.[59]

The Black Death and subsequent epidemics caused significant changes to occur in agriculture from the late fourteenth century. As already stated, land became relatively abundant and labour scarce. Landlords also leased out their former demesne lands, resulting in a transfer in decision-making from large landlords to smaller producers. A smaller population reduced the demand for cereals, but higher living standards resulted in the increasing consumption of livestock and dairy products, and cloth exports provided a continuing market for wool. High labour costs favoured animal husbandry, pastoral farming therefore grew at the expense of arable cultivation, and some areas and individuals prospered in this sphere. However, few were able to maintain, let alone increase, their farming incomes during the prolonged recession of the mid-fifteenth century. Some recovery from this slump had occurred by the 1480s,[60] but there is no evidence in many parts of England for a long-term rise in rents before the 1520s – indeed there is still evidence of falling rents and entry fines, vacant and neglected holdings, and arable land reverting to waste. Even after the 1520s, there was no single pattern of growth, and the income of many landlords failed to rise as quickly as prices. In the chalk area of Wiltshire, for example, rent rises varied considerably between different landowners and largely took the form of an increase in entry fines. Rents, fines and overall manorial revenues changed little between 1450 and 1575 on the manors of north-east Norfolk studied by Whittle.[61]

The slack demand for land enabled tenants to gain concessions over land tenures. Land previously held for labour services was converted to alienable and hereditary copyhold tenures. But entry fines were not fixed and could be raised to excessive

---

58 R.B. Outhwaite, *Inflation in Tudor and early Stuart England* (London, 2nd edn., 1982); Britnell, '1450–1550', pp. 107–8; R.A. Doughty, 'Industrial prices and inflation in southern England, 1401–1640', *Explorations in Economic History*, 12 (1975), 177–92; N.J. Mayhew, 'Population, money supply, and the velocity of circulation in England, 1300–1700', *EcHR*, 48 (1995), 238–57.

59 Hatcher, *Plague*, pp. 47–52; E.H. Phelps Brown and S.V. Hopkins, *A perspective of wages and prices* (London, 1981), pp. 13–59; D. Woodward, 'Wage rates and living standards in pre-industrial England', *Past and Present*, 91 (1981), 28–46.

60 Hatcher, 'Slump', pp. 247–59, 271.

61 I. Blanchard, 'Population change, enclosure, and the early Tudor economy', *EcHR*, 2nd ser., 23 (1970), 433–42; E. Kerridge, 'The movement of rent, 1540–1640', *EcHR*, 2nd ser., 6 (1953–4), 16–34; Whittle, *Agrarian capitalism*, pp. 64–82.

levels when the demand for land rose again in the sixteenth century. Many families also escaped from personal serfdom during the fifteenth century by negotiating with their lords, or by fleeing their manors to start a new life elsewhere, as on the Cambridgeshire manors of Cottenham, Oakington and Wilburton.[62]

The cloth industry was arguably one of the most dynamic areas of the later-fifteenth and early sixteenth-century economy. Cloth exports almost quadrupled between 1450–4 and 1540–4, and domestic sales also probably increased in the fifteenth century to meet demand from rising real incomes. Initially this growth was merely recovery from the mid-century depression, and cloth exports did not consistently exceed the totals of the 1440s until the first decade of the sixteenth century. Production, concentrated in the late fourteenth century in towns such as Colchester, York, and Coventry, was by the fifteenth century rivalled by smaller centres of production in parts of southern Suffolk, Devon, the Cotswolds, the West Riding of Yorkshire and the Lake District. Wealth generated in these areas was reflected in the rebuilding of houses, guild halls, and parish churches, and the presence of wealthy clothiers. Frequently, however, this localised economic development was at the expense of other areas of cloth production, and therefore seems to have been the consequence of entrepreneurial restructuring of trade and industry, rather than net economic growth. The greatest beneficiary of these developments was London. Exports were increasingly concentrated on the London–Antwerp axis, although this meant that when these markets were disrupted in the 1550s, cloth exports fell sharply.[63]

The timing of recovery within the economy between 1450 and 1560 varied considerably between different sectors, and it is very difficult to identify a general turning point. Population growth had begun by the 1520s, and intensified further in the 1560s. Prices began to rise in the 1510s, with the greatest increase between 1540 and 1560. Cloth exports grew during most of the period, with the most rapid rise in the early sixteenth century. There is no sign of a general agricultural recovery, measured by rising rents, until after the 1520s. William Harrison attributed the dramatic improvement in the livelihood of farmers to the later part of Henry VIII's reign.[64] The years after 1570 saw a rapid expansion in the volume of agricultural trade in regional markets.[65] Estimates of national income (deflated) suggest the most rapid growth in our period occurred between 1526 and 1546.[66] The pace of change also varied regionally, with, for example, some areas around London showing signs of

---

62 M. Bailey, 'Rural society', in R. Horrox, ed., *Fifteenth-century attitudes: perceptions of society in late medieval England* (Cambridge, 1994), pp. 150–9; F.W. Maitland, 'The history of a Cambridgeshire manor', *English Historical Rev.*, 35 (1894), 436–7; F.M. Page, *The estates of Crowland Abbey* (Cambridge, 1934), pp. 146–51.

63 Carus-Wilson and Coleman, *Export trade*, pp. 97–119; Britnell, '1450–1550', pp. 90, 95–7; F.J. Fisher, 'Commercial trends and policy in sixteenth-century England', in Corfield and Harte, eds., *London and the English economy 1500–1700*, pp. 81–103.

64 Hatcher, 'Slump', pp. 271–2.

65 A. Everitt, 'The marketing of agricultural produce, 1500–1640', in J. Chartres, ed., *Chapters from the Agrarian History of England and Wales, iv: Agricultural markets and trade, 1500–1750* (Cambridge, 1990), p. 51.

66 Britnell, '1450–1550', p. 100, from figures in Mayhew, 'Money supply', 244.

recovery earlier than other parts of the country. Nor can the possibility of limited growth in the later fifteenth century, checked in the early sixteenth, be dismissed, particularly if much of this was recovery from the extremely severe economic conditions of the mid-fifteenth century.

The debate over urban fortunes

The fortunes of the urban sector during the later fifteenth and sixteenth centuries became a subject of major debate in the 1970s and 1980s. Proponents of 'urban decline' pointed to contracting populations, declining trade and industry, and the flight of townspeople from holding civic offices. Dobson suggested that recession hit many towns, particularly from 1450 onwards, with little reversal until after 1550. Phythian-Adams found depression and decay, which seemed to reach its nadir in the years between 1520 and 1570, when the two main economic functions of towns, as centres of textile production and marketing, were eroded by rural competition. Clark and Slack also detected widespread urban decay by the middle of the sixteenth century, but extended their pessimistic assessment into the late seventeenth century, highlighting the escalating pressures of poverty, plague, and harvest failure, coupled with commercial depression, heavy financial burdens, and an influx of migrants.[67]

However, Bridbury championed a far more optimistic interpretation of urban fortunes in this period. He claimed that the later middle ages was a period of widespread urban prosperity, pointing to the enduring ability of towns to attract substantial numbers of immigrants, their continuing importance as centres of cloth production, and their increasing share of the nation's taxable wealth.[68] Goose has shown the underlying resilience of urban economies to the challenges of plague, harvest failure and poverty, and argued that as towns were interlocked into the wider economic and social system, there was no 'urban variable' preventing towns from sharing in the demographic recovery and economic expansion of the late sixteenth and early seventeenth centuries.[69]

The debate has now subsided, with an increasing awareness of the dangers of drawing broad generalisations from the experiences of different towns and different decades, and from failing to separate external and internal factors, and absolute and relative decline. Changes in population and wealth, for example, were not necessarily parallel. Most urban populations contracted in the later middle ages as the total population fell, but the prosperity of individual townsmen often increased with greater resources per head. Estimates of population and wealth generally rely on taxation records over a hundred years apart, which can hide medium- and short-term changes.

---

67 R.B. Dobson, 'Urban decline in late medieval England', in Holt and Rosser, eds., *Medieval town*, pp. 265–86; C.V. Phythian-Adams, 'Urban decay in late medieval England', in Abrams and Wrigley, eds., *Towns in societies*, pp. 159–85; P. Clark and P. Slack, *English towns in transition 1500–1700* (Oxford, 1976), pp. 13–16.

68 A.R. Bridbury, *Economic growth: England in the later middle ages* (London, 1962); A.R. Bridbury, 'English provincial towns in the later middle ages', *EcHR*, 2nd ser., 34 (1981), 1–24.

69 N.R. Goose, 'In search of the urban variable: towns and the English economy, 1500–1650', *EcHR*, 2nd ser., 39 (1986), 165–85.

Problems in civic government finances have not always been distinguished from problems affecting urban economies. Boroughs received income from a variety of sources, including tolls on trade and property rents, but these could be affected by external influences unrelated to economic factors.[70]

Urban economies responded to the changing patterns of internal and external trade. After the Black Death, there were fewer people with little or no land, so demand for food and raw materials in the countryside fell, leading to the decline and abandonment of many small markets. At the same time, the rising standard of living in both urban and rural society increased demand for merchant wares, and towns benefited from manufacturing and distributing consumer goods such as cloth, leather and metal wares in response. Consumers purchased more imported goods, and exported manufactures became increasingly significant, particularly cloth. This encouraged the expansion of cloth-making in particular towns and regions, with London merchants increasingly dominating networks of trade and credit. The sixteenth century saw trade becoming more concentrated within mercantile networks.[71]

Recent works have tended to stress the similarities of experiences in urban and rural economies, and to describe the changes taking place within the urban sector as relative readjustment rather than radical restructuring. Goose describes the years between the 1520s and 1570s as 'a period of readjustment, in both town and countryside', and Wrightson writes of a 'reshuffling of the existing urban hierarchy' in the sixteenth century in which the essential urban infrastructure remained intact.[72] Britnell argues that all the key features identified as 'urban decline' – depopulation, abandoned houses, falling rents, contracting traditional markets, reluctance to assume office – were also widespread features of rural life in the fifteenth and sixteenth centuries. Rising living standards were also enjoyed in both town and country. He argues for the need to leave aside independent consideration of the urban sector in order to investigate how relationships changed between towns and rural suppliers.[73]

Cambridge in the fifteenth and sixteenth centuries

Cambridge had grown where a road running along a chalk and gravel ridge crossed the navigable River Cam, leading to the Fens and the coast: 'the one bridge that gives name to a county'.[74] A castle that became the headquarters for the county's administration was constructed in the eleventh century. During the twelfth and thirteenth centuries the townspeople acquired various governmental privileges. From the thirteenth century onwards, the town corporation faced the challenges presented by the establishment of a university in Cambridge and the creation of a rival port at Lynn.[75]

---

70 R.H. Britnell, 'The economy of British towns 1300–1540', in *CUHB*, i, pp. 330–1.

71 Britnell, 'Urban demand', pp. 1–21.

72 Goose, 'Urban variable', 184; Wrightson, *Earthly necessities*, pp. 104–8.

73 Britnell, 'Urban demand', pp. 18–19.

74 F.W. Maitland, *Township and borough* (Cambridge, 1898), p. 37.

75 *VCH Cambs.*, iii, pp. 4–9; M.D. Lobel, 'Cambridge', in M.D. Lobel, ed., *The atlas of historic towns*, (London, 1975), ii, pp. 5–9.

Direct quantitative measures are frequently lacking, but a mass of anecdotal evidence would suggest aspects of decline in Cambridge's economy over the later fourteenth and fifteenth centuries and some elements of recovery by the mid-sixteenth century. The century after the Peasants' Revolt has been described as 'a period of retrogression and decay' in the town, with two severe fires, the continuing presence of plague, and the eviction of tenants and destruction of property to create the site for King's College. The corporation made pleas for the reduction of their fixed obligation to the crown – the borough fee farm – and for reductions in the town's tax quota.[76] By the later sixteenth century, though, the population seems to have been growing again. A paving act of 1544 described the town as well-inhabited and replenished with people. By 1584 the hazards posed by the density of population in the town led the privy council to instruct the vice-chancellor and mayor to restrict builders and landlords who divided single houses into many small tenements, and complaints of such subdivisions continued into the seventeenth century.[77]

The fifteenth century, however, also saw the development of the university. This became an increasing source of study and patronage, with its rival at Oxford tainted with the influence of the religious reformer John Wycliffe and his followers. Student numbers at Cambridge may have increased from between 400 and 700 scholars in the 1370s and 1380s to around 1,300 by the mid-fifteenth century, although in the absence of records of matriculation or graduation, such figures can be little more than intelligent guesses. During the fifteenth century, six new colleges were founded, including the royal foundations of King's and Queens', university schools and libraries for the higher faculties were constructed, and the complete rebuilding of Great St Mary's Church, largely at the cost of the university, was begun. Cambridge University became home to such distinguished patrons as John Fisher, Lady Margaret Beaufort, and a succession of monarchs. The university's alumni became more influential: in 1425, no Cambridge graduate sat on the bench of bishops, but a Cambridge graduate occupied every English see during some part of Henry VIII's reign. The century after 1450 saw the rise to ascendancy of the colleges, and the creation of an academic quarter between the High Street and the river.[78]

During the sixteenth century the university's expansion continued despite several setbacks. Before the later fifteenth century, most students were housed in hostels, but thereafter these disappeared and colleges expanded to take in their numbers. This necessitated new buildings or extensions, like the insertion of garret rooms into the roofs of Corpus Christi's Old Court during Henry VIII's reign.[79] Student numbers fell from the late 1530s as the dissolution of the monasteries ended the entry of monks and friars, and, for a while, there was despondency about the future of the colleges.

---

76 *VCH Cambs.*, iii, pp. 12–14.

77 RCHMC, p. xci; N. Goose, 'Household size and structure in early-Stuart Cambridge', in Barry, ed., *Tudor and Stuart town*, pp. 81–2.

78 T.H. Aston, G.D. Duncan and T.A.R. Evans, 'The medieval alumni of the University of Cambridge', *Past and Present*, 86 (1980), 11–28; A.B. Emden, *A biographical register of the University of Cambridge to 1500* (Cambridge, 1963), p. xxx; C. Brooke, R. Highfield and W. Swaan, *Oxford and Cambridge* (Cambridge, 1988), pp. 138–52.

79 RCHMC, p. lxxxiii.

The religious changes of Mary's reign led to a large number of exiles to the continent, but many of these returned after her death. By the beginning of Elizabeth's reign, numbers had returned to pre-Reformation levels, and an increasing proportion of sons of the nobility began to join the university.[80]

Historiography and sources

The town of Cambridge has received the attention of a number of distinguished medieval historians, perhaps most notably Maitland, whose work, over a century after its first publication, remains one of the most valuable studies of the legal development of the medieval borough.[81] The principal works on the economy and society of Tudor Cambridge are the unpublished theses by Goose and Siraut, but these both concentrate on the later sixteenth and seventeenth centuries rather than the 1450–1560 period.[82] There are recently published histories of the university,[83] while the magnificent surviving architecture has inspired a number of studies, including the extensive surveys by Willis and Clark and the Royal Commission on Historical Monuments.[84]

The county of Cambridgeshire is now fully covered by ten volumes of the *Victoria County History*, which provide the essential starting point for any academic research.[85] Taylor and Darby have described the landscapes of the county and fenland.[86] Specific studies of communities like Landbeach and Chippenham in this period have become models for local history research in their own right,[87] while the estates of some landowners have also been analysed.[88] Alison Taylor has provided

---

80 E. Leedham–Green, *A concise history of the University of Cambridge* (Cambridge, 1996), pp. 46–64.
81 Maitland, *Township*; *VCH Cambs.*, iii.
82 M.C. Siraut, 'Some aspects of the economic and social history of Cambridge under Elizabeth I' (unpublished M.Litt. thesis, University of Cambridge, 1978); N.R. Goose, 'Economic and social aspects of provincial towns: a comparative study of Cambridge, Colchester and Reading c.1500–1700' (unpublished PhD thesis, University of Cambridge, 1984).
83 D.R. Leader, *A history of the University of Cambridge*, i: *the university to 1546* (Cambridge, 1988); V. Morgan and C. Brooke, *A history of the University of Cambridge*, ii: *1546–1750* (Cambridge, 2004); Leedham–Green, *Concise history*; P. Zutshi, ed., *Medieval Cambridge: essays on the pre-Reformation university* (Woodbridge, 1993).
84 R. Willis and J.W. Clark, *The architectural history of the University of Cambridge and of the colleges of Cambridge and Eton*, 4 vols. (Cambridge, 1886, vols. 1–3 reprinted, 1988); RCHMC; N. Pevsner, *The buildings of England: Cambridgeshire* (London, 2nd edn., 1970).
85 *VCH Cambs.*, i–x.
86 C. Taylor, *The Cambridgeshire landscape* (London, 1973); Darby, *Fenland*; H.C. Darby, *Medieval Cambridgeshire* (Cambridge, 1977).
87 J.R. Ravensdale, *Liable to floods: village landscape on the edge of the Fens, A.D. 450–1850* (Cambridge, 1974); M. Spufford, *Contrasting communities: English villagers in the sixteenth and seventeenth centuries* (Cambridge, 1974).
88 Page, *Crowland Abbey*; J.A. Raftis, *The estates of Ramsey Abbey: a study in economic growth and organisation* (Toronto, 1957); E. Miller, *The abbey and bishopric of Ely* (Cambridge, 1951); F. Heal, 'The Tudors and church lands: economic problems of the bishopric of Ely during the sixteenth century', *EcHR*, 2nd ser., 26 (1973), 198–217.

comprehensive introductions to recent archaeological work undertaken in both the town and county, while more detailed reports are presented in the *Proceedings of the Cambridge Antiquarian Society*.[89]

The changing nature of the documentary sources is probably largely responsible for the lack of empirical work covering this period. Late medieval English scripts became increasingly irregular and informal with the mixing of cursive and *textualis* forms, evolving into the secretary hand of the early modern period. English gradually replaced Latin in many formal documents. The documents of neither central nor local government are particularly helpful for local studies in this period. Although the increasing activity of state government under the Tudors created new departments such as the Star Chamber, the Court of Wards and the Court of Augmentations, the amount of business relating to a single geographical area is usually small and difficult to locate.[90] As the estates of large landowners changed from being cultivated directly to being leased, accounts that formerly detailed cropping and livestock arrangements,[91] were replaced by terse entries recording rent payments. Many court rolls became increasingly formalised and uninformative, reflecting the contracting business of many manorial courts following the disappearance of personal serfdom and the growth of royal justice.[92] Probate inventories listing the possessions of the deceased only become widespread in the later sixteenth century. The parish registration of baptisms, marriages and burials, which allows detailed reconstitution of family relationships and population trends, did not begin until 1538.[93] The changing nature of the documentation invariably shapes the view we may obtain of the period.

However, the wide range of surviving sources from Cambridge and its region permits some of these difficulties to be overcome. As the records generated by individual groups are so often incomplete, no single series of documents will be viewed in isolation, but recourse will be made to the records of Cambridge colleges, the university and town government of Cambridge, central government, and local manors.

The college archives of Cambridge, which have been described as one of the greatest potential resources for future research by medievalists in this country, are especially informative. The secular colleges of Oxford and Cambridge, with the exception of the secular cathedrals, were among the few collegiate organisations that survived the Reformation, providing continuity in record keeping.[94] The college accounts cover a crucial period of price inflation, at a time when the other major record-generating institutions, the monasteries, were being dissolved. Valuable price and wage data can be found in several accounts, most notably those of King's Hall and

---

89 A. Taylor, *Archaeology of Cambridgeshire*, 2 vols. (March, 1997–8); A. Taylor, *Cambridge. The hidden history* (Stroud, 1999).

90 P. Riden, *Record sources for local history* (London, 1987), pp. 51–80.

91 See D. Stone, 'The productivity of hired and customary labour: evidence from Wisbech Barton in the fourteenth century', *EcHR*, 50 (1997), 640–56, for an exceptionally detailed series of accounts.

92 *The English manor c.1200–c.1500*, ed. M. Bailey (Manchester, 2002), pp. 105–11, 184–9; Whittle, *Agrarian capitalism*, pp. 46–63, 83–4.

93 Riden, *Record sources*, pp. 94–5, 106.

94 Zutshi, ed., *Medieval Cambridge*, pp. 3–4.

King's College. College accounts will be used to show the trade of Cambridge and its region, to determine the area from which the town secured supplies of food and fuel, and to explore the labour market.

The borough archives of Cambridge provide another important group of sources, although these are now very fragmentary compared to the collections from other medieval boroughs. Poor storage of the records over the centuries has undoubtedly led to the loss of many documents: the eighteenth-century antiquarian James Bowtell rescued the sixteenth-century treasurers' accounts, which were being offered for sale as waste paper, and bequeathed them to Downing College. Cooper published a wide range of extracts from the borough archives, together with material from the university and colleges in the mid-nineteenth century, but his sources are not always easy to identify today.[95] Palmer and Barnard catalogued the borough archives in the 1920s and published a collection of sources. On completion of this catalogue, they pragmatically told the corporation:

> Such records as are lost would not, if in existence, add one penny to your revenue, and if all the documents perpetrated by your clerks had now been in existence … you would have wanted a Muniment Room ten times as large as the present one, and it would have cost you 100 guineas instead of 10 guineas to get a report on them.[96]

But historians have reason to mourn the loss of most of the records of the court baron, court leet, the town pleas, and the bailiffs' accounts, which mean that only a partial picture can now emerge of the corporation's activities.

Of the surviving borough records, the treasurers' accounts form an important series, despite being incomplete and now split between two repositories, the County Record Office and Downing College. These accounts detail rents from property in the town and booths in Stourbridge Fair, fines from townsmen admitted to the freedom, and expenditure on fees, rewards and repairs.[97] The corporation accounts are used throughout this study, but particularly to examine the origins and occupations of freemen, the operation of the fairs, and the demand for property in the town. Other valuable documents include the borough charters, dating back to 1207, the 'Cross Book', a cartulary of important documents from the fourteenth to the early eighteenth centuries, and the Common Day Book, a general ledger of corporation business, beginning in 1544.[98] There are also a number of agreements and correspondence within the borough archive, many of which concern disputes with the university or the borough of Lynn, that can shed light on the economy of the town.

The archives of the university have also seen losses, although the Peasants' Revolt, when the university's muniments were allegedly burnt, was probably less significant than routine disposal and general negligence. Records of the court leet

---

95 *Annals*, i–v.

96 CCA, W.M. Palmer and E.A.B. Barnard, 'Cambridge Corporation Archives' (typescript catalogue, 1929), schedule ii; *CBD*.

97 *CBD*, p. xxxvi; CCA, X/70/1–10, X/71/1–10, X/71A, XVII/24A; CCTA, i–ii.

98 *Charters of the borough of Cambridge*, ed. F.W. Maitland and M. Bateson (Cambridge, 1901); CCA, I/4; Palmer/Barnard vol. 57.

survive only for the late fourteenth and late sixteenth centuries, and the records of the vice-chancellor's and commissary's courts begin only during the mid-sixteenth century.[99] The surviving documentation from the period 1450–1560 includes the series of Grace Books, the principal administrative registers of the university, which have been published. These include not only the graces (rulings dispensing individuals from the university's statutory requirements) but also the proctors' accounts, recording the university's receipts and expenditure.[100] Additionally, many loose documents survive that were collected and bound together thematically by the nineteenth-century registrary, Luard. The university archives have been used in this study mainly to detail the regulation of marketing in the town, which was under the control of the university after 1382.

Various central government and local records can supplement the archives of the colleges, university and borough government. Taxation records of 1334, 1377 and 1524, and deductions made during the fifteenth century, illustrate the changing population and wealth of the town and surrounding region, while the 1524 returns also supply information about the wealth of particular individuals. Chancery proceedings include many disputes referring to trade in the region, particularly relating to malt barley and saffron. There is also a wide array of manorial and ecclesiastical records. Using a range of documents, therefore, this study will examine the principal aspects of Cambridge and its region between 1450 and 1560: the population and wealth, society, trade, markets and fairs, food and fuel supplies, property and labour markets, and building projects of the town and hinterland.

---

99 H.E. Peek and C. Hall, *The archives of the University of Cambridge: an historical introduction* (Cambridge, 1962); D.M. Owen, *Cambridge University archives: a classified list* (Cambridge, 1988); E. Leedham-Green, 'The University Archives (what are they, anyway?)', in P. Fox, ed., *Cambridge University Library: the great collections* (Cambridge, 1998), pp. 197–210.

100 *Grace Book A, containing the proctors' accounts and other records of the University of Cambridge, 1454–88*, ed. S.M. Leathes, CASLMS, I, (Cambridge, 1897); *Grace Book B...1488–1511*, ed. M. Bateson, CASLMS, II-III, (Cambridge, 1903–5); *Grace Book [...1501–1542*, ed. W.G. Searle (Cambridge, 1908).

Chapter 2

Population and wealth

The later middle ages saw fundamental changes in the balance between population and land. The Black Death of 1348-9 and subsequent epidemics in the later fourteenth and fifteenth centuries halved the English population, making land much more abundant. The population did not recover significantly until the sixteenth century, and by the middle of this century was growing more rapidly, although still experiencing outbreaks of epidemic disease. The local impact of these general trends varied considerably, though, and historical studies are highlighting the varying regional and local pattern of population change in the fourteenth, fifteenth and sixteenth centuries.[1]

Changes in population and wealth have been used to examine the growth and decline of towns across the country, and to support the arguments of both proponents and opponents of the 'urban decline' debate. Many of these arguments have been constructed around the amounts of taxable wealth and numbers of taxpayers listed in the tax records of the fourteenth and sixteenth centuries. Comparing rates of urban and rural growth between the subsidies of 1334 and 1524–5, for example, Bridbury argued that the urban sector's relative share of national taxation increased over the period. Others have suggested that these figures were distorted by an undervaluation of urban wealth in 1334 and an overvaluation in 1524–5.[2] More recently, Dyer has proposed that urban growth between 1377 and 1524–5 was concentrated predominantly within the middle-ranking and smaller towns.[3] Historians have also been divided over whether urban populations regularly experienced natural decline from high rates of mortality, and over the extent to which plague and harvest failure affected towns in this period.[4] While overall trends are still debated, it is clear that changes in population and wealth were occurring at differing paces within different towns.

Population and wealth within Cambridge and its region can be examined in a number of ways. As the evidence is often patchy in survival and difficult to interpret, it is important to draw on a wide range of sources. Taxation returns show relative changes in population and wealth between Cambridge and neighbouring towns, Cambridgeshire and adjoining counties, and the different sub-regions and settlements

---

1. L.R. Poos, *A rural society after the Black Death: Essex, 1350–1525* (Cambridge, 1991), pp. 32–57, 89–182; Spufford, *Contrasting communities*, pp. 3–36; Bailey, *Marginal economy?*, pp. 266–315; J.N. Hare, 'Growth and recession in the fifteenth-century economy: the Wiltshire textile industry and the countryside', *EcHR*, 52 (1999), 1–26; Yates, 'Rural society'.
2. Bridbury, *Economic growth*, appendices 2–3; S.H. Rigby, 'Urban decline in the later middle ages: some problems in interpreting the statistical data', *Urban History Yearbook* (1979), 46–60; J.F. Hadwin, 'The medieval lay subsidies and economic history', *EcHR*, 2nd ser., 36 (1983), 210–13; S.H. Rigby, 'Late medieval urban prosperity: the evidence of the lay subsidies', and A.R. Bridbury, 'Dr Rigby's comment: a reply', *EcHR*, 2nd ser., 39 (1986), 411–22.
3. A. Dyer, '"Urban decline" in England, 1377–1525' in T.R. Slater, ed., *Towns in decline AD1000–1600* (Aldershot, 2000), pp. 266–88.
4. Clark and Slack, *English towns*, pp. 89–91; Goose, 'Urban variable', 178–9.

within the county between the fourteenth and sixteenth centuries. Reductions in tax quotas can help to identify areas that experienced particular contractions in population and wealth. Rental evidence can also reflect these changes.[5] Wills and parish registers provide indicators of trends in fertility and mortality but only begin during the sixteenth century.

Using sources to identify changes in population and wealth

The principal taxation records used to identify changes in population and wealth during the later middle ages are the lay subsidy of 1334, the poll taxes of 1377–81, and the lay subsidies of 1524–5.[6] The numbers of taxpayers and amounts of taxable wealth raised from towns and villages in Cambridgeshire by these three assessments are now available in published editions.[7] The lay subsidy of 1334 introduced tax quotas for each town and village, representing a fifteenth or a tenth of the total value of the moveable goods of all inhabitants. Royal demesnes and some boroughs paid the higher rate of one tenth. The 1334 subsidy therefore reveals the relative wealth of different communities, but not of individuals. These quotas remained in place, with certain reductions, which will be examined below, throughout the fifteenth century.[8] A recent study argues that this subsidy excluded many of the profits of the commercial and urban economy, so indications of the level of wealth must be treated with caution. The urban assessments favoured ports where imports and ships were effectively taxed, and undervalued inland towns where wool and cash escaped valuation.[9] The poll tax of 1377 assessed individuals, rather than communities, requiring all lay people over 14 years of age to pay 4d each.[10] No lists of individual taxpayers survive for Cambridgeshire, but the receipts of 1377 record the total number of persons taxed in each place, providing an indicator of population distribution. The Tudor lay subsidies assessed all individuals who fell within the thresholds of the tax. Among the most comprehensive were two subsidies granted in 1523 and collected in 1524 and 1525, which had a particularly low tax threshold, assessing all those with more than £1 in lands, £2 in goods, or £1 in wages. Taxpayers paid on whichever category of wealth would produce the greatest tax revenue, although this was complicated by differing rates of tax for each category.[11]

---

5   Rents in Cambridge are examined below, pp. 174–82.

6   M. Jurkowski, C.L. Smith and D. Crook, *Lay taxes in England and Wales 1188–1688* (Kew, 1998) provides a detailed guide to records of taxation.

7   *The lay subsidy of 1334*, ed. R.E. Glasscock, BARSEH, new ser., II (London, 1975); *The poll taxes of 1377, 1379 and 1381*, i: *Bedfordshire-Leicestershire*, ed. C.C. Fenwick, BARSEH, new ser., XXVII (Oxford, 1998); J. Sheail, *The regional distribution of wealth in England as indicated in the 1524/5 lay subsidy returns*, ed. R.W. Hoyle, List and Index Soc., special ser., XXVIII, 2 vols. (Kew, 1998).

8   *Lay subsidy*, pp. xv–xxxii. For the purposes of comparison, places in Cambridgeshire with wealth taxed at one tenth have been converted to one fifteenth.

9   P. Nightingale, 'The lay subsidies and the distribution of wealth in medieval England, 1275–1334', *EcHR*, 57 (2004), 1–32.

10 *Poll taxes*, i, pp. xiii–xxvi.

11 R.W. Hoyle, *Tudor taxation records: a guide for users* (London, 1994), pp. 3, 12–14.

The dates of the surviving tax returns present difficulties for an analysis of economic change over the 1450–1560 period. To gain an impression of the population and wealth of the region around 1450, one must look back to the fourteenth century. This is because the 1334 tax quotas remained in use, with some reductions allowed during the fifteenth century,[12] while the poll taxes of 1377–81 were not repeated because of their unpopularity. The 1334 tax quotas show the wealth of the country before the Black Death and the consequent economic upheaval: circumstances are therefore considerably different to those around 1450. Demographic trends in the fifteenth century are uncertain: population decline probably continued after 1377, with further decline or stagnation for much of the fifteenth century, and then growth, but with little impact in many areas until the early sixteenth century. But the population of the 1520s is unlikely to have been significantly larger than in 1377, and these figures can give the superficial impression that the population was almost stationary between the two dates.[13] When analysing changes in wealth between 1334 and 1524–5, and population between 1377 and 1524–5, it is usually impossible to specify what occurred before and after 1450.

As the taxes were assessed on different bases, it is necessary to examine relative rather than absolute rates of growth. The fifteenth of 1334 was based on assessments of moveable goods alone, and consisted of a fixed sum for each community. The poll tax of 1377 made a flat charge per person, irrespective of wealth, and the sixteenth-century lay subsidies assessed goods, incomes and wages. Over time, the accuracy of the assessments may have varied, the definition of the moveable goods to be assessed could have differed, and prices fluctuated. Absolute changes in population and wealth between the subsidies cannot, therefore, be measured accurately, and direct comparisons will not be made between the different records. However, *relative* rates of change can be examined. If each locality is ranked, using the number of taxpayers or amount of taxable wealth, from highest to lowest at two different dates, the change in rank order for each locality between the two dates provides a measure of relative change. Relative rates of growth and decline have been used to compare variations in the distribution of population and wealth between different counties, towns, and sub-regions.[14] While levels of accuracy and evasion may have varied considerably between taxes levied at different dates, it can be assumed that levels of accuracy and evasion did not generally vary significantly within the same assessment.

Other evidence can supplement trends revealed in the taxation records of 1334, 1377 and 1524. Population estimates can be derived from the bishops' census of 1563, which recorded the total number of families in each parish. Unfortunately, there are doubts surrounding the reliability of this census, as there appears to have been large differences in accuracy between dioceses, and some totals may have been rounded. So in this study, only population totals between sub-regions, rather than

---

12   See below, pp. 42–4.
13   Cornwall, 'English population', 42.
14   R.S. Schofield, 'The geographical distribution of wealth in England, 1334–1649', *EcHR*, 2nd ser., 18 (1965), 508–9; Dyer, *Decline and growth*, pp. 56–63; Yates, 'Rural society', 620–6.

individual parishes, will be compared using the bishops' census.[15] Other tax records, like the *Nonarum Inquisitiones*, a tax of one ninth on specific tithes in 1341, and reductions from the tax quotas of 1334 made in 1433 and 1446, reveal the extent of economic contraction in the region. The distribution of different groups of taxpayers in the various sub-regions of the county will be examined using the original returns from the 1524 lay subsidy, while the county's most prosperous inhabitants are also highlighted as contributors to a loan in 1522.[16]

Fluctuations in the number of wills registered, and in the number of children recorded in wills, can indicate trends in mortality and fertility. Such analysis is made more problematic, though, by the social selectivity and gender selectivity of wills. Willmakers were predominantly men and generally, although not entirely, comprised the wealthier inhabitants. Married women were not allowed to leave a will without permission from their husband. Despite their social bias, the number of wills proved can highlight major outbreaks of epidemic disease, while the number of children mentioned in wills can provide evidence of replacement rates among the will-making population.[17]

From 1538, the clergy were required to record every baptism, marriage and burial conducted in their parish. These parish registers provide a more detailed indication of demographic trends, although the figures relate to church ceremonies and not to actual births, deaths and marriages, raising questions about the completeness of registration. Wrigley and Schofield used the aggregated totals recorded in the registers of 404 parishes to reconstruct the population history of England from the sixteenth to the nineteenth century. However, the demographic experiences of individual parishes were far from uniform, and recent research has begun to examine local differences.[18] Parish registers are more difficult to use in urban areas, where under-registration was probably greater, and where towns were made up of many separate parishes, like Cambridge, with 14 parishes.[19] The survival of early parish registers also tends to be fragmentary. Although over a dozen parishes in Cambridgeshire have registers beginning in 1538, many of these contain breaks rather than continuous entries of both baptisms and burials through to 1570.

---

15 N. Goose, 'The ecclesiastical returns of 1563: a cautionary note', *Local Population Studies*, 34 (1985), 46–7; A. Dyer, 'The bishops' census of 1563: its significance and accuracy', *Local Population Studies*, 49 (1992), 19–37; N. Goose, 'The bishops' census of 1563: a re-examination of its reliability', *Local Population Studies*, 56 (1996), 43–53.

16 *LP*, iii (2), no. 2640, pp. 1116–19.

17 N. Goose, 'Fertility and mortality in pre-industrial English towns from probate and parish register evidence' in T. Arkell, N. Evans and N. Goose, eds., *When death do us part: understanding and interpreting the probate records of early modern England* (Oxford, 2000), pp. 189–200.

18 Wrigley and Schofield, *Population history*; R. Schofield, *Parish register aggregate analyses: the population history of England database and introductory guide*, Local Population Studies Supplement (Colchester, 1998), pp. 6–11.

19 N. Goose, 'Urban demography in pre-industrial England: what is to be done?' *Urban History*, 21 (1994), 276–84; Goose, 'Household size', p. 90.

Population of Cambridge

Attempting to calculate the population of the town of Cambridge demonstrates the difficulties in producing population estimates from taxation records. To convert the number of taxpayers recorded in the poll tax of 1377 into an estimate of population, a multiplier of 1.9 is generally accepted to account for those too young and too poor to be assessed, and those evading the tax. Converting the number of taxpayers listed in the 1524–5 lay subsidies is more difficult. Dyer proposes a multiplier of 6.0, which produces a population of 3,300 in Cambridge.[20] Goose uses a correlation of the two subsidy lists of 1524–5, and correction factors to allow for women, children, and those too poor to be taxed, to give a population of 2,600 for Cambridge in 1524–5.[21] The degree of under-enumeration in the bishops' census of 1563 has also been debated.[22] Finally, the university vice-chancellor made a population estimate of the town in 1587 following concern over food supplies.[23]

The situation is made more complex by the extent to which the university was included in tax assessments. The colleges could be subject to both lay and clerical taxation, while the university and colleges secured certain exemptions from tax for their scholars, employees and tenants.[24] Tax assessments for the town of Cambridge did not usually include the university. In 1377, all scholars at Cambridge were assessed separately from the townspeople, under the clerical poll tax as beneficed clergy: the university's size has been estimated at between 400–700 members, partly from these figures.[25] In the lay subsidies of 1524–5, the university scholars were again exempt. University employees were listed separately in returns of 1524, but not scholars.[26] Unfortunately, there are no records of the size of the university at this time: a list of valuations and taxes levied on university members, compiled in 1522, suggests that college accounts underestimate the number of members, but it contains too many illegible entries to use.[27] Given the expansion of the colleges, it is unlikely that the university in the 1520s was any smaller than in the mid-fifteenth century, when its size has been estimated at 1,300 members, based on estimates of the likely capacity of colleges and hostels.[28] Although student numbers appear to

---

20 Dyer, 'Urban decline', p. 275. This figure revises his earlier estimate of Cambridge's population of 3,575, based on a multiplier of 6.5, in *Decline and growth*, pp. 31, 65.
21 Goose, 'Household size', pp. 118–19; Goose, 'Economic and social aspects', pp. 242, 429–32.
22 Goose, 'Fertility', p. 192, produces a revised population estimate for Cambridge based on the 1563 census which includes a correction factor of 25 per cent to the original figure for the town.
23 Goose, 'Household size', p. 119.
24 T.A.R. Evans and R.J. Faith, 'College estates and university finances, 1350–1500', in J.I. Catto and R. Evans, eds., *The history of the University of Oxford*, ii: *late medieval Oxford* (Oxford, 1992), pp. 641–2, 659–61.
25 Aston, Duncan and Evans, 'Alumni', 12–13 and n. 8.
26 14 & 15 Henry VIII, c. 16: *SR*, iii, p. 240; TNA: PRO E 179/81/133, rot. 5.
27 *LP*, Addenda 1, Part 1, no. 357, pp. 105–10; Leader, *University*, pp. 258–9.
28 Aston, Duncan and Evans, 'Alumni', 19.

Table 2.1

Estimates of the town and university populations, 1377–1587

Town population			University population			Total population
Date	Source	Approx. no.	Date	Source	Approx. no.	
1377	Poll tax	3,614	1377	Clerical tax	400–700	4,000–4,300
1524–5	Lay subsidies	2,600 (3,300)	mid C15	Estimate	1,300	3,900 (4,600)
1563	Bishops' census	c.3,000	1564	University assessment	1,267	4,270
1587	Vice-Chancellor's estimate	5,000	1587	Vice-Chancellor's estimate	1,500	6,500

Sources: See text.

have fallen from the late 1530s, with the religious changes, notably the dissolution of the monasteries, they had recovered by 1564, when an assessment of the university recorded 1,267 members, while the vice-chancellor's estimate in 1587 included 1,500 scholars.[29] The student figures are very much a matter of intelligent guess work until the records of university matriculations begin in 1544. These show that numbers had almost doubled by 1570, from 150 to 300 per annum.[30]

Given these uncertainties, the total populations for the town and university set out in Table 2.1 can only be approximate. The estimates of the university's population strongly suggest that the expansion of the university in the fifteenth century helped Cambridge to avoid the worst effects of population decline. It seems likely, though, that some decline in the town's population occurred despite the university's growth, given the evidence of a significant tax reduction awarded to the town in 1465 and declining rents in the fifteenth century.[31] Therefore the lower figure for the town's population in 1524–5 appears more plausible, and an increase (rather than a decrease) in population during the second and third quarters of the sixteenth century seems more likely given the evidence, outlined in subsequent chapters, of some revival of economic activity in the town during this period.

Taxation assessments in other parts of the county were not significantly affected by the exemptions that some colleges secured. The colleges were freed from liability to pay the fifteenths and tenths by statute in 1512, although prior to this, some colleges gained writs of exemption for their estates in Cambridgeshire.[32] The recorded quotas of 1334, though, were produced when only five colleges had been founded with limited endowments. Although the colleges were also exempt from all the Tudor lay subsidies up to 1527,[33] outside Cambridge this dispensation was not

---

29 *Annals*, ii, pp. 206–7; Goose, 'Household size', p. 119. The 1564 figure included servants at King's and Trinity colleges.

30 J.A. Venn, *Oxford and Cambridge matriculations 1544–1906, with a graphic chart illustrating the varying fortunes of the two universities* (Cambridge, 1908); J. A. Venn, *A statistical chart to illustrate the entries at the various colleges in the university of Cambridge, 1504–1907* (Cambridge, 1908).

31 See below, pp. 43–4 and 174–82.

32 TNA: PRO E 179/81/107, E 179/241/318; R.S. Schofield, 'Parliamentary land taxation 1485–1547' (unpublished PhD thesis, University of Cambridge, 1963), p. 146.

33 Schofield, 'Parliamentary land taxation', pp. 146, 253.

significant. In any case, tenants were not assessed on lands held by copyhold or leasehold in the subsidies and surveys of the 1520s;[34] tenants of college properties do not appear to have been exempt from assessments on other lands and goods. Dame Elizabeth Payton of Isleham, for example, who held a lease from King's College of all lands in the lordship of Isleham for 15 years from 1519, was assessed at £80 in goods in 1524.[35] In practice, therefore, the exemption of the colleges' lands and goods does not affect the use of the lay subsidies for Cambridgeshire, apart from within the town of Cambridge.

Comparing urban centres

Using taxation returns, Cambridge's population and wealth can be compared with other urban centres: with the leading provincial towns across the country, the largest towns within a 50-mile region, and the smaller centres within 15 miles of the town. Such comparisons still risk errors, caused by variations in assessments between towns, the extent to which suburban development was included, and the unreliability of certain returns, but provide a starting point in the absence of better data.[36]

Among the ranks of the largest and wealthiest towns in England, Cambridge rose in terms of size, but fell in terms of wealth, between the fourteenth and sixteenth centuries. In the poll tax of 1377, Cambridge was the twenty-first largest town; by 1524–5 it had risen to the fifteenth largest town (including London). But in terms of ranking by urban taxable wealth, Cambridge fell from the twentieth to thirtieth place between 1334 and 1524–5. By the mid-seventeenth century, Cambridge had risen to the tenth largest town.[37]

Arguably more important than Cambridge's national standing, however, was the town's performance in relation to neighbouring towns, its potential competitors. The larger towns and regional centres[38] within a radius of 50 miles from Cambridge included towns of varying size and function. There were the ports of Lynn and Ipswich, the centres of county administration at Bury St Edmunds, Northampton and Huntingdon, the older textile centres of Stamford and Northampton, towns where cloth-making had developed more recently, as at Colchester, Bury and Hadleigh, and the smaller centres of Saffron Walden, Wisbech and Wymondham. Additionally, there were several major cities which lay just outside this 50-mile radius, but with which Cambridge had links: the regional capital of Norwich, the cloth-making city of Coventry, the university town of Oxford, and London. Of course, these straight-line distances give no indication of travelling time, and it is likely that several of these

---

34 Hoyle, *Taxation records*, p. 14; J.C.K. Cornwall, *Wealth and society in early sixteenth-century England* (London, 1988), p. 107.

35 KC, Ledger Book, i, fol. 248; TNA: PRO E 179/81/137, rot. 2v.

36 Dobson, 'Urban decline', pp. 282–3.

37 Based on the ranking of towns in Dyer, *Decline and growth*, pp. 56–63. In a slightly wider list of towns, Cambridge rose in rank by population from 22nd place in 1377 to 18th in 1524–5, and fell in rank by wealth from 21st place in 1334 to 35th in 1524–5: A. Dyer, 'Ranking lists of English medieval towns', in *CUHB*, i, pp. 755–68.

38 Defined here as towns with over 250 taxpayers in 1524–5.

Table 2.2

Taxpaying populations of major towns and regional centres within 50 miles of Cambridge, 1377 and 1524–5

	1377		1524–5		1377 – 1524–5
	Taxpayers	Rank order	Taxpayers	Rank order	Change in rank
Cambridge	1,902	4	550	3	1
Bury St Edmunds	2,445	3	645	2	1
Colchester	2,955	2	701	1	1
Ely	1,394[a]	7	300	12	–5
Hadleigh	917[b]	12	311	10	2
Huntingdon	1,384[a]	8	433	7	1
Ipswich	1,507	5	484	4	1
Lynn	3,127	1	330[b]	9	–8
Northampton	1,477	6	477	5	1
Saffron Walden	1,040[b]	11	380	8	3
St Albans	1,300[b]	10	463[c]	6	4
Stamford	1,340	9	308	11	–2
Wisbech	862	13	252	14	–1
Wymondham	786[b]	14	287	13	1

Source: From the 57 largest provincial towns in 1377 and 1524–5, listed in Dyer, *Decline and growth*, pp. 64–6, except where noted below.
Notes: [a] Revised figure from Dyer, 'Urban decline', pp. 273–6
[b] Estimate
[c] Revised figure based on a more careful urban/rural delineation from N. Goose, 'People and society in Hertfordshire's early modern towns' (forthcoming)

major centres, particularly London and Norwich, were easier and quicker to reach than smaller centres which were closer in distance. Nonetheless, for convenience, the 50-mile radius will be adopted here.

The period between 1377 and 1524–5 saw some adjustment within the urban hierarchy of larger towns, in terms of the total number of taxpayers, in the 50-mile region around Cambridge. As Table 2.2 shows, while the position of Cambridge remained relatively stable between these two dates, two larger centres of Lynn and Ely fell significantly in rank, and the smaller centres of St Albans, Saffron Walden and Hadleigh appear to have experienced relative growth. This pronounced relative decline of some larger centres and the relative growth of a number of smaller towns is a trend mirrored by comparisons of urban populations on a country-wide basis.[39]

Turning to comparisons of taxable wealth between the same group of towns in 1334 and 1524–5, shown in Table 2.3, the pattern is somewhat different. Although the 1334 returns may have inflated the position of ports over inland towns,[40] Lynn and Ipswich retained their leading positions in the ranking of wealth in 1524–5. This probably reflected the continuing overseas trade handled by these ports, and was despite Lynn's significant fall in ranking by the number of taxpayers. Colchester and

---

39 Dyer, 'Urban decline', p. 285.
40 Nightingale, 'Lay subsidies', 1–32.

Table 2.3

Taxable wealth of major towns and regional centres within 50 miles of Cambridge, 1334 and 1524–5

	1334 Wealth £	1334 Rank order	1524–5 Wealth £	1524–5 Rank order	1334 – 1524–5 Change in rank
Cambridge	31.07	3	96.53	7	–4
Bury St Edmunds	24.00	5	169.43	4	1
Colchester	17.43	10	215.90	3	7
Ely	23.84	7	69.23	10	–3
Hadleigh	8.50	12	108.52	5	7
Huntingdon	8.00	13	46.82	12	1
Ipswich	43.02	1	282.10	1	0
Lynn	33.33	2	267.55	2	0
Northampton	18.00	8	91.20	8	0
Saffron Walden	4.73	14	55.78	11	3
St Albans	17.70	9	104.13	6	3
Stamford	23.92	6	90.17	9	–3
Wisbech	27.30	4	44.16	14	–10
Wymondham	13.00	11	44.95	13	–2

Source: 1334: *Lay subsidy of 1334*; 1524–5: Sheail, *Regional distribution*, ii.
Notes: Figures are taxation assessments. Boroughs taxed at one tenth in 1334 have been converted to one fifteenth. The highest figure from the 1524 and 1525 assessments has been used.

Hadleigh increased substantially in ranking by wealth by the early sixteenth century, and in these two towns, as in Bury St Edmunds, this wealth came largely from the cloth industry. By the 1460s, Hadleigh and Bury were among the leading cloth markets in Suffolk, and Colchester was the largest cloth market in Essex. Lavenham and Long Melford produced even more striking examples of the wealth generated by the Suffolk cloth industry: despite having populations of less than 1,300, they had tax assessments of £180 and £65 respectively in the 1520s, greater than many large towns.[41] The relative increase in wealth at St Albans may be attributed to its role as a market for basic commodities to the capital and its rise as an innkeeping town, and the relative increase at Saffron Walden arguably reflected the development of the town as a marketing centre for saffron, which was cultivated in the vicinity.[42]

Cambridge, Ely, and Wisbech all declined in ranking by wealth between 1334 and 1524–5. To some extent, this may just reflect the concentration of wealth within the cloth-making regions. The substantial drop in relative wealth at Wisbech, though, may partly be due to the effects of flooding, which the surveyors of Wisbech hundred drew attention to in 1524.[43] Ely's relative decline in size and wealth may have reflected the downturn in the town's economy, which has been attributed to the cessation of major

---

41 Britnell, *Colchester*, pp. 189, 191; G.A. Thornton, *A history of Clare, Suffolk* (Cambridge, 1928), pp. 150–3; Sheail, *Regional distribution*, ii, p. 322.

42 N. Goose, 'People and society in Hertfordshire's early modern towns' (forthcoming); for Saffron Walden, see below, pp. 108–13.

43 Sheail, *Regional distribution*, i, p. 70.

Table 2.4

Taxable wealth of small towns around Cambridge, 1334 and 1524–5

	1334 Wealth £	1334 Rank order	1524–5 Wealth £	1524–5 Rank order	1334–1524–5 Change in rank
Ashwell	9.99	4	15.35	7	−3
Gamlingay	9.70	5	10.24	9	−4
Godmanchester	9.51[a]	6	35.58	1	5
Haverhill	6.79	9	5.73	11	−2
Linton	8.50[b]	7	12.52	8	−1
Mildenhall	11.50	3	19.40	5	−2
Newmarket	7.00[b]	8	9.57[c]	10	−2
Ramsey	6.10	10	28.97	3	7
Royston	3.50[d]	11	15.64[d]	6	5
St Ives	16.23[e]	1	21.20	4	−3
St Neots	12.92[b]	2	34.42	2	0

Source: 1334: Lay subsidy of 1334; 1524–5: Sheail, Regional distribution, ii.
Notes: Figures are taxation assessments. The highest figure is used from 1524–5 returns.
[a] Taxed at one tenth in 1334 and converted to one fifteenth
[b] Includes totals of neighbouring villages
[c] Includes Cambridgeshire and Suffolk assessments
[d] Includes Cambridgeshire and Hertfordshire assessments
[e] Includes St Ives with the soke of Slepe and the prior of St Ives' manor

building projects by the monastery, the slump of trade at the ports of the Wash and the decline of the town's trade in ale.[44] Cambridge's relative decline in wealth may to some extent be illusory, merely reflecting the greater share of the town's wealth that was in the hands of the university and colleges by the early sixteenth century, and not included in the taxation assessments.

The small towns that surrounded Cambridge also experienced relative changes in wealth between the fourteenth and sixteenth centuries. No poll tax schedules survive for Huntingdonshire to provide comparisons of change in size over the same period. Identifying small towns among rural settlements is difficult. They can be defined as compact and permanent settlements where high proportions of the inhabitants pursued non-agricultural trades, but the evidence is often incomplete.[45] Within a 20-mile radius of Cambridge, there were around 11 small towns with between about 80 and 200 taxpayers in 1524–5.

Among the eleven small towns, one of the largest relative increases in wealth between 1334 and 1524–5 occurred at Royston (Table 2.4). This can be attributed to the town's role in the malt barley trade, which developed during the fifteenth century.[46] The relative decline of wealth at Gamlingay may be due to competition from the neighbouring small town of Potton, to where Gamlingay's market was eventually

---

44 A. Koren, 'Ely in the late middle ages' (unpublished PhD thesis, Indiana University, 1977), pp. 343–5.
45 C. Dyer, 'Small towns 1270–1540', in CUHB, i, pp. 505–10.
46 See below, p. 105.

transferred.[47] In comparison with other parishes in Cambridgeshire, however, both Gamlingay and Linton increased in rank order by wealth and number of taxpayers, suggesting that they were growing at a faster pace than most of the countryside in Cambridgeshire.[48]

Many of the smaller urban centres which surrounded Cambridge were 'new towns' founded during the economic expansion of the twelfth and thirteenth centuries. Royston developed where a house of Austin Friars established a market and fair at the intersection of two major roads, and promoted the cult of St Rohesia's shrine. The abbots of Ramsey built a new bridge, obtained the grant of a fair, and brought the bones of St Ivo to their new town of St Ives. St Neots probably developed in a similar way: adjacent to a priory, at the shrine of St Neot, and by a river crossing. By 1137, St Neots held three annual fairs, but these never rivalled the fair at St Ives which became an international trading event during the thirteenth century.[49] According to local tradition, Newmarket was founded when the market was removed from nearby Exning on account of the plague: the Argentein family may have established it as a speculative market at the meeting-point of two important roads. At the ancient settlement of Linton, burgage tenements were laid out, and in the thirteenth century a diverse range of craft occupational names could be found among the burgage tenants.[50] Several of these towns were situated on important roads. Harrison classed Linton, Newmarket, Huntingdon, Royston and Saffron Walden as thoroughfare towns in the late sixteenth century, as they each possessed several inns to accommodate passing travellers. In the mid-sixteenth century, Royston had at least 11 inns.[51]

As these towns developed relatively late, their sites often crossed established boundaries. Newmarket and Royston both lay across county boundaries, with split administrations. This makes comparisons of population and wealth difficult, as parts of the towns were often assessed in different counties. Such towns, and others like Brandon and Thetford, by virtue of their positions on the borders of counties, were popular haunts for criminals, who in the middle ages were outlawed only in the county of their offence.[52] Many of these modest market centres, frequently on major transport routes, often assumed an economic role relatively late in the period of medieval expansion.[53]

---

47 *VCH Cambs.*, v, pp. 78–9.
48 Lee, 'Cambridge and its region', pp. 300, 303.
49 M. Beresford, *New towns of the Middle Ages: town plantation in England, Wales and Gascony* (London, 1967), pp. 454, 456; *VCH Huntingdonshire*, ii, pp. 214–16.
50 P. May, *Newmarket – medieval and Tudor* (Newmarket, 1982), pp. 1–4; J.H. Clapham, 'A thirteenth-century market town: Linton, Cambs.', *Cambridge Historical Journal*, 4 (1933), 194–202.
51 William Harrison, *The description of England*, ed. G. Edelen, Folger Shakespeare Library (Ithaca, New York, 1968), pp. 397, 399, 400, 403; *VCH Hertfordshire*, iii, p. 255.
52 *VCH Hertfordshire*, iii, p. 259; Bailey, *Marginal economy?*, pp. 169–70.
53 C. Phythian-Adams, 'Local history and societal history', *Local Population Studies*, 51 (1993), 43.

Table 2.5

Comparative county lay wealth in £,000 per acre, 1334 and 1515

	1334 rank	1515 rank	Rate of growth of wealth per acre, 1334/1515
Cambs.	11	21	2.44
Essex	25	3	5.51
Herts.	17	8	4.05
Hunts.	10	9	3.25
Norfolk	3	12	2.21
Suffolk	18	7	4.11

Source: Schofield, 'Geographical distribution', 504.
Note: Ranked in order of wealth, out of 38 English counties. Isle of Ely included with Cambs.

Comparing counties

Schofield has compared the distribution of wealth per acre in England on a county basis between the lay subsidy of 1334 and an assessment of 1514–15. The later subsidy was levied on moveable goods, incomes and wages, like the taxes of 1524–5, but individual assessments for towns and villages do not survive. In 1334, Cambridgeshire ranked as the eleventh wealthiest county out of a total of 38. By 1515 it ranked twenty-first, below the average. The counties bordering Cambridgeshire generally grew much more in their amount of wealth per acre over the same period, and by 1515 they all exceeded Cambridgeshire in rank, even though most had not been as wealthy as Cambridgeshire in 1334 (Table 2.5). Only Norfolk had a similar growth rate to Cambridgeshire and fell in ranking between the two dates.[54] Such analysis masks, however, the increases in wealth in parts of Cambridgeshire, which were comparable with the areas of largest growth elsewhere.

Changes in wealth per acre between 1334 and 1524–5 have also been examined across the country on a more detailed scale than the county, in 610 units covering most of England. The 1524–5 tax was expressed as a percentage of the assessed wealth of 1334, in the form of quintiles. The highest quintile, indicating the largest increase in wealth, occurred in Cambridgeshire only in the north-west corner of the Isle of Ely, around Chatteris. There were two areas with the lowest quintile showing the least growth in the south-western and central-southern parts of the county. In the adjoining counties there were areas with the highest growth in the area around Huntingdon in Huntingdonshire, Saffron Walden and Thaxted in Essex, and Bury St Edmunds and the Stour Valley in Suffolk. Increases in wealth across the country were generated by a variety of local factors and two main stimuli – the cloth industry and London's demand for foodstuffs.[55]

Comparisons of population levels in the 1377 poll tax and 1524–5 subsidies on a county basis, calculated as taxpayers per square mile, are similar to comparisons of wealth, with the East Midlands, including Cambridgeshire and Norfolk, revealing a

---

54 Schofield, 'Geographical distribution', 504–5.
55 H.C. Darby, R.E. Glasscock, J. Sheail and G.R. Versey, 'The changing geographical distribution of wealth in England: 1086–1334–1525', *Journal of Historical Geography*, 5 (1979), 257–61.

Cambridge and its economic region, 1450–1560

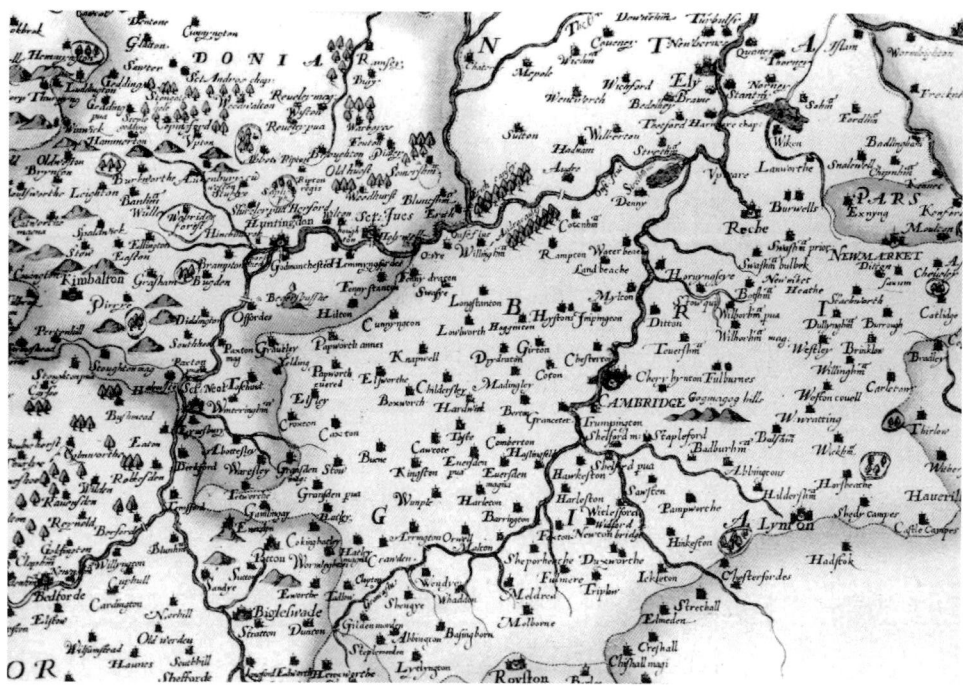

Figure 2.1 Cambridgeshire, from Christopher Saxton's map of 1576 (Cambridgeshire Collection)

lower rate of increase than Huntingdonshire, Hertfordshire, Essex, Suffolk and the south-east. In relation to 32 English counties, Cambridgeshire remained in the ranks of the upper half, with regard to the density of its population, but not in terms of population growth, between 1377 and 1524. Again, those counties experiencing growth often possessed expanding cloth industries or links with the London food market.[56]

Thus Cambridgeshire did not grow significantly in wealth or population between the fourteenth and early sixteenth centuries: in comparison to the country as a whole, or in comparison with most of its neighbouring counties, rates of increase in the county were low. The more detailed comparison of wealth, however, shows that the pace of growth varied significantly in different parts of the county: some areas matched the highest national rate of increase, other areas experienced the lowest national rate of growth. Furthermore, the Cambridgeshire fenland, a large area of sparse settlement, tended to deflate the county's wealth and population when measured by area, in comparison with counties of denser settlement. Only analysis on a more detailed level can show the significant variations in population and wealth between different sub-regions and villages in Cambridgeshire.

Comparing sub-regions and parishes

Administrative boundaries of counties or hundreds often failed to reflect important

---

56   Dyer, *Decline and growth*, pp. 32–4.

Population and wealth

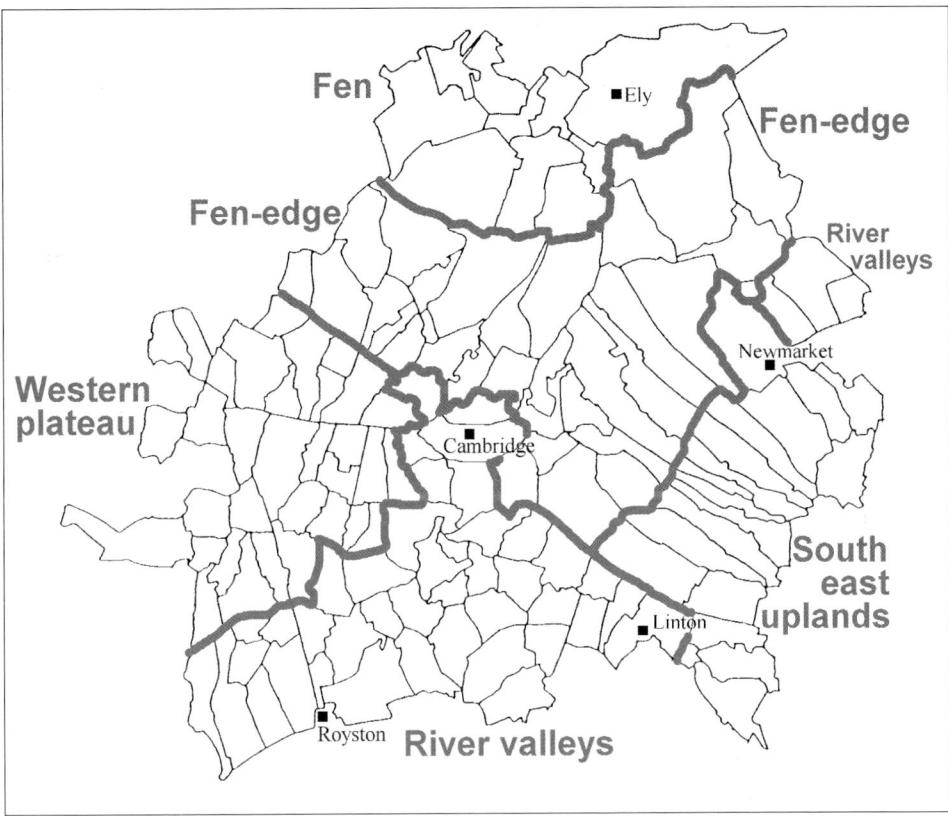

Figure 2.2 Cambridgeshire parishes grouped by sub-region

differences in soil type, relief, natural resources and access to markets, which placed significant constraints on the economic activities that could be practised. The exchange of agrarian products between these differing agricultural regions was the basis upon which Cambridge, like most other market towns, operated. Cambridgeshire was predominantly an agricultural county, but comprised important sub-regional contrasts in types of landscape, settlement and farming patterns.[57] Five sub-regions are defined in Figure 2.2. The allocation of parishes to sub-regions has had to be somewhat arbitrary, as in practice many parishes straddle more than one type of land. The area examined is the whole of the historic county of Cambridgeshire, together with the southern part of the Isle of Ely, going as far north as the parishes of Sutton, Mepal, Witcham and Wentworth. The urban parishes of Cambridge, Ely, Newmarket and Royston are excluded from this analysis.

Each of the Cambridgeshire sub-regions had a particular landscape, geology, and agricultural and settlement pattern. Pastoral farming predominated in the peat fen,

---

57 M. Spufford, 'General view of the rural economy of the county of Cambridge', *PCAS*, 89 (2000), 69–85.

Table 2.6

Taxable wealth per acre, by sub-region

	Tax £	Acreage	Pence per acre	Rank
1334				
fen-edge	242.25	108,025	0.54	3
fen	30.38	28,869	0.25	5
south-east uplands	70.58	42,932	0.39	4
river valleys	274.99	88,220	0.75	1
western plateau	184.78	60,703	0.73	2
Total	802.97	328,749	0.59	
1524				
fen-edge	166.50	86,181	0.46	4
fen	66.71	31,540	0.51	2
south-east uplands	57.49	37,581	0.37	5
river valleys	201.03	78,079	.62	1
western plateau	98.96	48,566	0.49	3
Total	590.70	281,947	0.50	

Source: 1334: *Lay subsidy*, pp. 23–8; 1524: Sheail, *Regional distribution*, ii, pp. 28–35; Acreage: *VCH Cambs.*, ii, pp. 136–40.
Notes: Acreage from the total of parishes with surviving returns. The column headed 'Pence per acre' has been calculated as ([Tax in £]*240)/Acreage.

while the inhabitants also exploited the fen through fishing, fowling, and the cutting of reeds, sedge, turves and rushes. Settlement was scattered and the parishes large. Dairy farming was also prominent in the fen-edge, where parishes shared fenland and chalkland, providing plentiful meadow and pasture. The river valleys, an area of much denser settlement, was a 'sheep-corn' region, where large sheep flocks were kept and barley cultivated, but there were also water meadows along the river. The western plateau of boulder clay, and the south-eastern uplands, with clay and chalk heath, were both regions of later and sparser settlement.[58] Arable cultivation was prominent, although several villages in the south-east also supplied firewood and charcoal during the later middle ages.[59] The Isle of Ely, comprising the peat fen and the silt fen lying further to the north-east, was a liberty in which the bishop of Ely enjoyed extensive powers and was one of the main landowners, the other being Ely Cathedral Priory. Outside the Isle there were few large estates, although the earl of Oxford had a number of manors based on Castle Camps, and it was generally a county of modest landholdings held by a range of owners from knights to wealthy local officials.[60]

The relative wealth of the Cambridgeshire sub-regions changed between 1334 and 1524 as Table 2.6 shows. The tax assessment for each vill in the sub-region has been added together, and divided by the total acreage of the sub-region to produce a figure

---

[58] Darby, *Fenland*, pp. 23–84; *VCH Cambs.*, v, p. 3, vi, p. 126, ix, p. 1; Taylor, *Cambridgeshire landscape*, pp. 24–5, 85–7.

[59] See below, pp. 156–61.

[60] A. Emery, *Greater medieval houses of England and Wales 1300–1500*, ii: *East Anglia central England and Wales* (Cambridge, 2000), p. 16.

Table 2.7

Taxpayers per acre, by sub-region

	Taxpayers	Acreage	Taxpayers per 100 acres	Rank
1377				
fen-edge	6,031	95,877	6.3	3
fen	1,389	31,540	4.4	5
south-east uplands	2,173	48,003	4.5	4
river valleys	5,116	64,295	8.0	1
western plateau	3,915	60,703	6.5	2
Total	18,624	300,418	6.2	
1524				
fen-edge	1,213	86,181	1.4	4
fen	662	31,540	2.1	2
south-east uplands	468	37,581	1.3	5
river valleys	1,660	74,066	2.2	1
western plateau	767	50,309	1.5	3
Total	4,770	279,677	1.7	
1563				
fen-edge	1,410	81,500	1.7	2
fen	525	31,540	1.6	3
south-east uplands	504	35,022	1.4	4
river valleys	1,611	79,457	2.0	1
western plateau	810	60,703	1.3	5
Total	4,860	288,222	1.7	

Source: 1377: *Poll taxes*, i, pp. 68–74; 1524: Sheail, *Regional distribution*, ii, pp. 28–35; 1563: BL, Harleian MS 594, fols. 198–200v; Acreage: *VCH Cambs.*, ii, pp. 136–40.
Notes: Acreage from the total of parishes with surviving returns.

of pence per acre. The sub-regions have then been ranked from 1 (the sub-region with the highest pence per acre) to 5 (the lowest).[61] The river valleys sub-region remained the wealthiest area in terms of pence per acre, but the positions of the other sub-regions moved between 1334 and 1524. The western plateau and south-east uplands, areas of heavier clay soils, both slipped in rank. The fenland showed a relative increase in wealth, which may reflect the better returns that could be generated from pastoral farming and the products of the fen during the later middle ages than from areas where arable farming was more dominant. Similar changes occurred in the distribution of population in the sub-regions, as Table 2.7 shows. The river valleys region remained the most densely populated region, but the relative size of the populations of the western plateau and south-east uplands contracted between 1377 and 1563. The fen and fen-edge generally grew in relative wealth at the expense of the areas of heavier soils.

Important sub-regional variations in growth occurred in Cambridgeshire during the later middle ages. With falling demand for arable produce for much of this period, the heavier soils of the western plateau and south-east uplands experienced a contraction

---

61 The technique is based on that used by M. Yates in 'Continuity and change in rural society c.1400–1600: West Hanney and Shaw (Berkshire) and their region' (unpublished D.Phil. thesis, University of Oxford, 1997), pp. 61–76.

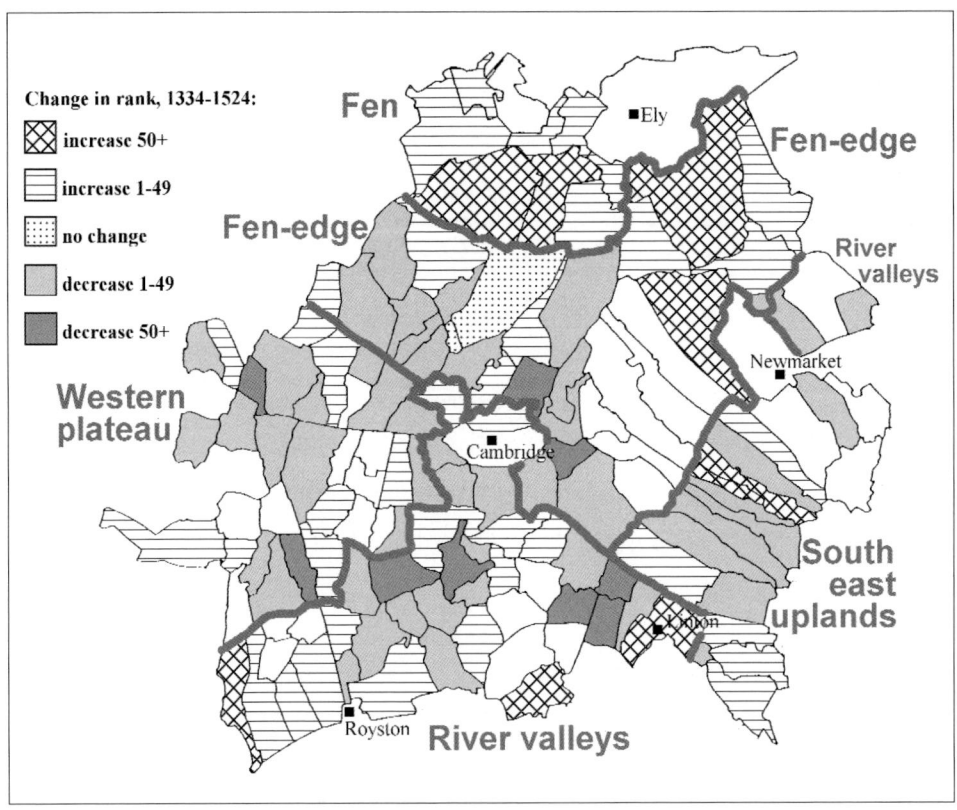

Figure 2.3 Changes in the ranking of parishes by wealth, 1334–1524
Source: See Table 2.6.

in settlement, and these areas experienced the greatest relative falls in population and wealth and the largest reductions in taxation within the county. In contrast, the greater opportunities for pastoral farming and other activities allowed the fen and fen-edge regions to maintain, and in some places to increase, their relative shares of wealth and population over the period. The river valleys region remained the wealthiest region in per acre terms and the most densely populated area of the county in 1524 as it had been in 1334.

Comparison of taxation returns on a parish basis, though, reveals that growth and decline were not as uniform as the sub-regional trends might suggest. The greatest increases in wealth, where parishes increased fifty or more places in rank order between the two dates, occurred on the fringes of the area of study, and were not confined to any one sub-region (Figure 2.3). They included Haddenham and Wilburton on the fen, Soham and Burwell on the fen-edge, Guilden Morden, Ickleton and Linton in the river valleys, and Burrough Green with Westley Waterless on the south-east uplands. The largest decreases occurred at Milton and Teversham on the fen-edge, Little Abington and Barrington in the river valleys, and Papworth Everard on the western plateau. The changes in the ranking of parishes by the number of taxpayers reveal a similar, but not identical, pattern to the changes in wealth (Figure 2.4). The greatest increases occurred in the fenland vills of Wilburton and Haddenham, with

Table 2.7

Taxpayers per acre, by sub-region

	Taxpayers	Acreage	Taxpayers per 100 acres	Rank
1377				
fen-edge	6,031	95,877	6.3	3
fen	1,389	31,540	4.4	5
south-east uplands	2,173	48,003	4.5	4
river valleys	5,116	64,295	8.0	1
western plateau	3,915	60,703	6.5	2
Total	18,624	300,418	6.2	
1524				
fen-edge	1,213	86,181	1.4	4
fen	662	31,540	2.1	2
south-east uplands	468	37,581	1.3	5
river valleys	1,660	74,066	2.2	1
western plateau	767	50,309	1.5	3
Total	4,770	279,677	1.7	
1563				
fen-edge	1,410	81,500	1.7	2
fen	525	31,540	1.6	3
south-east uplands	504	35,022	1.4	4
river valleys	1,611	79,457	2.0	1
western plateau	810	60,703	1.3	5
Total	4,860	288,222	1.7	

Source: 1377: *Poll taxes*, i, pp. 68–74; 1524: Sheail, *Regional distribution*, ii, pp. 28–35; 1563: BL, Harleian MS 594, fols. 198–200v; Acreage: *VCH Cambs.*, ii, pp. 136–40.
Notes: Acreage from the total of parishes with surviving returns.

of pence per acre. The sub-regions have then been ranked from 1 (the sub-region with the highest pence per acre) to 5 (the lowest).[61] The river valleys sub-region remained the wealthiest area in terms of pence per acre, but the positions of the other sub-regions moved between 1334 and 1524. The western plateau and south-east uplands, areas of heavier clay soils, both slipped in rank. The fenland showed a relative increase in wealth, which may reflect the better returns that could be generated from pastoral farming and the products of the fen during the later middle ages than from areas where arable farming was more dominant. Similar changes occurred in the distribution of population in the sub-regions, as Table 2.7 shows. The river valleys region remained the most densely populated region, but the relative size of the populations of the western plateau and south-east uplands contracted between 1377 and 1563. The fen and fen-edge generally grew in relative wealth at the expense of the areas of heavier soils.

Important sub-regional variations in growth occurred in Cambridgeshire during the later middle ages. With falling demand for arable produce for much of this period, the heavier soils of the western plateau and south-east uplands experienced a contraction

---

61 The technique is based on that used by M. Yates in 'Continuity and change in rural society c.1400–1600: West Hanney and Shaw (Berkshire) and their region' (unpublished D.Phil. thesis, University of Oxford, 1997), pp. 61–76.

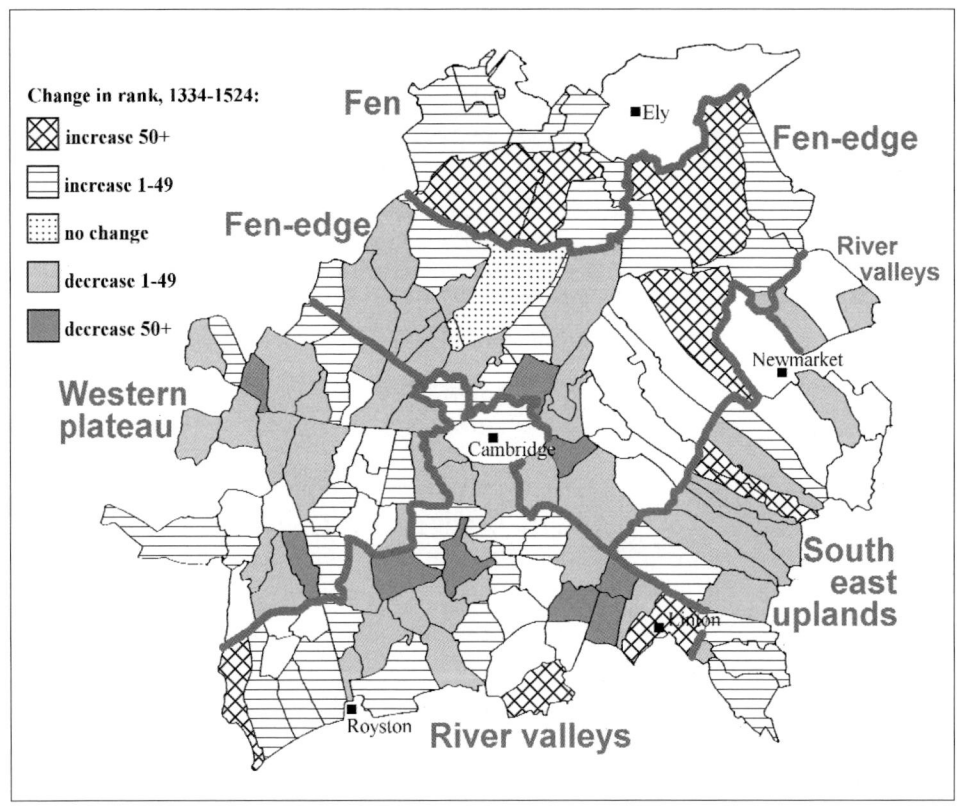

Figure 2.3 Changes in the ranking of parishes by wealth, 1334–1524
Source: See Table 2.6.

in settlement, and these areas experienced the greatest relative falls in population and wealth and the largest reductions in taxation within the county. In contrast, the greater opportunities for pastoral farming and other activities allowed the fen and fen-edge regions to maintain, and in some places to increase, their relative shares of wealth and population over the period. The river valleys region remained the wealthiest region in per acre terms and the most densely populated area of the county in 1524 as it had been in 1334.

Comparison of taxation returns on a parish basis, though, reveals that growth and decline were not as uniform as the sub-regional trends might suggest. The greatest increases in wealth, where parishes increased fifty or more places in rank order between the two dates, occurred on the fringes of the area of study, and were not confined to any one sub-region (Figure 2.3). They included Haddenham and Wilburton on the fen, Soham and Burwell on the fen-edge, Guilden Morden, Ickleton and Linton in the river valleys, and Burrough Green with Westley Waterless on the south-east uplands. The largest decreases occurred at Milton and Teversham on the fen-edge, Little Abington and Barrington in the river valleys, and Papworth Everard on the western plateau. The changes in the ranking of parishes by the number of taxpayers reveal a similar, but not identical, pattern to the changes in wealth (Figure 2.4). The greatest increases occurred in the fenland vills of Wilburton and Haddenham, with

Population and wealth

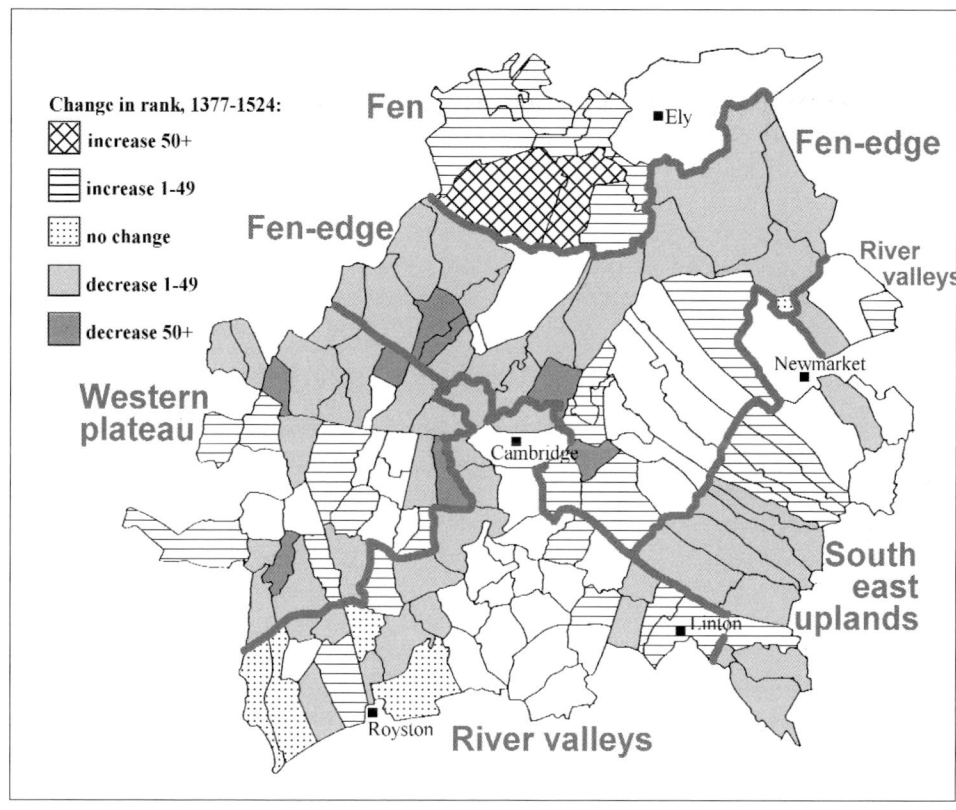

Figure 2.4 Changes in the ranking of parishes by number of taxpayers, 1377–1524
Source: See Table 2.7.

smaller pockets of growth taking place in all the sub-regions. The greatest decreases took place at Lolworth, Clopton, Papworth Everard and Barton on the western plateau, and Milton on the fen-edge.

Attempting to explain what caused these large relative increases in population and wealth in certain parishes between the fourteenth and sixteenth centuries is far from easy. Yates suggested three elements helped to determine the local pattern of economic development in West Berkshire during the later middle ages: ecological factors, types of lordship, and proximity to an expanding urban centre.[62] As the analysis of the sub-regions has shown, geological factors were of some importance, with the heavy clay soils of the western plateau and south-east uplands declining in wealth and population, and the river valleys generally experiencing growth, but such trends were not uniform within each sub-region. The urban centres of the region do not seem to have provided a significant stimulus for growth, although some parishes adjoining towns experienced a relative increase in wealth between 1334 and 1524. Some landlords offered greater opportunities for tenants to profit from their leases

---

62   Yates, 'Rural society', 617–37.

than others, and the fenland perhaps benefited from the inertia of institutional landlords more than the upland sub-regions, with more diverse patterns of lordship. At Wilburton, for instance, under the absentee bishop of Ely, tenants profited from fixed rents: in 1609 the rents of assize and demesne land were at almost the same level as a century before, and farm of the manor remained at the same sum as that received around 1426.[63] There were other local factors, such as the expansion of some settlements sited on major roads, or which supported markets, fairs, and non-agricultural trades. There was no single pattern of development, but a variety of local experiences, and from these, some trends can be identified.[64]

Additional evidence of areas of contracting population and wealth

The returns of the *Nonarum Inquisitionies*, a tax of one ninth levied on the value of corn, wool and lambs within each parish, indicate that a contraction of arable land occurred in Cambridgeshire between 1291 and 1341. The returns recorded vills with uncultivated land, which were proportionally most abundant in the south-east uplands and the western plateau, and much more scarce in the fen-edge and the fen sub-regions. So even before the Black Death, the expansion of land under cultivation that had characterised the twelfth and thirteenth centuries was coming to an end, and the majority of the vills within the county experiencing contraction were in the sub-regions of heavy soils and later settlement.[65]

Taxation reductions to the fifteenth and tenth were made in 1433 and 1446 and distributed among 'poor vills, cities and boroughs, desolate, wasted, destroyed or very impoverished, or otherwise too heavily burdened with tax'. While local commissioners apportioned these remissions within each county in differing ways, in at least some counties like Suffolk and Cambridgeshire, the reductions appear to have been allocated on the basis of need, and seem to provide an indicator of the extent of the relative decline in wealth and population since 1334.[66] Comparing the tax quotas for communities in Cambridgeshire in 1334 with the reductions allowed in 1443 and 1490–1 (the latter containing the additional reduction made in 1446), the western plateau and the south-east uplands gained the largest percentage reductions of the five sub-regions. The fen and fen-edge received the smallest proportions of relief. Although the parishes with the largest reductions were scattered across much of the county, there were concentrations on the western plateau and south-east uplands.[67]

Where populations fell substantially, ambitious landowners could consolidate and enclose their holdings. Childerely, Clopton, East Hatley and Shingay were among several Cambridgeshire villages which received large taxation reductions and

---

63 Maitland, 'Cambridgeshire manor', 432–9.
64 J.S. Lee, 'Tracing regional and local changes in population and wealth during the later middle ages using taxation records: Cambridgeshire, 1334–1563', *Local Population Studies*, 69 (2002), 39–41.
65 Ibid., 42.
66 D. Dymond and R. Virgoe, 'The reduced population and wealth of early fifteenth-century Suffolk', *Proceedings of Suffolk Institute of Archaeology*, 36 (1985–8), 73–100.
67 TNA: PRO E 179/81/80, E 179/81/120; Lee, 'Regional and local changes', 43–6.

experienced significant relative decline in population and wealth, and where arable lands had been turned to pasture and enclosures had taken place by the early sixteenth century.[68] Deserted medieval villages, which appear to have been abandoned during the population decline of the late fourteenth and fifteenth centuries, provide the most striking evidence of the contraction of population and land under cultivation. In Cambridgeshire, these sites tended to be found on the western plateau and river valleys. Very little enclosure or desertion of villages occurred in the fen or fen-edge sub-regions.[69]

The town of Cambridge petitioned for substantial reductions in its financial obligations to the crown during the fifteenth century, both for the annual fee farm paid by the borough corporation, and the total amount of tax paid by residents. Requesting a reduction to the fee farm in 1402, the burgesses stated that the town was wasted and impoverished following the loss of franchises after the Peasants' Revolt, damage from fire, and the diminution of people in the town since Richard II's reign. It was not until 1483, though, that a deduction of £10 was granted, and this does not appear to have continued after Henry VII's accession.[70] Cambridge received a reduction of only 40s, or 4 per cent of its total tax quota in 1433, but a much larger reduction of £26 12s 2½d was given in 1446 and confirmed in 1465. The burgesses had complained to parliament that a number of houses were standing empty and craftsmen were leaving, while the sites acquired for King's College and for students' lodgings were exempt from tax, unduly burdening the rest of the town.[71]

Many boroughs secured remissions of fee farm payments and taxation during the fifteenth century. Whether these concessions represent a genuine decline in urban wealth or merely the strength of civic lobbying has been a central point of contention within the 'urban decline' debate.[72] Borough income formed only a tiny part of the town's aggregate income, and its fluctuations could reflect political decisions rather than trends in the wider urban economy.[73] Cambridge lost part of the communal income that it had allocated to pay the borough fee farm in 1382 when, as a punishment for its involvement in the Peasants' Revolt, the corporation's profits from the regulation of foodstuffs and weights and measures were given to the university, and the town's fee farm was raised by just over £2 to £70 per year. However, the borough treasurers' income from property also declined considerably between the 1420s and 1480s, suggesting a more widespread downturn within the town's economy.[74] The petitions for a reduction in taxation also reflected the corporation's resentment towards the university's exemption from civic dues. The statement in

---

68 These enclosures should be distinguished from the enclosures of common pastures made during the mid-sixteenth century in densely populated parts of the county, such as at Cambridge and Landbeach: see below, p. 82.
69 Lee, 'Regional and local changes', 45–6.
70 *Annals*, i, pp. 148, 227; *VCH Cambs.*, iii, p. 35.
71 *Annals*, i, pp. 197, 214; *Charters of the borough of Cambridge*, pp. xxvi, 54–61.
72 Phythian-Adams, 'Urban decline', pp. 161–2; Bridbury, 'English provincial towns', 2–5; Dyer, *Decline and growth*, pp. 39–41.
73 Britnell, 'Economy of British towns', p. 331; Dobson, 'Urban decline', p. 277.
74 See below, pp. 177–8.

Table 2.8

Distribution of taxpayers by wealth in Cambridge, 1524–5

	<£2%	£2–4%	£5–9%	£10–19%	>£20%
Cambridge	55	28	5.2	7.1	4.7

Source: Goose, 'Economic and social aspects', p. 72, with thanks to Professor Nigel Goose for permission to reproduce this data from his unpublished thesis.

1446 that craftsmen were allegedly leaving the town as the number of scholars increased must be counterbalanced with the tremendous demand generated by the construction of new colleges like King's, whether in the form of building materials or consumer goods and services for college members. In the same period, Oxford put forward a contrary argument: a decline in artificers had resulted in students withdrawing from the town.[75]

Distributions of taxable wealth

Goose has analysed the social structure of Cambridge using the taxation returns of 1524–5. As Table 2.8 shows, the distribution of wealth recorded in these assessments formed a pyramid, with a broad base of poorer inhabitants and progressively fewer taxpayers in the higher bands of wealth. Other sixteenth-century towns had similar pyramids of wealth, but Cambridge had a broader base, with 83 per cent of taxpayers assessed on £4 or less, compared with between 67 and 79 per cent in nine other towns of comparable size. Cambridge's pyramid of wealth also had a lower peak, as the town's wealthiest taxpayers owned only 17 per cent of the total taxable wealth, compared to 43 and 53 per cent in the textile-producing towns of Colchester and Reading. This suggests that fortunes were more readily generated within the cloth-making towns than among the inland trade and service functions that dominated Cambridge's economy.[76]

Within Cambridgeshire, the distribution of the wealthiest inhabitants is most clearly shown through the loan of 1522, levied on all those with more than £20 in goods and lands, and totals for the sub-regions are displayed in Table 2.9. As no settlements in the Isle of Ely are recorded, it is probable that this area was assessed separately. In per acre terms, the river valleys sub-region contained the highest number of payers and the greatest amount of wealth. The combined wealth of Cambridgeshire's richest inhabitants was not large in comparison with many other counties: the county's yield per thousand acres from the loan was just over £6, placing Cambridgeshire in twentieth place out of 32 counties. As in a subsidy of 1515, the total for the county in 1522 was substantially lower than all the counties that bordered Cambridgeshire.[77] Cambridgeshire had very few noble families resident in the county,

---

75 *VCH Cambs.*, iii, p. 12; *Rotuli Parliamentorum*, v, pp. 337–8.
76 Goose,'Economic and social aspects', pp. 55–91.
77 W.G. Hoskins, *The age of plunder: the England of Henry VIII, 1500–1547* (London, 1976), p. 24.

Table 2.9

Contributors to 1522 loan, by sub-region

	Payers	Assessed wealth £	Acreage £	Payers per 1,000 acres	Wealth per 1,000 acres £
fen-edge	115	4,145	108,025	1.06	38.38
south-east uplands	42	1,714	48,003	0.87	35.71
river valleys	104	3,997	88,220	1.18	45.31
western plateau	39	1,549	60,703	0.64	25.51
Total	300	11,405	336,491	0.89	33.89

Source: *LP*, iii (2), no. 2640, pp. 1116–19.
Note: There are no entries for the Isle of Ely, so the fen sub-region is not recorded.

Table 2.10

Distribution of taxpayers by wealth in Cambridgeshire sub-regions, 1524

	<£2%	£2–4%	£5–10%	>£10%
fen-edge	35.4	39.9	16.5	8.3
fen	48.3	34.4	11.3	6.0
south-east uplands	50.5	31.6	13.5	4.5
river valleys	59.4	22.1	10.9	7.6
western plateau	48.6	29.7	14.3	7.4
Total	49.0	30.7	13.2	7.1

Source: 1524 lay subsidy returns: TNA: PRO E 179/81/126, E 179/81/129–130, E 179/81/132, E 179/81/134, E 179/81/136–7, E 179/81/161, E 179/82/220, part 2, E 179/82/224, part 2.
Note: Percentage of total number of taxpayers in each sub-region. All assessments, whether based on lands, goods, or wages, are used.

and, as in Cambridge, there were no wealthy merchant clothiers with large fortunes generated through the cloth trade.

The surviving 1524 tax returns for Cambridgeshire have been used to produce the totals of occupational wealth in Table 2.10 for the sub-regions. Categories of wealth follow those used by Spufford, Wrightson and Levine. Taxpayers assessed at under £2 were generally labourers and servants. Those assessed at £2–4 were perhaps holding tenements of up to a yardland (30–40 acres) and could be described as husbandmen or craftsmen; those assessed at £5–10 were substantial husbandmen, craftsmen, and yeomen, farming perhaps 50–60 acres, and often the most prosperous men in their village. Large farmers and the gentry had assessments of over £10.[78]

It is generally accepted that in addition to those who were assessed on wages in the muster of 1522 and the subsidies of 1524–5, those who were assessed at below 40s on goods should also be classed as wage-earners. These men lacked the minimum amount of land from which a family could support itself without other

---

[78] Spufford, *Contrasting communities*, pp. 28–36; K. Wrightson and D. Levine, *Poverty and piety in an English village, Terling 1525–1700* (London, 1979), pp. 33–4. Cornwall, *Wealth and society*, pp. 14–30, uses higher bands of wealth for his categories.

employment – in Cambridgeshire perhaps half a yardland of 14 to 20 acres.[79] Grouping those with assessments of less than 40s in goods together with those charged on wages, the average percentage of wage-earners in a sample of six counties was 36 per cent, with Rutland having the highest proportion of 41 per cent.[80] In three central Essex hundreds, this figure was 43 per cent of all taxpayers, and in West Berkshire, 43 per cent of all men.[81] In Cambridgeshire, 49 per cent of taxpayers were assessed on wages of less than 40s in goods, well above the averages of the other counties stated above, and in Cambridge this rose to 55 per cent. Cambridgeshire, like Essex and other parts of south and eastern England, had a larger proportion of wage-earners than counties further north or west.[82]

There were significant sub-regional variations in the distribution of different categories of taxpayer too. As Table 2.10 reveals, the fen and fen-edge had the smallest numbers of wage-earners and the largest numbers of smallholders, with between £2 and £4 in wealth. Similar trends have been found in other regions where pastoral farming predominated.[83] Assessments of less than £2 occurred most frequently in the Cambridgeshire river valleys, where 10 per cent more taxpayers were charged at this rate than in the whole county. This sub-region was the wealthiest and most densely populated, and had seen the greatest increases in relative population and wealth between the fourteenth and sixteenth centuries. With large numbers of poor labourers together with some wealthier yeomen, the river valleys sub-region was similar to parts of Norfolk and Berkshire. All these regions were major corn-producing areas that transported grain to London.[84]

Fertility and mortality

Changes in the numbers of children recorded in wills provide an indicator of trends in fertility, which Goose has used to analyse trends in Cambridge between 1500 and 1700, and to compare with evidence from parish registers. The data indicate small increases in the average numbers of children and sons per male in wills proved in 1540–59, and more substantial increases in 1560–79, before stabilising for the rest of the century. This suggests that, at least among the population wealthy enough to leave wills, population was achieving natural growth by the mid-sixteenth century, and the rate of growth quickened after 1560.[85]

Parish registers provide another indicator of fertility and mortality, and baptisms and burials have been totalled for those parishes in the town and county where

---

79 Spufford, *Contrasting communities*, pp. 34–5.
80 C. Dyer, *Standards of living in the later middle ages: social change in England, c. 1200–1520* (Cambridge, 1989), p. 214.
81 Poos, *Essex*, pp. 28–31; Yates, 'Continuity and change', 94.
82 Poos, *Essex*, p. 30.
83 Cornwall, *Wealth and society*, pp. 35–42.
84 Ibid., pp. 32–3. The supply of grain to London from the Cambridge region is examined in Chapter 4, below.
85 Goose, 'Fertility', pp. 196–7.

Table 2.11

Net surplus or deficit in baptisms compared to burials in Cambridge parishes, 1540–70

	St Benedict	St Edward	St Mary the Great	St Mary the Less	All Saints	Total
1541–5	−28				−18	−46
1546–50	−20					−20
1551–5	5					5
1556–60	−18	−5	10	−21		−34
1561–5	−17	22	28	−9		24
1566–70	−12	13	10	3		14

Source: Cambridge: All Saints 1540–5, St Benedict 1540–70, St Edward 1558–70, St Mary the Less 1558–70, St Mary the Great 1559–70. Entries are from CCRO parish registers.

registers survive between 1538 and 1570. Table 2.11 uses the baptism and burial totals to calculate the net surplus or deficit in parishes in Cambridge, in each quinquennium between 1540 and 1570. Only St Benedict's parish register contains continuous entries between these dates. This was a small parish in area, close to the market place, where the average of burials exceeded the average of baptisms throughout the period except for a short period during the mid-1550s. Burials peaked in 1547, 1550–1, 1562, 1565–6, and 1569. The parishes of St Mary the Great and St Edward tended to have more surpluses of baptisms over burials, while All Saints and St Mary the Less followed a similar pattern to St Benedict over the period. Studies have found marked variations in demographic experiences between different urban parishes, and such a small sample is not necessarily representative of the experience of the whole town. From the very fragmentary evidence available from Cambridge, it does appear that burials exceeded baptisms for most of the period between 1540 and 1560, but thereafter baptisms more frequently exceeded burials. Goose found a slight surplus of baptisms in Cambridge in the 1560s, followed by a period of natural increase to 1600.[86]

Table 2.12 provides quinquennial totals across the county's sub-regions. The totals for parishes in the western plateau show the same trends as the fen-edge parishes, with 1556–60 being the only period in both sub-regions that registered more burials than baptisms. Unfortunately, the parish registers of the river valleys and south-east uplands are incomplete, but those periods with data available show a positive balance of baptisms exceeding burials.

As the extent of net migration is not known, these surpluses and deficits in baptism and burial totals cannot be used to draw firm conclusions about the balance of fertility and mortality in Cambridge and its sub-regions. Imbalances may have been caused by considerable flows of migration into or out of parishes. However, the surpluses and deficits suggest certain possible trends. Among the 404 parishes examined by the Cambridge Group, while in aggregate deficits of baptisms to burials were recorded in only two decades over more than three centuries, among individual parishes, such deficits were particularly prominent in marshland communities, market towns, and London parishes. The size of these deficits suggests that there was a

---

86   Goose,'Economic and social aspects', pp. 258–76.

Table 2.12

Net surplus or deficit in baptisms compared to burials in Cambridgeshire sub-regions, 1540–70

	Cambridge	Fen-edge	Fen	South-east uplands	River valleys	Western plateau
1541–5	−46	9	−24		9	24
1546–50	−20	6	2		12	13
1551–5	5	17	−13			42
1556–60	−34	−40	−99			−31
1561–5	24	77	154	108	22	69
1566–70	14	66	117	66	65	79

Source: Cambridge: as Table 2.11.
Notes: Fen-edge: Landbeach 1540–70*, Cherry Hinton 1540–50 and 1561–70, Willingham 1559–70*, Fulbourn St Vigor 1560–70;
Fen: Elm 1540–70*, Stretham 1558–70, Ely Holy Trinity 1559–70*, Sutton in the Isle 1559–70;
South-east uplands: Balsham, Dullingham, Horseheath, Shudy Camps (all 1561–70);
River valleys: Coton 1540–52, 1559–64, Hinxton 1560–70, Melbourn 1561–70, Fowlmere 1562–70*, Linton 1566–70*;
Western plateau: Croxton 1540–70, Elsworth 1540–70, Madingley 1540–53, 1560–70, Arrington 1550–6, 1560–4.
Entries are from CCRO parish registers, except those marked *, which are from data held by the Cambridge Group for the History of Population and Social Structure, Department of Geography, University of Cambridge. I am grateful to Dr Richard Smith for making this data available to me.

difference between fertility and mortality in certain urban and marshland areas, compared to more isolated and better-drained rural parishes.[87]

Recent studies have shown that pre-industrial towns were not invariably 'urban graveyards' suffering net deficits of baptisms to burials, although some did show higher levels of mortality than the rural average.[88] While burials exceeded births in the surviving Cambridge parish registers for all the five-year periods between 1540 and 1560 except 1551–5, births exceeded burials from the 1560s and continued to do so in every quinquennium but one through to 1600.

Research has revealed that death rates in marshland parishes were excessively high compared to other places in early modern England, and only a constant flow of incomers to these areas prevented complete demographic decline. Malaria was endemic in the marshlands and fens, and this, together with other water-borne diseases prevalent in these low-lying areas, produced what has been described as an outstanding 'contour of death' in south-east England. The Cambridge Group found March in Cambridgeshire had one of the highest infant mortality rates in their national sample of parishes.[89] The five-year totals from the four parishes in the fen sub-region up to 1560 show regular deficits of burials over baptisms, suggesting similar conditions may have prevailed. The figures from the other sub-regions suggest a more expanding population, particularly in the fen-edge, where there was a net surplus in every quinquennium except 1556–60.

---

87   Schofield, *Parish register aggregate analyses*, p. 9.
88   Goose, 'Urban demography', 280; C. Galley, *The demography of early modern towns: York in the sixteenth and seventeenth century* (Liverpool, 1998).
89   M.J. Dobson, *Contours of death and disease in early modern England* (Cambridge, 1997), pp. 176, 343, 493–4.

Dramatic increases in burials indicate periods of crisis mortality, usually caused by epidemic disease. Goose has highlighted years of crisis mortality in Cambridge using parish registers and probate records.[90] The small number of wills proved in the early sixteenth century make it difficult to draw clear trends, but numbers were well above average in Cambridge in 1521 and over the years 1529 and 1532. There was a sharp rise in the number of wills proved in Cambridge in 1544–5, and the highest annual total for the whole sixteenth century was reached in 1545. Parish register evidence suggests that mortality rose by a factor of 2.3 in 1547. The early and mid 1540s also saw increases in wills proved in Colchester and Reading, and successive years of high mortality in the national sample of parish registers.[91] Few parish registers from the Cambridgeshire sub-regions cover this period, and although there were noticeable increases in the burials in Elm and Landbeach in the mid 1540s, these were not sufficient to be classed as periods of crisis mortality.

Two major epidemics occurred in Cambridge during the 1550s. Sweating sickness, probably a type of viral infection, prevailed at Cambridge, as in many other parts of the country in 1551. Henry Brandon, Duke of Somerset, and his brother Charles left Cambridge University to escape the sickness, but died in Huntingdonshire. Henry Dylcock, fellow of Christ's College, made his will 'in the time of the sweat ... daylye seinge and howrlye hearing tell of soden death every where'. While this epidemic created only a slight rise in the annual total of wills proved in Cambridge in 1551–2, surviving parish registers from the town suggest that mortality increased by a factor of 1.9.[92] The 'influenza' epidemic of the late 1550s may have been a combination of typhus and plague after harvest failures in 1555 and 1556. Historians have identified this as one of the most severe periods of mortality during the sixteenth century, but the magnitude of the crisis and its causes are still debated.[93] In Cambridge, a number of prominent members of the borough and university died. University matriculations fell from more than 200 to 59 between 1554 and 1557, before recovering, although the religious upheavals of Mary's reign, as well as the epidemics, probably contributed. In the two Cambridge parishes where data survives, burials rose by a factor of 2.3 in 1558, but the annual total of wills proved in Cambridge suggests that the epidemic lasted from 1556–9.[94] Table 2.12 shows that the period 1556–60 was one of natural decrease in all Cambridgeshire sub-regions with surviving registers. Corn prices in the town rose sharply and the borough and university authorities made provision to assess the poor for relief.[95] Yet these setbacks appear to have been

---

90   Crisis mortality is measured using the conventional multipliers of twice the normal number of burials for a major crisis, and 1.5 times for a minor crisis.

91   Goose, 'Fertility', pp. 201–2, 206.

92   *Annals*, ii, p. 59; P. Slack, 'Mortality crises and epidemic disease in England, 1485–1610', in C. Webster, ed., *Health, medicine and mortality in the sixteenth century* (Cambridge, 1979), pp. 25–7; Goose, 'Fertility', pp. 205–6.

93   F.J. Fisher, 'Influenza and inflation in Tudor England', in Corfield and Harte, eds., *London and the English economy*, pp. 163–72; J.S. Moore, 'Jack Fisher's "flu": a visitation revisited', *EcHR*, 2nd ser., 46 (1993), 280–307; Wrigley and Schofield, *Population history*, pp. 234, 333, 651, 671; Dyer, 'Bishops' census', 21, 24; Slack, 'Mortality', pp. 27–32.

94   Leedham-Green, *Concise history*, pp. 62, 90; Goose, 'Fertility', pp. 202, 205–8.

95   See below, pp. 167–70.

temporary: the overall total of baptisms exceeded burials among the town parishes in the 1560s and the evidence from wills indicates increases in replacement rates during the 1550s, which intensified in the following two decades. The impact of plague in Cambridge, as in other towns in the sixteenth century, appears to have been temporary rather than prolonged, suggesting an underlying resilience in urban economies.[96]

Conclusion

Identifying trends in the population of Cambridge in this period is complicated by the different multipliers used by different historians to estimate urban populations, by the difficulties in estimating the size of the university and by the unknown incidence of migration. It seems more likely that the general trend in Cambridge's population between 1377 and 1524–5 was decline rather than growth, given the evidence of declining rents in the fifteenth century discussed below and the large tax reduction that the town received in 1465, even if not all the complaints made by the burgesses of Cambridge in their petitions for reductions to their subsidy quota and fee farm during the fifteenth century can be accepted at face value. It also seems more likely that the town's population grew slightly, rather than contracted, between 1524–5 and 1563. Admittedly, the evidence from wills and parish registers outlined in this chapter is not conclusive. On the one hand, there is evidence from wills of a slight increase in 'replacement' rates during 1540–59, and a larger increase during 1560–79, while on the other hand, the surviving parish registers show a surplus of burials over baptisms in most town parishes up to 1560, with natural increase in most parishes thereafter. However, there is evidence, outlined in subsequent chapters, to suggest some revival of economic activity in at least some decades between 1510 and 1560 occurred within the town. The population estimates further suggest that the university expanded significantly over the fifteenth century, and this growth is also apparent from the evidence of building work.[97] This expansion may have helped Cambridge to avoid the worst effects of population decline which hit many towns during the fifteenth century. Indeed, the town retained its position within the regional urban hierarchy.

Within the Cambridge region, the taxation returns reveal important sub-regional variations in growth between the fourteenth and sixteenth centuries. The fen and fen-edge experienced some relative increases in population and wealth. Within the fen in particular, however, growth probably had to be sustained by substantial immigration, given the unhealthy natural environment. The south-east uplands and western plateau experienced the greatest relative declines in population and wealth, and contraction in land under cultivation and settlement. These were areas of later settlement, which were less accessible and more difficult to cultivate. By the fifteenth century, the rising cost of labour, and restricted market for agricultural produce, particularly cereals, meant that agricultural investment in these areas could no longer be justified. The river valleys sub-region retained its lead, in terms of both population and wealth per acre

---

96   Goose,'Urban variable', 178–80.
97   See below, Chapter 7.

Population and wealth

between 1334 and 1524. This sub-region contained the most 'capitalist' social structure, with the largest number of wealthiest taxpayers, and the greatest proportion of wage-earners, reflecting the agricultural, marketing and employment opportunities available. A large number of poorer inhabitants, gaining income from wages rather than land, suggests a considerable demand for buying and selling foodstuffs and goods. This required markets for exchange, and many markets and fairs were found in this sub-region, while the growth of the malt barley and saffron trades also tended to be concentrated within the Cambridgeshire river valleys during the later fifteenth and early sixteenth centuries.[98]

---

[98] See below, Chapters 4 and 5.

Chapter 3

Cambridge and its society

The close links between the ranks of urban and rural society in medieval England have led a recent historian to state, 'Town and country were not separate worlds, between which a choice had to be made, but integrated elements of a single society'.[1] Many different groups of people made their home in medieval Cambridge, including burgesses, non-franchised residents, university scholars, privileged persons, clergy, members of religious orders, and aliens. Each group had social networks which linked the town with a variety of areas beyond. The dichotomy between town and gown has been a common theme in the historiography of the town of Cambridge. This approach has tended to emphasise the hostility between townsmen and scholars, which has been described as the '700 years' war in Cambridge' and a state of 'endemic border warfare, with recurrent crises'.[2] While there were undoubtedly tensions, periodically erupting into hostilities, this chapter will show that the society of Cambridge could never have been as polarised as some commentators seem to suggest, and some aspects of the town's society, notably the parish churches and guilds in the medieval period, could provide shared foci for members of both town and university. As a recent study of the town in the early modern period has shown, town and gown were part of a more complex network of community relations and identities.[3]

A few studies have assembled biographical details for some residents of medieval Cambridge, including university members, mayors and prominent burgesses, and members of parliament, while Siraut has examined the merchant community of the Elizabethan town.[4] Much more analysis remains to be undertaken, however, from wills, civic and university records, taxation returns, guild and churchwardens' accounts, and other surviving records. Wills are among the most valuable documents for this purpose, providing an indicator of the range of contacts within the town and region, through references to family and property, bequests to people and institutions, debts, witnesses and executors. Examining the wills of Cambridge and its region is complicated, however, by the range of different courts in which wills were registered, the pattern of surviving records, and the different repositories in which they are now

---

1 R. Horrox, 'The urban gentry in the fifteenth century', in J.A.F. Thomson, ed., *Towns and townspeople in the fifteenth century* (Gloucester, 1988), p. 36.

2 R. Parker, *Town and gown: the 700 years war in Cambridge* (Cambridge, 1983); *VCH Cambs.*, iii, p. 76.

3 A. Shepard, 'Contesting communities? "Town" and "gown" in Cambridge, c.1560–1640', in A. Shepard and P. Withington, eds., *Communities in early modern England: networks, place, rhetoric* (Manchester, 2000), pp. 216–34.

4 Emden, *Biographical register*; J. Milner Gray, *Biographical notes on the mayors of Cambridge* (Cambridge, 1921); *CBD*, pp. 145–59; J.C. Wedgewood, *The History of Parliament: biographies of the members of the Commons House, 1439–1509* (London, 1936); S.T. Bindoff, ed., *The House of Commons 1509–1558*, The History of Parliament, 3 vols. (London, 1982); Siraut, 'Cambridge', pp. 191–200.

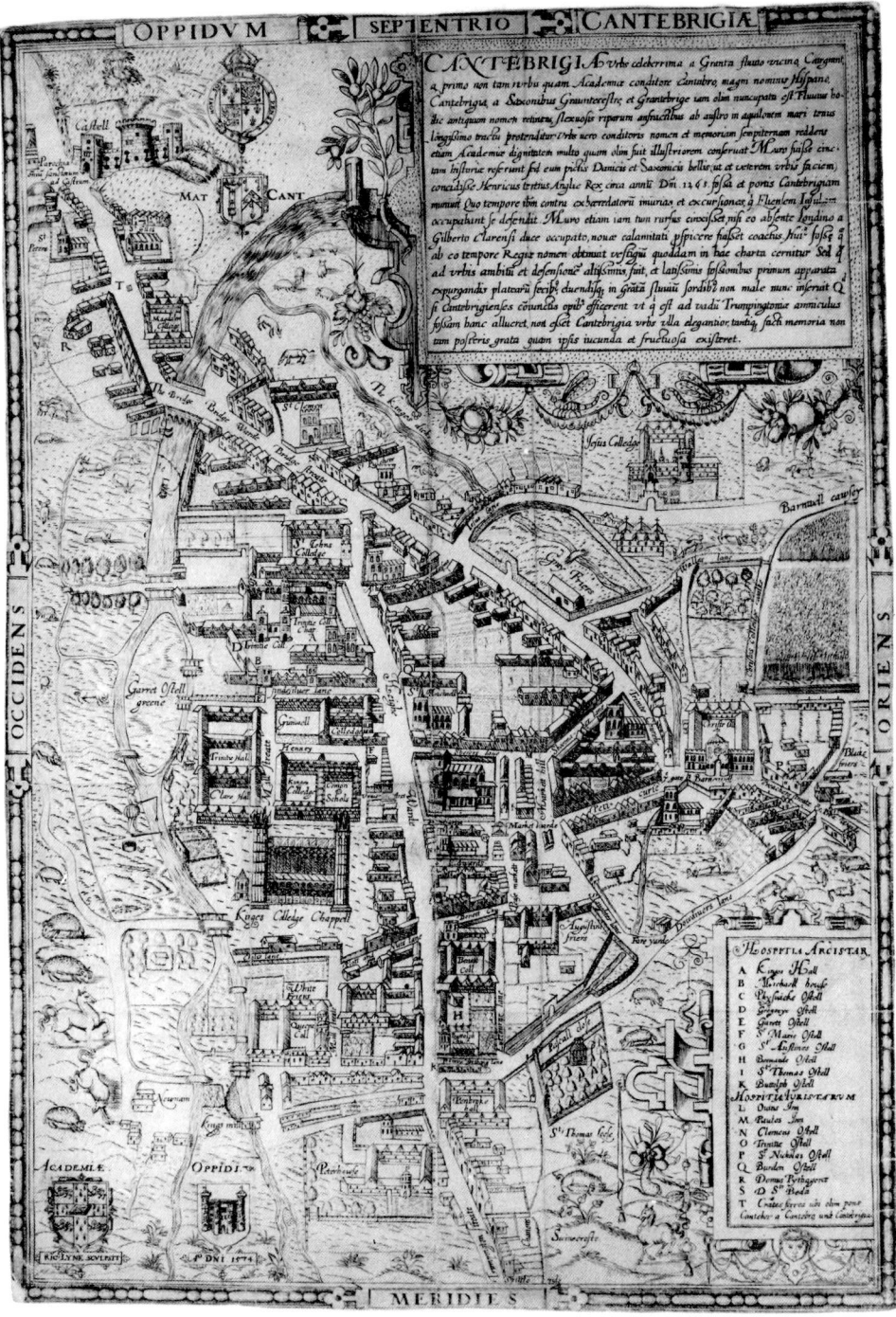

Figure 3.1 Richard Lyne's map of Cambridge, 1574 (Cambridgeshire Collection)

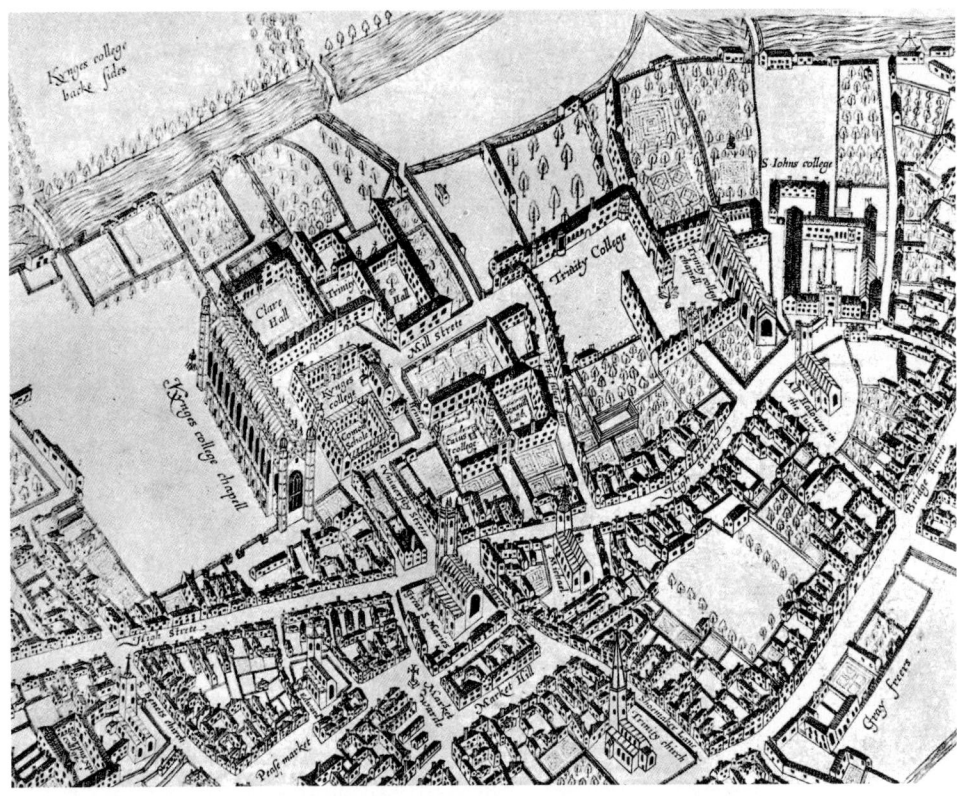

Figure 3.2 Central section of John Hamond's map of Cambridge, 1592 (Cambridgeshire Collection)

housed.[5] The wealthiest testators tended to use the prerogative court of Canterbury.[6] Ely Consistory Court included most of the county, but the court of the archdeaconry of Ely covered the town of Cambridge and parishes in south-west Cambridgeshire.[7] The vice-chancellor of the university proved wills of scholars and others with connections to the institution, notably those townsmen known as 'privileged persons' who served the academic community.[8] Enjoying the status of a peculiar, King's College was able to prove the wills of its college members and associates.[9] Cambridge Corporation also

---

5   J. Gibson, *Probate jurisdictions: where to look for wills* (Solihull, 3rd edn., 1989), pp. 8–9.

6   TNA: PRO PROB 11.

7   Held at CCRO and indexed in C. Thurley and D. Thurley, eds., *Index of the probate records of the Archdeaconry of Ely, 1513–1857*, British Record Soc., LXXXVIII (London, 1970) and E. Leedham-Green and R. Rodd, eds., *Index of the probate records of the Consistory Court of Ely, 1449–1858*, British Record Soc., CIV, CVI–CVII (London, 1994–6). BL Add. MS 5861 contains extracts from the Ely consistory court wills.

8   CUL, UA, WILLS, i, 1501–58.

9   KC, Ledger Book, i, 1449–1558.

made copies of the wills of some burgesses who bequeathed property to the borough.[10]

An examination of the topography of medieval Cambridge also reveals how the different groups that co-existed within the town shaped its layout and appearance. Richard Lyne's map of 1574 provides a starting point, as the earliest extant plan of Cambridge. It is, however, far from accurate: most churches and many college courts are represented in identical form, while the scale is enlarged in the town centre and compressed around the town fringes. John Hamond's map of 1592 provides greater detail and accuracy, but only a central portion survives in good condition.[11]

Occupational structure

Taking occupations recorded in wills between 1500 and 1579, Goose has shown that 47 per cent of Cambridge's population were engaged in providing food, drink, clothing and housing (see Table 3.1). This was a far higher proportion than the 23 and 24 per cent employed in the same trades in the towns of Colchester and Reading, or some 35 to 40 per cent in Coventry, Leicester and Northampton, although the proportion rose to 50 per cent at York and 67 per cent at Oxford. Westminster was another predominantly service-based economy, meeting the demand of the royal palace and Benedictine abbey, but this London suburb possessed a more transient and affluent market than the university towns, with courtiers, suitors, members of parliament and pilgrims passing through. Oxford, Westminster and Cambridge were all centres of hospitality, with their alehouses and inns, victuallers, building craftsmen, specialist trades such as those of goldsmiths and printing, and very small manufacturing sectors.[12] Service-based economies were perhaps, during the fifteenth and sixteenth centuries, more resilient than those based on manufacturing, particularly cloth, which were highly susceptible to fluctuations in trade.[13]

Reflecting the predominance of service-based occupations, the most commonly recorded occupations in Cambridge wills between 1500 and 1579 were bakers, shoemakers, tailors, drapers, cooks, brewers and carpenters. Using a larger sample of wills over a longer period, Goose suggests that only 35 per cent of Cambridge's occupied population worked in manufacturing, compared to 50 per cent or more in ten other provincial towns.[14] This reflected Cambridge's role as an inland trading centre with a major market and river port, as well as demand generated by the university.[15]

---

10   CCA, Palmer/Barnard vol. 57.
11   J.W. Clark and A. Gray, *Old plans of Cambridge 1574 to 1798* (Cambridge, 1921), i, pp. 1–17.
12   *VCH Oxfordshire*, iv, pp. 40–8, 101–9; G. Rosser, 'London and Westminster: the suburb in the urban economy in the later Middle Ages', in Thomson, ed., *Towns and townspeople*, pp. 45–61; G. Rosser, *Medieval Westminster, 1200–1540* (Oxford, 1989), pp. 119–64, 201–16.
13   e.g. the urban economies of Colchester or Coventry: Britnell, *Colchester*, pp. 163–80; Phythian-Adams, 'Urban decline', pp. 162–3, 169.
14   Goose, 'Economic and social aspects', pp. 121–7; Goose, 'Pre-industrial urban economies', pp. 65, 70.
15   The specific employment opportunities created by the colleges and religious houses, and the specialist academic trades are examined in Chapter 6. Markets and trade are examined in Chapter 4.

Table 3.1

Occupations recorded in wills in Cambridge, 1500–79

Category of occupation	%
Food and drink	22.4
Textiles	8.2
Clothing	17.2
Leather (raw)	1.7
Household	10.8
Tools and armour	1.7
Housing	7.3
Transport	3.0
Services	13.8
Education	2.6
Medicine	3.9
Miscellaneous and unattributed	7.3

Source: Goose, 'Economic and social aspects', p. 121. I am grateful to Professor Nigel Goose for permission to reproduce this data from his unpublished thesis.

The county administration, based at the castle, provided additional custom for the service trades of the town. Founded by the first Norman sheriff, Picot, and enlarged by Edward I, Cambridge Castle had no military function by the later middle ages, but still housed the gallows, gaol and county administration. The sheriff accounted for repairs to the castle in 1440 and 1523/4.[16] The shire house, rebuilt in 1572, had a central office for the sheriff and his staff, and accommodation for the county courts.[17] Parliamentary elections for knights of the shire were also held in the castle. During a disturbed and unruly election in 1439, all the inns in the streets leading to the castle were occupied. Cambridge also returned two members of parliament, and was the only borough in the county to do so.[18]

Cambridge's commercial centre lay along two main streets. The High Street (now comprising Trumpington Street, King's Parade, Trinity Street and St John's Street) and Bridge Street (now Sidney Street) both joined before leading to the Great Bridge (now known as Magdalene Bridge) and the castle. A third thoroughfare, Milne Street, was cut in two when Henry VI acquired an enlarged site for King's, which he granted to the college in 1449, leaving two stretches remaining outside Queens' College, Trinity Hall and Clare College.[19]

---

16 TNA: PRO E 101/553/10–11, E 101/553/15.

17 P.H. Reaney, ed., *The Place-names of Cambridgeshire*, pp. 39–40. Kermode, 'Greater towns', p. 452; M.H. Mills, 'The medieval shire house' in J. Conway Davies, ed., *Studies presented to Sir Hilary Jenkinson* (London, 1957), pp. 254–71.

18 R. Virgoe, 'The Cambridgeshire election of 1439', *Bulletin of the Institute of Historical Research*, 46 (1973), 95–101; Bindoff, *House of Commons*, i, p. 42.

19 Willis and Clarke, *Architectural history*, i, pp. 334–46.

Cambridge and its society

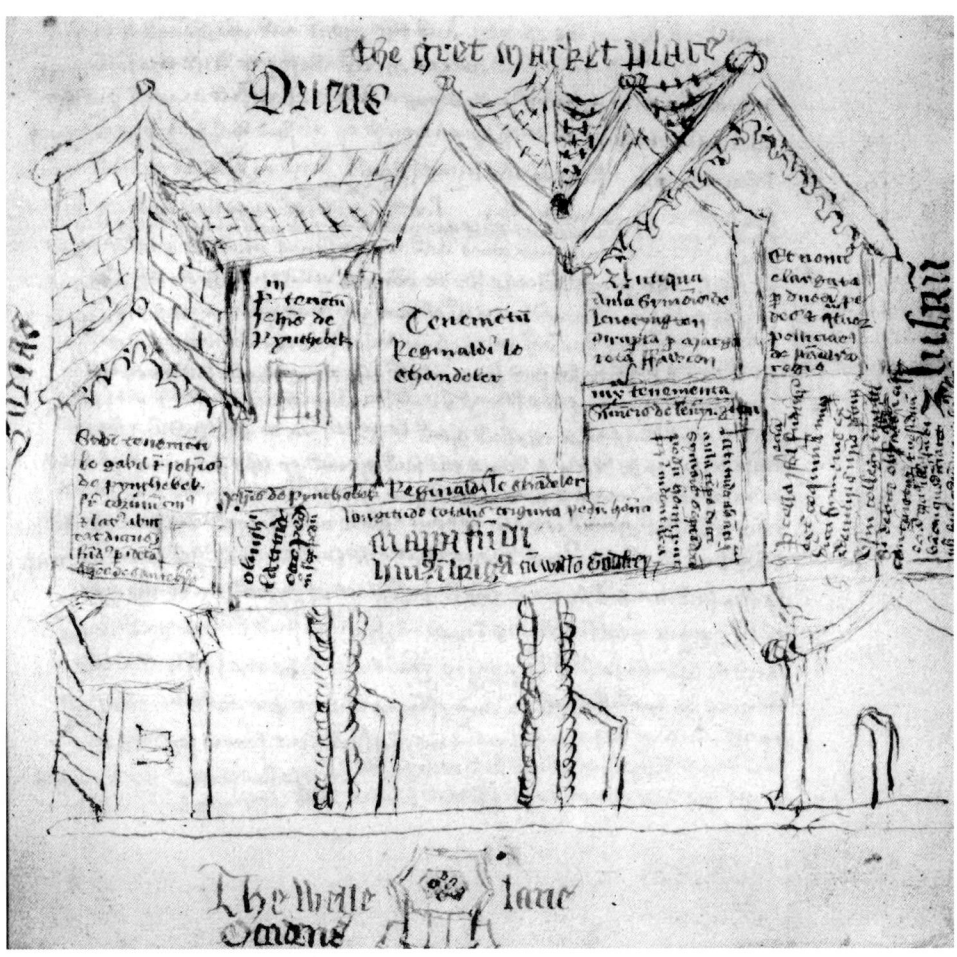

Figure 3.3 Sketch of Cambridge market place, mid-fifteenth century. This shows shops and houses to the east of Great St Mary's Church, in the northern part of the market place. The area to the east (at the top of the plan) is described as 'the gret market place' and the street to the west as 'Welle Lane'. From the 'Liber Albus' of John Botwright, Master of Corpus Christi College, 1443–74 (by permission of the Master and Fellows of Corpus Christi College, Cambridge)

Within the market place at Cambridge stood the tollbooth or guildhall, town gaol, stocks and pillory, and market cross. Around the central marketing area lay the Butchery, Butter Row, Cordwainers' Row, Petty Cury, and a fish market. As in many larger market towns,[20] separate parts of Cambridge market place were reserved for the trading of particular commodities, including corn, peas, cheese, leather, malt, milk and oats. Freshwater fish was sold from tubs on the market hill, while livestock were

---

20 Everitt, 'Marketing', p. 29; Britnell, *Commercialisation*, p. 85.

traded in the fairyard near the slaughterhouse.[21] The market place was symbolically the heart of the medieval town: the location of the civic administration, and a public space used to disseminate news and perform punishments. The Duke of Northumberland proclaimed Mary Tudor to be Queen at the market cross, having previously tried to place his daughter-in-law, Lady Jane Grey, on the throne.[22] Robert Barker, found to be in possession of a book and instruments of the black art, was ordered in 1466 to walk round the market places of Ely and Cambridge barefooted, holding the books and wand, with the plates and charts round his neck, and the instruments were afterwards to be burned in Cambridge market place.[23]

The river side provided another focus for commercial activity. The River Cam was navigable through the fens to the coast at King's Lynn. Cambridge's Great Bridge provided the main crossing point over the river. One indication of the importance of the bridge and shipping to the town's economy is their representation on the town corporation's common seal of 1423.[24] The town mills were located further upstream, and are shown on Lyne's map. The corporation owned the King's Mill and during the sixteenth century held the other town mills on leases from the bishop of Ely and Gonville Hall, and sub-leased them to farmers at a profit.[25] By the sixteenth century, the main loading and unloading point for water-borne goods was the quay next to the Great Bridge. Hithes had formerly lay along the Cam south of the Great Bridge, connected by lanes from Milne Street and the High Street, with names indicating some of the goods unloaded there: Cholleshethe, Salthithelane, Blancwyneshithe, Flaxhythe, and Cornehithe.[26]

Burgesses

The burgesses comprised the more substantial traders and craftsmen, and dominated the economic activity of the town. A burgess or freeman was entitled to trade in the town without paying toll, received preferential treatment in the borough courts, and in Cambridge acquired the right to hold a booth in Stourbridge Fair without charge. But burgesses were also liable to borough taxes and office holding, which could make the privilege expensive and time-consuming.[27]

The career of Hugh Chapman, who died in 1536, demonstrates how some of the biographical details of the leading burgesses of Cambridge can be pieced together

---

21 Reaney, *Place-names of Cambridgeshire*, pp. 44–50; *LP*, xii (2), g. 1008 (17), p. 352; CCA, Palmer/Barnard vol. 57, fol. 9; *CBD*, map facing p. 168; P. Bryan and N. Wise, 'A reconstruction of the medieval Cambridge market place', *PCAS*, 91 (2002), 73–87.

22 J. Masschaele, 'The public space of the market place in medieval England', *Speculum*, 77 (2002), 383–421; T.D. Atkinson and J.W. Clark, *Cambridge described & illustrated being a short history of the town and university* (London, 1897), p. 98.

23 'Ely episcopal registers', *Ely Diocesan Remembrancer* (1907), 95.

24 *CBD*, frontispiece.

25 Maitland, *Township*, pp. 206–8; CCA, X/56.

26 Reaney, *Place-names of Cambridgeshire*, pp. 41–2.

27 R.B. Dobson, 'Admissions to the freedom of the city of York in the later Middle Ages', *EcHR*, 2nd ser., 26 (1973), 15.

from surviving documents. Hugh's will reveals that he was not a native of the town, but born in Shouldham, Norfolk.[28] Religious bequests illustrate the geographical spread of Chapman's interests, with donations to religious houses in Norfolk, Denny Abbey in Cambridgeshire, the Cambridge churches of Great St Mary's and Holy Trinity, and the Cambridge friars. He served in a succession of public offices in the borough as treasurer, bailiff, mayor, and alderman. Two of his relatives may also have served as mayor: John Chapman, possibly the 'cousin' described in Hugh's will, and Robert Chapman, possibly Hugh's son.[29] Over the course of his career, Hugh leased a range of properties from the corporation, including a shop occupying a prime location under the tollbooth in the market place for the substantial sum of 13s 4d in 1500/1 and 1503/4, and fish stalls in the market in 1513/14, as well as a lane from the market and Newnham Mill.[30] While there does not appear to be a record of Hugh's trade or business, the properties he leased suggest that he traded in a variety of products. The poll tax returns of 1512 reveal that Hugh held lands and tenements worth between £20 and £40 per year, and movable goods worth between £100 and £200; he paid the second largest tax assessment in Market Ward, making him one of the wealthiest men in the town.[31] Hugh's will made provision for a priest to pray for the souls of John and Ann Essewell, a neighbouring grocer and tavern keeper, and Henry Vessey, an apothecary, whose son occupied a house fronting the market place.[32]

While Chapman's interests were largely based in Cambridge, other leading burgesses had wider networks. George Foyster, mayor in 1523, made his will in London and had it witnessed by William Blande, a haberdasher of the city, described as his cousin, together with a London grocer and two gentlemen.[33] John Bell, five times mayor of Cambridge between 1494 and 1512, was a native of Earith (Huntingdonshire) but had important ties to Lynn: he was a member of the guild merchant of the Holy Trinity of Lynn, and requested to be buried in the chapel of St Nicholas there. He also left money to pay for gravel to repair ways between Wotton Cross and Gaywood near Lynn. One of his executors was from Bury St Edmunds. Bell appears to have had a number of business interests: he owned an osier yard in Waterbeach and a beer brewhouse beside the Great Bridge in Cambridge, and leased Copped Hall barn in the town which he may have used for corn dealing. Described as a pikemonger in one document, Bell leased the fishponds of St John's Hospital for over thirty years and was involved in a dispute over fishing rights in Barnwell Pool.[34]

Fifty-four men, including the three members of the Chapman family, Foyster and

---

28 I am grateful to Honor Ridout for sharing details of her research and her transcript of Hugh Chapman's will. The original will is in CCRO, Archdeaconry of Ely, Will Register 1, fol. 88.

29 Milner Gray, *Biographical notes*, pp. 20, 22–4.

30 CCRO, CCA, X/71/10, X/71A, XVII/24A; CCTA, i, fols., 54–54v, 56v, 74–5, 88–9, 105v–106, 118v–119, 129v.

31 *CBD*, p. 113.

32 Milner Gray, *Biographical notes*, p. 19; T.D. Atkinson, 'On the house of the Veysy family in Cambridge', *PCAS*, 7 (1893), 93–103.

33 Milner Gray, *Biographical notes*, pp. 21–2; CCRO, Archdeaconry of Ely, Will Register 1, fol. 143.

34 TNA: PRO PROB 11/21, fols. 117v–118; *CBD*, pp. 136, 146; E. Miller, 'Fishponds close and its pondyards', *The Eagle* (Magazine of St John's College), 59 (1963), 353–62.

Bell, served as mayors of Cambridge between 1450 and 1560. Those men who served most frequently as mayor during the period were John Belton (1453–6, 1461–3), Robert Coope (1464–5, 1467–9, 1476), John Bell (1494–5, 1501, 1504, 1512), Robert Morehouse (1497–9, 1502–3), and Thomas Hayrman (1450–2, 1457–8).[35] These dates when mayors served multiple years of office are concentrated within the later fifteenth century and first decade of the sixteenth century, when the treasurers' accounts show a downturn in the corporation's property income.[36] This may be suggestive of a time of financial hardship for the borough, when it was particularly difficult to find men who would accept the office of mayor. Indeed, when John Hessewell was re-elected mayor in 1490, he was described as having 'borne many great importune charges and inbodily labour' while occupying the office previously. To induce him to accept the office for a further two years, the corporation discharged Hessewell from all liability to serve and penalties from refusing to serve in the future.[37] The reluctance of leading townsmen to take up office was a problem faced by many late medieval town corporations, but in Cambridge the problem was compounded by the many tradesmen who sought the status of privileged person, thereby placing themselves outside the jurisdiction of the borough council and its civic dues and duties.[38]

As Chapman's career illustrates, a man who was born outside the town could still attain the leading office of the borough. The admissions of burgesses to the freedom of the borough give an indication of a medieval town's ability to attract skilled and prosperous migrants and therefore some indication of general economic fortunes. At Colchester and York, the numbers of new burgesses elected annually were consistently higher in the later fourteenth century than in the 1330s and 1340s, reflecting the increased economic opportunities in these towns, while the declining applications by the late fifteenth century mirrored the contraction of local trade and industry.[39]

Admissions of freemen in Cambridge are only recorded in detail in the corporation's Common Day Book, which begins in 1544. Before this date, the treasurers' accounts include income from freemen's admissions, and sometimes list the names of those admitted. Admissions tended to cluster in a few years, with intervening years characterised by relatively few admissions, with totals usually in single figures. The averages presented in Table 3.2 therefore conceal a large range of figures. There was a noticeable increase in admissions in the four decades between 1490 and 1530, when a large amount of building work was under way in the town.[40] Few building craftsmen appear to have become freemen, apart from John Morley, slater, and possibly John Bury, mason,[41] but the construction work may have

---

35 Milner Gray, *Biographical notes*, pp. 18–28.
36 See below, Chapter 7.
37 Milner Gray, *Biographical notes*, p. 19.
38 See below, pp. 67–9.
39 Dobson, 'Urban decline', p. 281; Bartlett, 'York', esp. 22–3; Britnell, *Colchester*, pp. 96, 203–5, 279–80.
40 See Table 7.4.
41 CCA, X/71/9; CCTA, i, fol. 92; J. Harvey, *English medieval architects: a biographical dictionary down to 1550* (Gloucester, 1984), pp. 41–2.

Table 3.2

Burgesses admitted to freedom of Cambridge, 1422/3–1560

	Treasurers' accounts			Common Day Book		
	No. of years with admissions	Total freemen admitted	Yearly average admitted	No. of years with admissions	Total freemen admitted	Yearly average admitted
1421–30	4	34	9			
1431–40	2	7	4			
1481–90	3	11	4			
1491–1500	3	44	15			
1501–10	2	35	18			
1511–20	3	32	11			
1521–30	4	49	12			
1531–40	6	56	9			
1541–50	9	72	8	7	69	10
1551–60	5	59	12	10	104	10

Source: Treasurers' accounts: CCA, X/70/1–10, X/71/1–10, X/71A, XVII/24A; CCTA, i; Common Day Book: CCA, Palmer/Barnard, volume 57.

generated a general increase in economic activity. Another rise in admissions during the 1550s coincided with an increase in the corporation's urban rents. This could indicate an upturn in economic activity and migration into the town, although a reduction of fees for admission to the freedom in 1544 may also have encouraged more men to apply. This reduction may have been made in response to the severe mortality of 1544–5, the later year exhibiting the highest number of wills proved in any year during the sixteenth century.[42] The increased number of admissions may therefore reflect mortality among the burgesses, as at York, where high entry rates followed years of plague mortality.[43] In Cambridge, freedom of the borough could be obtained through birth, apprenticeship, purchase, or gift. In 1534 the mayor urged all foreigners in the town to become freemen, 'affyrmynge that they had as good a corporatyon as london had'. Unless this was an effort to raise support against the university, it seems that the freedom was not in great demand, and the reduction of entrance fees for burgesses' sons in 1544 and 1576 suggests that this was indeed the case.[44]

The places of residence of those admitted as freemen reveal the areas from which towns could draw migrants. Unfortunately, the Cambridge treasurers' accounts rarely state the residence of those becoming freemen. From the few surviving references three groups emerge. Firstly, many men came from surrounding villages, like Barnwell, Bourn, Girton, Madingley, Over and Waterbeach in the 1520s and 1530s.[45] Secondly, a few London merchants became freemen like Thomas Taylor, fishmonger,

---

42 Goose, 'Fertility', pp. 201–2.
43 Dobson, 'Admissions', 17.
44 *Grace Book A*, p. 230; *VCH Cambs.*, iii, p. 47.
45 CCTA, i, fols. 9v, 57v, 91v, 93v, 154.

(admitted in 1525), and William Sympson, draper (1523),[46] possibly so that they could hold booths in Stourbridge Fair.[47] Thirdly, a handful of men from overseas also became burgesses, as discussed below.[48] The residence of freemen admitted in Cambridge is recorded much more frequently from the mid–sixteenth century: Siraut's analysis has shown that just under one-third of freemen came from Cambridge, 18 per cent from Cambridgeshire, 23 per cent from adjoining counties, and 18 per cent from the north.[49] Wills sometimes highlight the links that freemen who had immigrated to Cambridge retained with their birthplaces. John Wood, born in Bottisham, and admitted freeman in 1551, left bequests in his will to Bottisham Church and the poor there, while stating that he lived in Cambridge and wished to be buried there.[50]

The occupations of freemen admitted to the borough are recorded infrequently in the late fifteenth and early sixteenth centuries, although more occupations are listed in the 1520s. Among the admissions, butchers predominated, and other service trades were also represented, such as drapers, fishmongers, a baker, a brewer, an innholder and hosteler.[51] Textile and leather workers also received the freedom, including a dyer, a weaver, a tanner, a shoemaker and a glover,[52] while a few more unusual occupations, like a goldsmith, a 'hardware man', a 'farecariar', a minstrel and a holy water clerk are recorded.[53] These trades reflected the town's strong service economy.

Leading burgesses also had important links with members of the nobility and gentry, which connected both town and country. Six of those admitted as freemen between 1520 and 1560 were styled gentlemen, together with three 'experienced knights at law'. Another country gentleman providing legal counsel for the corporation was John Hynde of Madingley (c.1480–1550), who had probably attended King's College before training as a lawyer at Gray's Inn. Hynde was also a major landowner, purchasing Anglesey Priory in 1539 and the manor and advowson of Girton in 1543.[54] From 1529, the borough also appointed and paid a high steward, mainly to defend their interests against the university: the Dukes of Norfolk, Somerset, and Northumberland held this post during the reigns of Henry VIII and Edward VI. While many English boroughs were represented in the House of Commons by county gentlemen rather than resident burgesses in the fifteenth century, all the Cambridge MPs between 1442 and 1558 were burgesses, except John Battisford of Chesterton in 1442 and Sir John Say of Broxbourne (Hertfordshire) in 1447.[55] Burgesses were also likely to have enjoyed contact with the sons of county families who resided in

---

46 CCTA, i, fols. 78, 93v.
47 Thomas Taylor held a double booth in Stourbridge Fair in 1525/6: CCTA, i, fol. 91.
48 See below, p. 80.
49 M. Siraut, 'Physical mobility in Elizabethan Cambridge', *Local Population Studies*, 27 (1981), 66.
50 CCA, Palmer/Barnard vol. 57, fols. 54, 145v.
51 CCTA, i, fols. 57v, 77v, 92–4.
52 CCTA, i, fols. 77v, 92, 92v, 133.
53 CCA, X/71/6; CCTA, i, fols. 78, 91v–92, 108v.
54 Bindoff, *House of Commons*, ii, pp. 432–4.
55 Dobson, 'General survey', p. 284; Wedgewood, *History of Parliament*, pp. 620–1; *VCH Cambs.*, iii, p. 60.

towns. Described as the 'urban gentry', these were men such as Clement Cotton, a member of the Cotton family of Landwade, who held a tenement in the Shraggery in Cambridge, and requested in his will of 1502 to be buried in St Mary's Church.[56] Like many towns, the corporation also presented gifts such as wine, spices and fish to lords, gentlemen and senior clerics when they visited the town, in the hope of securing their favour and political influence.[57]

University

For the first two centuries of its existence, the university developed discreetly within the Cambridge townscape. The hostels and early colleges were generally small and largely unobtrusive. Corpus Christi College, for example, stood on a small site in Luthburne Lane, now the Old Court, and houses occupied the frontage on Trumpington Street until the creation of the New Court in 1823.[58] However, the clearance of a section of the town between the High Street and the river to create King's College in the mid-fifteenth century, together with the foundation of Queens', St John's and subsequently Trinity College, created a new academic quarter. This transformation of the townscape was symbolic of the way in which the colleges came to dominate the university during the fifteenth and sixteenth centuries.[59]

The medieval colleges were generally established to secure perpetual prayers for their founders and families, and to increase the supply of graduates to church and state. Bishop Hugh de Balsham of Ely founded the first Cambridge college, Peterhouse, in 1284 and seven other colleges were founded during the course of the fourteenth century.[60] Crowland Abbey established a Benedictine hostel in 1428 to accommodate their monks while they studied at the university, which subsequently became known as Buckingham College, while Godshouse was founded in 1439 to train grammar school teachers. Robert Wodelarke, provost of King's, founded St Catharine's College in 1473, and John Alcock, Bishop of Ely, converted the dissolved priory of St Radegund into Jesus College in 1496.[61]

Between the mid-fifteenth and mid-sixteenth centuries, new colleges with royal foundations added to the prestige of the university and the importance of the colleges. Henry VI founded King's College in 1441 to provide education for his scholars from Eton, and subsequently granted the college an enlarged site in 1449. Queens' College, originally founded by Andrew Doket, vicar of St Botolph's in 1446, subsequently became a royal foundation of Queen Margaret of Anjou and then of Queen Elizabeth Woodville. Lady Margaret Beaufort, mother of Henry VII, refounded Godshouse as Christ's College in 1505, and her executors realised the foundation of St John's

---

56 TNA: PRO PROB 11/13, fol. 77v; *CBD*, p. 149; Horrox, 'Urban gentry', pp. 22–44. These predated the seventeenth-century 'pseudo-gentry' identified by Everitt by over a century: A. Everitt, 'Introduction', in A. Everitt, ed., *Perspectives in English urban history* (London, 1973), pp. 7–9.
57 R.B. Dobson, 'General survey 1300–1540', in *CUHB*, i, p. 283; *VCH Cambs.*, iii, p. 13.
58 Willis and Clarke, *Architectural history*, i, pp. 241–50.
59 Morgan and Brooke, *History*, pp. 21–4.
60 King's Hall, Michaelhouse, Clare, Pembroke, Gonville Hall, Trinity Hall and Corpus Christi.
61 Leader, *History*, pp. 60, 78–88, 225–7, 270–5.

Figure 3.4 Arms and statue of Lady Margaret Beaufort on the great gate of Christ's College

College, on the site of the town's hospital, in 1509–11. Henry VIII created Trinity College in 1546 by absorbing Michaelhouse, King's Hall and Physwick Hostel.[62]

Around 1450, when the size of the university has been estimated at around 1,300 members, comparatively few scholars resided within a college. The colleges had around 225 places according to their statutes, although these limits were rarely

---

62 Leader, *History*, pp. 228–9, 281–90.

Table 3.3

Geographical origins of known scholars of the University of Cambridge during the fifteenth century

Dioceses of origin	English population in 1377	Cambridge: non-collegiate scholars	Cambridge: collegiate scholars
	%	%	%
Northern: York, Durham, Carlisle	16	39	25
Eastern: London, Ely, Norwich	20	27	33
Lincoln	20	15	25a
Coventry-Lichfield	7	10	
Southern: Salisbury, Winchester, Chichester, Rochester, Canterbury	36a	5	11
Western: Hereford, Worcester, Bath and Wells, Exeter		4	6

Source: Aston, Duncan and Evans, 'Medieval alumni', 28–34, based on 879 scholars of known geographical origin.
Note: a Combined totals for the two groups of dioceses

reached. Some scholars may have lived in private lodgings in the town, although the university legislated against this practice in 1495.[63] The majority lived in hostels: there were approximately 17 hostels accommodating 800 scholars. These were more than simple boarding houses, and some had halls, chapels, libraries and galleries. Yet the hostels never had the resources of even the poorer colleges, and from the late fifteenth century they began to decline as colleges took in undergraduates.[64] The beginnings of a tutorial system, with fellows serving as tutors to pupils whom they supervised, appeared at King's Hall in the 1430s. Salaried college lectureships and tutorial arrangements made the colleges more attractive for undergraduates. As a result of these, and possibly other factors, such as the increased accommodation available within colleges, their growing prestige and courtly links, and perhaps a desire by the university authorities for greater control over their students, the colleges expanded and the hostels gradually disappeared.[65]

The social and geographical origins of university members have been traced through the records of alumni. Medieval students began their courses at the university in their early teens, and worked for at least seven years for a first degree, and for a further ten if they wished to progress to a master's degree. The majority of students seem to have come from modest backgrounds such as the more affluent peasantry and yeomanry, lesser gentry, leading town merchants and property owners.[66] The University of Cambridge appears to have recruited predominantly from the northern and eastern counties in the fifteenth century, as Table 3.3 shows. The low percentage

---

63 Aston, Duncan and Evans, 'Medieval alumni', 14–19.
64 Leader, *History*, pp. 45–8.
65 A.B. Cobban, 'Commoners in medieval Cambridge colleges', in Zutshi, ed., *Medieval Cambridge*, pp. 47–64; Leader, *History*, pp. 257–9; Morgan and Brooke, *History*, p. 24.
66 Aston, Duncan and Evans, 'Medieval alumni', 41–50.

from the south-east is surprising given the concentration of wealth and population in this region. Some colleges, though, also had statutory preferences which would have drawn more recruits from the south-east: at King's College, for example, these included candidates from parishes where the college or Eton College had property, and for those born in Cambridgeshire or Buckinghamshire.[67]

The century before the Reformation also saw an increasing number of monks and canons studying at Cambridge. The majority of these came from eastern England: Benedictine monks from Ely and Norwich, and to a lesser extent, from Bury St Edmunds, Crowland, Thorney, Spalding and St Benet of Hulme, and Augustinian canons from Walsingham and St Osyth in Essex. After 1450, however, the university also attracted a growing number of monks and canons from most regions of England, apart from the area around and to the west of Oxford.[68]

Adding to the diversity of the medieval academic population were commoners. These included older men, many of graduate status, and undergraduate commoners. The colleges valued commoners for the income they generated through room charges and board. The undergraduate commoners lived mainly in hostels until the second half of the fifteenth century, when they began to transfer to the colleges. Mature commoners included ex-fellows, who had vacated their fellowships but continued to reside in college, beneficed clergy, who had obtained episcopal licence to attend a university, and those using the accommodation as a base from which to pursue an administrative career. Commoners also included a handful of noblemen engaging in academic studies, and those in monastic orders. The mature commoners provided a broad social spectrum and linked the colleges with the wider community.[69]

The origins and backgrounds of university members were much wider than those of many other townspeople, and their wills reflect this. Some scholars had families in the surrounding villages, like John Nede, clerk of King's College, who left books to the churches at Trumpington and Grantchester, and gifts to his sister-in-law at Somersham, and sister and brother-in-law at Shelford in 1519.[70] Others had far more distant links, like Hugh Chaderton of Clement Hostel, who wanted to be buried in Portsmouth in 1543.[71] Many ties arose from the ecclesiastical careers that many medieval graduates pursued. In his will of 1502, John Scarlett, a doctor in canon law, requested burial in Holy Trinity parish, Cambridge, made bequests to the Norfolk churches of West Raynham, where he was rector, and Tunstead, where he was vicar. He also described books that he held at Norwich. Robert Clyfton of Michaelhouse was rector of Bucknall in Lincolnshire when he died in 1508; he left donations to his church, college and to Lincoln Cathedral, and asked to be buried in St Michael's,

---

67 Aston, Duncan and Evans, 'Medieval alumni', 28–34; A.B. Cobban, *English university life in the Middle Ages* (London, 1999), pp. 16–17.

68 R.B. Dobson, 'The monastic orders in late medieval Cambridge', in P. Biller and R.B. Dobson, eds., *The medieval church: universities, heresy and the religious life*, Studies in Church History Subsidia, XI (Woodbridge, 1999), p. 256.

69 Cobban, 'Commoners'; Cobban, *University life*, pp. 95–118.

70 KC, Ledger Book, i, fol. 249.

71 UA, WILLS, i, fol. 66.

Cambridge.[72] In several cases, like the bequest by the vicar of Barrington to fellows at Michaelhouse in 1545, the college held the rectory and would have appointed the vicar.[73] The colleges also developed links with the people of the town and surrounding region as consumers, employers and landlords.[74]

Privileged persons

The university exercised jurisdiction over its own members and certain persons serving the academic community, known as scholars' servants or privileged persons. The university courts, which undertook proceedings against moral offenders and breaches of the peace, and had oversight of regulations relating to weights, measures and foodstuffs, could also hear personal pleas involving members or employees of the university.[75] Privileged persons, being subject to the chancellor and so exempt from the duties and charges of the borough and the authority of the borough courts, were particularly resented by other townsmen who did not share these concessions. Protection of the chancellor's court may have been used as a shield from enemies in the town, or to gain a speedier and cheaper recovery of debts.[76] A scholar's servant swore obedience to the chancellor and vice-chancellor and promised to maintain all ordinances, customs and liberties of the university.[77]

An agreement made between the university and town in 1503 classed the following as scholars' servants:

> all Bedells... Mancipills, Cooks, Butlers, & Launders of everye Colledge, Hostell & other places... & all appotycares, Stacioners, Lymners, Schryveners, Parchment-makers, Boke bynders, Phisitions, Surgeons, & Barbers in the said Universitie.

Classifying who came under the definition of a privileged person could nonetheless be difficult, and a schedule of people who enjoyed the privilege was attached to the award.[78] In 1526 the definition was extended to include every household servant of a scholar.[79] In the first half of the sixteenth century, those who registered wills in the vice-chancellor's court, thereby claiming the privilege, included an apothecary, baker, butler, draper, freemason, glover, maid, stationer, surgeon, and cooks from five colleges.[80]

In 1503 the town complained that the university had 'accepted & toke everye

---

72   Ibid., fols. 2v, 24v; Emden, *Biographical register*, pp. 144, 510.
73   BL Add. MS 5861, fol. 29.
74   See below, Chapters 6 and 7.
75   A. Shepard, 'Litigation and locality: the Cambridge university courts, 1560–1640', *Urban History*, 31 (2004), 5–28.
76   C.I. Hammer, 'Oxford town and Oxford University', in J. McConica, ed., *The history of the University of Oxford*, iii: *the collegiate university* (Oxford, 1986), p. 85; A.B. Cobban, *The medieval English universities: Oxford and Cambridge to c.1500* (Aldershot, 1988), pp. 269–71.
77   See the oaths of scholars' servants in UA, C.U.R. 36.2 and UA, Collect.Admin.5, fol. 15v.
78   UA, Luard 143b (72 people listed), Luard 145b (68 people listed).
79   CCA, X/20, printed in *Annals*, i, pp. 323–4.
80   UA, WILLS, i.

person at their pleasure, as their Servaunts and Commen Ministers'. Under the terms of the agreement made in the same year, menial servants living with or retained by scholars, were to be regarded as scholars' servants only during the time of their service. Unfortunately, a complaint drawn up c.1530 by the town suggests that this ruling was open to abuse. It argued that former students of the university, who had since moved elsewhere, had retained various craftsmen such as skinners, tailors and shoemakers in the town, as their servants, by purchasing a livery or riding coat for them, or paying very small wages. These servants seldom if at all attended on their masters, who were not resident in the university.[81]

The willingness of the university to accept regulation of the number of scholars' servants may have stemmed from their liability to cause disorder. Evidence from the chancellor's court at Oxford points to the 'chronic unruliness' of cooks, manciples and private servants employed by the friaries and monastic houses, who were frequently involved in intercollegiate brawls and affrays.[82] Several clauses in the Cambridge agreement of 1503 detail the procedure for the arrest and trial of privileged persons, all stressing that this was to be conducted by the university authorities and not the town.[83]

From the town's point of view, the privileged persons were not, as was stated during the 1530s, contributing anything towards the finances and government of the borough:

> bearyng no maner of Skott lott offices nor other imposityons and Charges belongyng to the saide Towne to the no lytill hyndrannce and impoverisshment of the said Mayer baylyffes and burgesses by reason that their dayly lyving is taken from them by the saide persons.[84]

Similarly in 1554, it was claimed that the extension of the privilege of scholar's servant to men who did not serve in that function was leading to the 'decaie' of the town, the diminishing of sums due in subsidies, and a reduction in soldiers available in times of war.[85] Medieval towns demanded considerable obligations from their inhabitants in money and time: to serve in municipal office and to contribute to the financial needs of the town's complex infrastructure and ceremonies. As urban populations contracted in the later middle ages, these burdens fell on fewer heads and became increasingly onerous. Many citizens became reluctant to bear these burdens and evaded or refused serving in municipal office.[86] A growing number of scholars who were exempt from taxation placed an increasing burden on the other inhabitants of the town. Cambridge secured a reduction of its fixed taxation assessment in 1446 and

---

81 CCA, X/38.
82 R.B. Dobson, 'The religious orders 1370–1540', in J.I. Catto and R. Evans, eds., *The history of the university of Oxford*, ii: *late medieval Oxford* (Oxford, 1992), p. 565.
83 UA, Luard 145a, printed in *Annals*, i, pp. 262–5.
84 CCA, X/38; see also X/69(ii).
85 CCA, X/3, printed in *Annals*, ii, p. 88.
86 Phythian-Adams, 'Urban decay', pp. 174–7; Dobson, 'Urban decline', pp. 278–9. Kermode, however, has argued that the increasing numbers of fines for refusing office in York reflected exploitation by the corporation, rather than an increased unwillingness to serve: J.I. Kermode, 'Urban decline? The flight from office in late medieval York', *EcHR*, 2nd ser., 35 (1982), 179–98.

1465, partly on the basis that many houses, formerly inhabited by craftsmen, were now occupied by scholars and not chargeable.[87] The growth of privileged persons increased the size of the community not participating in civic offices, town courts, or contributing to the borough's fee farm. For the town council, it was particularly annoying to see fellow tradesmen treated as privileged persons who were 'of right goode substance and valewe mette apte and able to bear thoffices of bayliff or mayer ... and to Susteyn the charges therof'.[88]

Parish churches and guilds

The parish churches of medieval Cambridge generally lay adjacent to the two main streets of the town. Along or near the High Street were St Mary the Less (called St Peter without Trumpington Gate until 1352), St Botolph, St Benedict (or St Bene't), St Edward King and Martyr, St Mary the Great, St Michael, and All Saints by the Hospital (or All Saints Jewry). On the other main parallel street lay St Andrew the Great and Holy Trinity; while from Bridge Street to Castle Hill lay Holy Sepulchre, St Clement, St Giles, and St Peter by the Castle. To the east, St Andrew the Less comprised a precinct of Barnwell Priory. Cambridge lost two other parishes during the later middle ages: the church of All Saints by the Castle was abandoned after the Black Death when the parish merged with St Giles, and St John Zachary (the Baptist) in Milne Street was demolished to provide part of the new site for King's College.[89]

The foundation of Cambridge's parish churches can rarely be dated precisely, but all existed by the thirteenth century. Most were probably built and supported by groups of citizens or landowners, to be status symbols and centres of devotion for their communities.[90] The abundant evidence of additions and alterations during the fifteenth and early sixteenth centuries suggests that these churches remained foci for their communities.[91] These parish communities also sub-divided the society of the town more by geography than social status, and they included both town and gown.

The colleges founded in the fourteenth century generally used neighbouring parish churches as places of worship, often adapting the buildings to meet their particular requirements. The fellows of Peterhouse rebuilt the chancel of St Mary the Less on the model of Merton College Chapel, Oxford. Bursar John Leedes and masters Thomas Lane, Henry Horneby and John Warkworth made additions to the church in the fifteenth century. Hervey de Stanton, founder of Michaelhouse, rebuilt St Michael's Church dividing two-thirds into a chancel for the college, and one-third for the nave for the parishioners, while Gonville Hall may have used the north choir aisle of the church. Corpus Christi College worshipped in St Bene't's, adjacent to the college, where a surviving memorial brass commemorates Richard Billingford, master

---

87 *Charters*, pp. xxvi, 55–61.

88 CCA, X/38.

89 C.N.L. Brooke, 'The churches of medieval Cambridge', in D. Beales and G. Best, eds., *History, society and the churches: Essays in honour of Owen Chadwick* (Cambridge, 1985), pp. 69–72.

90 Ibid., pp. 52–4, 69–73; R. and M. Lovatt, 'The religious life of the townsmen of medieval Cambridge', in N. Rogers, ed., *Catholics in Cambridge* (Leominster, 2003), pp. 8–9.

91 See below, Chapter 7.

Figure 3.5 Memorial brass of Richard de Billingford, Doctor of Divinity and Master of Corpus Christi College, 1398–1432, in the south aisle of St Bene't's Church. The inscription and scroll are missing

of the college from 1398 until his death in 1432. A later master, Thomas Cosyn (1487–1515), built a south vestry and chapel with a gallery linking the church and the college's Old Court. Chapels for Trinity Hall and Clare were added to the church of St Edward King and Martyr between 1446 and 1466 to replace chapels lost with the demolition of the church of St John Zachary.[92]

Several colleges, however, began to construct oratories and chapels within their own precincts, as at Pembroke and Gonville Hall during the second half of the fourteenth century, and at King's Hall in the mid-fifteenth.[93] King's College Chapel, begun in 1446, was granted an exceptional range of privileges, including exemption from the authority of the archbishop, bishop and archdeacon, independence from all parish rights, and rights of burial. Some college chapels had also acquired burial rights. Edmond Chollerton requested in 1526 to be buried in King's Hall Chapel 'yf the felowes be content therewith' or else in the Grey Friars Chapel. At King's College, the college statutes restricted burial within the precincts of the church to 'a fellow of the

---

92 Brooke,'Churches', pp. 64–8; *RCHMC*, pp. 264, 271, 281; Emden, *Biographical register*, pp. 61–2.
93 Brooke,'Churches', pp. 74–5.

college, or some person of noble rank or a special friend'.[94] Nicholas Francis, a joiner, requested in 1536 to be buried 'in hallow ground within Jesus in Cambridge' and his will was witnessed by Master Bull, curate of Jesus College.[95] After the Reformation, the new college foundations included a chapel, and the older colleges gradually abandoned using their parish churches and added chapels, Corpus doing so in 1579 and Peterhouse in 1628.[96]

Despite these developments, the early parish registers show that many colleges retained links with their parish churches. Children of Doctors Sands and Parker, of Corpus Christi College, were baptised at St Bene't's in 1549 and 1550, and William Sowode, master of the college, was buried there in 1544. Fellows of Peterhouse were buried at St Mary the Less in 1558 and 1559, while a butler and member of Trinity Hall, and a fellow and scholar of Clare Hall were all buried at St Edward's.[97]

The process of appropriation – through which monasteries and colleges acquired the income from the parish that had previously supported the rector, together with the right to present the incumbent – meant that the colleges also appointed many of the clergy that served in churches in the town and county, generally from among their fellowships. In Cambridge, St Mary the Less was appropriated by Peterhouse, St Michael by Michaelhouse, St Mary the Great by King's Hall, St Bene't by Corpus Christi, and St Edward's by Trinity Hall.[98]

Great St Mary's Church had particularly strong links with both the university and leading burgesses. The university used the church for ceremonial occasions: degrees were conferred there until the Senate House was built in 1730. The nave of Great St Mary's was rebuilt around the 1490s in what was probably a co-operative venture between the university and townspeople. Subscribers to the work included Richard III, Lady Margaret Beaufort, Archbishop Thomas Rotherham, 10 bishops, and 30 heads of religious houses. John Alcock, Bishop of Ely, preached a sermon lasting more than two hours for the building fund, and the expenses of the junior proctor in 1493 included letters requesting support.[99] At least 18 mayors between 1450 and 1560 had connections with Great St Mary's, 8 serving as churchwardens or in another office for that church.[100] This no doubt reflected the central position of the parish, and taxation returns show that many of the town's wealthiest inhabitants resided in this area.[101]

Many medieval parishes in Cambridge and surrounding villages accommodated guilds or fraternities. These were essentially socio-religious, rather than economic organisations: 'among their functions were the jobs now done by the Rotary Club, the Women's Institutes, mutual insurance companies, the Amateur Dramatic Society,

---

94 TNA: PRO PROB 11/22, fol. 71v; Willis and Clark, *Architectural history*, iii, pp. 514–15.
95 CCRO, Archdeaconry of Ely, Will Register 1, fol. 25.
96 Willis and Clark, *Architectural history*, iii, pp. 501–16.
97 CCRO, parish registers.
98 Willis and Clark, *Architectural history*, iii, pp. 484–98.
99 Morgan and Brooke, *History*, p. 16; W.D. Bushell, *The church of St Mary the Great: The university church at Cambridge* (Cambridge, 1948), pp. 10–20, 34–7.
100 Milner Gray, *Biographical notes*, pp. 18–28.
101 Goose, 'Economic and social aspects', pp. 79–81.

sickness insurers, the Parish Council, the Freemasons, the Internal Drainage Board, and (most important of all) a burial club.'[102] Guilds provided funerals and commemorative rites for their deceased members: a church service, often with a procession or commemorative sermon, was followed by a meal with distribution of alms to the poor. It appears that the less prestigious urban guilds were open to craftsmen and artisans, while the most expensive guilds in Cambridge were restricted to wealthier citizens. Most guilds were open to men and women, although women did not hold office or generally become involved in decision-making.[103]

While those town guilds that required wealth and social respectability for membership could be divisive, some Cambridge guilds also brought together members of town and gown. The membership of Holy Trinity Guild in the early sixteenth century included a doctor of law from the university, a father of the president of Queens' College, a university bedell and six mayors of Cambridge.[104] The guilds of Corpus Christi and the Blessed Virgin Mary amalgamated in 1352 to found an academic college, Corpus Christi College. Although the united guild is last recorded in the 1370s, the college inherited its property and public functions, notably the Corpus Christi procession, in which leading members of the university and corporation both participated.[105] The ceremony was stopped during Edward VI's reign, revived under Queen Mary, and finally abolished by Elizabeth, after vigorous protests from the townspeople. Other college feasts on religious festivals, like that held on Holy Innocents' Day at King's Hall, brought together scholars and townsmen including the mayor, and also college tenants and friars.[106] The Corpus Christi procession, like the religious ceremonies and plays in other medieval towns, was an important expression of civic unity and cohesiveness. The guilds themselves had been foci of community life and after their suppression in 1547 the townspeople had to forge new social and religious relationships.[107]

Religious houses

Travellers to early sixteenth-century Oxford were more likely to be impressed by the concentration of ten different religious houses around the town, rather than the university and its collegiate buildings.[108] In Cambridge, too, the cluster of monastic

---

102 O. Rackham, 'Why Corpus Christi?' in M.E. Bury and E.J. Winter, eds., *Corpus within living memory: life in a Cambridge college* (London, 2003), p. 10.

103 V. Bainbridge, *Gilds in the medieval countryside: social and religious change in Cambridgeshire c.1350–1558* (Woodbridge, 1996), pp. 41–50.

104 M. Siraut, 'Accounts of Saint Katherine's Guild at Holy Trinity Church, Cambridge: 1514–37', *PCAS*, 67 (1977), 114–15.

105 Rackham, 'Why Corpus Christi?'; C.P. Hall, 'The gild of Corpus Christi and the foundation of Corpus Christi College: an investigation of the documents', in Zutshi, ed., *Medieval Cambridge*, pp. 65–91.

106 M. Underwood, 'Religion and the university to 1535', in Rogers, ed., *Catholics*, pp. 23–4; Cobban, *University life*, p. 208.

107 V. Harding, 'Reformation and culture 1540–1700', in *CUHB*, ii, pp. 263–88.

108 Dobson, 'General survey', p. 286.

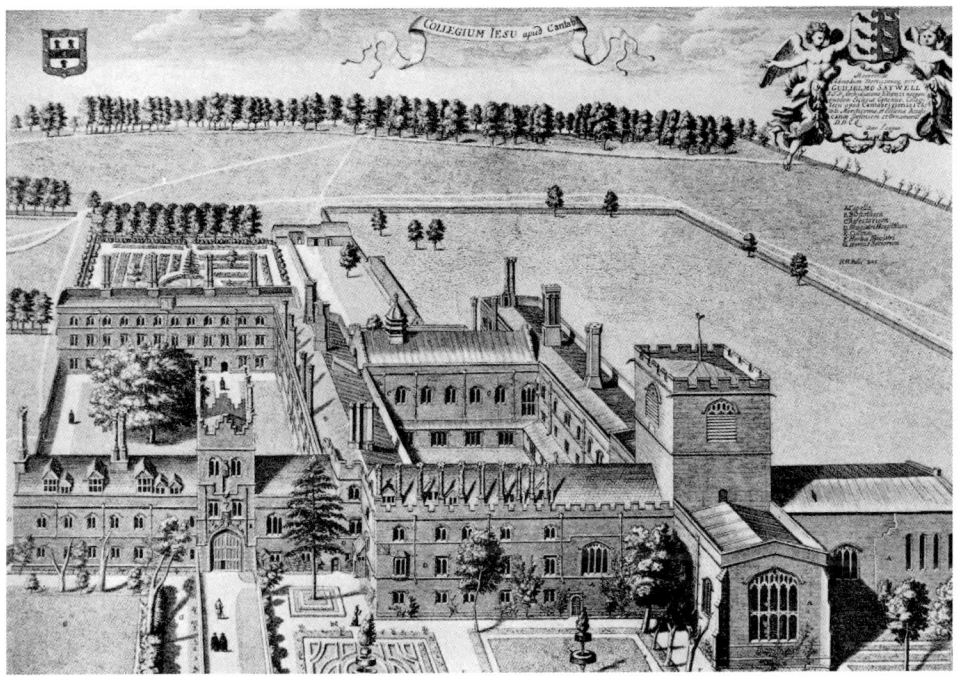

Figure 3.6 Jesus College from David Loggan's *Cantabrigia Illustrata* of 1690. The buildings of the Benedictine nunnery of St Radegund, including the church, were adapted for the college (Cambridgeshire Collection)

and mendicant houses were significant features of the medieval townscape. Barnwell Priory, a house of Augustinian canons, lay east of the town. It often housed visitors of importance, including the king and his court during the Cambridge Parliament of 1388, and bishops of Ely in the fifteenth and early sixteenth centuries.[109] St Radegund's Priory of Benedictine nuns was founded in the mid-twelfth century, and dissolved by Bishop Alcock of Ely in 1496 to found Jesus College. Friaries were essentially urban phenomena, dependent on the alms-giving of concentrated populations, and Cambridge accommodated the four major orders – the Franciscans (Grey friars), Dominicans (Black friars), Carmelites (White friars) and Augustinian (or Austin) friars. Hospitals were another religious institution characteristically found in towns to treat the urban poor and destitute. Cambridge's two leper hospitals occupied customary sites outside the boundaries of the town: the hospital of St Mary Magdalene, founded in the mid-twelfth century, fell out of use by the thirteenth century, but its chapel and fair on Stourbridge Common survived; the hospital of St Anthony and St Eligius (or St Eloy) was founded before 1361 outside Trumpington Gate and became an almshouse after 1526. The hospital of St John was established around 1200 as a symbol of Christian welfare in the heart of the Jewish quarter of Cambridge, and dissolved in

---

109 *VCH Cambs.*, ii, pp. 244–6.

1509–11 to create St John's College.[110] The religious houses, like the colleges, were linked to the town and surrounding region through their ownership of urban and rural estates, by employing staff and consuming goods and services, and by appointing clergy to benefices and collecting tithes.[111] Barnwell Priory, for example, received the tithes of the three parishes north and west of the river – St Giles, St Peter and All Saints by the Castle, and St Radegund's received the tithes of St Clement's and All Saints Jewry.[112]

The friaries had very small endowments and relied largely on alms from the town and surrounding region. This region was, at least in theory, clearly delineated. In 1395, the friars of Cambridge complained that their territory was being invaded by the friars of Ware (Hertfordshire), and the Pope forbade the latter group from seeking alms or preaching where the Cambridge friars had sought, or to extend their boundaries more than five miles, except to the town of Puckeridge (Hertfordshire).[113] They also received pilgrims and tourists from further afield. The prior of the Black Friars in Cambridge reported that an image of Our Lady in his house drew much pilgrimage, especially when Stourbridge Fair was held.[114]

While the pastoral role of the canons of Barnwell and the nuns of St Radegund's in the town is obscure,[115] the friars were popular with lay people for hearing confessions and preaching, and many Cambridge townspeople left them bequests. Some families had clearly built long-standing relationships over several generations: Hugh Rankyn requested in 1521 to be buried in the Grey Friars' Church in Cambridge under the same stone as his grandfather and father were buried, and left bequests to four orders of friars.[116] The friars also attracted bequests from many villages around Cambridge: between 1515 and 1527 these included at least 18 villages stretching from Guilden Morden in the west to Weston Colville in the east, and from Over in the north to Ickleton in the south. Many were small gifts like the one comb of barley left by John Sereman of Boxworth to the orders of friars in Cambridge to pray for his soul, in 1521.[117] Cambridge residents also made bequests to neighbouring religious houses, including the monasteries of Ely, Denny, Ickleton, and St Osyth, and friaries in Lynn and Sudbury.

The hospital of St John received gifts to maintain beds, provide lights for the sick and support the poor, such as the money left by John Archer in 1504 for 'reparacio of

---

110 Brooke, 'Churches', pp. 59–60, 74; M. Rubin, *Charity and community in medieval Cambridge* (Cambridge, 1987).

111 See below, Chapters 6 and 7.

112 *The West Fields of Cambridge*, ed. C.P. Hall and J.R. Ravensdale, Cambridgeshire Records Soc., III (Cambridge, 1976), p. 76.

113 J.R.H. Moorman, *The Grey Friars in Cambridge 1225–1538* (Cambridge, 1952), p. 69.

114 *LP*, xiii (2), no. 224, p. 85. The church of Our Lady of the Assumption and the English Martyrs, Cambridge, contains a mid-sixteenth century image of the Virgin and Child, traditionally from Emmanuel College, the site of the Dominican Friary: *RCHMC*, p. 300.

115 Brooke, 'Churches', pp. 57–8.

116 TNA: PRO PROB 11/20, fol. 135.

117 BL Add. MS 5861, fols. 21–77v; CCRO, Archdeaconry of Ely, Will Register 1*, fol. 44.

Bedding for the poor people that be lodged within the place'.[118] It provided corrodies or pensions in food and clothing for laymen, lodgings for some members of the university, and was used by a town congregation for masses, having acquired parochial rights independent of the neighbouring church of All Saints. The hospitals of St John, and St Anthony and St Eligius, being the only houses in Cambridge or within 13 miles of the town, were the obvious places to which the poor and sick of Cambridge and surrounding villages would resort for help.[119]

Almshouses and charitable bequests from individuals and guilds also provided relief for the poor in the town. Thomas Jakenett, a burgess of Cambridge, and Agnes, his wife, founded almshouses for the parish of St Mary the Great in the later fifteenth century. Several members of the university left bequests for charitable support. John Hogekyns, fellow of King's College, managed almshouses which were handed over to the college in 1504/5, and Andrew Doket, president of Queens', founded almshouses through his will, proved in 1485.[120] Thomas Colyer, fellow of Michaelhouse, bequeathed a load of wood each to the two poorest almshouses in Jesus Lane, and 3s 4d to the tollbooth and castle in his will of 1506. William Adams, bachelor in law, left 40s for building a house for the lodging and relief 'of very pore people lyeng in the streetes of Cambrige that may not help them selff'.[121] In addition to the resident poor, strangers passed through the town seeking relief, perhaps like 'Old John came out of the north', buried at St Bene't's in 1539 and 'James Base, of a stranger borne in the streete' baptised at All Saints, Cambridge in 1541.[122]

Many of the religious orders had members who studied at the university. The friars played a major role in establishing Cambridge as a university and especially in the study of theology there.[123] Barnwell Priory's influence is less apparent: it seems that it was not until the early sixteenth century that the community accommodated two or three university graduates. The history of St Edmund's Priory, founded in 1290 as a convent for Gilbertine canons studying in Cambridge, is also obscure. After the mid-fourteenth century, the house rarely had more than three or four brethren in residence, and very few of these canons appear to have attended the university. The hostel founded by Crowland Abbey, which developed into Buckingham College, helped to accommodate an increasing number of Benedictine monks studying at Cambridge from the 1470s. By the early sixteenth century, Benedictine monks and Augustinian canons 'had never been so much in evidence at Cambridge', reflecting the growing academic prestige of the university and the increasing emphasis placed on the value of a higher university degree by the monastic orders.[124]

The fate of Cambridge's religious houses at the dissolution was closely tied to the university. The refounding of St Radegund's Priory as Jesus College and St John's

---

118   TNA:PRO PROB 11/14, fol. 125v.
119   Rubin, *Charity and community*, p. 175; Underwood, 'Impact', pp. 169–70.
120   *VCH Cambs.*, ii, p. 146; *RCHMC*, p. 316.
121   CUL, WILLS, i, fols. 11, 16v–17v.
122   CCRO, Cambridge St Bene't's and All Saints parish registers.
123   Zutshi, ed., *Medieval Cambridge*, p. 8.
124   Dobson, 'Monastic orders', pp. 240–59.

Hospital as St John's College had provided precedents. Buckingham College survived to be re-established by Thomas, Lord Audley of Walden, as Magdalene College. The friary precincts were still marked on Lyne's map of 1574, showing that there had been little development in over 30 intervening years since their dissolution. The Dominican and Franciscan friaries eventually became the sites of Emmanuel and Sidney Sussex Colleges, founded in 1584 and 1594 respectively. Queens' College incorporated the adjacent precinct of the Carmelite friars and the Austin friary buildings later became the Perse Grammar School. As occurred elsewhere, some laymen also profited from the disposal of church lands. Barnwell Priory, too far from the university to be used as the site of a college, was bought by Thomas Wendy of Haslingfield in 1553, whose heir gave most of the stone to build Corpus Christi College Chapel.[125] Ralph Bicardyke, a Cambridge burgess, obtained the site of the Gilbertine house of St Edmund's in 1544.[126]

At the dissolution, many urban corporations became direct owners and managers of the former lands and resources of monastic foundations, chantries and fraternities, gaining fuller control over the jurisdiction of their respective towns. In Norwich, for example, the city gained the Dominican friary, while Colchester Corporation purchased former chantry lands, and in Coventry the borough council acquired the city lands of the Benedictine cathedral priory. Cambridge Corporation, however, was unable to gain any substantial part of the former monastic sites in the town, reflecting the influential connections which the university held with the royal court.[127] The mayor and aldermen met Thomas Wendy 'to commune with him concerninge of ye byenge of Barnwell', but had to content themselves with gaining possession of the lands belonging to St Edmund's and the sites of two hermitages.[128]

Aliens

While foreign immigration formed only a small part of the total migration in Cambridge and its region, it is particularly well-documented by the subsidies levied on aliens residing in the county. These accounts survive from the mid-fifteenth century onwards; the most detailed are assessments for the first subsidy, granted in 1440.[129] Foreigners living in Cambridge and Cambridgeshire were also recorded in letters of protection issued to 'Flemings' in England in 1436,[130] and in the lay subsidies of 1513 and 1524.[131] Unfortunately, these subsidies varied in their coverage of different

---

125 P.V. Danckwerts,'The inheritors of Barnwell Priory', *PCAS*, 70 (1980), 211–34.
126 *VCH Cambs.*, ii, p. 256.
127 Harding,'Reformation', pp. 264–5; Goose,'Urban variable', 181; Morgan and Brooke, *History*, pp. 10–11.
128 CCA, Palmer/Barnard, vol. 57, fol. 93v; *CBD*, pp. 137, 144.
129 TNA: PRO E 179/235/4 is the clearest copy, with assessments for the 1440 alien subsidy for the Isle of Ely, Cambridgeshire, and Cambridge. The same names are recorded in E 179/81/85, inquest for Cambridge and E 179/81/87, inquests for 10 Cambridgeshire hundreds. The alien subsidy return examined in *CBD*, p. 105 seems to have been an assessment made in 1441: E 179/235/3.
130 *CPR, 1429–36*, pp. 537–9, 541–88.
131 *CBD*, pp. 110–31; E 179/81/129, E 179/81/132–3, E 179/81/137.

Table 3.4

Nationalities of aliens in Cambridgeshire, 1440

	Cambridge	Number of aliens Cambridgeshire	Isle of Ely
'Dutch'	59	24	2
French	6	37	2
Scots	4	1	0
Irish	9	6	1
Other	1	0	0
Not stated	5	2	23

Source: TNA: PRO E 179/235/4.

nationalities of aliens over time and so precise comparisons cannot be made.[132]

Aliens comprised less than 1 per cent of the country's total population in the mid-fifteenth century, but were more prominent in some areas, such as port towns and above all in London, where they formed at least 6 per cent of the population of the city and its suburbs. The scale of this immigration can be measured crudely by expressing the number of aliens in 1440 as a percentage of the number of taxpayers in 1377. By this measure, aliens comprised 4 per cent of Cambridge's population, a similar proportion to towns in west Wiltshire, but they formed a negligible part of the total population in the rest of Cambridgeshire.[133]

The nationalities of aliens in Cambridge and its county in 1440 are shown in Table 3.4. The majority of aliens in Cambridge were described by the blanket term, 'Ducheman' or 'Duchewoman', which covered Flemish, Dutch and German migrants.[134] The town still contained a predominance of 'Dutch' and a smaller number of French and Scottish immigrants in the early sixteenth century: 9 'Dutchmen', 4 Scots and a Norman were listed in 1513, and 29 'Dutch', 5 Scottish, and a French taxpayer in 1524.[135] In the county in 1440, however, French migrants outnumbered the 'Dutch'. The proportions of different nationalities varied across the country, but a similar predominance of Dutch and Flemish immigrants were found in other parts of East Anglia and in London. Economic opportunities in England and the opportunity to escape political instability and religious persecution in The Netherlands attracted these migrants from across the North Sea.[136] Scots in England were largely concentrated in

---

132 *The alien communities of London in the fifteenth century: the subsidy rolls of 1440 & 1483–4*, ed. J.L. Bolton (Stamford, 1998), pp. 3–4.

133 S.L. Thrupp, 'A survey of the alien population of England in 1440', *Speculum*, 32 (1957), 266, 271; *Alien communities*, p. 8; Hare, 'Growth and recession', 15; *Poll taxes*, p. 69.

134 Thrupp, 'Alien population', 271; S.L. Thrupp, 'Aliens in and around London in the fifteenth century', in A.E.J. Hollaender and W. Kellaway, eds., *Studies in London history presented to Philip Edmund Jones* (London, 1969), p. 259.

135 *CBD*, pp. 110–31; TNA PRO E 179/81/133.

136 Thrupp, 'Alien population', 266–7; *Alien communities*, pp. 6–7, 28–34; N. Goose, 'The Dutch in Colchester in the 16th and 17th centuries: opposition and integration', in R. Vigne and C. Littleton, eds., *From strangers to citizens: the integration of immigrant communities in Britain, Ireland and colonial America, 1550–1750* (London, 2001), pp. 88–98.

Table 3.5

Occupations of aliens in Cambridge, 1440

Occupation	Number of aliens
cordwainer's servant	20
wife	16
servant	14
not stated	12
cordwainer	8
university member	6
webster	2
bookbinder	1
cobbler	1
currier	1
fisher	1
labourer	1
patternmaker	1

Source: TNA: PRO E 179/235/4.
Note: The patternmaker may have worked in either the textile or iron industries: *OED*, xi, p. 358.

East Anglia, Kent and London, reflecting east coast trading routes and the hostility displayed towards them in northern cities such as York.[137] Foreigners from more distant parts occasionally appeared in the Cambridge region. In 1460, Corpus Christi College gave alms to two Greeks, presumably refugees, after the Turkish capture of Constantinople.[138] A 'Spanyard' resided at Fulbourn in 1524.[139]

Many aliens found employment in towns, particularly the Flemish, Dutch and German migrants, who tended to work in crafts that were largely urban-based, such as the leather and textile industries. In Wiltshire, alien immigration was a particular feature of the towns and cloth-making hundreds of the county, while in Norfolk, aliens clustered in Norwich, Lynn and Yarmouth.[140] In Cambridgeshire, aliens congregated mainly in Cambridge, with a few minor clusters in some small towns, and a sprinkling across the countryside. In 1436, of the 49 'Flemings' receiving letters of protection in the county, the largest concentrations were at Cambridge (25 aliens), Huntingdon (5 aliens) and Ely (3 aliens). In 1440, 84 aliens were assessed in Cambridge, 7 in Wisbech, 6 in Ely, and 85 in 55 villages spread across the county and Isle of Ely. In 1524, 35 aliens were assessed in Cambridge and 7 in other parts of the county, at

---

[137] J.A.F. Thomson, 'Scots in England in the fifteenth century', *Scottish Historical Rev.*, 79 (2000), 1–16; R.B. Dobson, 'Aliens in the city of York during the fifteenth century', in J. Mitchell, ed., *England and the continent in the middle ages* (Stamford, 2000), pp. 249–66.

[138] P. Zutshi, 'John Botwright master of the college, 1443–1474', *Letter of the Corpus Association*, 77 (1998), 17.

[139] TNA: PRO E 179/81/132.

[140] Thrupp, 'Alien population', 267; Hare, 'Growth and recession', 15–16; N.J.M. Kerling, 'Aliens in the county of Norfolk, 1436–1485', *Norfolk Archaeology*, 33 (1965), 205.

Table 3.6

Occupations of aliens in Cambridgeshire, 1463

Occupation	Number of aliens
servant	5
husbandman	4
weaver	4
shoemaker	2
labourer	1
smith	1

Source: TNA: PRO E 179/81/111.

Burwell, Bassingbourn, and three villages in Flendish hundred – Fulbourn, Fen Ditton and Cherry Hinton.[141]

Occupations are not recorded consistently in the alien subsidies, but some accounts provide sufficient entries to give a rough breakdown of the main areas of work. Aliens in Cambridge tended to enter leather working, as Table 3.5 shows, with cordwainers, cobblers and curriers listed in the subsidy of 1440. There were four cordwainers among the Flemings who resided in Cambridge in 1436.[142] Occupations have not been inferred from surnames in the 1440 subsidy, but the surnames Barbour, Coryour, Girdelere and Sadeller may indicate trades in which aliens participated. Robert Browne, tailor, was a Scot assessed in Bridge Ward in 1524; his will of 1540 mentions his shop board, two pairs of tailors' shears and a pressing iron.[143] The occupations of aliens in the county are not recorded in 1440, but a subsidy of 1463 suggests that the majority of aliens were employed in agricultural work or weaving (Table 3.6). Several aliens resided with local landowners. In 1440, two Frenchmen lived in the household of William Alington, owner of Horseheath manor, and another Frenchman with Henry Somer of Grantchester, who also employed Welshmen on his estate for ditching work. John Fermour of Elsworth, whose family held the lease of Ramsey Abbey's demesne in the village, had a French servant in 1441.[144]

Some aliens in Cambridge were, by the standards of the time, substantial employers. In 1440, Giles Ducheman, cordwainer, employed 5 Dutchmen, and Elie Ducheman employed 6 alien servants; in 1513, 3 Dutchmen had a number of employees: Nicholas Williamson, shoemaker, had 6 servants and 2 apprentices, Nicholas Symond, goldsmith, had 4 servants and an apprentice, and Richard Cole had 5 servants.[145] Even larger units of production were found among aliens in London.[146] Successive parliamentary legislation tried to restrict the numbers of apprentices,

---

141 Of the 1524 lay subsidy returns for Cambridgeshire listed in the bibliography, only three list alien taxpayers: TNA: PRO E 179/81/129, E 179/81/132, E 179/81/137.
142 *CPR, 1429–36*, pp. 545, 588.
143 CCRO, Archdeaconry of Ely, Will Register, 1, fol. 150.
144 TNA: PRO E 179/235/4, E 179/235/3; KC, GRA/658–9; *VCH Cambs.*, v, p. 206, vi, p. 71, ix, p. 311.
145 TNA: PRO E 179/235/4; *CBD*, pp. 104–5, 111, 115, 117.
146 *Alien communities*, pp. 20–2.

servants and journeymen kept by foreign artificers, although strangers of the universities of Oxford and Cambridge were initially exempted.[147]

Whilst some communities of aliens experienced hostility in the later middle ages, such as the infamous 'evil May Day' riots of 1517 in London, outbreaks of xenophobia in Cambridge are not apparent from the surviving records. Some aliens became well-integrated within the town. Dutchmen Nicholas Symond, Francis van Horne and William Johnson became freemen of Cambridge in the 1520s and 1530s, as did seven men during the 1540s and 1550s who were described as from *dominium domini Imperatoris* (the dominion of the lord emperor - presumably from a territory belonging to the Holy Roman Emperor).[148] Nicholas Symond's burial in 1533 involved many of the religious organisations in the town. A dirge and mass were to be held in St Bene't's, then friars from the four orders in Cambridge were to bear his body to the Grey Friars' Church for burial. Twelve torches carried with the hearse were afterwards to be distributed to every parish church in the town.[149]

Six university members were assessed as aliens in 1440.[150] Although during the course of the sixteenth century the university attracted such eminent foreign scholars as Desiderius Erasmus, Martin Bucer and Paul Fagius,[151] the university's recruitment from overseas in the fifteenth century was extremely limited. Wales, Scotland and Ireland supplied only 1 per cent of the university's recorded alumni up to 1500, while the continent provided another 1 per cent, the largest number being German and Italian. The majority of continental scholars were friars. Contacts with other institutions of learning outside England were also very restricted, although a few scholars had studied at continental universities before coming to Cambridge, and some Cambridge men migrated overseas, most frequently to Italy.[152]

Demand from the university encouraged migrants skilled in specialised crafts such as printing and brewing to settle in Cambridge. A number of aliens were stationers, bookbinders, or printers, including Gerard Wake, an Irish bookbinder listed in 1440, and Garret Godfrey, Nicholas Speryng (or Spierinck), John Siberch, Sygar Nicholson and Nicholas Pilgrim, who came to Cambridge from The Netherlands during the first half of the sixteenth century.[153] Men from the Low Countries also brought skills in beer brewing and aliens often operated the first breweries producing beer.[154] The fifteenth-century alien subsidies do not record any immigrants brewing in Cambridge, but in the sixteenth century Francis van Horne and stationers Nicholas Speryng and

---

147 14 & 15 Henry VIII, c. 2, 21 Henry VIII, c.16, 32 Henry VIII, c. 16: *SR*, iii, pp. 208–9, 298–300, 766.
148 CCTA, i, fols. 57v, 77v, 123; CCA, Palmer/Barnard vol. 57, fols. 23, 35, 51, 75, 98, 122, 125v.
149 CCRO, Ely Consistory Court, Will Register 7, p. 120.
150 E 179/81/85.
151 Leedham–Green, *Concise history*, pp. 34, 52.
152 Aston, Duncan and Evans, 'Medieval alumni', 35–6.
153 TNA: PRO E 179/235/4; G.J. Gray, *The earlier Cambridge stationers and bookbinders and the first Cambridge printer*, Oxford Bibliographical Soc. Illustrated Monographs XIII (Oxford, 1904), pp. 10–65.
154 *Alien communities*, p. 21; Britnell, *Colchester*, pp. 195–7; J.M. Bennett, *Ale, beer and brewsters in England: women's work in a changing world, 1300–1600* (Oxford, 1996), pp. 79–81.

Sygar Nicholson held a 'beerebruehouse' by Magdalene Bridge in Cambridge.[155] Some aliens found work in the colleges. Corpus Christi College employed Dutchmen and Flemings as casual workmen in the mid-fifteenth century and Janyn Frensshman worked as a cook at Trinity Hall in 1441.[156]

Disputes

Several historians have emphasised the conflict between town and gown in later medieval Cambridge, and the surviving sources certainly reveal an extensive catalogue of disagreements. Many of the matters in dispute related to the market, including weights and measures, regulation of butchers and chandlers, and tolls levied on goods entering the town.[157] Other areas of contention included the town commons, where the borough corporation claimed that scholars inter-commoned their cattle on the town commons, but refused to be assessed for their animals, and the river, where the scholars allegedly over-fished.[158] The university did not have its own prison in this period, and so depended on the co-operation of the townspeople to use the tollbooth or castle, but this was not always forthcoming.[159] The search for and punishment of suspect persons was a further area of confusion and disagreement during the sixteenth century, with the chancellor holding the authority to banish all prostitutes sinning within the university and precincts, while the corporation punished waifs and strays.[160]

The most violent attack on the university in Cambridge occurred during the Peasants' Revolt of 1381. The revolt comprised a complex mixture of national and local grievances, which in Cambridge included not only hostility towards the university, but expressions of anti-clericalism, the burden of the poll tax, and long-standing local disagreements. The revolt was marked in Cambridgeshire, as elsewhere, by activity that revealed close political networks between the inhabitants of the town and its surrounding villages. Cambridge residents joined a group of country rebels in an attack on the manors of Thomas Haselden at Steeple Morden and Guilden Morden, 15 miles south-west of the town. Rebels in the town also allied with rebels in the country to attack the university, targeting the house of William Wigmore, a university bedell, and Corpus Christi College, as well as destroying the university's charters of privileges held in chests in Great St Mary's Church and the Carmelite friary. While the two groups may have had different motives for this attack, with the townspeople keen to end the university's privileges, and the rural rebels arguably viewing the same privileges as symbolic of a system that restrained the unfree, they formed a common interest.[161] A combined force from the town, country and other counties attacked Barnwell Priory,

---

155 *CBD*, pp. 83, 155.
156 E.C. Pearce, 'College accounts of John Botwright, master of Corpus Christi, 1443–74', *PCAS*, 22 (1917–20), 82; TNA: PRO E 179/235/3.
157 Siraut, 'Cambridge', pp. 30–50, and see below, Chapter 4.
158 CCA, X/69(iii), X/3.
159 *Annals*, ii, p. 3.
160 *CPR 1452–61*, p. 502; CCA, X/66, m. 6; UA, Collect.Admin.5, fol. 27.
161 Cobban, *University life*, pp. 195–7.

partly to affirm rights of driftway and pasture in meadows which the priory had enclosed. The homes of some Cambridge burgesses also fell victim to the rebels, though, notably those of Roger Harleston at Cottenham, and John Blankpayn in Petty Cury, Cambridge; both men probably attracted resentment through serving as parliamentary representatives in 1377. There were also outbreaks of violence across the county, including riots at Ely, the plunder of property at Burwell, Bottisham, Chippenham and Reach, and the destruction of court rolls at Balsham, Ickleton and West Wratting.[162]

Fear of attack in 1460, during the Wars of the Roses, prompted at least one college to fortify its premises. Corpus Christi College made payments for saltpetre, sulphur, artillery and arrows, for guarding the college treasury and jewels, and for defending the windows. Most of the external windows of the Old Court may have been blocked at this time. The college accounts also mention a riot against the king on 10 July, the same day as the defeat of Henry VI's forces at the battle of Northampton.[163]

Protests against the enclosure of common land in 1549 brought the non-burgesses of the town into conflict with both the burgesses and colleges, with complaints voiced against leading burgesses, former mayors, and the colleges of King's, Queens' and Trinity. The mayor temporarily allied with the vice-chancellor when protestors pulled up fences enclosing parts of the commons around Cambridge on 10 July 1549. The town treasurers made payments for watchmen, carrying out the gallows, and mending the prison 'after the prisoners brake out', while a curious ballad attacked 'the false flattering freemen of Cambridge, the open and secret enemies of the poor'.[164] This was part of a number of disturbances across East Anglia during early July: camps were established at Downham Market, Ipswich and Bury St Edmunds, and rebels under the leadership of Robert Kett reached Norwich and later took possession of the city. As in 1381, there were links between the protests, and Diarmaid MacCulloch suggests that planning by townspeople and yeomen may have been conducted under the cover of sporting competitions, and mass support gathered at the feast of St Thomas the Martyr at Wymondham or the fairs at Sudbury and Stowmarket.[165] Similar grievances to those made in Cambridge were voiced at nearby Landbeach, where villagers alleged that Richard Kirby, lord of Brays manor, had overstocked the commons, impounded villagers' cattle, and demanded excessive fines to release them.[166]

The extent of town-gown hostility should not be overstated, though. Appeals to important figures at the royal court during the sixteenth century, like Lady Margaret Beaufort, Cardinal Wolsey, Thomas Cromwell and Protector Somerset, offered an

---

162 E. Powell, *The rising in East Anglia in 1381* (Cambridge, 1896), pp. 41–56; R.B. Dobson, *The Peasants' Revolt of 1381* (London, 2nd edn., 1983), pp. 239–42.

163 Pearce, 'College accounts', 89–90; Zutshi, 'Botwright', 16; Rackham, 'Why Corpus Christi?', p. 16.

164 CCC, MS 106, pp. 312–15, 405–7; U.A., Collect.Admin. 5, fol. 119v–121; *Annals*, ii, pp. 38–44, v, pp. 286–7; *VCH Cambs.*, iii, p. 14.

165 D. MacCulloch, 'Kett's rebellion in context', *Past and Present*, 84 (1979), 36–59; A. Fletcher, *Tudor rebellions* (Harlow, 3rd edn., 1983), pp. 54–132.

166 *VCH Cambs.*, ix, p. 147; J.R. Ravensdale, 'Landbeach in 1549: Kett's rebellion in miniature', in L.M. Munby, ed., *East Anglian studies* (Cambridge, 1968), pp. 94–116.

opportunity for grievances to be aired, which might otherwise not have come to light. The surviving evidence is therefore biased towards highlighting moments of conflict, often separated by years of more peaceful co-existence. There was nothing in Cambridge to equal the St Scholastica's day riot at Oxford in 1355, where a tavern brawl escalated into three days of street battles between the university and townspeople. Town and gown in Cambridge were not completely united among themselves. There were potential conflicts of interest between the burgesses who dominated trade and politics, and other inhabitants, while parish, craft and guild loyalties could also divide. Among the student population, as well as differences of age, wealth, degree and college or hostel, riots between northern and southern students were common until the sixteenth century.[167] Even the corporation and university authorities could co-operate officially when major problems presented themselves. A paving leet was held jointly by the mayor and vice-chancellor from 1544, and both leaders worked together during major outbreaks of epidemic disease in 1556 and the early seventeenth century.[168]

Conclusion

The society of Cambridge had a complex range of links with its region and beyond. This hinterland for social contact can be compared with those of other medieval towns. In sixteenth-century Worcester, an urban centre of similar size to Cambridge, references in wills to relatives, properties and birthplaces, and bequests to rural parishes, were concentrated within an area extending between 10 and 25 miles from the city,[169] while at the larger city of York, 50 per cent of freemen admitted in the sixteenth century came from within 25 miles of the town, and 20 per cent from between 12½ and 25 miles away.[170] London, by virtue of its size and economic influence, was able to draw on migrants from the whole country. The birthplaces of London merchants recorded in wills made between 1450 and 1515 included between 24 and 28 per cent each from the Home Counties, the east, and the midlands, and 10 per cent from the north, while nearly half of the apprentices to the skinners' and tailors' companies at the end of the fifteenth century came from northern England.[171] Cambridge's connections, however, were much wider than those of Worcester townsmen by virtue of the university. Indeed, the university drew migrants from a similar range of regions as London merchants, recruiting heavily from the northern and eastern counties. This widened the town's links considerably, as most of the burgesses admitted to the borough came from surrounding villages, although some had links with major towns and rural landowners. The university's presence also brought members of religious orders to reside in the town, as well as specialist

---

167 Cobban, *Universities*, p. 273; Cobban, *University life*, p. 193.

168 Peek and Hall, *Archives of the university*, pp. 61–2; *Collection*, p. 190; Shepard, 'Contesting communities', pp. 223–4.

169 A. Dyer, *The city of Worcester in the sixteenth century* (Leicester, 1973), pp. 183–4.

170 D.M. Palliser, 'A regional capital as magnet: immigrants to York, 1477–1566', *Yorkshire Archaeological Journal*, 57 (1985), 113–15.

171 S.L. Thrupp, *The merchant class of medieval London* (Chicago, 1948), pp. 208–13.

craftsmen who had migrated from overseas. These links increased with the expansion of the university during the fifteenth and early sixteenth centuries.

All medieval towns contained a diverse social and economic mix of people. Cambridge was not alone in containing two particular groups with different objectives, providing the potential for tension and dispute. A number of medieval towns had the presence of a large number of ecclesiastics. Cathedrals and large religious houses often held jealously guarded rights of government, disputed by civic authorities, and could become the focus for material grievances, as occurred in several monastic boroughs like Bury St Edmunds and St Albans during the Peasants' Revolt. Indeed, most large towns in medieval England included ecclesiastical and other franchises in their midst, and townspeople could occasionally resort to violence against these territorial jurisdictions.[172] During the most serious disputes in Cambridge in 1381 and 1549, town and gown hostility merged with, and often became subsumed by, other grievances. The links between the town and its surrounding region, though, continued to be evident through the closely concerted activity of urban and rural rebels.

Between 1450 and 1560 the society of Cambridge experienced significant changes, with the growth in size and prestige of the university, and the loss of the religious houses and guilds. Yet there were also important continuities. Despite changing social and political circumstances, and the existence of two distinct institutions of government – the university and borough authorities – the society of Cambridge continued to be characterised by complex alliances and interests, and the mutual interdependence of town and gown, throughout the fifteenth and sixteenth centuries and beyond.[173]

---

172 Holt, 'Introduction', pp. 4–14; Dobson, *Peasants' Revolt*, pp. 234–6, 267–77; Dobson, 'General survey', p. 287.

173 Shepard, 'Contesting communities', pp. 216–34.

Chapter 4

Markets and trade

Medieval trade was conducted through both formal and informal markets. The formal trading institutions of weekly markets in towns and villages, also described as 'the open market', provided sites where traders and their wares could be regulated. Formal markets were outlets for agricultural produce, foodstuffs, and basic craft and household goods, where small households largely made their purchases. Private marketing and informal trade operated outside these formal markets, ranging from small and local exchanges to large consignments and long-distance trade.[1]

Much of the evidence relating to marketing refers to formal markets, with charter grants recording their foundation, and court rolls and accounts documenting their operation and regulation. The archives of the university and borough corporation contain documents relating to Cambridge market, as both bodies were involved in the regulation and management of this market. Informal trading is more difficult to trace, and a large amount was probably never recorded. Credit arrangements could be registered, with smaller debts arising from local trade recorded in manorial and town courts, and larger debts from regional trade recorded in London courts. Transactions could be disputed, and legal proceedings like the Chancery petitions reveal examples of informal trade. Within the Cambridge region, fairs provided other marketing opportunities, while the colleges developed their own sources of supply, frequently making agreements directly with producers, and these particular networks are examined in Chapters 5 and 6. Evidence relating to the marketing and trading networks in Cambridge and its region is therefore disparate and needs to be pieced together from a variety of sources.

Marketing networks changed significantly in the later middle ages with the abandonment of many markets in villages and small towns. This decline partly reflected the fall in population, with fewer people to trade. The extent of the contraction may have been exaggerated because market grants recorded only the foundation of a market, not its operation, so some markets that received grants may never have been established successfully.[2] The most important factor behind the decline of rural markets, though, was the improvement in living standards after the Black Death. This reduced the numbers of cottagers and smallholders, who had been the greatest source of demand in village markets in the pre-plague period, and increased demand for consumer goods handled by merchants at the expense of local manufacturers. This meant that even when the population began to grow again significantly during the sixteenth century, and the number of smallholders increased,

---

1 Everitt, 'Marketing', p. 15; C. Dyer, 'The hidden trade of the Middle Ages: evidence from the West Midlands of England', *Journal of Historical Geography*, 18 (1992), 141–57; Britnell, *Commercialisation*, pp. 81–101, 161–4.

2 Britnell, *Commercialisation*, pp. 156–61; J. Masschaele, 'The multiplicity of medieval markets reconsidered', *Journal of Historical Geography*, 20 (1994), 255–71.

most former markets did not reappear and only a core of the former medieval markets remained.[3]

The rising standard of living in both the town and countryside during the later middle ages increased demand for foodstuffs and manufactured goods of higher quality and greater variety. Producers of agricultural and industrial commodities responded in a variety of ways. More barley was grown and sales of the crop became more commercialised, while new links developed between rural graziers and urban butchers in the meat trades. Growing demand for merchant wares stimulated urban industries such as cloth-making and leather-working and also led to the import of a growing range of goods from overseas. A new structure of mercantile networks developed to distribute these goods, increasingly dominated by London traders.[4] This chapter examines how the networks of both formal and informal marketing in the Cambridge region responded to these wider economic changes over the 1450–1560 period. The changes affected the markets of villages, small towns, and Cambridge, together with local and regional networks of trade and credit.

Grants of markets in the Cambridge region

Traditionally, the principal sources used to trace formal markets have been charter grants of their foundation. Although trading did not require a formal market to be instituted, a market grant signified that such exchanges were, or could become, substantial enough to benefit from official organisation. Royal charters licensed markets and fairs at specified times and places, and entitled the recipients to collect rents for stalls and tolls for trading. There was a remarkable growth in the number of weekly markets across England between the Norman Conquest and the Black Death of 1348–9, although many of these foundations failed to survive into the fifteenth and sixteenth centuries.[5]

Figure 4.1 attempts to plot the distribution around Cambridge of markets known from their foundation charters.[6] It also highlights those markets that still appear to have operated in the 1450–1560 period.[7] Several markets are known only from their foundation charters: the editors of the *Victoria County History* could find no further evidence for the operation of the markets and fairs at Burwell, Great Abington, Great Wilbraham, Hildersham, Impington, Milton and Wicken. Other markets in the region are definitely known to have contracted or ceased during the later medieval period, like Bassingbourn market and fair, where the site of the stalls was empty in 1435.[8]

---

3   Britnell,'Urban demand', pp. 9–21.

4   Ibid; J.A. Galloway, 'Town and country in England, 1300–1570', in S.R. Epstein, ed., *Town and country in Europe 1300–1800* (Cambridge, 2001), pp. 114–16.

5   R.H. Britnell, 'The proliferation of markets in England, 1200–1349', *EcHR*, 2nd ser., 34 (1981), 209–21.

6   See the map in H. Ridout, 'Markets and fairs', in T. Kirby and S. Oosthuizen, eds., *An atlas of Cambridgeshire and Huntingdonshire history* (Cambridge, 2000), ch. 44, for the periods when Cambridgeshire markets were chartered.

7   Markets listed in Everitt,'Marketing', p. 23 and *VCH Cambs.*, iv–x, *passim*.

8   *VCH Cambs.*, vi, pp. 13, 66, viii, p. 23, ix, pp. 135, 180, x, pp. 314, 353, 567.

Markets and trade

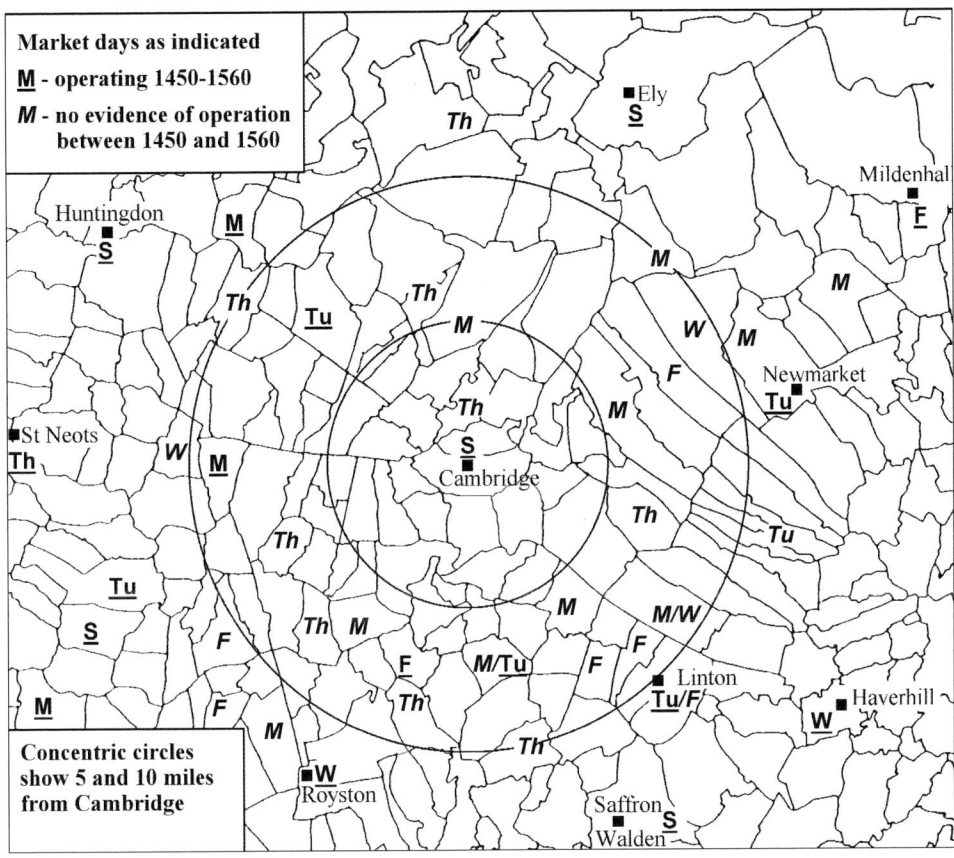

Figure 4.1 Markets of Cambridge and its region
Sources: VCH Cambs., iii-x; S. Letters with others, *Gazetteer of Markets and Fairs in England and Wales to 1516*, 2 vols. (London, 2003), available online at the Centre for Metropolitan History website http://www.ihr.sas.ac.uk/cmh/gaz/gazweb2.html.
Note: Where market days were changed after the initial grant, the final day chosen is shown.

The high density of population and intensity of trade in East Anglia led to an exceptional concentration of markets in this region before 1350, compared with other parts of the country.[9] Within Cambridge's region, markets were particularly concentrated along the river valleys. This reflected the density of settlement in these fertile and accessible areas, and also the social structure, as shown by the lay subsidies of 1524–5, with the largest proportion of wage-earners in the county, requiring markets to obtain foodstuffs and other goods.[10] Bracton, a legal treatise of

---

9 Britnell, 'Markets', 210; Poos, *Essex*, pp. 35–6.
10 See Chapter 2.

the mid-thirteenth century, stated that six and two-third miles was the normal limit for a day's journey to market and back.[11] Even by the sixteenth century, few, if any, parts of Cambridgeshire lay further from a market than this, at least measured by a straight-line distance. In practice, though, people were prepared to travel further to reach specific markets.

The timing of weekly markets in and around Cambridge appears to have had significance, as in other counties. Saturday markets were usually held at larger towns, as at Cambridge, Huntingdon, Ely and Saffron Walden, while market days in smaller towns and villages were spread across the week: such a pattern, it has been suggested, allowed traders to visit several smaller markets in a week, and sell their combined purchases at the more extensive markets.[12] It was rare for the day on which a market was held to be changed, as to do so usually required the expense of obtaining another charter. It did occasionally happen, though: relatively soon after the initial grant at Balsham and Brinkley, and at a later date at Walden.[13] Neighbouring markets were sometimes founded on the same days, like the Friday markets at Great Abington and Hildersham, both located north-west of Linton, but such markets rarely survived long in close proximity.

The markets that survived into the later middle ages in the Cambridge region, as elsewhere, tended to be the older establishments, created before 1250, and located in the larger settlements of the region.[14] During the 1450–1560 period, available evidence suggests that there were no markets operating within 5 miles of Cambridge. Between 5 and 10 miles from the town, the only markets known to have been operating were at Caxton, Foxton, Linton and Swavesey, and possibly at Whittlesford. Although it was less important for village markets to be located in particularly accessible areas in the twelfth and thirteenth centuries, when most traders were travelling only a short distance, those markets which survived into the fifteenth and sixteenth centuries around Cambridge tended to be on major roads.

The distribution of market grants provides a rough indicator of the market area of a town by showing what other formal markets were available. Such a picture, though, gives no indication of the extent to which town hinterlands overlapped, or the ability of larger towns to poach trade from smaller centres.[15] The variety of marketing opportunities available in Cambridge meant that very few village markets were ever established close to Cambridge, and none appear to have operated in the fifteenth and sixteenth centuries. Cambridge market therefore dominated the formal marketing infrastructure of the region.

---

11 Britnell, *Commercialisation*, p. 83.

12 Unwin, 'Towns and trade', pp. 137–8; R.M. Smith, 'A periodic market and its impact on a manorial community: Botesdale, Suffolk, and the manor of Redgrave, 1280–1300', in Z. Razi and R. Smith, eds., *Medieval society and the manor court* (Oxford, 1996), p. 461; Masschaele, *Peasants*, pp. 180–3.

13 *VCH Cambs.*, vi, pp. 132, 138; Richard, Lord Braybrooke, *The history of Audley End* (London, 1836), p. 160.

14 Ridout, 'Markets'.

15 H.B. Rodgers, 'The market area of Preston in the sixteenth and seventeenth centuries', *Geographical Studies*, 3 (1956), 49–50.

Cambridge market

Major urban markets, like Cambridge, were regulated through a complicated mixture of royal statutes and local bylaws. Weights and measures were checked locally, to standards enforced by the crown. Market authorities sought to secure a competitive market price and prevent monopolies by several particular means. They restricted the location and timing of trading. Priority was given to consumers over producers, such as bakers and brewers, and burgesses often had some claim on incoming supplies at an agreed public price. Market authorities also attempted to regulate supplies and acted against those who attempted to restrict goods or fix prices. So the authorities prohibited, for example, the interception of goods before they reached the market, known as forestalling, or the buying and then reselling of goods in the same market, known as regrating. The quality and price of key commodities was regulated through the assizes of bread and ale, which kept prices to a minimum while ensuring producers and traders earned a 'reasonable' income. Tolls were usually levied on outsiders and non-burgesses: they were generally fixed by custom, with the only check on owners that demands should be reasonable. The enforcement of these regulations was mainly left to local courts. Essentially, such mechanisms sought to maintain the commercial advantages of the town's own burgesses, control quality and raise revenue.[16]

The situation at Cambridge was complicated, though, by the presence of a large community requiring foodstuffs and other goods to be available in abundance at a cheap price, but who were not producing goods themselves – the university. Difficulties were compounded by the fact that the borough and university authorities administered different elements of the market. As a punishment for their part in the Peasants' Revolt of 1381, the king took control of the market from the burgesses of Cambridge, including the assize of bread, wine and beer, with the custody of weights and measures and cognisance of forestalling and regrating, and granted these privileges wholly and forever to the university.[17] Cambridge Corporation continued to collect income from market stalls and tolls from those bringing goods into the town. This shared control over marketing was the source of many disputes between town and gown.

Income from market stalls appears to have fallen during the fifteenth century and then increased during the sixteenth century, with the provision of additional stalls, suggesting an increase in activity within Cambridge market. The corporation's treasurers accounted for £5 or more from the farm of the *tabula regis* (king's table) in the 1420s and 1430s. It is assumed that this rent was recorded as the farm of the fish and flesh stalls in the market, fixed at £4 and described variously as *tabula piscis*, *fishbordes*, and later as the flesh stalls, in the subsequent series of treasurers' accounts from 1483/4 until 1551/2. Additional fish stalls brought in 8s from 1515/16,

---

16 Britnell, *Commercialisation*, pp. 90–7; Kowaleski, *Exeter*, pp. 180–92; J. Davis, 'Baking for the common good: a reassessment of the assize of bread in medieval England', *EcHR*, 57 (2004), 465–502; J. Davis, 'The representation, regulation and behaviour of petty traders in late medieval England' (unpublished PhD thesis, University of Cambridge, 2001), pp. 120–214.

17 *VCH Cambs.*, iii, p. 32.

Figure 4.2 Inspection of weights and measures, c.1587. The vice-chancellor, three bedells with their maces, and other university officials supervise the inspection and destruction of false weights and measures (U.A. Hare A.1, fol. 276v: by permission of the Syndics of Cambridge University Library)

16s after 1521/2, and 20s from 1552/3.[18] In 1551/2, the town corporation erected two houses for butchers, each containing fourteen standings. In the first year of their operation, 27 rents of between 3s 4d and 7s each were collected for half a year's rent. In subsequent years, a farm of £14 13s 4d was collected from these flesh shambles.[19] Country butchers could hire the new standings to sell flesh on Tuesdays and Saturdays, and men from Balsham, Dullingham, Girton, Waterbeach and Wilbraham initially occupied these standings.[20] The additional income produced by the new stalls suggests that trade within Cambridge's market place was growing during the mid–sixteenth century, after the decline between the 1430s and 1480s.

The borough corporation collected tolls for water-borne goods unloaded at the town's hithes, for carts and beasts driven through the town, and for the use of the town's mills and markets. Tolls were a major source of income for the borough corporation of Cambridge: the bailiffs accounted for over £48 in tolls in 1510/11, compared to less than £18 in income from property and the farm of the fish and flesh stalls received by the treasurers in 1500/1.[21] Indeed in 1330, the burgesses had stated in a petition to parliament that they had no certain means to pay their annual fee farm

---

18   CCA, X/70/1–10, X/71/1–10, X/71A, XVII/24A; CCTA, i, *passim*.
19   CCA, Palmer/Barnard vol. 57, fol. 81; CCTA, i, fols. 342, 356–356v, 370v, 385v, 399.
20   CCTA, i, fols. 342, 356–356v.
21   *CBD*, p. liii; CCA, X/71/10.

Markets and trade

to the king except by small tolls and customs from strangers who brought merchandise on market days. The university disputed many of the borough's charges, testifying in 1420 that although all the colleges were exempt from tolls on building materials, fuel, and victuals, by land and water, they were being charged on such goods, and protested in 1491 about the exactions taken from victuallers. The agreement made between the town and university of Cambridge in 1503 agreed that no charge would be made for persons bringing pigs or poultry, dairy produce, freshwater fish, fruit, or other victuals 'in ther hands, or at ther Bakke, or on horse backe in baggs or panyers without a wombtie (girth)'.[22] Thomas Cromwell accused the town of forcing scholars to pay tolls and ordered them to stop taking charges from university members in 1537.[23] The collection of tolls was the main means by which the town corporation could profit from and possibly even regulate trade in the town and at Stourbridge Fair after it had lost its market rights to the university. Perhaps because of this, the tolls were particularly onerous; certainly Cambridge Corporation was also involved in disputes during the first half of the sixteenth century with the towns of Hertford, Huntingdon, Lynn, Northampton and Walden over tolls it tried to levy.[24] These disputes also show that Cambridge's market hinterland stretched to other major towns and regional centres in neighbouring counties.

The university's proctors and taxors ensured the use of correct measures, the maintenance of quality, and the avoidance of excessive profits, and had regulations for

---

22 UA, Luard 133, Luard 145a; *Annals*, i, pp. 84–5, 163–4.
23 *Annals*, i, pp. 388–9.
24 CCA, X/103, printed in *Charters*, pp. 202–3; *Annals*, i, pp. 302, 304, 310, 376–7, ii, pp. 2, 36, 55–8.

a range of traders including millers, bakers, brewers, innholders, butchers, fishmongers, cooks, taverners, spicers, weavers and tanners.[25] Surviving records from the court leet in the late fourteenth and late sixteenth centuries include amercements of bakers and brewers, for hostellers selling hay, oats and victuals at excessive prices, for those regrating candles, selling corrupt meat and fish, selling ale and not displaying a sign, and for millers taking excessive tolls.[26] The university commonly complained that burgesses broke the assizes and used false measures, and were disobedient towards correction.[27] The town, in turn, claimed that university officers took excessive charges from victuallers when measuring and gauging their wares.[28] The university controlled the sale of certain commodities particularly closely. It prohibited butchers from selling tallow in the market, except to inhabitants dwelling within the university precincts, and ordered chandlers to sell candles of higher quality to scholars and aldermen than to any other person from the town or country.[29] The demand for candles by scholars must have placed pressure on supplies and led to the danger of shortages. In 1537 the proctors mounted a night watch to stop candles being carried out of the town and retrieved four barrels that had been sent to London.[30]

Through its regulation of the market, the university exercised jurisdiction not only over the townspeople of Cambridge, but also over those traders who had come from the surrounding region. By 1503, the university courts heard most actions concerning contracts of victuals, and in 1526 oversight of all contracts of victuals bought or sold within Cambridge was granted to the chancellor.[31] Records of the university's court leet from the early fifteenth century list villagers from around Cambridge, including men from Hinxton, Ickleton and Stow-cum-Quy who sold using the auncel,[32] and men who came to sell ale in Barnwell ward, probably at Stourbridge and Midsummer fairs.[33] A book of acts of the vice-chancellor's court, recording a variety of pleas and presentments for breaches of market regulations between 1552 and 1557, lists men from the Cambridgeshire villages of Barton, Chesterton, Shepreth, Stapleford, Thriplow, Wilbraham, Wilburton and Whittlesford, from Bury, Stratford-le-Bow in London, and Norfolk.[34] While the majority of traders had therefore travelled only a few

---

25 UA, Collect.Admin.2, fols. 105v–107v.
26 UA, C.U.R. 17.
27 UA, Luard 133; Collect.Admin.5, fols. 22–23v.
28 CCA, X/66, mm. 2–3; X/90, printed in *Annals*, i, pp. 356–8.
29 UA, Collect.Admin.2, fol. 116v; UA, V.C.Ct.I.24, fol. 19v.
30 *Grace Book B*, ii, pp. 204, 207.
31 UA, Luard 145a, printed in *Annals*, i, pp. 265–6; CCA, X/20, printed in *Annals*, i, p. 324. The university courts after 1560 are examined in Shepard, 'Litigation'.
32 UA, C.U.R. 17, fol. 13. The auncel was a weighing device for small merchandise, liable to be falsely manipulated by fraudulent traders. It was banned outright in 1351–2, but continued to be used: Davis, 'Representation', pp. 163–4.
33 See below, pp. 124, 130.
34 UA, V.C.Ct.I.1, fols. 2–19v.

Markets and trade

Figure 4.3 Linton guildhall. In 1507 Nicholas Wickham, the parish priest, left two marks towards building a new guildhall; the building was nearly complete in 1523 (Cambridgeshire Collection)

miles from surrounding villages, a few had travelled greater distances, generally from towns outside the local area.

The origins of witnesses who gave depositions for the court of Star Chamber in 1534 provide further evidence of the local area served by the market. This concerned a riot that had occurred in the market square in Cambridge on Saturday 11 April 1534, and the witnesses can generally be assumed to have visited the market on that day. They included men from Barton, Bottisham, Chesterton, Dry Drayton, Girton, Grantchester, Histon, Rampton, Shelford, Thriplow and Trumpington – all villages lying between 1 and 7 miles from Cambridge.[35]

Rural marketing in Linton, Foxton and Whittlesford

Regulations similar to those in major urban markets governed markets and petty trading in small towns and villages, and were largely enforced by local courts, as the trading offences recorded in the court rolls of Linton, Foxton and Whittlesford show. Linton was a small town situated 9 miles south-east of Cambridge with about 89 taxpayers in 1524. Foxton, lying 7 miles south-west of Cambridge, contained 43 taxpayers, and Whittlesford, 7 miles south of Cambridge, had 55 taxpayers in 1524–5. Lying on mainly chalk soils in the river valleys sub-region, these three communities

---

35 G.R. Elton, *Star Chamber stories* (London, 1958), p. 75.

Table 4.1

Bakers, brewers and butchers amerced at Foxton, Linton and Whittlesford

	No. of courts with amercements	Bakers		Brewers/ ale sellers		Butchers	
		Total	Average	Total	Average	Total	Average
Foxton							
1491–1500	7	3	0.4	8	1.1	0	
1501–10	4	0		10	2.5	4	1.0
1511–20	11	12	1.1	22	2.0	12	1.1
1521–30	7	13	1.9	15	2.1	2	0.3
1531–40	6	12	2.0	19	3.2	0	
1541–50	7	13	1.9	14	2.0	0	
Linton							
1511–20	7			16	2.3*	6	0.9
1521–30	7			26	3.7*	14	2.0
1531–40	9			56	6.2*	21	2.3
Whittlesford							
1471–80	3	2	0.7	23	7.7		
1511–20	4	4	1.0	13	3.3		

Sources: CCRO, L63/17–18, L64/1–4; CCRO, R59/14/11/7A–B; CCRO, 488/M, Huddleston MSS, Whittlesford manorial records box 5, court rolls 1461–83, 1513–23.
Note: * includes bakers and brewers

stood on important medieval routes, including branches of the Icknield Way and other main roads.[36]

Each community had been granted several formal markets and fairs before 1300, but significant evidence of continuing operation in the period 1450–1560 only survives for the market and fair at Linton.[37] The market place there included an open area and permanent stalls. Various shops in the 'midelrow' and 'Butcheryrow' were held at rents of between 7d and 2s per annum in the 1530s and 1540s, and 20s was left towards the building of a market house in 1528.[38] The manor court amerced traders for regrating a quarter of barley and a barrel of herring, and for selling defective herring and whiting in the market.[39]

Bread and ale were usually sold outside formal markets, often from the producer's home. Foxton manor court ordered anyone selling ale, bread or other victuals to put a sign outside their door.[40] Trade in bread, ale and meat occurred in many villages without markets, as in Shepreth – a parish adjoining Foxton – where bakers and

---

36 Sheail, *Regional distribution*, ii, pp. 30, 33–4; Taylor, *Archaeology of Cambridgeshire*, i, pp. 49–51, 108–110, ii, pp. 55–60.
37 Linton Fair is examined below, pp. 117, 119.
38 C.C. Taylor, 'Medieval market grants and village morphology', *Landscape History*, 4 (1982), 22–3; CCRO, R59/14/11/7A, mm. 25, 29d, courts 1531, 1534; R59/14/11/7B, m. 4, court 1549.
39 R59/14/11/7A, m. 27, court 1532; R59/14/11/7B, m. 8d, court 1552.
40 CCRO, L64/3, court 1542.

brewers were amerced.[41] While only Linton appears to have had an active formal market in this period, leet courts in Foxton, Whittlesford and Linton made presentments for breaking the assize of bread and ale.[42] A seller of fish and butter was also amerced at Foxton.[43] Amercements for infringing the assizes of bread and ale appear frequently in court rolls. Brewing required only the resources of the household kitchen, and as the average output was unlikely to vary much, the numbers of brewers amerced can be used as a rough indicator of population trends and living standards. So in the late fourteenth century, a rise in the number of amercements at Colchester reflected the growth of the population and a rise in living standards, while the falling numbers recorded in many Breckland villages reflected the drop in trade and declining population.[44] The number of bakers, brewers and butchers amerced at these three Cambridgeshire market courts over the period are shown in Table 4.1. During the early sixteenth century, the number of bakers and brewers at Foxton and Linton rose, and the number of brewers at Whittlesford fell considerably. However, the decline at Whittlesford may have been compensated by the development of informal trading 1 mile to the east at Whittlesford Bridge.[45]

In all three places, a number of women were amerced for brewing ale, although sometimes the courts amerced their husbands, rather than the women themselves. Women had dominated the brewing of ale, which required little capital investment and could be pursued at home, but during the fifteenth and sixteenth centuries, male brewers gradually replaced them. To some extent this shift may have been due to legal changes, whereby the husband was indicted while the wife continued to do the brewing. It has also been claimed, though, that men dominated the new technology of beer brewing, while women lacked the capital to compete, had no legal autonomy when married, and suffered from negative images of the corrupt tradeswoman.[46]

The places of residence of the traders, when recorded, reveal the hinterlands served by these rural markets. At Foxton, William Walles, baker, from Fowlmere (2 miles away) was recorded on 14 occasions, and bakers John Browne and Gill of Cambridge (7 miles away) on 8 occasions and 3 occasions respectively. There were also single visits from bakers from Cambridge, Fowlmere and Sawston (5 miles). At Linton, a butcher visited from Hadstock (1½ miles away) and another from Haverhill (7 miles distant). At Whittlesford, brewers came from Whittlesford Bridge and Sawston (1 mile away) and Great Shelford (3 miles), together with a baker from Walden (7½ miles). John Dale of Cambridge paid for admission to the market green at Whittlesford

---

41 L63/17, m. 7v, court 1498; L63/18, mm. 2, 3v, 4, courts 1510–12; Britnell, *Commercialisation*, p.98.
42 L63/17–18, L64/1–4; R59/14/11/7A–B; CCRO, 488/M, Huddleston MSS, Whittlesford manorial records box 5, court rolls 1461–83, 1513–23.
43 L63/18, m. 6d, court 1513.
44 Britnell, *Colchester*, pp. 89–90, 93–5; Bailey, *Marginal economy?*, pp. 259–62.
45 See below, pp. 96–7.
46 Bennett, *Ale*, pp. 145–57; M. Mate, *Women in medieval English society* (Cambridge, 1999), pp. 38–45.

in 1488, and men from Walden occupied two shops at Linton in the 1540s.[47] Butchers and bakers generally travelled from further afield than brewers, as meat and bread were easier to transport than ale. The hinterlands of these smaller markets seem to have stretched to nearly 8 miles for suppliers from towns, down to around 5 miles for suppliers from local villages.

Many food retailers were poorer inhabitants, trying to earn a few additional pence. At both Foxton and Linton, the social structure of the village in 1524–5 was fairly extensively differentiated. Those with assessments of under £2 comprised 54 per cent of the taxpaying population at Foxton and 75 per cent at Linton, compared to 39 per cent at Whittlesford. Many of these poorer inhabitants must have relied on the market to obtain foodstuffs and other supplies, as they lacked sufficient land to support themselves. Even more prosperous peasant households often found it convenient to make purchases in the market.[48]

Indeed a number of these traders can be identified as local inhabitants, by matching the names of those who were amerced for baking and brewing at the three markets with taxpayers in the lay subsidy of 1524–5 and a list of tenants and their holdings in the Foxton court rolls of 1507.[49] Among those amerced at Linton were four men each assessed on goods of 20s, and one man assessed on goods of £4. At Foxton, Robert Verley, a butcher, with £3 in goods, and Thomas Welles, a miller, with £5 10s 0d in goods, and three holdings and a mill, both had wives who brewed ale. The Symton and Rayner families, with assessments from 20s to £4, had members involved in brewing. At Whittlesford, John Scote, with £3 in goods, Richard Saddeler with 40s in goods, and John Whiteby with 20s in wages, were fined for breaking the assize of ale. Thus most of the food retailers amerced were labourers, craftsmen and husbandmen, with goods of £4 or less in 1524–5. Those like William Beton, brewer, of Shepreth, holding a cottage in 1507, and assessed on goods of 40s in 1524, probably did not hold enough land to support their families, and the production and retailing of food and drink would have been a valuable additional source of income for these households. Similar social groups of market traders were found at Botesdale, Suffolk, in the late thirteenth century: many of the tenants with holdings in that market place were artisans and tradesmen, and nearly half were landless.[50]

Another focus of trade may have been at Whittlesford Bridge where the Newmarket to Royston road crossed the River Cam. Cambridge Corporation owned most of the bridge tolls, and must have viewed the bridge as a valuable source of income and important piece of infrastructure, given that the council expended the considerable sum of £40 8s 4d on rebuilding in 1565, before leasing the bridge and

---

47 CCRO, 488/M Huddleston MSS, Whittlesford manorial records box 5, rental 1487/8; VCH Cambs., viii, p. 173.

48 TNA: PRO E 179/81/130, E 179/81/134, E 179/81/147; C. Dyer, 'Were peasants self-sufficient? English villagers and the market, 900–1300', in E. Mornet, ed., Campagnes médiévales: l'homme et son espace (Paris, 1995), pp. 660–1.

49 TNA: PRO E 179/81/130, E 179/81/134, E 179/81/147; CCRO, L63/17, m. 12–12d, court 1507.

50 Smith, 'Periodic market', pp. 466–81.

tolls for a £4 fine and 30s annual rent the following year.[51] The lord of Whittlesford manor had been granted the right to collect the tolls of Whittlesford Bridge on Tuesdays – the day of the market granted in 1206 – throughout the year, and although these were worth only 12d a year in 1460, a description of manorial profits c.1450 lists a tariff of potential charges for horses, colts, cattle, sheep, malt, wheat, fish, woolpacks, and other wares. 'Franchised men' with merchandise were charged 1d to set up a stall, presumably at either the bridge or in Whittlesford market place.[52] A small hamlet grew around the bridge and the hospital of St John the Baptist, which probably provided accommodation for passing travellers. A fair was reported as belonging to the hospital in 1279, but was not recorded later.[53] The White Lion Inn took over the provision of hospitality in the sixteenth century, using the former hospital as its barn. Inns, providing rest and refreshment for travellers, often developed as informal centres of trade outside formal market places.[54] There was no single authority to control or profit from the trading activities at Whittlesford Bridge: the bridge tolls were split between two owners, and the hamlet was said to lie within four parishes in 1279. This may have encouraged the growth of informal trading, in a similar way to the informal market that developed at Buntingford in Hertfordshire.[55]

Masschaele has proposed that the marketing structure that had been formed by 1300 functioned chiefly to supply the needs of the fifty largest English towns. Rural markets acted as nodes in this supply network. Britnell, however, has argued that the marketing system remained largely localised and poorly integrated, with rural markets existing primarily for smallholders and labourers to obtain foodstuffs and raw materials and dispose of their surplus produce, rather than to supply merchants from larger towns.[56] Only a handful of men from Cambridge and Walden appear in the records of Foxton, Linton and Whittlesford, and they may have been selling their own produce, rather than coming to obtain supplies. The numerous traders, particularly victuallers, found in many towns would not have gained enough custom only within their town, and also supplied villagers in the neighbourhood.[57] The majority of traders in the small town and villages examined above were local labourers, craftsmen and husbandmen, from their own communities and other villages up to 5 miles away, suggesting that

---

51 *Annals*, i, p. 253, ii, p. 216; CCA, XVIII/12, no. 4.
52 Description of manorial profits c.1450, printed in T.F. Teversham, *A history of the village of Sawston*, 2 parts (Sawston, 1942–7), part ii, p. 26. The present whereabouts of this document is not known – it is not catalogued among the Huddleston MSS at CCRO; *VCH Cambs.*, vi, p. 270.
53 *VCH Cambs.*, vi, pp. 202, 215.
54 *VCH Cambs.*, vi, p. 202; Dyer, 'Hidden trade', 149–50; A. Everitt, 'The English urban inn, 1560–1760' in Everitt, ed., *Perspectives*, pp. 91–137.
55 M. Bailey, 'A tale of two towns: Buntingford and Standon in the later middle ages', *Journal of Medieval History*, 19 (1993), 358.
56 Masschaele, *Peasants*; Britnell, 'Urban demand', pp. 1–21.
57 Dyer, 'Were peasants self-sufficient?', pp. 662–4.

these and other rural markets were principally serving local demand, not larger urban centres.

Debt cases in local courts

Debt litigation reveals patterns of credit that facilitated trade. Credit stretched throughout the medieval economy, from the small debts of peasants in manorial courts to the loans made to leading noble families and the international transactions of merchants.[58] Manorial and borough courts could be used for debts of up to 40s and so recorded predominantly local and small-scale trade, mostly in food, clothes, leather goods and other necessities. Cases relating to trade on a larger scale or over long distances were usually heard in larger borough courts, while many creditors sought recovery of debts in London courts. Records of debts may only state the names of individuals involved and their place of residence, and not the reason for the debt, which might arise not only from sales, but also from rents, services, loans, pledges, or damages. But even if these pleadings did not result from a sale, the social contact is still reflective of a town's sphere of influence.[59]

The use of manorial courts to record pleas of debt, detention of chattels and broken agreements had declined by the close of the fifteenth century. At Whittlesford, a handful of pleas were made in the late fifteenth century, mainly relating to the agricultural economy and including debts for small quantities of barley, rents and arrears of account. A couple of defendants came from Thriplow, a mile to the south-west. The only debt case that appears to have included someone with wider connections involved John Godyn in 1461, a London brewer, who owned a tenement and 14 acres at Whittlesford Bridge.[60] Debts are not found in the sixteenth-century court rolls. At Linton, a few debts were sued in the manorial court, including debts for barley and saffron.[61] The decline in debt cases was a general feature of many manorial courts, and it seems that peasants must have increasingly turned to other borough or ecclesiastical courts to pursue their debts.

Although most of the records of Cambridge's borough courts have been lost, a book of pleas for 1389–90 survives. Just over 300 cases are recorded: the majority, about 189, are pleas of debt; 76 are pleas of trespass, 24 for detention of chattels, 17 for broken contracts, and 2 are pleas of account. Of the few debt pleas where further details are given, the cases involve leather, peas, locks, malt barley, a horse and half a

---

58 Dyer, *Standards*, pp. 38–40, 178–80; Kermode, *Merchants*, pp. 226–30.
59 Kowaleski, *Exeter*, pp. 202–8; Dyer, 'Market towns', 21–30; Britnell, *Colchester*, pp. 100–1, 108–9, 208.
60 CCRO, 488/M, Huddleston MSS, Whittlesford manorial records box 5, compotus 1463/4 and court rolls 1461–83, m.1, court 1461; *Calendar of Wills proved and enrolled in the Court of Husting, London A.D.1258–A.D.1688*, ed. R.R. Sharpe (London, 1890), ii, p. 549.
61 CCRO, 488/M, Huddleston MSS, Whittlesford manorial records box 5, court rolls 1461–83, mm. 1–2d, 4–5, 7–8d; R58/14/11/7A, mm. 12, 15, courts 1516, 1518.

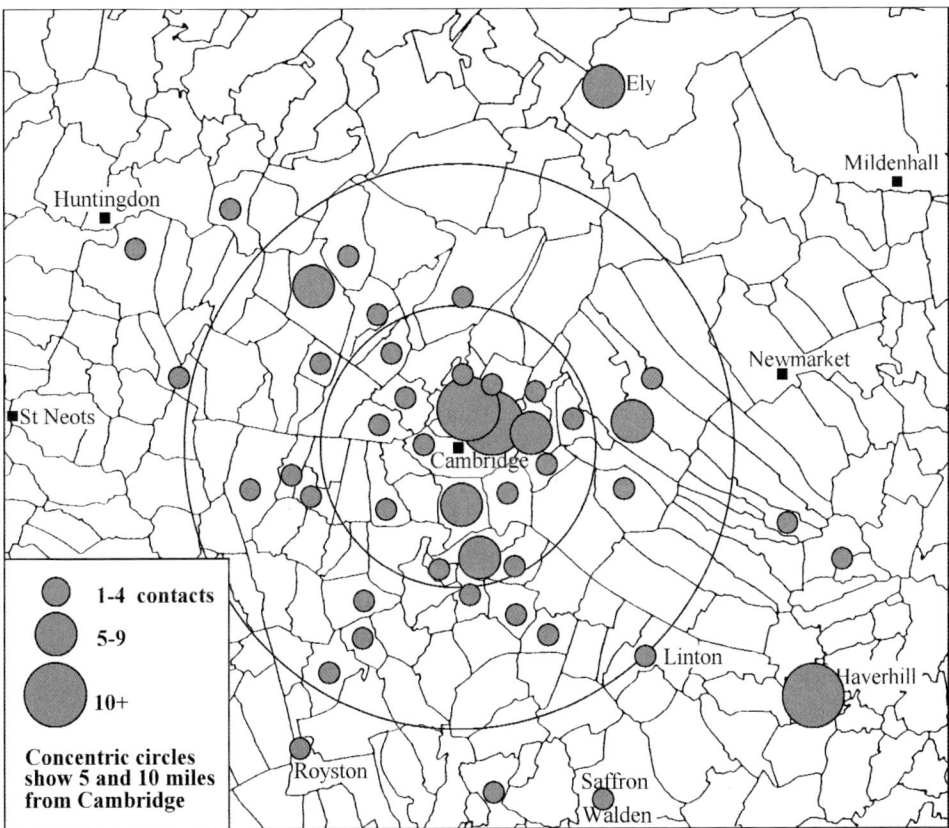

Figure 4.4 Cambridge town pleas, 1389–90
Source: CCA, Palmer/Barnard vol. 1.

barrel of ale.[62] While the borough court heard cases involving the prior and a canon of Barnwell, and the prioress of St Radegund's,[63] no university members were specifically identified, because cases involving masters, students, scholars' servants and university members could be moved to the university courts.

Figure 4.4 illustrates the geographical distribution of participants involved in pleas at Cambridge Borough Court in 1389–90. The vast majority of contacts resided within a 10-mile radius of Cambridge, and of these, just over half came from within a 5-mile radius. The most numerous contacts were with Barnwell, Chesterton and Haverhill, and then with Ely, London, Shelford, Swavesey and Trumpington – a mixture of adjacent villages and larger towns. The spatial spread of contacts was fairly evenly distributed around Cambridge, showing that the town operated as a gateway market for all the surrounding sub-regions.

---

62 CCA, Palmer/Barnard vol. 1, fols. 9v, 10v, 11v, 17v, 32v.
63 Ibid., fols. 1, 34v.

Similar trade in food, clothes, leather goods and other necessities is found in the fifteenth-century debt cases from the town courts of Newmarket, Saffron Walden and Godmanchester, on the edge of Cambridge's region. The hinterlands of these towns generally complemented Cambridge's sphere of influence for pleas, with slight overlapping at the edges. At Walden, for example, traders generally came from villages south of Shelford, east of Royston and west of Haverhill, while at Newmarket traders generally originated from places east of Cambridge and north of Haverhill, although a few stretched beyond Cambridge to Bedford, St Neots and Newport Pagnell (Buckinghamshire).[64]

The hinterland of Cambridge's borough court for debt cases was comparable with the areas served by other medieval towns. The debt cases recorded in a dozen small towns across England, as well as in larger centres like Gloucester and Exeter, show that around 50 per cent of debtors and traders came from within 6.2 miles, and the great majority within 15.5 miles. The limited power of local courts, which could usually only deal with debts below 40s, were not suited to trade on a larger scale or over a larger distance. They therefore give only a partial view of the trade of a town, confined to low value and largely retail transactions, and tending to exclude higher value and longer distance trade for more specialist goods and services.[65]

The most distant participants in the Cambridge borough courts lay outside the boundaries of the map in Figure 4.4. These were men from the Norfolk villages of Bridgham and Wiggenhall, 'Well', possibly Upwell in the northern fenland, and the towns of Bury, Lynn, Northampton and Thaxted. The maximum distance of contact was just over 50 miles, as Londoners were involved in eight cases, mainly pleas of debt. One might expect these towns to be more prominent among the court cases, but most of their trading transactions probably exceeded the 40s limit for actions in the borough court. Like the origins of those amerced by the university courts for breaching market regulations, the town pleas show that surrounding villagers, from up to 10 miles away, although often closer, used Cambridge as a marketing centre, together with a smaller number of more distant traders, and suggest that this hinterland for basic retail trade altered little between the late fourteenth and sixteenth centuries.

Debt cases in London courts

Although central government records tend to be too voluminous to locate cases relevant to the region with ease,[66] pardons of outlawry for not appearing to answer pleas of debt in the royal courts, recorded in the Patent Rolls, do give an indication of

---

64 D. Cromarty, 'Chepying Walden 1381–1420, a study from the court rolls', *Essex Journal*, 2 (1967), 126–7; P. May, 'Newmarket and its market court, 1399–1413', *Proceedings of Suffolk Institute of Archaeology*, 35 (1981), 32–3; Davis, 'Representation', pp. 216–22; J.A. Raftis, *Early Tudor Godmanchester: survivals and new arrivals* (Toronto, 1990), pp. 135–49, 170–83.

65 Dyer, 'Market towns', 23–4; Dyer, 'Small towns', pp. 517–18.

66 Samples of debt litigation in the Court of Common Pleas are analysed in D. Keene, 'Changes in London's economic hinterland as indicated by debt cases in the Court of Common Pleas', in Galloway, ed., *Trade*, pp. 59–81, and Galloway, 'Town and country', pp. 111–12.

Table 4.2

Most common residence of creditors, by county, making loans to Cambridgeshire men, 1450–1509

Creditor county	No.	Average £
Not stated	47	10.08
London	21	13.85
Norfolk	10	11.23
Cambridgeshire	7	8.10
Suffolk	3	7.22

Source: CPR, 1446–1509.

Table 4.3

Most common residence of Cambridgeshire debtors, 1450–1509

Debtor place	No.	Average £
Cambridge	14	19.74
Wisbech	9	6.26
Ely	4	4.81
Fulbourn	4	15.71
Newton by Leverington	4	18.24

Source: CPR, 1446–1509.

the pattern of credit. From these records, all 109 cases between 1450 and 1509 involving debtors, creditors, or both, stated to be from Cambridgeshire, have been extracted for analysis.[67] Cambridgeshire men acted as debtors in 98 cases, and 18 involved Cambridgeshire men as creditors. Fewer cases were recorded as the fifteenth century progressed: there were 510 pardons for not appearing to answer pleas of debt in the Patent Rolls between 1450 and 1454 and 15 of these involved Cambridgeshire men; there were 109 pardons between 1501 and 1505 and 4 involved Cambridgeshire men. The proportion of Cambridgeshire debt cases remained around 3–4 per cent of the total at the beginning and end of the period, despite the dwindling number of cases recorded. Cambridgeshire debt cases ranged from 20s to £100 in size, and the average debt was just under £12, similar to the average sum found in debt cases in the Court of Common Pleas involving Exeter residents during the later fourteenth century.[68]

The principal locations of the creditors lending money to Cambridgeshire men are shown in Table 4.2. They reveal a core of regular dealing by Cambridgeshire men with London, which comprised larger average debts than those with creditors elsewhere, and a smaller degree of contact with other parts of East Anglia. In addition, there were creditors in the Home Counties, the Midlands and Yorkshire. There was no concentration of creditors from a particular centre, apart from London, although most came from towns of varying size, which in East Anglia included Norwich, Bury St

---

67 CPR, 1446–52, 1452–61, 1461–7, 1467–77, 1476–85, 1485–94, 1494–1509.
68 Kowaleski, *Exeter*, p. 215.

Edmunds, King's Lynn, Hadleigh, Walden and Wisbech. A similar concentration of residents from urban centres was found amongst the Cambridgeshire men who received these loans, as Table 4.3 reveals. Medieval towns acted as focal points for financial services, offering the ability to register debts, and a wide range of people to act as pledges.[69] Cambridge was clearly the leading financial centre within the county.

Cambridgeshire men acted as creditors to men from a similar geographical area to those to whom they owed debts: namely, to men in Walden, Essex; Baldock, Buntingford and Hitchin, Hertfordshire; Caistor, Lincolnshire; Stow Bardolph, Norfolk; Bury St Edmunds, Suffolk, and to seven people in Cambridgeshire. In cases involving Londoners, though, Cambridgeshire men were always debtors rather than creditors.

The most common occupations among the Cambridgeshire debtors were husbandmen, yeomen and gentlemen. Many of these debts may have arisen from agricultural transactions, and reflect a regional economy heavily based on agriculture. Most cases heard before the Court of Common Pleas in 1424 and 1570 involved one or more parties that were dependent on landed income. The counties where such groups dominated debt cases tended to have local economies in which the supply of primary agricultural produce to London was more significant than commerce or manufacturing.[70] That said, the terms yeoman and husbandman were often used generically, and such individuals did not always receive the majority of their income from land – London merchants were sometimes described as yeomen.[71] Among the Cambridgeshire debtors were two drovers from Haddenham and Willingham, two adjoining parishes on the edge of the fenland, with abundant pasture for raising cattle. Fewer trade occupations were listed, but there was one debt each from a baker, brewer, chandler and vintner, all from Cambridge, reflecting the predominance of the service trades in the town, while some of the clerks and chaplains recorded may have been university members.

Among the occupations of creditors, mercantile occupations were more strongly represented than among the debtors, and these included mercers and drapers. Several prominent clerics acted as creditors, a trend found in debt cases elsewhere, and they may have been acting for themselves or for their institutions.[72] The handful of Cambridgeshire creditors comprised three clerks, two burgesses and a prior, a parson, a mercer, a bailiff, a baxter and a wife.

Gifts of goods and chattels provide further evidence of credit networks. These may have been a legal way to avoid distraint of goods for debt, or pledges against the repayment of a loan, and their use appears to have increased during the monetary

---

69 Kermode, *Merchants*, pp. 245–6.
70 Keene, 'Changes', pp. 72–3.
71 Thrupp, *Merchant class*, pp. 217–18.
72 Kermode, *Merchants*, pp. 236–7; H. Swanson, *Medieval artisans: an urban class in late medieval England* (Oxford, 1989), pp. 147–8.

scarcity of the 1440s.[73] London citizens are prominent in cases involving Cambridgeshire men. In association with townspeople of Cambridge, Londoners received gifts of goods and chattels from a resident of Newmarket, and from husbandmen of Comberton and Great Shelford.[74] Cambridgeshire residents received gifts of goods and chattels from a fishmonger, tailor, haberdasher, 'upholder', and mercer of London, a draper from Waltham Cross, Hertfordshire and the rector of Upminster, Essex.[75]

Admittedly, one would expect to find a greater number of Londoners in courts based in the capital than at provincial courts, but the same pattern is found in local records across the country, including Godmanchester, Romford, Chester and in Yorkshire. As a larger group than those in provincial towns, London merchants were better placed to survive the monetary scarcity and trade depression of the mid-fifteenth century, and their increasing role in debt cases reflected the growing dominance of the capital in both internal and export trade during this period.[76] London's trading links extended across the country and included many different commodities. The prevalence of agricultural and landholding occupations among the Cambridgeshire debtors, though, suggests that the county's trade with London was predominantly based on the supply of agricultural produce. The Cambridge region developed trade with London in two particular commodities during this period – malt barley and saffron.

Regional trade: malt barley and saffron

While debt cases in London courts illustrate the range of regional trading links, legal records such as the Chancery proceedings provide more detail about specific transactions that were disputed. These proceedings were petitions to the chancellor complaining of alleged wrongs and requesting the offender to be summoned to answer, because the courts of common law were unable to resolve the matter. They can often be dated only approximately, by the title of the chancellor addressed in each bill. From the beginning of the sixteenth century, there was a great increase in the work of Chancery as an equity court, and suits were heard concerning inheritance, landed property, and family business, as well as trade.[77] Most of the cases relating to trade refer to private transactions, made outside formal market places.

---

73   J.I. Kermode, 'Money and credit in the fifteenth century: some lessons from Yorkshire', *Business History Review*, 45 (1991), 493–5; P. Nightingale, 'Monetary contraction and mercantile credit in later medieval England', *EcHR*, 2nd ser., 43 (1990), 573–4.

74   *CCR, 1454–61*, p.168; *CCR, 1468–76*, no.813, p. 219, no.922, p.250.

75   *CCR, 1447–54*, pp.328, 353; *CCR, 1461–8*, p.405; *CCR, 1468–76*, no.1441, p.403; *CCR, 1485–1500*, no.286, p.77, no.861, p.252; *Calendar of Plea and Memoranda Rolls of the City of London, 1437–1457*, ed. P.E. Jones (Cambridge, 1954), p.179.

76   Raftis, *Godmanchester*, pp.162–5; J.I. Kermode, 'The trade of late medieval Chester', in Britnell and Hatcher, eds., *Progress and problems*, p.300; M.K. McIntosh, 'Money lending on the periphery of London 1300–1600', *Albion*, 20 (1988), 566; Kermode, 'Money and credit', 496–501.

77   Riden, *Record sources*, pp.73–4; *Select cases in Chancery 1364–1471*, ed. W.P. Baildon, Selden Soc., X (London, 1896), pp.xii–xxix. For cases relating to trade, see L.F. Salzman, *English trade in the middle ages* (Oxford, 1931), *passim*; Everitt, 'Marketing', p.93.

Chancery proceedings and other evidence show that the two most important trading links in the Cambridge region were with Lynn and London. Lynn, readily accessible from Cambridge via the Cam and Great Ouse, had overseas links to the Low Countries, Scotland, Iceland, the Baltic and France. The port also provided access along the East Coast, and inland to the counties of Warwickshire, Leicestershire, Northamptonshire, Rutland, Bedfordshire, Buckinghamshire, and Huntingdonshire.[78] Like Boston, the other major port of the Wash, trade at Lynn was hit during the fifteenth century through warfare, embargoes and sea level changes, which caused the silting of the haven, and the port lost trade to London.[79] The principal foreign traders at Lynn were the Hansards, who imported bulk commodities from the Baltic like timber, iron, flax and wax, and exported cloth, grain, cheese and wool. Despite interruptions to trade, most drastically during the Anglo-Hanseatic war of 1468–74, Hansard commercial links remained strong at the port during the later fifteenth century.[80] After a temporary trade boom between 1490 and 1510, Lynn, like other East Coast ports, was overshadowed in foreign trade by London. But the growth of London's trade provided employment for coastal shipping, and the amount of shipping carried in English vessels increased substantially.[81] London was Cambridge's other major trading centre, and could be reached both overland, and by water via the coast from Lynn. London lay just over 50 miles distant from Cambridge, and in parliamentary writs was considered a day's journey.[82] Carriers linked the two centres by road, delivering goods such as pike and butts of malmsey.[83] London was not immune to the population decline of the fifteenth century, but was able to compensate by increasing involvement in the marketing and distribution of goods across the country.

While the total demand for cereals fell in the later middle ages as the population declined, rising living standards and greater leisure time led to increased ale consumption. Barley malt replaced oats in the brewing industry as customers became more discerning. This led to major shifts in the areas supplying grain to urban hinterlands, most notably those supplying London. Cambridgeshire was a major cereal-growing region throughout the middle ages, with fertile soils, a favourable climate and accessible waterways, and was therefore well placed to meet this new demand. At the turn of the fourteenth century, contacts between London and East Anglia had been neither strong nor regular, but from the later fourteenth century onwards, the region supplied barley more regularly to the capital. A parliamentary ordinance of 1394 named Cambridgeshire as a source of malt, which should be carried to London and sold there

---

78 J.D. Fudge, *Cargoes, embargoes and emissaries. The commercial and political interaction of England and the German Hanse 1450–1510* (Toronto, 1995), pp. 147–9; Salzman, *English trade*, p. 209.

79 E.M. Carus-Wilson, 'The medieval trade of the ports of the Wash', *Medieval Archaeology*, 6–7 (1962–3), 201; S.H. Rigby, '"Sore decay" and "fair dwellings": Boston and urban decline in the later middle ages', *Midland History*, 10 (1985), 47–61.

80 Fudge, *Cargoes*, pp. 31–5, 105–10, 145–9, 163–4.

81 G.V. Scammell, 'English merchant shipping at the end of the middle ages: some East Coast evidence', *EcHR*, 2nd ser., 13 (1961), 327–41.

82 *VCH Cambs.*, iii, p. 1.

83 TNA: PRO C 1/19/469, C 1/232/32.

scarcity of the 1440s.[73] London citizens are prominent in cases involving Cambridgeshire men. In association with townspeople of Cambridge, Londoners received gifts of goods and chattels from a resident of Newmarket, and from husbandmen of Comberton and Great Shelford.[74] Cambridgeshire residents received gifts of goods and chattels from a fishmonger, tailor, haberdasher, 'upholder', and mercer of London, a draper from Waltham Cross, Hertfordshire and the rector of Upminster, Essex.[75]

Admittedly, one would expect to find a greater number of Londoners in courts based in the capital than at provincial courts, but the same pattern is found in local records across the country, including Godmanchester, Romford, Chester and in Yorkshire. As a larger group than those in provincial towns, London merchants were better placed to survive the monetary scarcity and trade depression of the mid-fifteenth century, and their increasing role in debt cases reflected the growing dominance of the capital in both internal and export trade during this period.[76] London's trading links extended across the country and included many different commodities. The prevalence of agricultural and landholding occupations among the Cambridgeshire debtors, though, suggests that the county's trade with London was predominantly based on the supply of agricultural produce. The Cambridge region developed trade with London in two particular commodities during this period – malt barley and saffron.

Regional trade: malt barley and saffron

While debt cases in London courts illustrate the range of regional trading links, legal records such as the Chancery proceedings provide more detail about specific transactions that were disputed. These proceedings were petitions to the chancellor complaining of alleged wrongs and requesting the offender to be summoned to answer, because the courts of common law were unable to resolve the matter. They can often be dated only approximately, by the title of the chancellor addressed in each bill. From the beginning of the sixteenth century, there was a great increase in the work of Chancery as an equity court, and suits were heard concerning inheritance, landed property, and family business, as well as trade.[77] Most of the cases relating to trade refer to private transactions, made outside formal market places.

---

73 J.I. Kermode, 'Money and credit in the fifteenth century: some lessons from Yorkshire', *Business History Review*, 45 (1991), 493–5; P. Nightingale, 'Monetary contraction and mercantile credit in later medieval England', *EcHR*, 2nd ser., 43 (1990), 573–4.

74 *CCR, 1454–61*, p.168; *CCR, 1468–76*, no.813, p. 219, no.922, p.250.

75 *CCR, 1447–54*, pp.328, 353; *CCR, 1461–8*, p.405; *CCR, 1468–76*, no.1441, p.403; *CCR, 1485–1500*, no.286, p.77, no.861, p.252; *Calendar of Plea and Memoranda Rolls of the City of London, 1437–1457*, ed. P.E. Jones (Cambridge, 1954), p.179.

76 Raftis, *Godmanchester*, pp.162–5; J.I. Kermode, 'The trade of late medieval Chester', in Britnell and Hatcher, eds., *Progress and problems*, p.300; M.K. McIntosh, 'Money lending on the periphery of London 1300–1600', *Albion*, 20 (1988), 566; Kermode, 'Money and credit', 496–501.

77 Riden, *Record sources*, pp.73–4; *Select cases in Chancery 1364–1471*, ed. W.P. Baildon, Selden Soc., X (London, 1896), pp.xii–xxix. For cases relating to trade, see L.F. Salzman, *English trade in the middle ages* (Oxford, 1931), *passim*; Everitt, 'Marketing', p.93.

Chancery proceedings and other evidence show that the two most important trading links in the Cambridge region were with Lynn and London. Lynn, readily accessible from Cambridge via the Cam and Great Ouse, had overseas links to the Low Countries, Scotland, Iceland, the Baltic and France. The port also provided access along the East Coast, and inland to the counties of Warwickshire, Leicestershire, Northamptonshire, Rutland, Bedfordshire, Buckinghamshire, and Huntingdonshire.[78] Like Boston, the other major port of the Wash, trade at Lynn was hit during the fifteenth century through warfare, embargoes and sea level changes, which caused the silting of the haven, and the port lost trade to London.[79] The principal foreign traders at Lynn were the Hansards, who imported bulk commodities from the Baltic like timber, iron, flax and wax, and exported cloth, grain, cheese and wool. Despite interruptions to trade, most drastically during the Anglo-Hanseatic war of 1468–74, Hansard commercial links remained strong at the port during the later fifteenth century.[80] After a temporary trade boom between 1490 and 1510, Lynn, like other East Coast ports, was overshadowed in foreign trade by London. But the growth of London's trade provided employment for coastal shipping, and the amount of shipping carried in English vessels increased substantially.[81] London was Cambridge's other major trading centre, and could be reached both overland, and by water via the coast from Lynn. London lay just over 50 miles distant from Cambridge, and in parliamentary writs was considered a day's journey.[82] Carriers linked the two centres by road, delivering goods such as pike and butts of malmsey.[83] London was not immune to the population decline of the fifteenth century, but was able to compensate by increasing involvement in the marketing and distribution of goods across the country.

While the total demand for cereals fell in the later middle ages as the population declined, rising living standards and greater leisure time led to increased ale consumption. Barley malt replaced oats in the brewing industry as customers became more discerning. This led to major shifts in the areas supplying grain to urban hinterlands, most notably those supplying London. Cambridgeshire was a major cereal-growing region throughout the middle ages, with fertile soils, a favourable climate and accessible waterways, and was therefore well placed to meet this new demand. At the turn of the fourteenth century, contacts between London and East Anglia had been neither strong nor regular, but from the later fourteenth century onwards, the region supplied barley more regularly to the capital. A parliamentary ordinance of 1394 named Cambridgeshire as a source of malt, which should be carried to London and sold there

---

78 J.D. Fudge, *Cargoes, embargoes and emissaries. The commercial and political interaction of England and the German Hanse 1450–1510* (Toronto, 1995), pp. 147–9; Salzman, *English trade*, p. 209.

79 E.M. Carus-Wilson, 'The medieval trade of the ports of the Wash', *Medieval Archaeology*, 6–7 (1962–3), 201; S.H. Rigby, '"Sore decay" and "fair dwellings": Boston and urban decline in the later middle ages', *Midland History*, 10 (1985), 47–61.

80 Fudge, *Cargoes*, pp. 31–5, 105–10, 145–9, 163–4.

81 G.V. Scammell, 'English merchant shipping at the end of the middle ages: some East Coast evidence', *EcHR*, 2nd ser., 13 (1961), 327–41.

82 *VCH Cambs.*, iii, p. 1.

83 TNA: PRO C 1/19/469, C 1/232/32.

Markets and trade

for the benefit of the royal household, noble households, and the whole population. John Paston reported Cambridgeshire malt on sale in London in 1465.[84]

Cambridge merchants traded in malt and malt barley through the port of Lynn, supplying markets in both London and overseas. Cambridge had long been a centre for collecting and marketing cereals exported from the county: fines were imposed on over sixty townsmen in 1177 for the unlicensed carriage of grain.[85] Chancery proceedings from the early sixteenth century show that David Johnson of Cambridge was involved in transactions in malt at Lynn, and William Richardson of Cambridge had agreed to supply 60 quarters of malt to William Cokkes and Thomas King, grocers of London, at Lynn.[86] James Fletcher, a grocer, baker and trader in malt barley, introduced a parliamentary bill 'against malt bills' while serving as Cambridge's member of parliament in 1553. The details of this measure are not known, but the town corporation paid him 3s 4d for his efforts. Cambridge merchants also exported grain overseas. James Fletcher was accused of illegally exporting malt from Lynn to Middelburg in 1542. During the 1550s, Thomas Ventris of Cambridge was arrested for the non-payment of customs on barley exported to Antwerp, and Henry Serle of Histon was sued for the non-delivery of 180 quarters of barley at Dover.[87]

Cambridgeshire grain could also be taken overland and down the River Lea to London, and towns along this route like Enfield, Ware and Royston show increasing involvement in the malt trade during the late fifteenth and early sixteenth centuries. In a court declaration of 1512, it was stated that the men of Standon had always delivered their malt at Ware, and men of Enfield and other places had carried this malt to London. From 1559 onwards, the city of London took various measures to improve the navigation of the Lea to stimulate the grain trade from Hertfordshire and Cambridgeshire.[88] John Leland remarked in the mid-sixteenth century that the market at Royston was 'mervelusly frequentid, espetially with corne'. Another marketing centre for corn developed on the River Ouse at St Neots, during the early years of Elizabeth's reign.[89] The emergence of these specialised arrangements for marketing and carriage show how the trade was becoming more commercialised.

Further evidence of barley being supplied to London brewers comes from the accounts of Grantchester manor in the 1430s and 1440s. Henry Somer, Chancellor of

---

84 J.A. Galloway, 'Driven by drink? Ale consumption and the agrarian economy of the London region c.1300–1400', in M. Carlin and J.T. Rosenthal, eds., *Food and eating in medieval Europe* (London, 1998), pp.92–9; Britnell, *Colchester*, p. 144; Campbell et al., *Medieval capital*, pp.70, 181; *PL*, i, p.130.

85 *VCH Cambs.*, iii, p. 6.

86 TNA: PRO C 1/293/59, C 1/687/35.

87 Bindoff, *House of Commons*, ii, p. 151; Siraut, 'Cambridge', pp.162, 166; N.J. Williams, *The maritime trade of the East Anglian ports, 1550–1590* (Oxford, 1988), pp.56–7, 151–9.

88 D.O. Pam, *Tudor Enfield: the maltmen and the Lea navigation*, Edmonton Hundred Historical Soc., Occasional Papers, new ser. XVIII (not dated), pp.1–9; K. Fairclough, 'A Tudor canal scheme for the River Lea', *London Journal*, 5 (1979), 218–27.

89 *The itinerary of John Leland*, ed. L. Toulmin Smith, 5 vols. (London, 1907–10), i, part 3, p.328; Everitt, 'Marketing', pp.41, 51–2.

the Exchequer, bought Burwash and Jaks manors in this village, lying 2 miles southwest of Cambridge. He resumed direct farming of most of the demesne, employing up to 14 workers, and was able to draw nearly £60 a year in cash from the proceeds of his sales.[90] The quantities of Grantchester malt bought by Londoners were large. In 1435/6, London brewers Thomas Yole and John Stone purchased 127 quarters of malt barley, from a total of 140 quarters sold by the bailiff. In 1436/7, most of the malt barley sold again went to London brewers Yole, Stone and Thomas Gildrigg. Another large sale, possibly to a London brewer, was made to John Mark of 400 quarters in 1444/5.[91] Such sales were undoubtedly facilitated by Somer's residence in London.

Indeed a number of links were established between London and Grantchester manor under Somer's ownership. Regular payments were made for journeys between the two locations, and costs were probably reduced because manorial transport and labour was being used. For example, Thomas Rangyll of Harston was paid 8d for carting various stock from London to Grantchester before Easter 1444. London suppliers, including a fishmonger and grocer, supplied the manor with fish, garlic and cloth. The farm regularly took on additional local labour at harvest time, but in 1437, men from London were sent down to assist, possibly suggesting a local shortage of cheap labour.[92] Had it not been for Somer's links, however, it seems unlikely that the manor would have drawn supplies of food and even labour from the capital. The links came to an end in 1452 when King's College purchased the manor and used it to provision the college, rather than relying on the small quantities of produce available in the market place in Cambridge.[93]

A century later, another Cambridgeshire landowner supplied the London market with corn. In 1546 Edward North, later Lord North, sold barley and wheat to London corn merchants from his farms at Kirtling and Ashley cum Silverley in the far east of the county. Some of the same crop was sold in nearby Newmarket, and the rest was consumed by his household.[94]

The extent of the grain exports from Cambridge to London occasionally generated complaints that this created shortages for the town and university. In 1439, William Bodevyle, brewer, produced testimonial letters before the mayor and aldermen of London, from the chancellor of Cambridge University, stating that William had 'been defamed by a malicious and false story that he had engrossed and bought at an excessive price 8,000 quarters of malt and other grains in Cambridge and surrounding townships' to the harm of the university and inhabitants of the town and country.[95] In 1565, the university asked the Privy Council to halt the transport of corn from Cambridge to Lynn, protesting that it was 'to the pinching of

---

90 *VCH Cambs.*, v, p. 206.
91 KC, GRA/656–9, GRA/661, GRA/676.
92 KC, GRA/657, GRA/661.
93 KC, GRA/657; J. Saltmarsh, 'A college home-farm in the fifteenth century', *Economic History*, 3 (1936), 155–72.
94 *VCH Cambs.*, x, pp. 36, 71.
95 *Calendar of plea and memoranda rolls of the City of London*, pp. 8–9.

Markets and trade

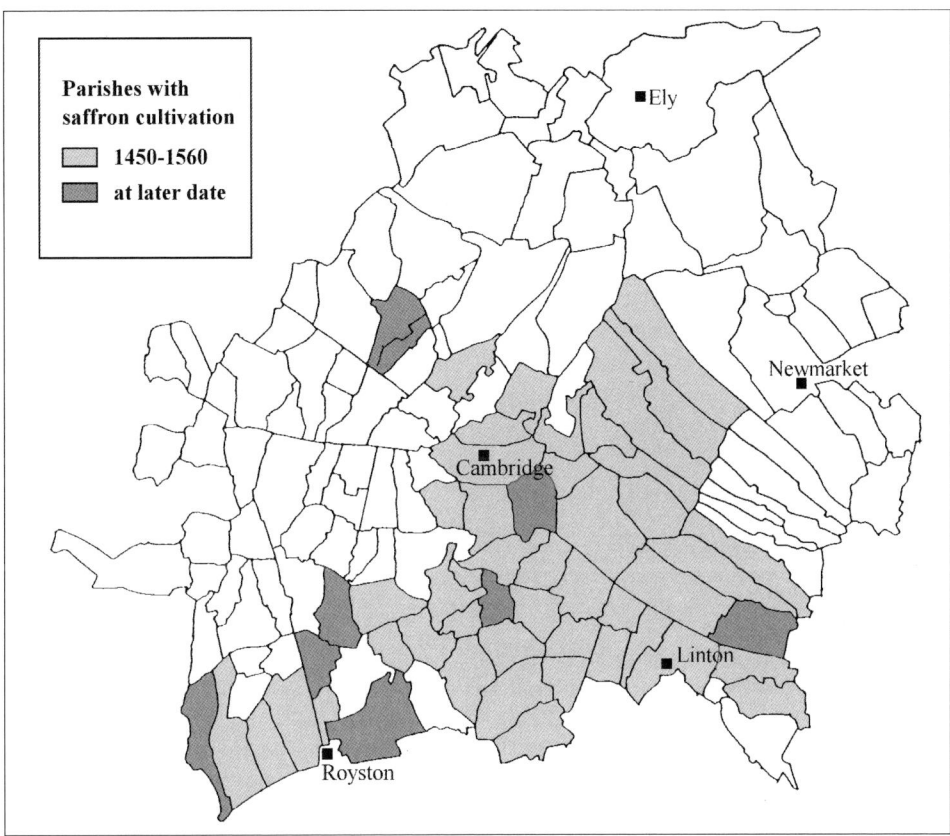

Figure 4.5 Saffron cultivation in Cambridgeshire parishes
Sources: BL, Add. MS 5861; *VCH Cambs*.

poor scholars' bellies'. In reply, the Privy Council revealed the regularity of this trade, stating that the 'sheire of Cambridge and others adjoyninge thereto have yearlie bene accustomed to utter and convey their graine by Water that waye to Lynne, and frome thence have brought it hither to London to the victuallinge of this citye'.[96] London's commercial networks had become more extensive over the fifteenth and sixteenth centuries, even though its overall demand as a consumer of basic commodities had probably declined.

London also appears to have been an important stimulus behind the saffron trade, which developed across many parts of southern Cambridgeshire and northern Essex in the 1450–1560 period. The saffron crocus, *crocus sativus*, is not a native flower, but originated in the Middle East, India and China. The saffron crocus was grown for its deep orange stigmas that were dried, and used as a dye, a pigment in

---

96   UA, Collect.Admin.5, fol. 163; N.S.B. Gras, *The evolution of the English corn market from the twelfth to the eighteenth century* (Cambridge, Mass., 1915), p. 109, n. 1.

manuscripts, and as a flavouring and colouring in cookery. Perceived medicinal benefits may have increased demand.[97] Thorold Rogers ascribed a dramatic rise in the price of saffron after the Black Death to its supposed medical virtues against the plague, but authors of books on medicinal herbs were inconsistent, recommending its use for a variety of ailments.[98] The decline of saffron cultivation in the eighteenth century was attributed to the import of foreign saffron and its diminishing use in medicine.[99] Aristocratic households and institutions had long purchased imported saffron, but from the middle of the fifteenth century, saffron was increasingly cultivated in the Cambridge region.

Saffron was grown in many villages in north-east Essex and south Cambridgeshire, mainly in areas of light, chalky soil, and particularly in parishes in the river valleys sub-region. Evidence of cultivation is found in field names, in bequests of saffron plots in wills, and from tithe disputes (see Figure 4.5). As with many alternative crops, saffron may have been cultivated for many years for household use and not tithed, but when it began to be grown commercially, rectors and vicars claimed tithed payments.[100] So the disputes and agreements concerning the tithes of saffron at Walden in 1445, Linton in 1473, Thriplow in 1475, Ickleton in 1516, Hinxton in 1524, and Babraham and Hauxton in the 1530s, probably mark the beginning of commercial cultivation in these parishes.[101] A lease of Barrington rectory of 1575 reserved the whole tithe of saffron in the closes and the moiety of the saffron tithe in the fields.[102] Saffron was also cultivated in neighbouring counties, including Godmanchester (Huntingdonshire), Newmarket (Suffolk), Sawbridgeworth (Hertfordshire), and the infirmary garden at Norwich Cathedral Priory,[103] but the crop was concentrated within north Essex and south Cambridgeshire.

In Cambridge, saffron was cultivated in several college gardens,[104] while around 1500, St John's Hospital paid for saffron heads, the digging of their saffron ground, and the pairing, picking and drying of saffron.[105] In the corporation treasurers'

---

97 J. Thirsk, *Alternative agriculture: a history from the Black Death to the present day* (Oxford, 1997), p. 66.

98 J.E.T. Rogers, *A history of agriculture and prices in England*, 7 vols. (Oxford, 1866–1902), i, pp. 631, 641; *Farming and gardening in late medieval Norfolk*, ed. C. Noble, C. Moreton and P. Rutledge, Norfolk Record Soc., LXI (Norwich, 1997), p. 8. *The grete herball which geueth parfyt knowlege and understandyng of all maner of herbes...* (Southwark, 1526), Ca. ciii; William Turner, *A new herball*, part 1 (1551), ed. G.T.L. Chapman and M.N. Tweddle (Cambridge, 1989), part 1, p. 290; Harrison, *Description*, pp. 354–5.

99 *VCH Essex*, ii, p. 364.

100 Thirsk, *Alternative agriculture*, p. 69.

101 *VCH Essex*, ii, p. 360; *VCH Cambs.*, vi, p. 99; 'Ely episcopal registers', *Ely Diocesan Remembrancer* (1907), 27 and (1911), 150, 167; *Cambridgeshire in the sixteenth century*, ed. W.M. Palmer (Cambridge, 1935), pp. 17–18, 23–5.

102 Trinity College, Cambridge, Lease Book, 1547–85, fols. 197–198v.

103 Raftis, *Godmanchester*, p. 150; May, *Newmarket*, p. 54; *VCH Hertfordshire*, iii, pp. 332, 346; Willis and Clark, *Architectural history*, iii, p. 579, n. 6; *Farming and gardening*, p. 8.

104 Peterhouse Computus rolls, 1470/1; Willis and Clark, *Architectural history*, iii, pp. 578–81.

105 SJC, D106.2, fols. 8, 11, 16.

accounts of 1530/1 and 1531/2, over twenty rents were paid for the liberty to plant saffron in Barnwell and Cambridge fields, at a cost of one penny per rood. Although these payments became decays of rents in the following year's accounts, this perhaps denoted a change in accounting procedure rather than an abandonment of cultivation.[106] In the late 1540s it was stated that the 'Radegun tythe', held by Jesus College, consisted of the tithe of grain, hay and saffron growing in the fields of Cambridge on the castle side of the river.[107]

During the fifteenth century, at a time of high wages, the large amounts of labour and small amounts of land required to grow saffron suggest that its cultivation was concentrated on peasant holdings. These could employ family labour at no additional cost. This is also the impression gained from examining Cambridgeshire wills recording bequests of saffron grounds.[108] The testators include husbandmen, widows, a carpenter and a vicar; frequently, the only possessions recorded are a few roods of saffron, a handful of goods and perhaps a few acres of land. Other documents describe saffron being grown by small farmers, like the obligation made by two husbandmen of Ickleton to supply the vicar there with 17½ lbs of English saffron over four years in 1515, and the action brought against William Gilson of Stapleford, husbandman, in the vice-chancellor's court in Cambridge concerning the detention of a rood of saffron.[109] Linton manor court ordered no one to throw 'lez Saffron Flowres & le drose' in the king's highway, and fined several men for doing so.[110] It was notable that the countrymen of Norfolk and Suffolk, who protested against enclosures in Kett's rebellion of 1549, were willing to allow existing saffron closes to remain, because of the expense of planting them.[111] Perhaps many of the rebels held saffron plots too. Saffron may be an early example of a cash crop which small farmers grew on holdings mainly devoted to subsistence: plants such as rape, flax, hemp, woad, tobacco and madder were increasingly cultivated during the sixteenth and seventeenth centuries to supply industry or satisfy particular consumer demands.[112]

London marketing links were evident in the saffron trade, as several Chancery proceedings from the early sixteenth century show. Thomas Hodylston, haberdasher of London, purchased 14 lbs of saffron at Fulbourn, and the Londoner later leased part of the village's demesne lands to cultivate the crop. John Capon, stockfishmonger of London, contracted with William Elyott of Cottered in Hertfordshire at Stourbridge Fair, Cambridge, to obtain saffron. Another contract to deliver saffron was made at the Swan Inn, Newmarket.[113] Robert Goldwyn of Hertfordshire, haberdasher, brought a

---

106 CCTA, i, fols. 122, 132v, 145v.
107 TNA: PRO C 1/1270/103.
108 BL, Add. MS 5861.
109 Trinity College, Cambridge, Box 21, item 45; UA, V.C.Ct.I.1, fol. 2.
110 CCRO, R59/14/11/7A, mm. 15, 16, courts 1518, 1519; R59/14/11/7B, m. 8d, court 1553.
111 Thirsk, *Alternative agriculture*, pp. 17, 68.
112 J. Thirsk, *Economic policy and projects* (Oxford, 1978).
113 TNA: PRO C 1/264/8, C 1/489/28, C 1/596/37–9; *VCH Cambs.*, x, p. 145.

Figure 4.6a Saffron crocus in the church of St Mary the Virgin, Saffron Walden. The representation is carved in a spandrel of an arch in the south aisle and dates from the late fifteenth century (Saffron Walden Museum)

plea against John Howsden of Grantchester, yeoman, who had failed to deliver 40 lbs of saffron to him, which he had planned to sell to a London grocer. The saffron was to have been brought to 'Colle fayre', which was probably Cold Fair, held at Newport, Essex.[114] At Trinity College's manor of Ickleton in 1483, John Catby of London held a plot of saffron.[115] Saffron was one of the commodities traded by the Grocers' Company of London, but as the examples above illustrate, other merchants came to be involved. It was perhaps significant that in 1471 the Grocers' Company relaxed its rule that members could only buy saffron from merchant strangers at the Great Beam in London: increasingly saffron was being obtained from country producers.[116]

Although saffron was cultivated across much of southern Cambridgeshire, the small Essex town of Walden became the centre of the industry, rather than Cambridge. Saffron cultivation in the area may have begun in Walden, stimulated by a number of dyeworks that existed in the town in the 1380s.[117] It was only during the

---

114 TNA: PRO C 1/809/45; Harrison, *Description*, p. 253, n. 9.
115 Trinity College, Cambridge, Box 21, item 39.
116 P. Nightingale, *A medieval mercantile community: the Grocers' Company and the politics and trade of London, 1000–1485* (New Haven, 1995), p. 548.
117 Cromarty, 'Chepying Walden', 109–11.

Figure 4.6b Saffron "walled-in" from the borough seal of 1549 (Saffron Walden Museum)

late fifteenth and early sixteenth centuries, though, that the industry really seems to have flourished, when the town adopted the flower as its symbol and as the prefix to the town's name. Saffron flowers were represented on a late fifteenth-century spandrel of an arch in the south aisle of the parish church, on the town's coat of arms, in Henry VIII's charter of 1514, and on the new town seal of 1549, while the corporation of Walden presented royal dignitaries with gifts of saffron.[118]

Saffron Walden was one of a group of small towns around London which developed specialised crafts or markets in response to the demands of the capital. Nearby Thaxted developed a large cutlery trade, in which nearly one third of the townsmen worked by 1381, combining local resources such as a skilled workforce, low labour costs and plentiful firewood, with investment from London cutlers. At High Wycombe in Buckinghamshire, bakers produced simnel bread which was sold as a speciality in the capital. Other small towns in the Home Counties developed specialised markets in grain, livestock and fuel, which supplied the capital.[119] As in the textile industry in this period, growth centred on small towns and villages, which were arguably more attractive to London capital and enterprise than the established

---

118 Saffron Walden Museum, *Saffron Walden local history activity guide* (Saffron Walden, rev. edn., 1997), pp. 7–13; *VCH Essex*, ii, pp. 359–64; Braybrooke, *Audley End*, pp. 145–7; A. Clark, 'Saffron and Walden', *Essex Review*, 19 (1910), 61–3.

119 K.C. Newton, *Thaxted in the fourteenth century* (Chelmsford, 1960); D. Keene, 'Small towns and the metropolis: the experience of medieval England', in J-M. Duvosquel and E. Thoen, eds., *Peasants and townsmen in medieval Europe* (Ghent, 1995), pp. 223–38, esp. pp. 234–6; Dyer, *Making a living*, p. 307.

Figure 4.7 Detail from Henry VIII's charter of 1514 to establish the guild of Holy Trinity, Saffron Walden. Saffron crocuses decorate the left-hand margin. The charter is now part of the Town Council's archives and is displayed in Saffron Walden Museum (by permission of Saffron Walden Town Council; with thanks to Saffron Walden Museum)

provincial towns, with their regulations, costly institutions of government, and existing mercantile networks.[120]

Conclusion

Cambridge's formal market served a hinterland that was largely local. The area can be identified from the origins of those holding stalls or fined for breaking market regulations. Additional evidence is provided by the residences of those making pleas in Cambridge Borough Court, where just over half of those recorded came from places up to 5 miles away, and the majority from within a 10-mile radius of Cambridge. Furthermore, no other formal markets operated within 5 miles of Cambridge. Within this local region, smaller towns and villages such as Linton, Foxton and Whittlesford attracted traders from surrounding villages up to 5 miles distant, and from nearby towns like Cambridge and Walden.

Informal trade took place within the Cambridge region at both a local and regional scale. Petty trading occurred outside formal market places, as at Foxton and Whittlesford Bridge. Cambridge, together with smaller towns like Newmarket and Walden, were centres for local credit networks, while townspeople, and particularly Londoners, dominated larger debt cases. Longer-distance trade linked Cambridge with

---

120 Britnell, 'Economy of British towns', pp. 332–3.

Lynn and London and other major towns in East Anglia and the Midlands, as toll disputes, town pleas, and debt cases show.

The changes that occurred in the marketing networks of the Cambridge region between 1450 and 1560 reflected longer-term trends in the English economy. The rise in living standards for many after the Black Death of 1348–9 and the subsequent development of new mercantile networks led to the decline of rural markets and increasing regional specialisation, particularly in agriculture. In the Cambridge region, the demise of countryside markets reflected the national trend, while the expansion of malt barley production and the emergence of saffron cultivation responded to growing demand. Sales of these commodities became less localised and more commercialised.

Cambridge benefited from some of these trends. With the contraction of the marketing network, the regional importance of Cambridge's market seems to have been enhanced. While income from stall lettings in Cambridge market appears to have fallen between the 1430s and 1480s, additional stalls generating extra income were added in the 1510s, 1520s and 1550s. Cambridge merchants marketed malt and malt barley to London grocers and overseas. The stimulus for the growth in the malt barley and saffron trades, however, seems to have come from outside the region rather than from within, and particularly from London. Walden rather than Cambridge emerged as the centre of saffron cultivation, and like many areas of growth in the English economy in the later fifteenth century, this was probably a consequence of London mercantile links.

Chapter 5

Fairs

Complementing the network of markets in Cambridge and its region was a group of fairs. Whereas local and retail trade predominated in markets, which were held weekly and lasted only one day, wholesale and regional trade dominated fairs, which were annual events, held over several days. Fairs generally attracted buyers and sellers who came from greater distances and who dealt in more valuable items than those attending markets. So while markets provided the opportunity to buy and sell basic foodstuffs and household goods, in addition fairs generally offered the chance to buy livestock, farming equipment, non-staple and luxury items.[1]

Three fairs were held in Cambridge, and others operated in towns and villages across the region. Being annual, transient events, fairs did not encourage the keeping of records, and for many fairs, only the charter grant licensing the fair survives. At Cambridge, though, a considerable amount of additional evidence exists, mainly relating to the town's Stourbridge Fair. Many colleges, together with other ecclesiastical and noble households, made purchases at this fair, illuminating trade from the perspective of the consumer. Records also survive from the town corporation which owned many of the booths in the fair, and from the university authorities that had oversight of some trading offences, while more serious disputes appear in the Chancery proceedings. These sources provide evidence of the buyers, sellers, and products being traded at fairs in Cambridge and its region, and reveal the growth of Stourbridge Fair, which by the mid-sixteenth century was the largest fair in the region and of national importance.

Late medieval fairs

Despite the recent attention paid to several aspects of medieval marketing, fairs remain a relatively under-researched subject, and so a brief general survey of English fairs in the later middle ages may help to place the fairs of Cambridge and its region in a broader perspective. Many fairs, like markets, disappeared with the dramatic reduction in population after the Black Death, and most of those that remained experienced a contraction in profits. Particularly severe was the decline of the larger English fairs at Boston, St Ives, Westminster and Winchester, which at their height in the mid-thirteenth century, had attracted traders from many parts of England and Europe. These international fairs had already begun to be eclipsed in the early fourteenth century by towns that offered year-round trading in luxury goods and the distribution of cloth, and after the Black Death they slid into obscurity.[2]

---

1 Kowaleski, *Exeter*, p. 41; D.L. Farmer, 'Marketing the produce of the countryside, 1200–1500', in E. Miller, ed., *The agrarian history of England and Wales, iii: 1348–1500* (Cambridge, 1991), p. 345.
2 Britnell, *Commercialisation*, pp. 155–61; E.W. Moore, *The fairs of medieval England: an introductory study* (Toronto, 1985), pp. 217–22; J.Z. Titow, 'The decline of the fair of St Giles, Winchester, in the thirteenth and fourteenth centuries', *Nottingham Medieval Studies*, 31 (1987), 58–75; Rosser, *Medieval Westminster*, pp. 97–115.

With the decline of the international fairs and the widespread contraction in marketing, medieval historians have focused little attention on English fairs in the later medieval period.[3] But this is in contrast to the importance that has been attributed to these institutions in the early modern period. Everitt has described the mass of different business transacted at fairs in the late sixteenth and early seventeenth centuries, reflecting population growth and the development of private marketing institutions. He has claimed that in terms of trade, luxury goods, news and ideas, fairs were probably more important for most provincial people than the London market.[4] Other writers have pointed to the vitality of fairs during Elizabeth's reign, the extensive network of fairs that served the horse and livestock trades, and to the fact that their widespread demise only occurred in the nineteenth century.[5] Nonetheless, the role of fairs in the century before Elizabeth's accession remains obscure.

The later middle ages saw major changes in the levels and distribution of incomes which in turn led to major shifts in the composition of demand and the structure of marketing. In some regions, certain sectors of the late medieval economy flourished, such as livestock farming, fishing, cloth production and lead mining, and fairs developed to serve these areas of growth. Welsh cattle drovers met West Midland graziers at the fairs of Birmingham and Coventry. Exeter's Lenten Fair, founded in 1374, mainly served as a market for the expanding fisheries of the south-west.[6] In the West Riding of Yorkshire, fairs in Bradford, Halifax and Wakefield provided an outlet for the cloth made in those districts, and the rapid decline in the income from Ripon's fairs at the end of the fifteenth century may have been a result of the decline of cloth production there.[7] Wye Fair was a major centre for the sale of cloth in Kent in the later fourteenth century. Despite a slump in the 1390s, the purveyor for the Calais garrison bought cloth there in the mid-fifteenth century, and it was described as a 'great fair' by Leland in Henry VIII's reign. Peasant workers in the Mendip lead mining industry in the late fifteenth century may have used fairs in the locality to engage in inter-regional trade.[8]

---

3   An older survey of English fairs is provided in C. Walford, *Fairs, past and present: a chapter in the history of commerce* (London, 1883). Continental European fairs are examined by O. Verlinden, 'Markets and fairs', in M.M. Postan, E.E. Rich and E. Miller, eds., *Cambridge economic history of Europe*, iii: *Economic organisation and policies in the middle ages* (Cambridge, 1963), pp. 150–3.

4   Everitt, 'Marketing', pp. 81–92; Everitt, 'Introduction', p. 6.

5   M.T. Hodgen, 'Fairs of Elizabethan England', *Economic Geography*, 18 (1942), 389–400; P.R. Edwards, 'The horse trade in Tudor and Stuart England', in F.M.L. Thompson, ed., *Horses in European economic history: a preliminary canter* (Reading, 1983), pp. 113–31; J.A. Chartres, 'Markets and fairs in England and Wales, 1500 to 1860', University of Leeds, School of Business and Economic Studies, Discussion paper ser., G93/03 (Leeds, 1993), pp. 11–16.

6   Britnell, *Commercialisation*, p. 160; M. Kowaleski, 'The expansion of the south-western fisheries in late medieval England', *EcHR*, 53 (2000), 447.

7   K.L. McCutcheon, *Yorkshire fairs and markets to the end of the eighteenth century*, Thoresby Soc., XXXIX (Leeds, 1940), pp. 51, 110, 131, 135; H. Heaton, *The Yorkshire woollen and worsted industries from the earliest times up to the industrial revolution* (Oxford, 2nd edn., 1965), pp. 71, 75, 145.

8   M. Mate, 'The rise and fall of markets in southeast England', *Canadian Journal of History*, 31 (1996), 69, 77; I. Blanchard, *International lead production and trade in the "Age of the Saigerprozess" 1460–1560* (Stuttgart, 1995), pp. 307–9.

Many towns held fairs, and some civic corporations even obtained charters licensing additional fairs in this period. As Exeter's commerce expanded between the 1370s and 1460s, five new fairs were founded in the city. Two new fairs were introduced at York in 1502, which were advertised in towns across the county. The city's merchants also attended the major fairs of Beverley and Howden, the latter attracting traders from London and the West Riding.[9] A statute of 1487 described the 'meny feyers for the comen welle of your seid lege people' at Salisbury, Bristol, Oxford, Cambridge, Nottingham, Ely, Coventry, and elsewhere, where all groups in society could purchase church ornaments, linen, woollen cloth, brass, pewter, bedding, iron, flax and wax, 'and many other necessary things'.[10]

Epstein has recently suggested that the increased per capita trade in higher quality goods and foodstuffs led to the growth of many regional fairs in late medieval Europe. In England, which had a very dense network of markets and fairs before 1350, the marketing network became more integrated and rationalised, and regional fairs 'tended to fuse into complex, integrated networks spanning one or more agricultural regions'.[11]

Fairs of Cambridge and its region

The fairs of Cambridge and its region can been traced, like markets, through grants of their foundation, and in lists compiled by early modern writers and travellers.[12] Table 5.1 lists the distribution around Cambridge of fairs known from their foundation charters, and highlights those fairs which still appear to have operated in the fifteenth and sixteenth centuries, the principal source being the list of fairs compiled by William Harrison in his *Description of England* published in 1577.[13] The survival rate of fairs in Cambridge's region was very similar to that of the markets: by the later middle ages, about 40 per cent of fairs continued to operate. Like the surviving markets, the remaining fairs tended to be concentrated in the towns of the region.

The varying times at which the region's fairs were held suggest that they may have operated in a temporal cycle over the year, like the circuit of local markets functioning over a week. In origin, many fairs were held at the times of church festivals, thus linking with holidays. Fairs tended to be concentrated in the summer months, when travel was easier. Seasonal peaks also matched the needs of production and trade. Cattle and sheep fairs, for example, tended to be clustered in spring, and to a lesser extent in autumn. Exeter's Lenten Fair and Yarmouth's autumn herring fair coincided with major imports of fish.[14] The great fairs of eastern England operated in an annual

---

9   Kowaleski, *Exeter*, p. 68; D.M. Palliser, 'York under the Tudors: the trading life of the northern capital', in Everitt, ed., *Perspectives*, pp. 52–3.

10   Henry VII, c. 9: *SR*, ii, p. 518.

11   S.R. Epstein, 'Regional fairs, institutional innovation, and economic growth in late medieval Europe', *EcHR*, 47 (1994), 459–82.

12   Britnell, *Commercialisation*, pp. 11–19, 81–90; Everitt, 'Marketing', pp. 16–26; Hodgen, 'Fairs', 389–400.

13   Harrison, *Description*, pp. 392–6.

14   Farmer, 'Marketing', pp. 339–41; Davis, 'Representation', pp. 26–8; Chartres, 'Markets and fairs', pp. 14–16; Kowaleski, 'Fisheries', 447.

Table 5.1

Dates of fairs of Cambridge and its region

14–16 Feb	Ickleton
Mid Lent Sunday	**Saffron Walden**
Easter, 8 days at	Impington
Wednesday in Easter week, 8 days at	**St Ives**
Monday before Ascension, 10 days from	**Huntingdon**
Lady Days	**Huntingdon**
Vigil of Ascension, 22 days from	Ely
Ascension, 3 days at	**St Neots**
Eve of Whitsun, for week	Saffron Walden
Monday in Whitsun week, 15 days from	Burwell
Whitsun week	**Royston**
Trinity, 3 days at	Balsham, Orwell, Swavesey
Trinity	Whittlesford
Monday in Rogation week	**Reach**
Translation of St Edmund (29 Apr), 2 days at	Mildenhall
7 May	*St Neots*
Translation of St Nicholas (9 May), 2 days at	Royston
St Barnabas (11 Jun), 8 days at	Newmarket
St Etheldreda (23 Jun) 7 days at	**Ely**
Midsummer (24 Jun), 4 days at *	**Cambridge, Midsummer Fair**
St John the Baptist (24 Jun), 3 days at	Fowlmere
Decollation of St John (29 Aug), 5 days at	Swaffham Prior
SS Peter and Paul (29 Jun), 3 days at	Cottenham
SS Peter and Paul (29 Jun), 3 days at	Foxton
SS Peter and Paul (29 Jun), 8 days at	Bassingbourn, Fenstanton
St Thomas the Martyr (7 Jul)	**Royston**
St Margaret (20 Jul), 3 days at	Barrington, Hildersham, Kingston, Linton
St Mary Magdalene (22 Jul), 5 days at	**Ickleton**
St James the Apostle, 2 days at *	**Saffron Walden**
St Neot (31 Jul), 3 days at	**St Neots**
St Peter ad Vincula (1 Aug), 3 days at	**St Neots**
St Peter ad Vincula (1 Aug), 3 days at	Trumpington
St Peter ad Vincula (1 Aug)	Mildenhall
4 Aug	*Linton*
5-6 Aug	Walden
St Lawrence (10 Aug), 3 days at	**Linton**
St Lawrence (10 Aug), 3 days at	Foxton, Great Abington, Wicken
St Lawrence (10 Aug), 8 days at	St Ives
Assumption of Mary (15 Aug), 2 days at *	**Cambridge, Garlic Fair**
15 August	Haverhill
St Bartholomew (24 Aug), 3 days at	Whittlesford
Nativity of St Mary (8 Sept), 9 days at	Great Wilbraham
Nativity of St Mary (8 Sept), 3 days at	Milton
Exaltation of Holy Cross (14 Sept), 2 days at *	**Cambridge, Stourbridge Fair**
St Lambert (17 Sept), 15 days at	Ely
21 Sept	*St Ives*
Michaelmas (29 Sept), 3 days at	Brinkley
Michaelmas, 2 days at	Chippenham
St Leodegarius (2 Oct)	Fordham
13 Oct	*Royston*
St Luke's even (17 Oct)	*Ely*
St Luke (18 Oct), 3 days at	Kingston
21 Oct	*Saffron Walden, Newmarket*
SS Simon and Jude (28 Oct), 3 days at	**Newmarket**
St Andrew (30 Nov), 3 days at	Foxton
Date not known	Rampton

Sources: VCH Cambs., iii–x; Letters, *Gazetteer.*
Notes: Entries in bold indicate fairs operating 1450–1560; entries in italic indicate dates given by Harrison which differ from earlier grants and may reflect changes of dates rather than additional fairs.
* Subsequently extended.

Figure 5.1 Stourbridge Chapel, Newmarket Road, Cambridge. The only surviving building from the leper hospital of St Mary Magdalene, this twelfth-century chapel later provided storage for booths from the fair

cycle from Lent to November during the thirteenth century, as did the fairs held in Champagne and Flanders.[15] It seems likely that Cambridge's fairs comprised one or more self-contained local cycles, but Stourbridge Fair, the largest fair in the region, may have been part of a wider cycle which stretched over several regions, as many of its participants came from outside the town's immediate hinterland.

As befitted its status as the leading centre of trade, Cambridge hosted the largest number of fairs in the region.[16] Stourbridge or Sturbridge Fair, held on Stourbridge Common on the outskirts of the town, had been granted to the leper hospital of St Mary Magdalene by King John. After the hospital was dissolved in the mid-thirteenth century, the fair continued, with the town corporation taking oversight. The fair had initially been held on 13–14 September, but by 1516 it lasted from 24 August to 29 September.[17] Midsummer Fair, also known as St John's or Barnwell Fair, was granted to the canons of Barnwell in 1211. This fair was to be held on 22–25 June, but it continued over fourteen days by 1498. By the sixteenth century the fair had given its name to the common, formerly known as Greencroft, on which it was held. A fair on

---

15 Masschaele, *Peasants*, p. 143; Verlinden, 'Markets and fairs', pp. 125–7.

16 Similarly, Exeter had the most numerous and largest fairs and markets in Devon: Kowaleski, *Exeter*, p. 60.

17 J. Nichols, *The history and antiquities of Barnwell Abbey, and of Sturbridge Fair*, Bibliotheca Topographica Britannica, no. XXXVIII (London, 1786), pp. 73–80; *VCH Cambs.*, pp. 92–3.

the vigil and feast of the Assumption of the Blessed Virgin Mary was granted to St Radegund's Priory in Cambridge by King Stephen, and a third day added during Henry VI's reign. It was known as Garlic Fair by the later sixteenth century.[18] No recorded purchases have been found which were made at this fair. Yet the priory appointed toll collectors, bought a lock and key for the fair gates, and drew an annual profit of 5s from the event in the 1450s.[19]

Outside Cambridge, but within the county, several fairs continued to operate in the fifteenth and sixteenth centuries. Ely Fair was an important market for fish, cloth, cattle, and local basketry products. Held during the feast of St Etheldreda, whose shrine was housed in the cathedral, the fair also sold tawdry lace: these silk laces or neckties were held in veneration as having touched St Etheldreda's shrine. A student of Clare Hall, Cambridge, sent tawdry lace from Ely Fair to Thomas Cromwell in 1533.[20] Reach Fair at Rogationtide was proclaimed by the mayor of Cambridge but held at Reach, 8 miles north-east of the town, where boats came up Reach Lode from the Cam, and was particularly important as a horse fair.[21] The fair held on the feast of St Mary Magdalene at Ickleton, and an August fair at Linton, were recorded by Harrison in his late sixteenth-century list of fairs, together with a number of fairs in towns just outside the county's borders.[22]

Other fairs in the region have left little trace. Although some are known to have decayed in this period,[23] others continued to be granted and confirmed, showing that these rights were still valued by their owners, even if they were not necessarily in operation. The bishop of Ely was granted a Friday market and February fair at Ickleton in 1556, the date of Swavesey Fair was altered in 1505, and the fair at Rampton confirmed in 1534, but so far, no evidence has been found to prove that these fairs were ever held.[24] Like weekly markets, charters may have been obtained for fairs which never functioned.

Not all the fairs described by early modern travellers were significant trading institutions either. William Harrison acknowledged that some of the fairs he listed in his *Description of England* had 'little else bought or sold in them more than good drink, pies, and some peddlery trash; wherefore it were no loss if divers of them were abolished'. There were other fairs, however, which he considered to be 'not inferior to the greatest marts in Europe, as Sturbridge fair, near to Cambridge, Bristol fair, Bartholomew fair at London, Lynn mart, Cold fair at Newport Pond for cattle, and divers other'.[25]

---

18 *VCH Cambs.*, iii, p. 92; *Annals*, i, p. 249; *Place-names of Cambridgeshire*, pp. 42–3.
19 *St Radegund*, pp. 147, 156, 163, 167.
20 *OED*, xvii, p. 675; *LP*, vi, no. 1264, pp. 315–16; *VCH Cambs.*, iv, p. 50.
21 *VCH Cambs.*, iii, p. 91, x, p. 227.
22 Harrison, *Description*, pp. 392–6.
23 *VCH Cambs.*, vi, p. 270, viii, p. 23.
24 *VCH Cambs.*, vi, p. 241, ix, pp. 216, 390.
25 Harrison, *Description*, pp. 253, 392.

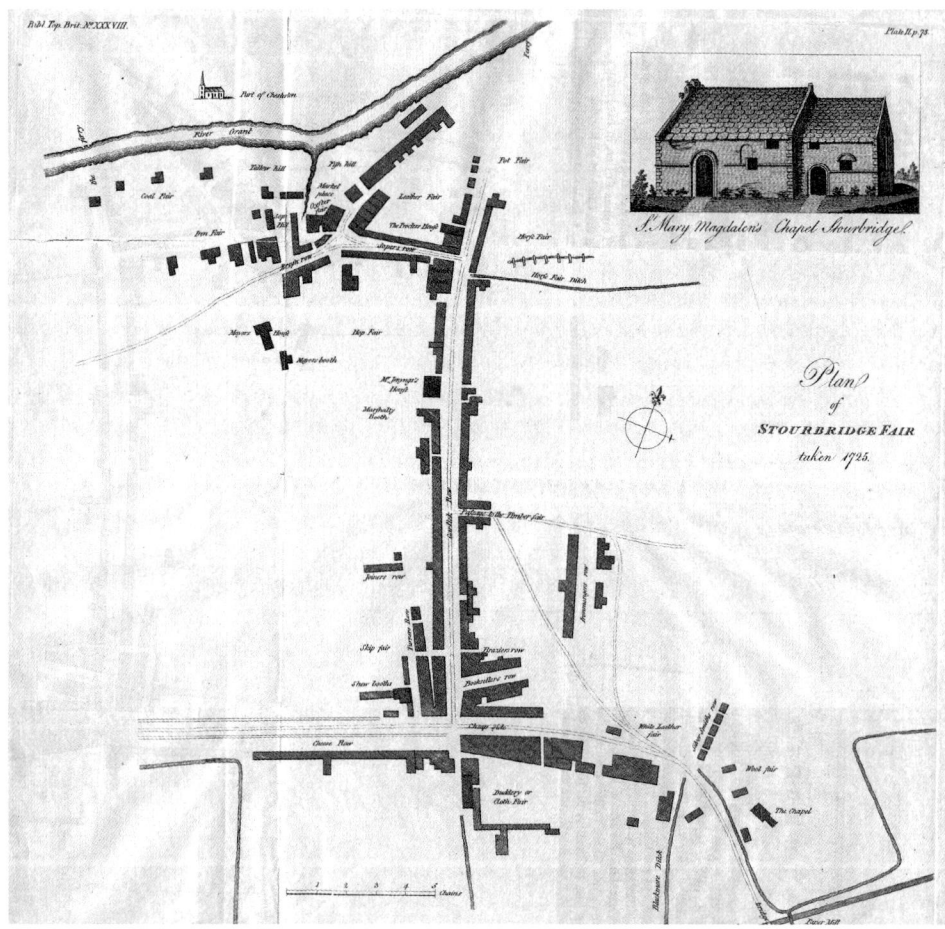

Figure 5.2 Plan of Stourbridge Fair, 1725, showing the 'streets' or rows of booths (Nichols, *History*, p. 71: by permission of the County Record Office, Cambridge)

Traders

A notable feature of Stourbridge Fair, and an indication of its size and the commodities traded, was the names given to groups or streets of booths within the fair. These included the 'Duddery', where woollen cloth was sold, Water Fair, Garlic Row, Petty Mercery, Ironmonger Lane, Stockfish Booths, Cordwainer Row, and Timber Fair. The Lenton Fair at Nottingham in 1516 had a similar range of street names.[26] Three of the names at Stourbridge Fair – Birchin Lane, Cheapside and Soper Lane – were also London streets, where drapers, mercers, haberdashers, pepperers and grocers could be found; these names may have reflected the prominence of Londoners at the fair

---

26 CCA, Palmer/Barnard vol. 57, *passim*; *Records of the borough of Nottingham 1155–1547*, ed. W.H. Stevenson, 3 vols. (London, 1882–5), ii, pp. 349–52.

and in these particular rows.[27] Many of the street names occur in a plan of the fair drawn in 1725, and the topographical details given in the sixteenth-century leases suggest that at least some of these streets were in the same position in both periods. Garlic Row, for example, ran roughly north to south, with booths on either side opening towards the east or west; Cheese Row opened to the north.[28] Remarkably, by the mid-sixteenth century, the size of the fair was such that the layout of the booths bore many similarities to the fairground in the eighteenth century.

The booths were substantial items, like covered stalls or tents. Timber, hair cloth, skins, packthread, penny nails and 'trasshes' were used by the corporation to repair its booths, and a tailor was occasionally employed.[29] Booths were often given elaborate names, which sometimes reflected the commodity traded, but more often were just for identification. Five booths in the Water Fair in 1544, for example, were known as 'le holybusshe, le wullffles, le Mayden hedde, le buckes hedde, et le rammes hedde'.[30] At some fairs such as Winchester, booths were permanent structures like shops, but at Stourbridge they were dismantled every year at the end of the fair, so that the common field could revert to cultivation, and the owners of the strips profited from the manure provided by the refuse of the fair.[31] Implements for building the booths were to be delivered to the new treasurers of the town every year by indenture.[32] Despite being temporary constructions, many owners regarded their booths as valuable items and treated them like property. The court of Chancery heard disputes over the ownership of booths, while John Manfeld was assessed at £10 and Margaret Gryme at £6 for their booth rents in the Cambridge subsidy returns of 1524.[33] Booths were also bequeathed in wills, and some amounted to significant sums in value, like the booths and standings left by George Foyster to provide a yearly annuity of 20 nobles for his son in 1539.[34]

Many Cambridge burgesses held booths in Stourbridge Fair. These booths were treated 'as copyhold property "held of" the corporation by the burgess', even though 'the material booth only existed for a few weeks in the year'. Every burgess with booths in the fair might give, sell, or surrender booths in the court of the mayor and burgesses, with 4d fine paid for every booth transferred.[35] These transfers began to be recorded regularly in the corporation treasurers' accounts from 1525/6, and the number of transactions per year has been extracted from these records (Figure 5.3).

---

27   John Stow, *A survey of London*, ed. C.L. Kingsford, 2 vols. (Oxford, 1908), i, pp. 81, 199, 261, ii, pp. 306, 330; CCTA, i, fols. 58v–59, 79A–79Av, 123v–124.
28   CCA, Palmer/Barnard vol. 57, fols. 26v, 31, 58v, 60v, 68, 92.
29   CCA, X/71/6, X/71/9–10; *CBD*, p. 166.
30   CCA, Palmer/Barnard vol. 57, fol. 2.
31   Salzman, *Trade*, p. 152; Maitland, *Township*, p. 80.
32   CCA, Palmer/Barnard vol. 57, fol. 98v.
33   TNA: PRO C 1/562/20–1, C 1/708/32, C 1/715/25, C 1/719/23, E 179/81/133.
34   CCRO, Archdeaconry of Ely, Will Register 1, fol. 143. The noble was an English gold coin; by 1550 its value had settled at 6s 8d: *OED*, x, p. 452.
35   Maitland, *Township*, p. 80. Additional ordinances relating to Stourbridge Fair booths are recorded in CCA, I/4, fols. 5b, 8b, 10b, 11b, 77b–79a.

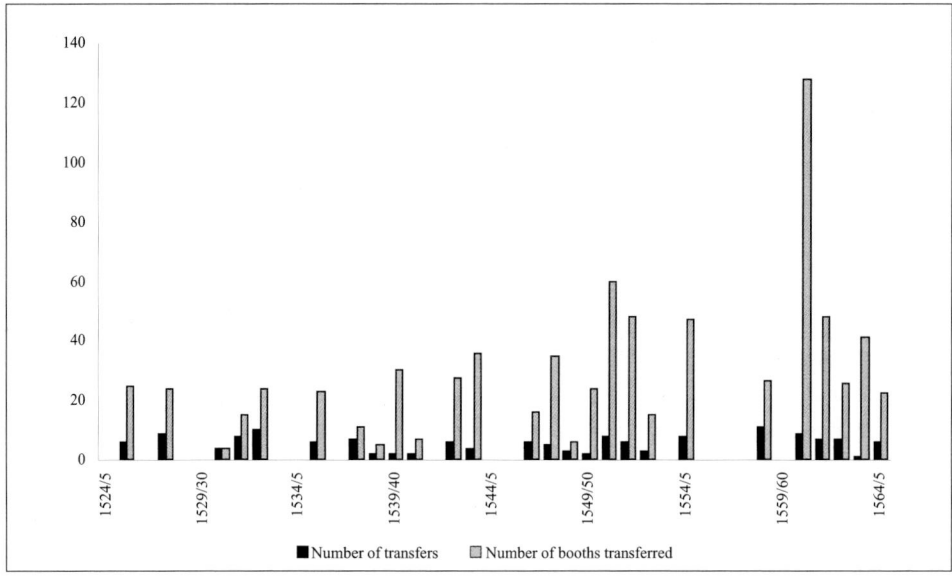

Figure 5.3 Transfers of booths in Stourbridge Fair held by Cambridge burgesses
Source: CCTA, i–ii.

There are gaps even when the accounts survive, and in these years it is not clear whether there were no surrenders or if the income was recorded elsewhere. Although the series is not continuous, making comparisons difficult, there appears to have been an increase in the number of transactions in the 1550s and 1560s, when the number of booths surrendered annually regularly exceeded 40. This increase alone is not a clear indicator of any particular trend, but, as will be discussed below, it may in fact have been a time of growth in demand. The graph also shows how numerous the booths were. In 1560/1, a total of 128 booths were surrendered, although a group of 28 were exchanged twice.

There were also treasurers' booths, let for a yearly rent by Cambridge Corporation, mainly to traders who were not Cambridge burgesses.[36] The total and average income from these booths, adjusted for inflation, is shown in Figure 5.4.[37] Unfortunately, it is not clear what proportion of all the stalls at the fair are represented. In the mid 1520s, the average and gross income from the corporation's booths increased substantially. Income from booths may have been a more profitable source of income than property rents at this time, as several Cambridge burgesses chose to bequeath booths to the corporation to provide funds for masses after their deaths.[38] These revenues came to the crown with the dissolution of the chantries, but most of the income was re-granted to the town in 1557.[39] The rise in the 1520s is particularly

---

36   CCTA, i–ii.
37   Using the price index of a shopping basket of consumables in Phelps Brown and Hopkins, *Perspective*, pp. 13–59.
38   *Annals*, i, pp. 210, 222, 246, 259.
39   TNA: PRO SC 11/90; *Charters*, pp. 205–9.

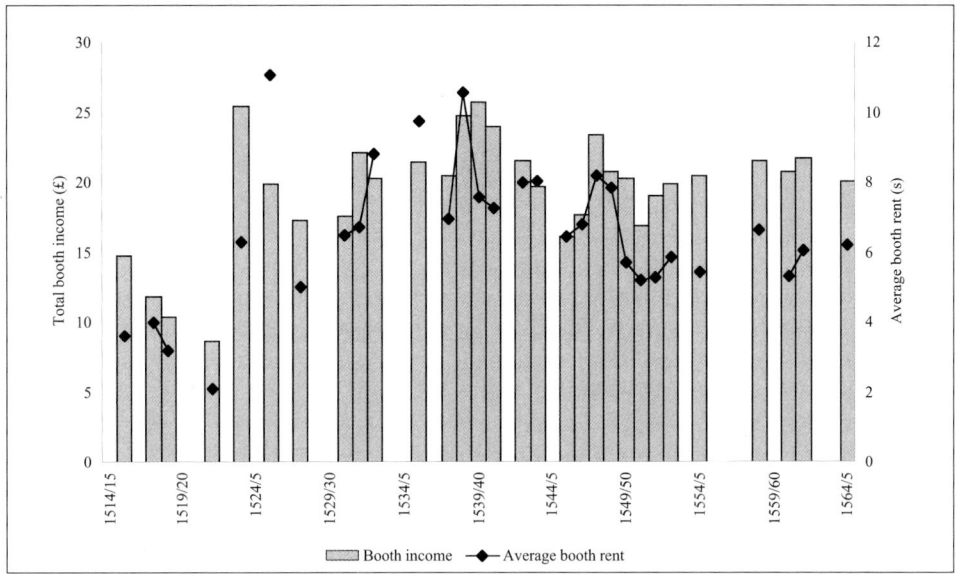

Figure 5.4 Income from treasurers' booths in Stourbridge Fair (adjusted for inflation)
Source: CCTA, i–ii. Adjusted for inflation using the Phelps Brown and Hopkins price index (1451–75 = 100).

interesting as it coincided in Cambridge with a large number of college building projects and some traces of rising wage rates for labourers and building craftsmen.[40] While booth rents continued to fluctuate thereafter, other evidence of the growth is suggested by Cambridge Corporation's introduction of fines, levied on leases of their own booths. Christopher Hoddesson paid 2s 4d fine for a booth in 1543/4, and Francis Pope paid 20s for a lease in the Duddery in 1546/7,[41] and during the 1550s, fines were regularly collected when leases of booths were taken up. These fines rose to as much as £6 13s 4d for two booths let to Francis Hynde, esquire, at 5 marks annual rent in 1555, an astonishing amount for property only used for a month every year.[42]

Many of the traders who attended Stourbridge Fair can be identified from the treasurers' accounts and some can be traced further using other records. Payments were taken for 'pakkes' – bundles of goods carried by pedlars, often containing cloth.[43] Among the 'pakkes' listed in the corporation accounts were men assessed for 'clothis', 'a remnante' and broad cloths.[44] 'A Treatise concerning the Staple', written c.1519–35, describes how 'sixty years agoo old merchaunts bought all ther clothes of cloth makers in the country by the holl sortes in pakkes', while at the time the author was writing, pedlars and chapmen took imported merchandise, 'from fair to fair, from

---

40 See below, Chapter 7.
41 CCTA, i, fols. 238v, 267.
42 CCA, Palmer/Barnard vol. 57, fols. 41v, 58, 62, 63v, 77, 82v, 98, 106.
43 OED, xi, p. 39.
44 CCTA, i, fols. 47, 80–80v.

markett to markett, carieth it to sell in horspakks and fote pakks'.[45] Packs were carried to other fairs: the Lent Fair in Bridgwater had a common house for packs, and the churchwardens organised a night watch over the packs at St James's Fair, Bristol. Similar security measures may have been taken in Cambridge, as two men were paid 20d each to 'wait upon the packs' for six days in the accounts of 1519/20.[46] In 1564/5 a payment was taken from 'certain poor pedlars that sold pins on the banks'.[47] These pedlars who came to Stourbridge and other late medieval fairs were probably similar to the chapmen described by Spufford a century later, who made frequent visits to fairs, often travelling outside their local marketing area to reach particular fairs, and selling textiles, haberdashery, and ready-made clothing accessories such as stockings, gloves, caps, handkerchiefs and neckcloths.[48] Other smaller traders at Stourbridge Fair included a barber, first appearing in 1548/9, and tanners from Potton in Bedfordshire, Walden in Essex, and Chesterton, recorded in 1521/2.[49]

Even at a large and important regional fair like Stourbridge, ale sellers, brewers and other small food retailers were present. Surviving records of the university's leet courts from the 1390s and early 1400s show that large numbers of brewers and petty traders were fined at the autumn court for selling ale and victuals within Barnwell Ward, explicitly at Stourbridge Fair.[50] Ale booths, often held by ale wives, were listed in the treasurers' accounts during the 1520s. Rents were between 3s and 4s, far greater than the charges made for pedlars. Holders of ale booths included Robert Bayseley of Bury, John Coleson of Bury, and possibly Agnes Turnour of Depden, assessed on goods of 5 marks, £2, and £5 respectively in the lay subsidy of 1524.[51] However, these ale sellers and their booths disappeared from the accounts during the late 1520s, and although the occasional ale booth is listed thereafter, the retailing of ale appears to have become a more minor part of the fair. This change may reflect the declining role of women in brewing and selling ale, the growth of larger-scale production, and an increasing demand for beer.[52] Kitchens gave additional refreshments and were provided in at least seven different booths. Alewives also attended Reach Fair in the fourteenth and fifteenth centuries. Even St Radegund's Priory took on an extra cook at the time of their fair.[53]

The Cambridge borough treasurers also collected rents from 'Hadleigh men' at Stourbridge Fair, who came from the vicinity around that Suffolk town: men from Bury,

---

45 *Tudor economic documents*, ed. R.H. Tawney and E. Power, 3 vols. (London, 1924), iii, pp. 108–9.
46 N.F. Hulbert, 'A survey of Somerset fairs', *Proceedings of the Somersetshire Archaeological and Natural History Soc.*, 82 (1936), 142; *CBD*, p. xliii.
47 CCTA, ii, fol. 50v.
48 M. Spufford, *The great reclothing of rural England: petty chapmen and their wares in the seventeenth century* (London, 1984).
49 CCTA, i, fols. 59, 293v.
50 UA, C.U.R. 17, fols. 2, 3, 4, 6v, 7v, 10v.
51 CCTA, i, fols. 59, 79Av; *Suffolk in 1524*, ed. S.H.A. Hervey, Suffolk Green Books, X (Woodbridge, 1910), pp. 283, 352, 355.
52 Bennett, *Ale*, pp. 77–97.
53 CCA, Palmer/Barnard vol. 57, fol. 80v; *St Radegund*, p. 167; *VCH Cambs.*, x, p. 227.

Sudbury, Waldingfield and Monks Eleigh ('monkisylle') were recorded in 1521/2.[54] The Suffolk traders recorded in the treasurers' accounts for that year can be traced further using the 1522 muster survey for Babergh hundred and the 1524 lay subsidy. Many of the traders had occupations in the textile industry: John Colman of Cornard Magna was a weaver,[55] William Jacob of Sudbury, clothmaker,[56] Robert Glaswright of Waldingfield Magna, clothmaker,[57] Thomas Holton of Nayland, sherman,[58] and William Turnour of Hadleigh, weaver.[59] These traders also had a range of different incomes. William Aleyn of Hadleigh was assessed on wages of less than 40s per annum in the 1524 subsidy, William Turnour, weaver, of Hadleigh, assessed for £2 in goods, and Richard Braddeway and Walter Mannyng of Stowe, assessed for £40 and £50 in goods.[60] A flourishing cloth-making industry had developed in southern Suffolk at this time, and the presence of these Suffolk textile workers strongly suggests that these men used the fair to market their own cloth. Although rents from Hadleigh men continued to be received by the town treasurers, from the 1530s onwards a smaller number of larger rents were recorded. While this may merely reflect a change in recording practice, it could also reflect a change in the cloth trade, with a smaller number of wealthier traders visiting the fair.

Cloth producers from even more distant textile regions may have visited the fair. Adam Wolford and Patrick Bryket, both described as 'kendalmen' in 1523/4, were probably bringing cloth that had been manufactured in the Lake District, where another vigorous textile industry had developed at the close of the fifteenth century. 'Kendalmen' transported packs of cloth to Southampton in the 1490s and 1520s and returned with imported foodstuffs, dyes and canvas.[61]

The fifteenth-century ulnage accounts provide earlier evidence of cloth sales at Stourbridge and Ely fairs. Unfortunately, these accounts present many difficulties in their use: the Suffolk and Cambridgeshire returns become unreliable from 1473–4, with entries copied almost exactly from the previous year and rounded totals, although in the late 1460s there had been a determined attempt to improve efficiency.[62] Cloth sales in Cambridgeshire in the 1460s were very small, a mere fraction of those in

---

54   CCTA, i, fol. 59v.
55   *The military survey of 1522 for Babergh hundred*, ed. J. Pound, Suffolk Records Soc., XXVIII (Woodbridge, 1986), p. 72; 'of Sudbury' in treasurers' accounts, but Cornard Magna adjoins Sudbury.
56   Ibid., p. 24; 'Jacob of Sudbury' in treasurers' accounts; there was also a John Jacob of Sudbury: ibid., p. 22.
57   Ibid., p. 55; 'Roger Glassowyke of Waldyngfeld' in treasurers' accounts.
58   Ibid., p. 32; no place–name is given in the treasurers' accounts.
59   *Suffolk in 1524*, p. 154; another William Turnour of Hadleigh is assessed on wages: ibid., p. 156.
60   *Suffolk in 1524*, pp. 154, 156, 316.
61   CCTA, i, fol. 79A; Britnell, *Closing of the Middle Ages?*, p. 214; B.C. Jones, 'Westmorland packhorse men in Southampton', *Transactions of the Cumberland and Westmorland Antiquarian and Archaeological Soc.*, new ser., 59 (1959), 65–84.
62   E.M. Carus-Wilson, 'The aulnage accounts: a criticism', in E.M. Carus-Wilson, *Medieval merchant venturers* (London, 1954), pp. 279–91; Thornton, *Clare*, pp. 144–54; Britnell, *Colchester*, pp. 78–81, 187–9. Ulnage was a subsidy on the sale of cloth.

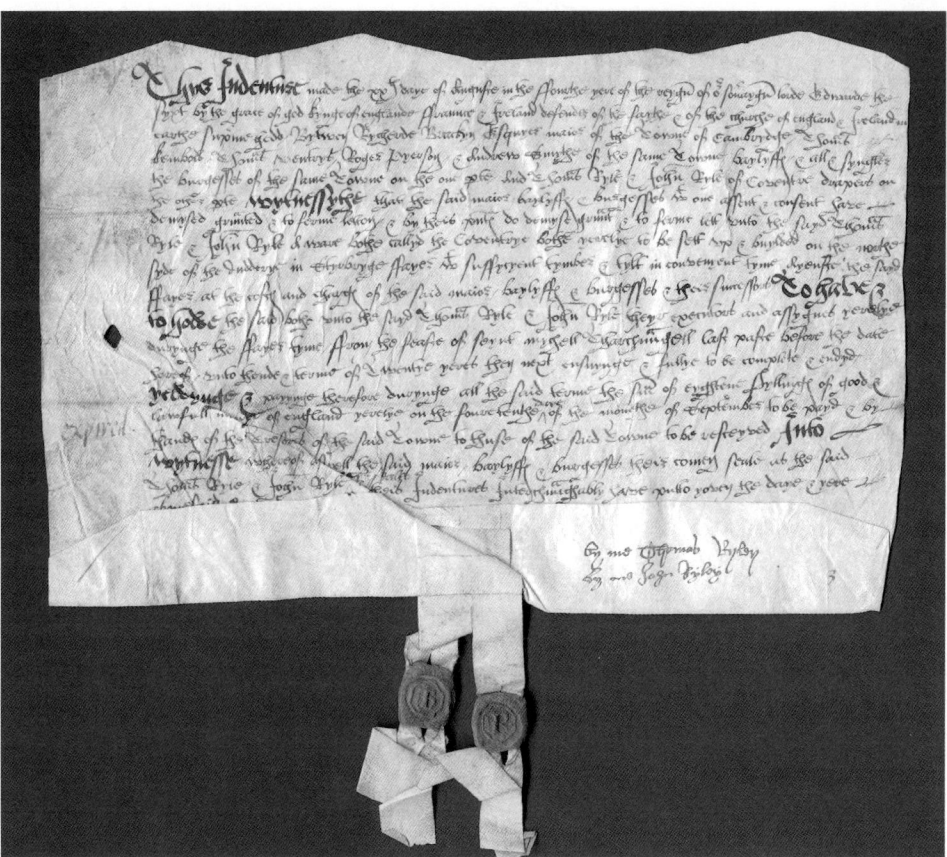

Figure 5.5 Indenture for the lease of a booth at Stourbridge Fair, 20 August 1550. The mayor and bailiffs of Cambridge lease the Coventry booth on the north side of the Duddery to Thomas and John Ryley of Coventry, drapers, for 20 years at a rent of 18s per year (CCA, III/10A, part 1: by permission of the County Record Office, Cambridge)

Suffolk and Essex,[63] and concentrated in the towns of Cambridge and Ely and at Stourbridge and Ely fairs. Subsidy was paid on 27 cloths and 4 kerseys at Stourbridge Fair in 1465–6, 15 cloths in 1469/70, and 40 in 1473/4.[64] These totals, covering a fair that lasted perhaps four weeks of the year, were of similar size to, or greater than, the total subsidies from the town of Cambridge, which were generally collected throughout the year. More significantly, the fairs attracted traders from a greater area. Although sales in Cambridge occasionally listed clothmakers from outside the town, like the men from Wisbech and Lynn who sold cloth there in 1465–6, most of the sales were by the townspeople. In contrast, traders from Stratford, Higham, and Nayland in Suffolk were assessed at Ely Fair in 146–5, while men from London and

---

63   Heaton, *Woollen and worsted industries*, pp. 85–6.
64   TNA: PRO E 101/338/9, E 101/343/7, E 101/343/9.

Leicester came to Stourbridge Fair in 1464–5 and 1466.[65] Earlier ulnage accounts from the 1390s also record cloth sales at Stourbridge and Ely fairs, but these comprised only a small part of the total sales during the year.[66]

Stourbridge Fair also attracted traders from Ipswich, Needham Market and Stowmarket. Several men from these towns held booths in the chapel ground in 1521/2, and their taxable wealth in 1524 varied from £2 to £50 in goods.[67] William Raynbald held a fish booth in the Water Fair during the 1540s and 1550s. Assessed at £60 in a lay subsidy of the 1540s, Raynbald was an Ipswich merchant who had offered substantial wages for a voyage to Iceland which attracted complaints from the bailiffs of Southwold. Henry Tooley of Ipswich, merchant adventurer, frequently came to Stourbridge Fair, although his usual area of internal trade extended only as far west from his home port as to Bury St Edmunds and Thetford.[68]

Merchants from larger and more distant towns also came to Stourbridge Fair. A couple of Coventry merchants paid rent for two booths owned by the corporation, known as the Woolfleece and Horseloaf. These drapers and mercers were often prominent office holders in the civic government there. In 1521/2 Masters Trussell and Banwell of Coventry held these booths: Thomas Trussell was warden of Coventry Corporation in 1520, sheriff in 1524, and bailiff in 1525; Thomas Banwell was draper and mayor in 1524, and William Banwell a Coventry mercer.[69] Grafton Owellyng and John Sanders of Coventry held two booths in the Duddery in 1527/8. Christopher Waren and Thomas Ryley, drapers, who rose through the council ranks to become mayors of Coventry in 1542 and 1555, held the two Duddery booths in the 1530s and 1540s.[70] Julian Nethermyll, draper, one of the richest men in Coventry in 1524, was trading at the fair in 1529.[71]

London merchants were also important traders at the fair. As early as 1403, Cambridge Corporation ordained that any bailiff or burgess leasing or lending the place called the tollbooth in Stourbridge Fair to any citizen of London was to be heavily fined and to lose his freedom.[72] Several of the leading London merchant companies had representatives in the fair. Richard Hunt, mercer, was riding to Stourbridge Fair when he came to blows with Edward Grene in 1522; Hunt was one of three mercers holding six standings in the fair in Cheapside in 1523/4.[73] Mr Warner, holding an 8s booth in

---

65 E 101/338/9, E 101/343/1, E 101/343/7.
66 E 101/338/3.
67 CCTA, i, fol. 60; *Suffolk in 1524*, pp. 121, 316, 358.
68 CCA, III/10A, part 1; J. Webb, *Great Tooley of Ipswich: portrait of an early Tudor merchant*, Suffolk Records Soc., V (1962), pp. 7, 77–8, 122, 142, map facing p. 93.
69 CCTA, i, fol. 58v; *The Coventry Leet Book*, ed. M. Dormer Harris, Early English Text Soc., 4 vols., CXXXIV, CXXXV, CXXXVIII, CXLVI (London, 1907–13), iii, pp. 601, 667, 686, 688, 690–1.
70 CCTA, i, fols. 124, 134v, 144, 216v, 227, 237, 251v, 293v; CCA, III/10A, part 1; *Coventry Leet Book*, iii, pp. 767, 811.
71 TNA: PRO C 1/660/33; Hoskins, 'Provincial towns', 6.
72 *Annals*, i, p. 149.
73 *Acts of the court of the Mercers' Company, 1453–1527*, ed. L. Lyell and F.D. Watney (Cambridge, 1936), pp. 547, 699; CCTA, i, fol. 79A.

1521/2, was possibly a mercer.[74] Mistress Bankes of London, silkwoman, held the farm of a little booth in Soper Lane in 1523/4, alongside mercers, grocers, and founders from the capital who also rented booths that year. Another London silkwoman had died whilst away at Stourbridge Fair in the late fifteenth century.[75] Chancery proceedings give further examples of these London traders. John Robinson, tailor of Westminster, rode with two hosiers of that town to Stourbridge in the early 1480s to gather cloth as they 'muste nedis occupye in thair saide occupations'. The wife of Thomas Barneby of London, haberdasher, brought caps, hats and other haberdashery wares to be sold in the fair, worth over £100 when seized for a debt. Richard Robynson, a London draper, claimed in the 1530s to have occupied a booth for 24 years selling embroidery products. Drapers, a mercer, linen draper, haberdasher, girdler, 'brocer' and barber surgeon, all from the capital, took leases of booths in the 1550s.[76]

By the 1540s and 1550s, the range of traders coming to the fair had grown even wider. Two men from Bristol paid for booths in Cheapside in 1552/3. Fines taken from traders at Stourbridge in 1550 and 1553 included men from neighbouring towns like Huntingdon, Bury, Bedford and Walden, as well as from Bristol, Stow-on-the-Wold and Stafford, showing that the fair was drawing traders from both the surrounding region and much further afield.[77] John Stablehill, 'devenshire manne' and 'an yryshe man' were renting treasurers' booths in the early 1550s.[78] Using court records from the last two decades of the sixteenth century, Siraut has shown that 40 per cent of sellers at Stourbridge Fair came from counties neighbouring Cambridge and 25 per cent from London and the south-east.[79]

The chief distributing crafts, the London mercers and grocers, used fairs extensively for their trade, but their companies often adopted a hostile attitude to major provincial fairs like Stourbridge. At times they felt strong enough to prohibit their members from trading at fairs, but on other occasions they feared losing trade by boycotting these events. The Grocers' Company levied fines on members selling at fairs in the early fifteenth century, but some grocers found it more profitable to continue trading.[80] The mercers forbade their members from attending fairs or markets outside London in 1376. This issue was raised several times by the fellowship during the late fifteenth century, as their rivals, the haberdashers, had become very successful through trading at fairs.[81] An ordinance of the common council of London made in 1487 forbade freemen from sending wares to any fair or

---

74 CCTA, i, fol. 59. My thanks to Dr Anne Sutton for this suggestion.
75 CCTA, i, fol. 79A; M.K. Dale, 'The London silkwomen of the fifteenth century', EcHR, 4 (1932–4), 327.
76 TNA: PRO C 1/61/350, C 1/471/12, C 1/708/32; CCA, III/10A, part 1.
77 CCTA, i, fol. 355; CCC, MS 106, pp. 103, 109–10, partly printed in Nichols, *History* (Appendix of Sturbridge Fair), pp. 31–2.
78 CCTA, i, fols. 324, 340.
79 Siraut, 'Cambridge', p. 114.
80 Nightingale, *Grocers' Company*, p. 439.
81 *Mercers' Company*, pp. xvi–xvii, 100, 116, 138–9, 158, 160, 219–20.

market in the realm for seven years, on pain of £100, but a month later the ordinance was suspended, and parliament subsequently annulled it.[82] Action by the London crafts continued however: in 1491 the mercers prepared to present a bill before parliament to reform 'the great abusion of fairs, strangers & other &c., used to the great hurt of this city'.[83] Cambridge Corporation attributed a fall in the rent of a group of booths from 60s to 20s in 1499/1500, to the withdrawal of London merchants from the fair, and for the same reason reported in 1500/1 that a large part of the farm of the chapel ground could not be collected.[84] It would appear that richer members of the merchant companies wished to maintain London prices and avoid being undercut by other traders, and wanted to pass on the transaction costs of acquiring goods to provincial merchants. They therefore encouraged provincial traders to come to London to buy their goods, rather than at the fairs.

The London companies also complained of the poor quality of goods sold at fairs and tried to obtain powers of search. As early as 1419, the city of London and the university of Cambridge appeared in a suit before the king's council, where both bodies claimed the custody of assize and assay of bread, wine and beer, and supervision of the measures and weights of London citizens coming to Stourbridge Fair.[85] In 1423, parliament was requested to allow the wardens of the embroiderers power of search in the fairs of Stourbridge, Ely, Oxford and Salisbury, where many embroiderers from the city and suburbs of London sold embroidery of insufficient quality. The wardens of the Horners' Company were given authority to search for defective wares in Stourbridge and Ely fairs in 1464, and to seize defective manufactures.[86] Two London pewterers disputed the university's right to examine pewter in Stourbridge Fair in 1550,[87] and in 1557 the university was ordered to prevent unlawful searches taking place at the fair, after a complaint had been made by the drapers, merchant tailors and clothworkers of London.[88] The London merchant companies may have thought that gaining powers of search over provincial fairs was a more acceptable alternative to banning their members from trading at these fairs.

The fairs at Ely also drew traders from a wide area, as records of the piepowder courts held in 1438, 1439 and 1441 show.[89] Traders came from the port of Lynn, the fenland villages of Haddenham, Aldreth, March, Sutton and Wicken, and Cambridge, Bury St Edmunds and London. The court heard pleas of debt for mercery goods, coverlets, a boat and a horse. Reflecting the opportunities for pastoral farming, particularly cattle rearing and dairying in the fenland, the fairs attracted cattle traders from significant distances. The butcher Richard Petrisburgh bought cows and steers

---

82 *Calendar of Letter-Books preserved among the archives of the Corporation of the City of London, 1275–1498*, ed. R.R. Sharpe, 11 vols. (London 1899–1912), vol.'L', pp. 240, 242.
83 *Mercers' Company*, pp. 219–20.
84 CCA, X/71/9, under *Recepte Forinsece*; X/71/10, under *Reparaciones*.
85 *Annals*, i, p. 163.
86 *Rotuli Parliamentorum*, Record Commission, 6 vols. (London, 1783), iv, p. 254, v, p. 567.
87 CCC, MS 106, pp. 105–10, printed in Nichols, *History* (Appendix of Sturbridge Fair), pp. 28–30.
88 UA, Collect.Admin.5, fols. 138, 140v; CCC, MS 106, p. 503.
89 CUL, EDR E1/1(3), E1/1(6).

through his agent at Ely in 1394, 67 miles distant from his home of Colchester. John Capell, farmer of Porter's Hall in Stebbing (Essex) bought 'northern steers' at the fairs of Woolpit (Suffolk) and Ely in the early 1480s. Thetford Priory sent representatives 20 miles to Ely Fair each year to buy basketry products, nails and expensive foodstuffs and spices.[90] Travel over a far greater distance appears to have been undertaken by Henry Gyll, servant of Lord Dacre of Gilsland, and residing at Cumrew in Cumberland, who sold 20 steers to John Girlinge of Stradbroke, Suffolk, on 7 September 1536, and agreed to collect most of the payment on 17 October at Ely Fair.[91]

Several fairs in the Cambridge region also served the fish trade. A statute of 1534 against forestalling and regrating of fish applied particularly to Stourbridge, St Ives and Ely fairs 'being the most notable faires within this Realme for provysions of fysshe'. This act was repealed in 1544 after merchants of London, Coventry and elsewhere had ceased to purchase fish at the coast and carry it to the fairs. Two fairs granted to King's Lynn in 1537 allegedly damaged the 'Provysion of Salt fyshe & Heryng' at Ely, Stourbridge and other fairs in Cambridgeshire and Huntingdonshire, leading the royal grant to be revoked in 1542. When the possibility of reviving the fair at Lynn arose again in 1556, Cambridge Corporation sent a letter of objection to the bishop of Ely.[92]

The limited information available for other Cambridgeshire fairs suggests that they attracted tradesmen from less extensive areas. In the July leet courts in 1391 and 1395, sellers of ale from nine Cambridgeshire villages and from Lynn were amerced at Barnwell – they had probably come to Midsummer Fair, as so many amercements were not made in the ward at other times of the year.[93] Proceedings of the court of Reach Fair in 1508 list merchants from Bury St Edmunds and Bottisham, and husbandmen from Fordham, Steeple Bumpstead and Wethersfield, Essex.[94] The smallest village fairs seem to have been very minor occasions and may have attracted only local residents. John Bruett of Ickleton listed trestles and pulleys belonging to Mary Magdalene Fair, Ickleton, among the agricultural tools left in his will of 1541.[95] The trading hinterlands of these smaller fairs were not much larger than those of the weekly markets held in small towns and villages.

Consumers

Among the most prominent consumers at larger fairs were noble, ecclesiastical and collegiate households, of varying size and wealth, stocking up with bulk purchases of non-perishable goods and foodstuffs. The household book of the earl of Northumberland in 1512 recommended buying supplies for the house for the whole year at fairs, such as wine, wax, beef, mutton, wheat and malt. Similarly in the early

---

90   Britnell, *Closing of the Middle Ages?*, p. 221; *Thetford Priory*, i, p. 44.
91   TNA: PRO C 1/804/31.
92   25 Hen. VIII, c. 4; 33 Henry VIII, c. 34; 35 Henry VIII, c. 7: *SR*, iii, pp. 440–1, 873, 964; CCA, Palmer/Barnard vol. 57, fol. 93v.
93   UA, C.U.R. 17, fols. 2v, 4v.
94   CCA, X/6.
95   A.R. Goddard, 'Ickleton church and priory', *PCAS*, 11 (1903–6), 192.

sixteenth century, the prior of Royston used Stourbridge Fair, 'for the provision & store of his said house for all the whole year following'.[96] Many of the Cambridge colleges made regular purchases at local fairs. King's Hall, for example, between 1521 and 1544, annually spent between 5s 6d and 56s 6d at Midsummer Fair, Cambridge, and between £7 6s 0d and £22 7s 0d at Stourbridge Fair.[97] These figures were roughly similar to the amount spent on fish and spices at other times during the year. The main items purchased at the fairs by King's Hall and other Cambridge colleges, large and small, were fish, spices, cloth, and hardware products.

Most of the fish sold in the fairs of Cambridge and its region was preserved fish. Available relatively cheaply, institutions could purchase supplies in bulk to last most of the year. King's Hall regularly purchased about one hundred each of cod, stockfish, and ling, and a barrel of salmon, and maybe also herring, lob, sturgeon, cat fish, and salted eels at Stourbridge.[98] The colleges of Trinity, King's, Queens', and Peterhouse, St Radegund's Priory, Thetford Priory, and the estate officials of the Crowland Abbey manors of Oakington, Cottenham and Dry Drayton also obtained fish at the fair.[99] Ely Fair was another major fish market, visited occasionally by Cambridge colleges like King's College and King's Hall.[100]

Despite the difficulties of preservation, some fresh fish and shellfish were also sold at Stourbridge Fair. Nichols, writing in the late eighteenth century, described the demand for Colchester oysters and white herrings at the fair, which had just come into season at the time the fair was held.[101] In 1534 and 1548 the townspeople of Cambridge complained of the charges put on carts laden with oysters entering the fair.[102]

Spices and other imported foodstuffs could be obtained in Stourbridge Fair and were purchased by the largest colleges and the aristocracy. King's Hall bought raisins, prunes, almonds, pepper, dates, cloves, mace, sugar, saffron and bay salt.[103] Peterborough Abbey purchased a similar range of spices at the fair in the early sixteenth century.[104] Most of these spices would have been imported from abroad, and entered via East Anglian ports, or through London merchants.

Cloth was another major item of expenditure at Stourbridge Fair for King's Hall, which often spent over £3 on the servants' liveries there.[105] The almoner and abbot's receiver of Peterborough Abbey, and members of Thetford Priory obtained various

---

96 TNA: PRO C 1/438/33; McCutcheon, *Yorkshire fairs and markets*, p. 130.
97 KH a/c, xxii–xxvi.
98 KH a/c, xxiv, fols. 67v, 97, 156, xxv, fols. 34, 75, 111v.
99 TCSB a/c, fols. 107, 189v, 220v; KCMB, ii, fol. 131, iv, fol. 20, xii, 1535/6, 1536/7, 1541/2 a/cs; QC, Magnum Journale, ii, fols. 26v, 53; Peterhouse Computus rolls, 1458/9 a/c; *St. Radegund*, p. 151; *Thetford*, i–ii, *passim*; CUL, QC10, views of accounts, 4 & 7 Hen VIII.
100 KCMB, ii, fol. 68, vii, fol. 23, xii, 1541/2 a/c; KH a/c, xxvi, fol. 151.
101 Nichols, *History*, p. 82.
102 UA, Collect.Admin.5, fols. 8v, 26v.
103 KH a/c, xxiii, fol. 194v; xxiv, fol. 97; xxvi, fol. 151.
104 *Account rolls of the Obedientiaries of Peterborough*, ed. J. Greatrex, Northamptonshire Record Soc., XXXIII (Northampton, 1984), pp. 180, 194.
105 KH a/c, xxiii, fol. 194v, xxiv, fol. 97, xxvi, fol. 151.

types of cloth at the fair.[106] Fines taken at the fair in the 1550s reveal a wide range of cloth and upholstery products, including kerseys, broad cloths, felts, caps, feather beds and mattresses.[107] The presence of drapers, hosiers, embroiderers and other merchants from important marketing centres for textiles like London and Coventry, as well as local cloth producers from Suffolk, provided a wide range of textiles.

A large number of hardware products were sold at Stourbridge and other fairs. Thetford Priory regularly bought basketry products, probably made in the local fenland, at Ely Fair, together with large quantities of nails of varying size and price, and kitchen and dining utensils. At Stourbridge Fair, the priory bought oil, tar, and on one occasion spent over £20 on lead and 15s 2d on its carriage.[108] King's Hall bought spades, shovels, and timber at Stourbridge and Midsummer fairs, and Trinity College later obtained nails and timber at these two fairs.[109] The churchwardens of Holy Trinity and Cambridge Corporation purchased timber at Midsummer Fair.[110] Around 1530, the following items of merchandise were also described as being sold at Stourbridge Fair:

> pewter brass hair girthwebbe[111] saddles bowgettes[112] males[113] silks furs beds and all other upholstery wares and all grocery wares whatsoever it be fuschions[114] worsteds sayes[115] Chaumblettes honey soap wax and all other wares.[116]

Clearly the traders who brought heavy, bulky products were confident that they would find customers at the fair.

Stourbridge Fair also offered a range of other specialist goods and services. Pewterers bought old or damaged pewter to reuse in producing new wares. St Radegund's exchanged vessels at the fairs in 1450/1 and King's Hall had vessels garnished or exchanged at the fair.[117] Goldsmiths are listed in the fines collected in 1550 and 1553, and York goldsmiths are known to have travelled to the fair.[118] Stourbridge Fair was also used to sell ornament and plate at the Reformation. In 1540, the churchwardens of Great St Mary's, Cambridge, sold a collar of gold and a relic of

---

106 *Book of William Morton, Almoner of Peterborough Monastery 1448–1467*, ed. P.I. King, Northamptonshire Record Soc. XVI (Northampton, 1954), pp. 124, 167; *Obedientiaries of Peterborough*, pp. 183, 197; *Thetford*, ii, pp. 534, 686, 705, 723.
107 CCC, MS 106, pp. 103, 109.
108 *Thetford*, i, pp. 260, 284–5, 297, 309, 319–20, ii, pp. 550, 568, 598, 618, 631.
109 KH a/c, xxiii, fols. 23, 161v, xxiv, fols. 28v, 67v, 96v; TCSB a/c, fols. 5, 102v, 147, 228v; TCJB a/c, fols. 148, 173v, 229.
110 CCA, P22/5/1, fol. 17v; CCA, X/71/3, X/71/5.
111 girthweb – woven material of which girths are made: *OED*, vi, p. 532.
112 bouget – (form of budget) a pouch, bag, wallet, usually of leather: *OED*, ii, p. 620.
113 mail – a bag, pack or wallet, a travelling bag: *OED*, ix, p. 212.
114 fustian – coarse cloth of cotton and flax: *OED*, vi, p. 292.
115 say – a cloth of fine textile resembling serge: *OED*, xiv, p. 542.
116 CCA, X/66, m. 5.
117 *St Radegund*, p. 167; KH a/c, xxiv, fols. 28v, 67v, xxvi, fol. 72v; J. Hatcher and T.C. Barker, *A history of British pewter* (London, 1974), pp. 181, 229, 239.
118 CCC, MS 106, pp. 103, 109; D.M. Palliser, *Tudor York* (Oxford, 1979), p. 182.

St Nicholas at the fair, and the fellows of Clare Hall, anticipating the dissolution of their institution, sold the college plate there in 1549.[119] The university and religious houses in particular created a demand for specialised products. Thetford Priory and Peterborough Abbey bought wax, paper and parchment at Stourbridge Fair.[120] The fair became a well-known market for booksellers in the later sixteenth century, but Joyce Pykegrome of London, bookseller, had been selling law titles there in the 1490s.[121] Fairs at university towns were probably important markets for books from an early date. One of the books in the stock of the Cambridge stationer Garrett Godfrey had been bought at a fair; the Oxford bookseller John Dorne sold books in the fairs of his university town in 1520.[122]

Some households which lay between 15 and 50 miles from Cambridge had little contact with the town or its immediate hinterland apart from attending Stourbridge Fair. Thetford Priory held manors in Cambridgeshire at Dullingham and Wood Ditton, provided a corrody to a former master of Corpus Christi College,[123] and occasionally made payments to poor scholars at Cambridge. But although agents from the priory regularly attended Stourbridge Fair, they rarely came to Cambridge on any other occasion.[124] Similarly at Peterborough Abbey, the abbot's receiver carried sweet wine from Cambridge on one occasion, and obtained lime from Reach and wheat from Burwell, but otherwise goods were not usually bought in Cambridge or its local region except at Stourbridge Fair.[125] Servants of the prior of Dunmow in Essex and Sir Thomas Vaux, Lord of Harrowden in Northamptonshire, also ventured beyond their usual shopping areas to make purchases at Stourbridge Fair in the 1530s.[126]

More distant households, which had no contact with Cambridge at other times of the year, also visited Stourbridge Fair. In the 1420s and 1430s, members came from the household of Sir William Mountford of Kingshurst, Warwickshire, and a servant from Greenwich, from the household of Thomas of Lancaster, Duke of Clarence. The Willoughby family of Wollaton Hall, Nottinghamshire, travelled to Stourbridge in the 1520s and 1540s for fish, spices and cloth.[127] Burcester Priory, Oxfordshire, purchased

---

119 *Churchwardens' accounts of St Mary the Great*, ed. J.E. Foster, CASOS, XXXV (Cambridge, 1905), p. 94; *Calendar of State Papers, Domestic Series, of the reign of Edward VI, 1547–1553*, ed. C.S. Knighton (London, 1992), no. 223, p. 101.

120 *Thetford*, ii, pp. 464, 481, 534, 582, 598, 618, 647, 686; *Obedientiaries of Peterborough*, pp. 178, 183, 194.

121 TNA: PRO C 1/218/2; D. McKitterick, *A history of Cambridge University Press*, i: *printing and the book trade in Cambridge 1534–1698* (Cambridge, 1992), pp. 14–17.

122 *Garrett Godfrey's accounts c.1527–33*, ed. E. Leedham-Green, D.E. Rhodes and F.H. Stubbings, Cambridge Bibliographical Soc. monograph, XII (Cambridge, 1992), p. 42; *VCH Oxfordshire*, iv, p. 311.

123 A corrody was a provision or allowance for maintenance paid annually by a religious house: *OED*, iii, p. 970.

124 *Thetford*, i, pp. 29–30, 274, ii, pp. 652, 710, 722, 737.

125 *Obedientiaries of Peterborough*, pp. 147, 179, 184.

126 *LP*, viii, no. 865, pp. 338–9, ix, no. 697, p. 234.

127 *Household accounts from medieval England*, ed. C.M. Woolgar, 2 parts, BARSEH, new ser., XVII–XVIII (Oxford, 1992–3), part 2, pp. 445, 449, 659, 667; *Report on the manuscripts of Lord Middleton preserved at Wollaton Hall, Nottinghamshire*, ed. W.H. Stevenson, Historical Manuscripts Commission (London, 1911), pp. 315–16, 362, 368, 372, 387, 403–4.

horse collars, silk, deal boards, and iron there in 1425, and in the first and second decades of the sixteenth century Oseney Abbey, Oxford, bought salted fish, herring, salmon, figs, raisins, oil, soap, wax and other goods, and paid six carters to go to the fair.[128]

While the Cambridge colleges rarely visited fairs outside Cambridge, as those in the town must evidently have satisfied the majority of their needs, for more distant households, Stourbridge was one of a number of fairs used. Thetford Priory relied on various local fairs in Norfolk and Suffolk within a 30-mile radius of the priory, but Stourbridge Fair was the third most regularly visited, after those at Ely and Bromehill, near Brandon, in Suffolk: the priory went to Stourbridge 21 times in the 41 years of accounts between 1498 and 1539.[129] In the mid-fifteenth century accounts of William Morton, almoner of Peterborough Abbey, purchases were made three times from fairs at Stourbridge, Ely and Peterborough Bridge, five times from Stamford Fair, and once from Deeping Fair, Lincolnshire.[130] The abbot's receiver of Peterborough Abbey bought cows and sheep at Coventry and Oundle fairs, keys at Peterborough and Stamford fairs, and fish and spices at Ely and Stourbridge fairs, during 1504/5 and 1505/6.[131] The Willoughby family visited a wide range of fairs in the Midlands, and also fairs in Kent and Yorkshire, as well as Stourbridge Fair.[132] Great households purchased luxury goods, bulk foodstuffs, and hardware products from fairs in the same way as they did from London. By purchasing in bulk and direct from leading merchants they could obtain goods at wholesale, rather than retail, prices.[133]

The smaller Cambridgeshire fairs appear only in the accounts of local households, and infrequently even in these. Some were used to buy livestock. Thetford Priory went to both Reach and Wisbech fairs twice between 1498 and 1540, to purchase a few horses or oxen. King's College occasionally visited St Thomas' Fair at Royston and Reach Fair for livestock and salt.[134] St John's Hospital in Cambridge once bought oxen and lambs at Cold Fair at Newport, Essex.[135] Commodities traded at Reach Fair in 1508 included a horse, a pair of shoes, 10½ quarters of barley, and various lengths of woollen cloth, and these were bought by local merchants, husbandmen, and labourers, rather than large institutions.[136] Smaller fairs probably relied, like so many lesser market towns and rural markets, on transactions of food, clothing, tools and livestock between small-scale producers and consumers for the bulk of their trade.[137]

---

128 *Annals*, i, p. 173; *Cartulary of Oseney Abbey*, vi, ed. H.E. Salter, Oxford Historical Soc., CI (Oxford, 1936), pp. 211, 219, 283.
129 *Thetford*, i, pp. 43–7.
130 *Book of William Morton*, pp. 34–167, *passim*.
131 *Obedientiaries of Peterborough*, pp. 172–200.
132 *Wollaton Hall*, pp. 329–93, *passim*.
133 C. Dyer, 'The consumer and the market in the later middle ages', *EcHR*, 2nd ser., 42 (1989), 308–10.
134 *Thetford*, ii, pp. 424, 432, 620, 700; KCMB, v, fol. 33, vi, fols. 21, 70.
135 SJC, D106.2, fols. 5–6.
136 CCA, X/6.
137 Britnell, 'Markets', 213–18.

So much of the evidence for medieval patterns of consumption comes from the accounts of aristocratic and institutional households that it is difficult to tell to what extent and for what purpose other groups in society visited fairs. One would assume that the peasantry purchased modest quantities and cheaper versions of the fish, spices, cloth, and hardware products available. Being only annual events, though, fairs were a very intermittent source of supply, unsuitable for consumers who wished to buy products in small and regular quantities, who were more likely to rely on the weekly market.

On the other hand, individual consumers of more substance must have been attracted by the range of imported and luxury goods available at the larger fairs, and an unusual source strongly suggests that scholars made purchases at fairs like Stourbridge. Remarkably, the fame of this fair was sufficiently well-known to be the subject of a schoolboy's exercise in a rival university town. A school book of English prose passages with model Latin translations, probably composed by a teacher of grammar at Magdalen School, Oxford, at the end of the fifteenth century, covers everyday activities of schoolboys in the town. One passage speaks specifically of Stourbridge Fair:

> Yff all thynge hade fortunede after my mynde I hade
> ben this day at stirbrige faire wher, as men say, a man may
> bye better chepe than enywher ellys.[138]

Other references to fairs in the schoolbook probably refer to St Giles' Fair in Oxford, but could equally apply to Stourbridge Fair. The presence of Londoners, and their deceptively attractive goods were subjects for translation:

> He that hath money enough to cast away lete hym
> pike hymselfe[139] to the faire and make a bargyn with the
> londyners, and I doubte not but er he depart thei shall
> make hym as clen from it as an ape fro tailys, for thei study
> nothyng in the worlde ellys but for to deceyve menn with
> fair spech.
>
> Many scholars of this universite wolde spende wast-
> fully all their fathers goodes in japys and trifulles this
> faire yf they myght have it at their liberte. for thies lon-
> dyners be so craftye and so wyly in dressynge their gere so
> gloriusly that they may deceyve us scholars lyghtly.[140]

Other passages mention a student who received a pen case and ink horn at the last fair from his uncle. Another schoolboy hoped that his mother and father would come when the next fair was to be held. A schoolboy saw many of his acquaintances at the

---

138 *A fifteenth century school book from a manuscript in the British Museum (MS Arundel 249)*, ed. W. Nelson (Oxford, 1956), p. 90.

139 pike hymselfe: be off.

140 Ibid., p. 54.

fair brightly apparelled in gold chains, brooches with gold, pearls and precious stones, probably bought from traders there.[141]

The other major role of larger fairs like Stourbridge was in wholesale transactions. Major merchants, and in particular Londoners, used fairs to sell goods to local tradesmen, who then resold retail in towns and markets in the locality. Pewter was distributed in this way, as were expensive spices, mercery goods, and cloth.[142] Nightingale has suggested that during the contraction of trade in the mid-fifteenth century, chapmen turned from provincial urban suppliers to London wholesalers in the capital and at fairs, with whom they could barter locally produced cloth for raw materials and luxury goods imported through London.[143] The evidence from Stourbridge Fair cannot give a date to this transition, but it would seem likely that a variety of urban merchants, including men from London, Coventry and elsewhere, obtained locally produced goods, particularly cloth, at Stourbridge, from the 'clothiers booths', 'packs' of 'broad cloths' and 'Hadleigh men' listed in the borough treasurers' accounts.

Subsequent references suggest that the wholesale cloth trade at Stourbridge Fair increasingly drew merchants from major cloth-producing regions in England. Julian Nethermyll of Coventry, draper, sold to William Richardson of Wakefield, draper, various cloth, including violet, muster and tawny colour and 'Kentishe Risett', for a total of £11 8s 2d in 1529. Matthew Hartley of York, draper, bought cloth worth over £27 from Andrew Yardlay of London, merchant tailor, at the fair, and tied William Harper of York, draper, into the transaction. Two London grocers were arrested for receiving broad cloths worth over £20, which were unstamped, from a London clothworker at the fair.[144] Matthew Goodwyn of Ipswich, who held a Hadleigh booth in the fair for at least twelve years, and Richard Cary of Bristol, fined at the fair, were also recorded at the main London cloth market at Blackwell Hall in 1561–2.[145]

Saffron was another commodity that was traded at fairs in the region. As in the cloth trade, fairs seem to have offered an opportunity for local men to buy and sell from London merchants.[146] In the mid-sixteenth century, the treasurers of Walden took forfeitures of saffron at the town's Ursula Fair, from traders which included a man from Walsingham and another from Suffolk.[147]

Visits to fairs also offered opportunities for conducting other transactions, like the settling of debts. John Smythe of Bristol collected £7 10s 0d for one pipe of wool oil at Stourbridge Fair in 1546, and gathered other debts at fairs in south-west England.[148] Some of Henry Tooley of Ipswich's debts matured at Stourbridge Fair, as did those of a

---

141 Ibid., pp. 14, 22, 90.
142 Hatcher and Barker, *Pewter*, p. 253.
143 Nightingale, *Grocers' Company*, p. 368.
144 TNA: PRO C 1/660/33, C 1/999/4, C 1/1094/40.
145 CCTA, i, fols. 171–398v, *passim*; CCC, MS 106, pp. 103, 109; G.D. Ramsay,'The distribution of the cloth industry in 1561–2', *English Historical Rev.*, 57 (1942), 364–5.
146 See above, Chapter 4, p.110.
147 Clark,'Saffron', 61.
148 *The ledger of John Smythe 1538–1550*, ed. J. Vanes, Bristol Record Soc. Publications, XXVIII (London, 1974), pp. 43, 56, 147, 164, 298.

London mercer in 1525, and the abbot of Peterborough's receiver collected rents from Lincolnshire, Northamptonshire, and Rutland, and payments for the sale of wood en route to, or at, the fair.[149] At least by the early modern period, the hiring of labour was conducted at fairs.[150] Fairs also provided news, recreation and entertainment. The Pastons awaited news from St Bartholomew's Fair, London, and bonfires were lit at Stourbridge Fair to celebrate the birth of Henry VIII's daughter, Princess Elizabeth.[151]

Regulation and ownership of the fairs

The university's control over marketing in Cambridge extended to the town's fairs. Stourbridge Fair in particular, given its size and the value of the goods being traded, required careful regulation. At the beginning of this fair, a proclamation or cry was given, detailing regulations by which all traders were to abide. Three versions, which vary slightly, have been attributed to the mid-sixteenth century,[152] while a fourth was produced while William Cecil, Lord Burghley was chancellor of the university (1559–98).[153] These proclamations included regulations for bakers, brewers, tiplers, gaugers, potters, vintners, fishmongers and butchers. No one was to regrate fish, wax, flax, osmund,[154] yarn, pitch, tar, cloth or any other merchandise under pain of forfeiture and imprisonment. The town corporation made regular complaints about the excessive fees taken by the university for searching and gauging goods brought to Stourbridge Fair.[155]

Every fair had the right to hold a court of pie-powder, which offered remedy for all contracts, trespasses, covenants, debts and other misdemeanours occurring within and during the fair. These were named after the dusty feet of the itinerant merchants who used the fairs. Cases were tried in front of a jury of traders on the spot, before the parties concerned had left for distant parts of the country. At Stourbridge Fair, the university held the chancellor's commissary court daily during the fair.[156]

Large gatherings also raised the possibility of disturbances, and the proclamation at Stourbridge Fair ordered everyone to 'make no fraye, crye, owtasse, scekinge, or ony other noys bythe which insurrectiones, coventicles, or gaderinge of people maybe made'. Strangers were to leave their weapons at inns, and innkeepers were required to warn their guests of this. All 'comyn women and mysbehavyng people' were

---

149 Webb, *Great Tooley*, p. 108; *Mercers' Company*, p. 699; *Obedientiaries of Peterborough*, pp. 172–7, 187–8, 191 – the phrase used in the Peterborough accounts is *erga Sturbridge*.

150 Chartres, 'Markets and fairs', pp. 16–17.

151 *PL*, i, p. 440, ii, p. 42; *Annals*, i, p. 360.

152 UA, Collect.Admin. 2, fols. 111v–117 is subdivided into 'The crye in Sturbrydge fayre', 'For the fissche fayre' and 'The Crye in the Towne' and ends 'God save ye King'. UA, Collect.Admin.9, pp. 342–7 has the same text, but without the subheadings and ending; printed in *Annals*, ii, pp. 18–21. A further copy is in CCC, MS 106, pp. 99–102.

153 UA, C.U.R. 67(1); *VCH Cambs.*, iii, p. 332.

154 A superior quality of iron imported from Baltic regions in small bars or rods: *OED*, x, p. 967.

155 UA, Collect.Admin.5, fols. 8v, 26v.

156 UA, Collect.Admin.2, fols. 115–115v.

ordered to keep away from the fair, and the proctors investigated and removed vagrants and prostitutes.[157] Other fairs in the region did not usually require these security measures. In 1395, though, probably mindful of the Peasants' Revolt 14 years before, Barnwell Priory feared great numbers of the commonalty and University of Cambridge going to Barnwell Fair, and the sheriffs were to proclaim that no unlawful assemblies were to be made.[158] Regular watches were organised by the proctors and townspeople while Stourbridge Fair was held: the colleges provided 20 watchmen with harnesses and weapons to serve the proctors in the night watch in 1550 and 1551.[159] The commissioners of the shire ordered the watches to be doubled and the university and town authorities to work together in 1555, noting the fair's national attraction: 'the resort and confluence ys from all parts of this realme'. Unfortunately, four years later, the two groups of watches came to blows at the fair.[160]

Cambridge Corporation strove to confirm and extend its ownership over the town's fairs in this period. Midsummer Fair had been granted to the prior and convent of Barnwell, but the borough corporation gradually acquired the rights to this fair, obtaining leases from the priory in 1496 and 1498, and tenure in perpetuity in 1506.[161] At Stourbridge Fair, the corporation obtained the land surrounding the former chapel of the leper hospital and the building itself, through agreements made in 1497 and 1544.[162]

The divided control at Stourbridge Fair, with the borough corporation controlling the rights to the fair but the university regulating marketing, inevitably caused disputes. It was not until 1589 that the position was clarified, through issuing new charters to the two authorities. The inspection and search of all wares except bread, wine, ale and victuals became the responsibility of both the mayor and vice-chancellor, who were to take turns at presiding at the fair's court and to divide the fines taken. Even then, the dissatisfied townsmen accused the mayor of betraying their interests.[163] But while the university generally fought to preserve its privileges in Stourbridge Fair, it did suggest offering these privileges for sale to the town in 1548 and 1558, although these proposals were never carried out.[164]

Stourbridge Fair was a valuable source of income for Cambridge Corporation, and the importance that the borough attached to their rights in the fair was highlighted when these rights were temporarily forfeited. In 1539 the king's attorney general challenged the town corporation in the court of the King's Bench to show by what warrant they claimed the right to hold fairs at Barnwell and Stourbridge and a court of pie-powder. As the corporation could not produce a title, the king seized the liberties, although in practice the town continued to draw income from the fair.[165] The

---

157 UA, Collect.Admin.2, fol. 112; *Grace Book B*, ii, p. 147.
158 *CCR, 1392–6*, pp. 426–7.
159 CCC, MS 106, pp. 322–3: printed in *Annals*, ii, p. 48.
160 *Annals*, ii, pp. 98–99, 154–7.
161 *Annals*, i, pp. 246, 249, 279.
162 *Annals*, i, pp. 248, 416; *LP*, xix (2), no. 261, p. 134.
163 *Charters*, pp. xxxi, 97–117, summarised in *VCH Cambs.*, iii, p. 93, n. 97.
164 *Annals*, ii, pp. 13, 143.
165 *Annals*, i, p. 393.

university may have prompted this action by stating in 1534 that the mayor and bailiffs had exacted over £500 a year in profits from the fair, 'Contrary to the kinges lawe prerogatyve and advantage as may more plenily appere by due and diligent examinacion of the townes charters grauntes and liberties'.[166] A charter was prepared for the town corporation at the huge cost of 1,000 marks, and it was agreed that the town should pay one half of the charge and the owners of booths the other half. This charter granted a pardon to the corporation and permitted them to continue holding the fair, but the document never apparently bore the great seal.[167] The matter was not settled until 1589, when a new charter stated that the corporation had held the fair from time immemorial.[168]

Conclusion

The charter of 1589 described Stourbridge Fair as 'by far the largest and most famous fair in all England' and its success was attributed to 'the laudable industry of the mayor, bailiffs and burgesses ... the convenience of the place itself, the neighbourhood of the university, and the favourableness of the time helping'.[169] This charter tried to settle long-running disputes between the town and university over the jurisdiction of trading offences in the fair, and so it was perhaps inevitable that both parties were congratulated. However, the factors mentioned in the charter can offer suggestions as to why Stourbridge Fair attracted consumers and traders from many parts of the country.

An important element in the success of any fair or market was its accessibility to customers by road or river. Cambridge stood at the intersection of a number of roads from London, the Midlands and East Anglia. In the 1430s, Sir William Mountford and John de Vere sent their 'chariots', vehicles kept for routine household journeys, to transport their purchases back from Stourbridge Fair.[170] Stourbridge fairground lay alongside the Cam, so was easily reached by water too. In 1550, Cambridge Corporation rebuilt the bridge near the fairground in stone, while further repairs were undertaken in 1553. A ferry provided access from Chesterton, and by the middle of the sixteenth century it made more than four-fifths of its yearly profits during the time of the fair.[171] Thetford Priory, Peterborough Abbey, King's Hall and Trinity College used boats to transport their purchases from Stourbridge and Ely fairs.[172] The increase in river traffic generated by the fair was discernible in the water bailiff's accounts at King's Lynn. The two towns made agreements regarding the fees for mooring boats at the fairground in 1518 and 1551. Wharves in the neighbouring villages of Fen Ditton

---

166 UA, Collect.Admin.5, fol. 11.
167 CCA, Palmer/Barnard vol. 57, fols. 66v–67, 82v; *LP*, xiv, no. 1188, p. 529; Nichols, *History* (Appendix of Sturbridge Fair), pp. 5–11.
168 *Charters*, p. xxxi.
169 *Charters*, p. 97.
170 Lobel, 'Cambridge', p. 1; *Household accounts*, part 2, pp. 449, 529; Dyer, 'Consumer', 310.
171 CCA, Palmer/Barnard vol. 57, fols. 39v, 64; *Annals*, ii, p. 47; *VCH Cambs.*, ix, p. 10.
172 *Thetford*, i, p. 93, ii, pp. 464, 534, 647, 686, 723, 738, 747; *Book of William Morton*, p. 125; KH a/c, xxv, fol. 75; TCSB a/c, fols. 142v, 189v, 220v; TCJB a/c, fols. 174v, 455v.

and Horningsea also provided landing stages for goods sold at the fair.[173] The fairs at Midsummer Common, Reach and Ely were also accessible by both road and river.

The university and colleges purchased large quantities of foodstuffs, in the manner of aristocratic households, as well as supplies of wax, parchment, paper and books. Stourbridge Fair was held in late August and September, just after harvest when money was plentiful, but before the onset of more difficult weather. For other fairs with a major trade in livestock, cattle could be supplied to drovers and graziers for fattening before slaughter. In fact, September was the most popular month among fairs chartered in England and Wales between 1227 and 1326.[174]

Although fairs could be held in country locations, most fairs in Cambridge's region, as elsewhere in England, were associated with towns. Allix claimed that 'the fair is a supplementary town, a parasite in a certain sense' and that fairs were of little benefit to towns, with which they had 'only superficial relations'.[175] Evidence from the Cambridge region does not support these claims. Fairs that continued to operate in the fifteenth and sixteenth centuries tended to be located in urban centres. Stourbridge Fair reflected the specialist occupations and trading contacts of Cambridge, with the presence at the fair of academic trades and links with Lynn and London. The fair also served as a cloth market, a trade which does not appear to have been significant in the town at other times of the year. One might assume that the attendance of so many merchants from other towns at Stourbridge Fair would be damaging to Cambridge traders. No protest, however, is recorded like that found at Bristol, when in 1542 the citizens claimed that due to the fair in the city's suburb of Redcliffe they were unable to dispose of wares and the presence of London and foreign cappers damaged their own industry.[176] Unlike the fair at Redcliffe, created in 1529, that at Stourbridge had been established for well over three centuries. Furthermore, many townspeople had a vested interest in Stourbridge Fair through the possession of booths, which also provided the town corporation with valuable income.

Stourbridge Fair had surpassed other local fairs by the sixteenth century because, like many of the expanding fairs of late medieval Europe highlighted by Epstein, its trade came from a variety of different regions. As it was put by Cambridge Corporation c.1530, Stourbridge Fair was:

> not onely the veray locke and keye of the saide Towne of Cambridge ... butt also a great and singuler Realeeff Succour and comforte aswell to all the inhabitants of the hole cuntreth thre as of diuerce and many other cuntres within this Realme to the same adjoynyng.[177]

The fair drew upon two particularly dynamic areas of the later medieval English economy – the textile trade and London. Cloth dealers from manufacturing and marketing centres like Coventry and Suffolk provided Stourbridge Fair with a wide range of textiles to be sold retail and wholesale, while profits gained from cloth sales

---

173 TNA: PRO C 1/316/65; CCA, X/42, X/50; Williams, *Maritime trade*, p. 56; *VCH Cambs.*, x, p. 118.
174 Farmer, 'Marketing', pp. 339, 341.
175 A. Allix, 'The geography of fairs: illustrated by Old-World examples', *Geographical Rev.*, 12 (1922), 543–4.
176 Salzman, *Trade*, pp. 158–60.
177 CCA, X/66, m. 5.

could also be spent on the range of hardware and luxury goods at the fair. Increasingly London was dominating not only the luxury trades, with its goldsmiths, pewterers and embroiderers, but also the distribution of wine and cloth, and general mercantile networks of trade and credit, while overseas trade was increasingly focused on the London-Antwerp link.[178] Stourbridge Fair was effectively becoming an extension of the London market.

Stourbridge Fair consolidated these advantages, and continued to flourish in subsequent centuries. One indicator of its importance was the attention it attracted from contemporary observers: John Evelyn climbed the roof of King's College Chapel to look at the stalls, Samuel Pepys' wife made a special journey from London to see the spectacle, and Daniel Defoe described it as the greatest fair in the world. It may have been the inspiration for the 'Vanity Fair' of John Bunyan's *Pilgrim's Progress*.[179] Stourbridge Fair continued to be a prominent trading event until well into the nineteenth century when improved communications, most notably the arrival of the railways, finally allowed traders to deal directly without the need to meet at a specified time or place.[180]

Thus large fairs like Stourbridge were able to combine many of the advantages of both the formal and informal markets. It was a regulated open market, where standards were controlled and redress was provided for buyers and sellers, providing security which was often much more difficult to obtain in private agreements. Fairs also offered economies of scale and scope for traders, and large institutions could buy in bulk and deal directly with larger merchants, rather than through middlemen. Traders benefited from low fixed costs and a wide range of potential contacts. Local tradesmen and merchants could buy products wholesale to be resold later retail in smaller markets. A wide range of products was offered, all on display at the same time and in the same place. In a pre-industrial economy, where the quality of goods could range enormously, only personal inspection could guarantee that the buyer's demands would be satisfied adequately. These advantages ensured that fairs were an important part of both the medieval and early modern marketing systems.

---

178 Britnell, '1450–1550', pp. 89–97.

179 Siraut, 'Cambridge', pp. 73–5; See also H. Ridout, 'Sturbridge Fair in the eighteenth century' (unpublished Certificate of Local History dissertation, Board of Continuing Education, University of Cambridge, 1992), appendix 1, pp. 28–9.

180 T. McIntosh, *The decline of Stourbridge Fair, 1770–1934*, Friends of the Department of English Local History, University of Leicester, No. 2 (Leicester, 1998).

Chapter 6

College consumption

Many medieval towns accommodated large aristocratic and ecclesiastical households, and townspeople profited from supplying goods and services to manor houses, castles, monasteries, cathedrals and colleges. In most towns, demand from these households was greatest before the Black Death, when the incomes of landowners were usually rising. By contrast, the declining real incomes of many large households in the fifteenth and early sixteenth centuries were not generally favourable to urban growth. Studies have charted the declining estate incomes of many late medieval households with urban residences, including the priories of Canterbury and Durham, the duchy of Lancaster, and the abbeys of Glastonbury and Leicester. Many noble and ecclesiastical houses sought economies through introducing tighter accounting procedures, cutting household staff, and reducing expenditure on buildings. Historians usually attribute the growth that did occur in some late medieval towns to demand from smaller and poorer households, such as wage-earners, or to demand from overseas markets, particularly for cloth.[1]

Cambridge, however, was an exception to this trend. During the fifteenth and early sixteenth centuries, the town witnessed the expansion of the university and the growing importance of the colleges. Seven new colleges were founded between 1420 and 1520, and the colleges accommodated an increasing proportion of the university's scholars, who had formerly lived in hostels or private lodgings. This created institutions with incomes and expenditure comparable with the wealthier aristocracy, increasing potential demand for foodstuffs, fuel and consumer goods within the town and region. This chapter seeks to explore the role of the colleges in late medieval Cambridge as consumers: firstly, by comparing the size and wealth of the colleges with their demand for goods and services, and secondly, through examining the provision of food and fuel from local producers. The colleges also required building materials and craftsmen, and these demands are examined in the next chapter.

The principal evidence for consumption comes from the accounts of the colleges. Like accounts from households of the nobility or monastic institutions, these generally record the provision of domestic services, although some deal more with the management of estates than internal organisation. All household accounts need to be used with caution. Entries vary in coverage, and are often imprecise. When regular payments cease, it is unclear if the payment has stopped, or if it has been placed under another heading. Most accounts are summaries of records of expenditure which have not usually survived, as indicated by phrases like 'at various times' and references to bills, tallies, and other accounts. The purpose of accounts was not

---

1   R.H. Britnell, 'The economy of British towns 600–1300', in *CUHB*, i, pp. 108–10; Britnell, 'The economy of British towns 1300–1540', in CUHB, i, pp. 313–14; Hatcher, *Plague*, pp. 36–44; Hatcher, 'Great slump', pp. 248–55, 264–6; Dyer, *Standards*, pp. 86–108.

usually to draw a profit/loss balance at the end of each year, but to watch and regulate income and expenditure.[2]

Surviving accounts from the Cambridge colleges vary considerably in their format. Some are in book form, like those of King's Hall; others as at Peterhouse, are in rolls. Some are fair copies, while others are working records with numerous corrections and erasures. The neatly organised Mundum Books of King's College contain subheadings and subtotals for different categories of income and expenditure, whereas the accounts at Corpus Christi College, even after the mid-fifteenth century reforms of Master John Botwright, list the whole income and expenditure for the year, regardless of category or price, together. With such differences, it has been necessary on many occasions to resort to selective quotation rather than systematic analysis.

Demand for goods and services

Recent research has shown that many medieval households were sophisticated and discerning consumers. Choices were influenced by price, availability, social status and fashion, and larger households in particular often purchased their products from a variety of different places.[3] Just as towns could be placed in a hierarchy of size and wealth, consumers also ranged in a social hierarchy of status and spending power, and there were significant links between the two. Great aristocratic and ecclesiastical households, like that of the bishop of Salisbury, with incomes of over £400 per annum, bought luxury and imported goods at the largest towns, and particularly at London, where the widest range of commodities and services could be procured. Knightly families, like the Paston family in Norfolk, and middle-ranking institutions with yearly incomes of between £200 and £400, sometimes bought directly from London, but were more likely to buy the same types of goods from provincial towns and ports, and made greater use of smaller towns. The gentry and institutions with incomes of under £100 per year used local market towns and villages for the bulk of their purchases, and obtained small quantities of more specialised goods from more distant towns. Small market towns and villages served the minor gentry, clergy, peasants, and artisans.[4] The relative abundance and diversity of surviving accounts in Cambridge, particularly those from the colleges, allows these differing patterns of consumption to be traced within a single region.

The colleges and other institutions in Cambridge varied considerably in size and wealth. As not all the college accounts survive, these features are shown most clearly in a survey of 1546, produced at Henry VIII's request by three commissioners recruited from the university.[5] At a time when the colleges' chantry lands, if not the

---

2 Dyer, *Standards*, pp. 50–3, 92–8; *Thetford*, i, pp. 5–8; *Household accounts*, part 1, pp. 3–65; A.B. Cobban, *The King's Hall within the University of Cambridge in the later middle ages* (Cambridge, 1969); *Domestic accounts of Merton College Oxford*, ed. J.M. Fletcher and C.A. Upton, Oxford Historical Soc., new ser., XXXIV (Oxford, 1996), pp. ix–xix.

3 M. Threlfall-Holmes, 'Monks and markets: Durham Cathedral Priory, 1460–1520' (unpublished PhD thesis, University of Durham, 2000), pp. 314–22; Dyer, 'Consumer', 305–27.

4 Dyer, 'Consumer', 305–27.

5 *LP*, xxi (1), no. 68, p. 28, no. 297, pp. 139–41; *Documents*, i, pp. 105–294.

Table 6.1

Wealth and size of Cambridge colleges, 1546

	Net income per annum £	No. of members
King's College	1,011	120
St John's	537	152
Christ's	287	72
Queens'	273	39
King's Hall	214	50
Corpus Christi	171	17
Pembroke Hall	171	29
Michaelhouse	142	21
Peterhouse	138	36
Clare Hall	132	28
Jesus	130	31
Gonville Hall	120	31
Trinity Hall	119	26
St Catharine's Hall	56	13
Magdalene	44	11
Total	3,546	676

Source: Documents, i, pp. 290, 292.
Note: members include all persons, scholars and servants, who received victuals, liveries, wages or fees.

colleges themselves, were threatened with dissolution, there is no doubt that the colleges wished to underplay their incomes and overstate their expenses to show that their revenues were not worth seizing by the king. Indeed on seeing the figures, Henry VIII reportedly said that 'he thought he had not in his realme so many parsons so honestly mayntened in lyvyng bi so little lond and rent'.[6] But although the survey has been described as 'a very long and creative piece of accounting',[7] the range of incomes are not dissimilar to those in the *Valor Ecclesiasticus* of 1535, while the totals for Queens' closely resemble the college accounts.[8] There is no reason to suppose that the variations in wealth between the colleges are not accurate. Similar impressions of relative size can be gained from comparing the number of statutory fellowships in respective colleges, although these statutory limits did not always conform to the actual number of fellows.[9]

Looking at the 1546 survey of Cambridge colleges presented in Table 6.1, a distinct hierarchy emerges. Generally, the wealthiest colleges contained the largest number of members. King's and St John's, with over 100 members and incomes in excess of £500, resembled the great aristocratic and ecclesiastical households, not only in their wealth, but also in the size of their households. Christ's, Queens' and King's Hall were

---

6   *Collection*, p. 60.
7   Leader, *University*, pp. 343–4.
8   *Valor Ecclesiasticus*, ed. J. Caley and J. Hunter, Record Commission, 6 vols. (London, 1810–34), iii, pp. 505–6; Evans and Faith, 'College estates', p. 655, n. 68, p. 682.
9   Emden, *Register*, p. xxix.

comparable with the more affluent knightly and gentry households, while most of the other colleges probably resembled, in wealth and in numbers, the lesser gentry, who usually had households of between 12 and 30 persons.[10] There was a distinct divide, therefore, between those colleges with royal foundations and endowments (which, with the exception of King's Hall, had all been founded between 1441 and 1511) and the others. No accounts survive from this period for the two poorest and smallest foundations, Magdalene and St Catharine's Hall, with incomes of less than £60 per annum. Records exist, though, from St Radegund's Priory and St John's Hospital, with incomes of between £70 and £80 in the later fifteenth century, before they were dissolved to found the colleges of Jesus and St John's. Much less is known about the consumption demands of the other religious houses in the town. Barnwell Priory, housing between 7 and 14 canons in the fifteenth century, and receiving an annual income of over £256 in 1535, was probably a sizeable consumer, while Cambridge's 4 friaries would have had more limited requirements.[11]

The purchases of King's College were similar to those of the grandest aristocratic households. Large quantities of fish, spices and other goods were obtained from London suppliers. These included eels, saltfish and red herrings in 1456/7, and sugar, pepper, dates and currants in 1468.[12] It is not always clear whether these purchases were actually bought in London, or from London merchants attending Stourbridge Fair in Cambridge. In 1509 and 1510, though, fish bought in London included separate payments for carriage from Westminster and from the warehouses of the Hanseatic traders at the Steelyard.[13] The college bought church furnishings and embroidery from London and used the services of Westminster and London pewterers.[14]

King's College, like many aristocratic families, owned two London mansion houses, in Baynard Castle, between the Thames and Blackfriars, known as the Garderobe Duke Humphrey and King's College Mansion. Such town houses served as residences when noble households visited London, provided purchasing bases and storage facilities when households bought goods in London, and could also generate income if leased out.[15] The Garderobe Duke Humphrey, formerly the town house of the Prior of Ogbourn and later of Humphrey, Duke of Gloucester, accommodated the provost on his visits to London, or while travelling to Eton College, and no doubt served as a depot for goods bought in the capital. The survey of 1546 recorded that King's College reserved the two *mansiones* in London for the use of the provost and scholars, and there was a 40s rent from another house in the city.[16]

---

10 Dyer, *Standards*, pp. 50–1.
11 D. Knowles and R.N. Hadcock, *Medieval religious houses: England and Wales* (London, 2nd edn., 1971), pp. 138, 146, 215, 224, 234, 241.
12 KCMB, iii, fol. 36, v, fol. 97.
13 KCMB, x, 1508/9, 1509/10 accounts.
14 KCMB, i, fols. 89v, 137; iii, fol. 113; G. Williams, 'Ecclesiastical vestments, books and furniture in the collegiate church of King's College, Cambridge, in the fifteenth century', *Ecclesiologist*, 20 (1859), 309–13.
15 C.M. Barron, 'Centres of conspicuous consumption: the aristocratic town house in London, 1200–1550', *London Journal*, 20 (1995), 1–16.
16 Williams, 'Vestments', 306–8; *Documents*, i, p. 262.

Figure 6.1 Trinity College, Great Court, looking south-east. King's Hall constructed the great gate tower and sections of the adjoining east range in the late fifteenth and early sixteenth centuries. The chapel was erected between 1555 and 1567. The early seventeenth-century octagonal fountain is supplied from a conduit that originally served the Franciscan friary

King's College obtained goods from other prominent towns, particularly ports and fishing centres, like the wax bought at Lynn in 1448/9 and candles from Huntingdon in 1535.[17] Fish was obtained from tradesmen from Lynn, 'Well', Ipswich, Lowestoft and Norwich. Some of these men may have attended Stourbridge Fair, but the college also bought fish in bulk on the East Anglian coast, as the Paston family did.[18] Cloth, including musterdevillers, green cloth, Kendal cloth and rays, was bought mainly from London, Salisbury and Winchester in the later fifteenth century. All these towns had important cloth industries in this period.[19]

The town of Cambridge was not used extensively for purchases by King's College. Cloth for liveries only occasionally came from Cambridge drapers.[20] During the late 1460s and 1470s, though, King's College bought substantial quantities of spices from a Cambridge apothecary, Richard Smyth. The relationship between the college and this supplier appears to have been particularly close: Smyth secured three leases of

---

17 KCMB, i, fol. 137v, xii, 1535/6 account.
18 KCMB, ii, fol. 68, xii, 1535/6, 1536/7, 1541/2 accounts, xiii, 1547/8 account, xiv, 1556/7, 1557/8 accounts; *PL*, i, p. 251, ii, pp. 357–8. 'Well' may refer to Wells-next-the-Sea, Norfolk.
19 KCMB, ii, fol. 112v, iii, fol. 115, iv, fol. 94, v, fol. 99, vi, fol. 25; Dyer, *Decline and growth*, pp. 13, 16. Musterdevillers – a mixed grey woollen cloth; rays – a striped cloth: *OED*, x, p. 143, xiii, p. 241.
20 KCMB, iii, fol. 115, iv, fol. 94v, vii, fol. 24.

Figure 6.2 Corpus Christi College, Old Court, north-west corner. The college was founded by the guilds of Corpus Christi and the Blessed Virgin Mary in 1352 and the court was constructed during the later fourteenth century

property in Great St Mary's parish from the college, and had his will proved by the college in 1504.[21]

King's College made large purchases every year, but only a small proportion of this expenditure was incurred locally. In the second half of the fifteenth century, on average about £11 a year was spent on fish, spices and kitchen utensils, probably most of which went to suppliers outside Cambridge. After some heavy expenditure of over £100 per annum in the 1450s, between 1460 and 1500, King's College generally spent between £50 and £70 per year on cloth for liveries. Nearly 70 per cent of this total, and sometimes more than 90 per cent, was spent on purchases made at London, Winchester and Salisbury.[22]

Similar types of suppliers appear to have been used by the other larger and wealthier colleges – King's Hall (which became part of Trinity College in 1546), St John's, Queens' and Christ's. St John's College, for example, bought a goblet and standing cup from a London silversmith in 1526/7. Queens' College sent canvas hangings from their hall to be repainted in Southwark in 1504/5.[23]

Smaller colleges, like smaller households, tended to make purchases from a more restricted area. At Corpus Christi College in the mid-fifteenth century, there were

---

21 KCMB, v–vii; KC Ledger Book, i, fols. 41v, 114, 126, 191v.
22 KCMB, ii–ix.
23 SJC, SB3.1; Willis and Clark, *Architectural history*, ii, p. 44.

between five and seven fellows, plus staff and other lodgers, and annual expenses were around £160 per annum, a situation not dissimilar to that in 1546. A goldsmith in Cambridge repaired the college's Eucharistic vessels, rather than a craftsman from London. Wine for the Mass was obtained from the nearby 'Angel' or 'New Tavern'. Like many small monastic households, no riding horses were kept, but they were hired when needed from local inns; by contrast, King's College had its own stables.[24] Like the larger colleges, though, Corpus made purchases at local fairs, particularly for timber.[25] Peterhouse, another smaller college, usually spent between £4 and £6 5s a year on fish, spices, and other commodities for the kitchen, and between £2 and £6 on cloth for liveries in the 1450s and 1460s. The accounts rarely state where these goods were purchased, but during the 1450s, wax and pepper were obtained from London and fish from Stourbridge Fair.[26]

The total annual expenditure of St John's Hospital in 1484/5 was just over £70, making it comparable with many minor monastic houses.[27] Purchases were generally made in Cambridge or other towns in East Anglia: fish were bought from Ely, barrels from Lynn and a wey of salt from Ipswich. The hospital had a landing stage by the river, with a crane or pulley, to unload goods transported by water.[28] The hospital did, however, journey as far as London for the exchange of its chalice in 1505/6. Like Corpus Christi College, the hospital bought wine for the Eucharist from local taverners, and a horse and cart may have been obtained from an inn, as payment was made to 'Jankyn of the Star'. Payments were made for the spinning of wool, and for the weaving, fulling, and shearing of cloth, suggesting an element of self-sufficiency.[29]

St Radegund's Priory was a small house containing around 11 nuns, with an annual income of £74 and £77 in two surviving account rolls from 1449/50 and 1450/1. The priory did not obtain goods from London: its main source of supply outside Cambridge was at Lynn, from where barrels of fish, linen cloth, timber and oil were procured. These purchases, together with fish from Ely Fair, were brought to Cambridge by boat.[30] The nuns also obtained supplies from neighbouring villages, including one dozen cheeses from Balsham, a horse from Bumpstead, two new ploughs from Fulbourn, and an axe from Sawston. The priory probably made more purchases in the town's market place than the larger colleges, including green peas, wheat, chickens, hens and other foodstuffs. The priory also appears to have been more self-sufficient than larger institutions. Candlewax was bought and then made into candles. Wool was spun and woven into cloth for the livery of the household servants by Roger Rede of Hinton, and this cloth was then fulled and sheared. A tailor at St Ives was used to make the garments.[31]

---

24   Zutshi, 'Botwright', 14, 16; Pearce, 'College accounts', 83, 86–7; Dyer, *Standards*, p. 71.
25   CCC, 'Liber Albus', fols. 76, 79, 97v; CCC, 'Registrum Accounts', fols. 221v, 226.
26   Peterhouse Computus rolls, 1456/7–1469/70.
27   Dyer, *Standards*, p. 70.
28   SJC, D106.9, fol. 9; D106.2, fols. 4, 12; Underwood, 'Impact', p. 171.
29   SJC, D102.3, fol. 8, D106.2, fols. 6, 10, 11; D106.9, fol. 9v.
30   *St Radegund*, pp. 150, 152, 157, 166, 167, 168, 173.
31   Ibid., pp. 151–2, 165, 167–8, 172.

The priory developed close relationships with two local suppliers of meat. William Rogger supplied a large amount of meat and held a Cambridge tenement from the priory. When the prioress and nuns were 'destitute of money' in 1478, Cambridge butcher Richard Wodecok supplied meat to the value of £21. As the priory could not settle his debt, he permitted the nuns to pay back in instalments of 19s per year.[32]

In addition to the institutional demand generated by the colleges and religious houses, there were also the needs of individual scholars. While most university scholars at this period did not come from the richest groups in society,[33] many accumulated some possessions. A scholar, clerk, and three masters of arts of King's College bequeathed a wide range of belongings in the 1460s and 1470s, including coverlets, linen sheets, blankets, robes, surplices, hoods, a mantle, mazer bowls, salt-cellars, pieces of silver, a counter (i.e. a table), a featherbed and books.[34] Some wealthy scholars relied, like the richest colleges, on London suppliers. So although a Cambridge vintner around 1511 supplied malmsey, rumney, bastard, red claret and white claret to five colleges and some forty private customers, these wines were not good enough for the discerning tastes of the scholar Erasmus, who sent for Greek wine from London.[35]

There is some evidence to suggest that the standard of living of college fellows increased in this period. In the fifteenth century, college fellowships were of limited value and many fellows were anxious to secure benefices that offered greater income. After 1500, though, fellows profited from a growing number of payments, the increasing availability of chantry chaplaincies, and more numerous fees from pupils. Another indicator of increasing prosperity may be the declining importance of college loan chests at this time. Loan chests provided scholars with interest-free loans, which were obtained by pledging items of greater value as security. Many loan chests experienced financial difficulties in the early sixteenth century, which have been attributed to their disuse by an increasingly wealthy fellowship. But the chests also suffered from the spread of the printed book, replacing the manuscript which had previously been the most common pledge, and the tendency for colleges to appropriate the capital of chests for their corporate use. In any case, the college fellows, numbering fewer than 200, formed only a small academic and wealthy elite among the total university population of over 1,000.[36]

The growth of the colleges also created new employment opportunities within the town. The survey of 1546 lists the servants employed by each college.[37] All colleges had a cook, and those with more than about 25 members employed an undercook.

---

32 *St Radegund*, pp. 41, 156, 159, 172, 175.
33 Aston, Duncan, and Evans, 'Alumni', 50.
34 KC, Ledger Book, i, fols. 58, 70v, 77, 107v.
35 'A Cambridge vintner's accounts, c.1511', ed. E.H. Minns, *PCAS*, 34 (1934), 50–8; *Erasmus and Cambridge: the Cambridge letters of Erasmus translated*, ed. D.F.S. Thomson and H.C. Porter (Toronto, 1963), pp. 85–6, 108, 176.
36 R. Lovatt, 'Two collegiate loan chests in late medieval Cambridge', in Zutshi, ed., *Medieval Cambridge*, pp. 129–65, esp. p. 144 and n. 66, pp. 153–4.
37 *Documents*, i, pp. 105–294.

Most colleges had a manciple or butler.[38] Servants were employed for the masters of St John's, Peterhouse and Queens', while King's employed a groom, cellarer, scullion, two stable boys and a bell ringer. Some fellows also kept private servants. The extent of this practice is unclear, but at King's Hall the number of personal servants began to increase around 1460, and by the sixteenth century half of the college's fellows supported servants.[39] Fees were paid for various professional services to stewards, auditors, clerks and recorders. In addition to the 83 college servants listed in the survey of 1546, other staff were hired on a casual basis when required, like gardeners, extra bakehouse and kitchen staff, and assistants for the laundress at King's Hall.[40] Several colleges also made payments for entertainment by minstrels. The widest range of performances occurred at King's Hall, which hosted folk players of All Saints, Cambridge, the town waites, minstrels from the royal and noble households, and the king's juggler and conjurer.[41]

The colleges offered few employment opportunities for women, though. Medieval college statutes stated that as far as possible, all domestic servants employed within the precincts of the college were to be male. King's College employed a laundress, but stated specifically in the college statutes that she was to live in the town, and at King's Hall the laundress received a higher stipend, probably to compensate for being unable to take board and lodging at the college.[42]

Relatively little is known about the servants of the religious houses in the town, but they would appear to have offered more limited scope for employment. A cook and a boy, a steward, a barber and an almsman served the master and 3 brethren of St John's Hospital in 1485. Barnwell Priory employed 11 servants, and the Black Friars engaged only a cook in 1513.[43] St Radegund's Priory retained a larger staff in the mid-fifteenth century, many of whom cultivated the monastery's estates: wages were paid to a confessor and chaplains, a collector of rents, a baker and brewer, and various workers in husbandry, including ploughmen, swineherds, maidservants, a shepherd and a yardwoman, while additional workers were hired when needed.[44]

Within Cambridge, a range of specialist trades developed to serve the academic community. Seventy-two tradesmen and servants, including parchment-makers, book binders, physicians, surgeons, stationers, apothecaries and the university mason, were classed as privileged persons in 1503, and therefore under the authority of the university rather than the borough.[45] An even wider range of specialist occupations were recorded in the tax returns of the 1520s including an organ player, freemason

---

38 Variously described as *promus, mancipius,* or *pincerna.*
39 Cobban, *King's Hall,* pp. 232–3, 242–4.
40 Lists of servants in monasteries compiled at the Dissolution probably omitted those servants who did not receive board from the house: B. Harvey, *Living and dying in medieval England, 1100–1540: the monastic experience* (Oxford, 1993), pp. 149–53.
41 Cobban, *University life,* pp. 207–9.
42 Cobban, *King's Hall,* pp. 235–6.
43 Rubin, *Charity and community,* p. 175; *CBD,* pp. 123, 129–30.
44 *St Radegund,* pp. 158, 174, 178.
45 UA, Luard 143b. For the extent of these privileges, see above, Chapter 3, pp. 67–9.

and collar-maker.[46] Thomas Browne of Cambridge (flourished 1508) was one of the few known organ-makers outside London in this period. John Siberch operated a printing press in Cambridge in 1521–2, and a paper mill existed by 1557.[47] Some university graduates in medicine stayed to practise as physicians in the town.[48] Cambridge attracted highly specialised craftsmen and the diversity of trades was wider than would have been justified by the size of the town alone.

Some of these specialist tradesmen also found markets beyond the university. Garrett Godfrey, bookseller and bookbinder in the 1520s and 1530s, supplied members of various monastic orders, a parson, and perhaps a schoolmaster, and had customers from Ely Priory, Crowland, Colchester, Peterborough, and possibly Ipswich.[49] Members of colleges and religious houses could also offer specialist services to the wider town. Holy Trinity church had an antiphonary bound and covered by a Friar Jeffrey in 1509/10, and an antiphonary, organ book, and missal repaired by Leonard of Christ's College in 1529–31.[50] A man from Christ's by the same name worked on vestments for St John's Hospital in 1510/11; this house also relied on the services of a friar to play their organ and repair its pipes.[51]

However, the development of a separate group of Cambridge tradesmen, classed as privileged persons or scholars' servants, meant that the university could assert its independence from the borough, through attempting to exclude miscreant traders from serving the colleges. In 1493/4, a letter from the corporation to the king asked the university chancellor to abolish prohibitions made within the university 'commanding thereby that no man should buy nor sell with divers burgesses of your said Town'.[52] This was a complaint against the practice of 'discommuning', whereby a trader who persistently refused to comply with the chancellor's regulations, or supplied commodities below standard and refused to pay the fine, had his name published in all colleges and students were forbidden to have dealings with him. Oxford University also used this tactic in 1533, and Cambridge had apparently revived the practice by the 1580s.[53] An even more far-reaching ban on trade with the town's burgesses was implemented in a university statute of 1532/3, which forbade scholars and scholars' servants from buying victuals of freemen, and required them to be bought from persons appointed by the masters of the colleges. Following bitter hostility, the university backed down the following year.[54] The university was able to

---

46   TNA: PRO E 179/81/133.
47   D.H. Boalch, *Makers of the harpsichord & clavichord 1440–1840* (Oxford, 3rd edn., 1995), pp. 27, 693–5; Gray, *Cambridge stationers*, pp. 54–5; *Annals*, ii, p. 132, n. 1.
48   C.H. Talbot and E.A. Hammond, *Medical practitioners in medieval England: a biographical register*, Publications of the Wellcome Historical Medical Library, new ser., VIII (London, 1965), pp. 17, 143–4, 353–4.
49   *Garrett Godfrey's accounts*.
50   CCRO, P22/5/1, fols. 26v, 107, 111.
51   SJC, D102.3, fol. 78; D106.2, fol. 11.
52   CCA, X/40, printed in *Annals*, i, p. 242.
53   Parker, *Town and gown*, p. 65; Hammer, 'Oxford town', p. 91; *Annals*, ii, p. 437.
54   *Grace Book A*, p. xiii.

make such threats by developing its system of privileged persons that supplied many of its needs, while larger colleges relied mainly on private agreements made with rural suppliers for essential foodstuffs.[55]

Nonetheless, despite these disputes, the growth of the university and colleges created an important increase in demand for a range of goods and services within Cambridge and its region over the 1450–1560 period. It is very difficult to quantify the combined demand of the colleges, but the 1546 survey shows that these institutions had a total net income of £3,500 per annum. That sum was three times the amount yielded from Cambridge and its county by taxation in 1524, or the equivalent of 500 to 700 building craftsmen earning between £5 and £7 per year.[56] Some of this demand was met from the town itself, but the larger and wealthier colleges looked further afield, and particularly to London, for purchases. For supplies of essential foodstuffs and fuel, though, the colleges were dependent on the surrounding region.

Food and fuel supplies

Grain constituted the most important element of the medieval diet and so trade in this commodity was particularly sensitive to changes in the size and wealth of the population, while cheap and accessible supplies of fuel, required for many household and industrial purposes, were essential for urban economies. Recent work has begun to illuminate the areas from which certain medieval towns drew basic commodities, and studies have examined the supply of foodstuffs to Colchester, Exeter, and London.[57] In many cases, though, the extent of urban hinterlands is still unclear. Yet if towns acted as promoters of economic growth, their impact was surely most keenly felt in those areas from which towns drew everyday supplies, while shortages of these commodities could seriously constrain urban development.

The Cambridge colleges could source their food and fuel supplies in several different ways: relying on their landed endowments (through drawing rents in kind, operating home farms, or receiving tithes), using the town market, or negotiating private contracts. The accounts of King's Hall and King's College show that for much of the period 1450-1560, these colleges relied on private agreements with local suppliers for most of their corn and fuel requirements. Although price and wage details from these accounts were collected by Thorold Rogers in the nineteenth century and the Beveridge Price History Group in the mid-twentieth century, the data recorded by these groups give only the prices and quantities of commodities bought, whereas the original documents often record in addition the name of the seller and his place of residence.[58] The places of residence of these suppliers can throw light on the town's hinterlands for corn and fuel supplies, and show how this region changed over

---

55 See below, pp. 155–66.

56 Sheail, *Regional distribution*, ii, p. 28; Dyer, *Standards*, p. 196.

57 Britnell, *Colchester*, pp. 35–47; Galloway et al., *Medieval capital*; M. Kowaleski, 'The grain trade in fourteenth-century Exeter', in E.B. DeWindt, ed., *The salt of common life: individuality and choice in the medieval town, countryside, and church* (Kalamazoo, 1995), pp. 1–52.

58 Rogers, *Agriculture and prices*; W. Beveridge, *Prices and wages in England, from the twelfth to the nineteenth century* (London, 1939).

time. A number of the suppliers can be traced further to show their wealth, status, landholding and commercial interests, thereby revealing the types of people who were supplying the Cambridge market, and the extent to which demand from the town impacted on the surrounding region. The fluctuating price of wheat can be studied over the period, and the impact of the severe crisis of 1556–9, when grain stocks were seriously depleted by two bad harvests and epidemic disease also struck, can be examined.

The colleges and other large landowners had to decide whether their rural estates should be cultivated for their own consumption, or placed on lease (often described as being 'farmed out') and the income used to purchase foodstuffs.[59] Around 1400, in response to falling grain prices and the rising cost of labour, many large landowners abandoned direct management of their estates and leased out most of the demesne lands which they had formerly cultivated. Manors or home farms near the residential centre might be retained to supply produce, and some rents could also be received in kind. For some large households, like Durham Priory, these still formed a major part of their supplies, but Cambridge colleges, like their counterparts at Oxford, generally appear to have leased out their estates and depended on market transactions.[60] King's Hall held relatively few estates, as royal exchequer allowances and appropriated churches supplied most of the college's income, but it occasionally received rents in kind from Chesterton.[61] King's College bought grain from some villages where it owned estates and sometimes from its own tenants. Between 1450 and 1480, for instance, farmers of the manors at Grantchester and Isleham supplied wheat and barley.[62] These prices, though, do not seem to have been any different to those charged by other suppliers. The position changed in the late 1550s, when the college introduced corn rents in its leases.[63]

While most of the estates of the Cambridge colleges were leased, a few manors around the town were cultivated directly for food during the later fifteenth century. Peterhouse owned a farm and rectory at Cherry Hinton, which during the 1450s and 1460s alternated between being leased out and cultivated directly by the college.[64] The rectory site comprised old and new halls, a malt house, bakehouse, dovecote, and chambers for wheat and barley. A schedule of land and stock attached to the 1459 lease lists over 44 acres of land and a range of equipment, including carts, ploughs, chains and a yoke, and oxen, sheep, hay and peas. When the rectory was not being leased, most of its produce probably supplied the college, but some was sold, including 42 quarters of barley and 120 quarters of malt barley in 1457/8.[65] The home farm of King's College at Grantchester operated between 1452 and 1466, when eight

---

59 The income the colleges received from their land holdings is examined in Chapter 7.
60 Threlfall-Holmes, 'Monks', p. 200; R.A. Lomas, 'A northern farm at the end of the middle ages: Elvethall manor, Durham, 1443/4–1513/14', *Northern History*, 18 (1982), 26–53; Evans and Faith, 'College estates', pp. 661, 671–4.
61 Cobban, *King's Hall*, pp. 202–7; KH a/c, xxv, fols. 110, 142v.
62 KCMB, iii, fols. 30–2, v, fol. 93, vi, fol. 66v, vii, fols. 19v, 32v.
63 See below, pp. 171–2.
64 Peterhouse, H1–H3; Peterhouse Computus rolls, 1455/6–1470/1.
65 Peterhouse, H2; Peterhouse Computus rolls, 1457/8.

full-time servants were employed to grow barley and wheat, and maintain a small amount of livestock and poultry to supply the college's kitchens. The college seems to have found the farm too expensive to operate, and subsequently leased it out. In the leases, though, King's reserved the right to pasture its flock of sheep on the demesne, and to use the gardens, orchards and fishponds of the manor. The college also reserved the use of the manor house, which may have provided a refuge for the fellows during outbreaks of plague in Cambridge; Christ's College repaired their manor house at Malton for the same purpose, following directions in the will of their foundress, Lady Margaret Beaufort. King's College also directly cultivated some land at Coton in 1508–10, when payment for seed and labour are recorded in the Mundum Books.[66] This was possibly a temporary expedient because another lessee could not be found immediately to cultivate the land.

St Radegund's Priory and St John's Hospital operated home farms based on their extensive holdings in the Cambridge fields. St Radegund's Priory cultivated mainly wheat and barley, but oats, peas, tares, mustard and 'le Bolymong'[67] were also grown. The sale of corn and livestock produced between £10 and £13 per year in the mid-fifteenth century, when wool was also sold to John Wolleman of Cambridge.[68] The farmstead owned by St John's Hospital included barns, stables, a dovecote, ponds, an oven and a kiln. Although by the later fifteenth century this property was generally leased out as a unit, payments in the accounts for livestock and agricultural work suggest that in some years at least, this or other land was being cultivated directly by the hospital.[69] Among the livestock purchased c.1500 were 10 horses, 8 oxen, 12 cattle, and 184 ewes and lambs. Six stone of wool was spun, and there were payments to a shearman and weaver. In 1507, there were payments for buying beans and barley for seed, and for fallowing, sowing, weeding, and gleaning.[70] The short-term nature of several home farms operating in the Forest of Arden has been noted; a similar flexible response appears to have been adopted by some Cambridge institutions.[71]

Another potential source of food was from the tithes and glebe produce of rectories, which many colleges owned. Corpus Christi College held the rectories of Grantchester and Landbeach, and in the mid-fifteenth century accounts, the college appears to have received some of its rents in wheat and barley, particularly from Grantchester, sometimes as part of the tithes along with peas, hay, capons, geese and wool.[72] Corpus also received some rents in kind in wax, timber and cloth in 1462.[73]

---

66 Saltmarsh, 'Home-farm', 155–72; M.K. Jones and M.G. Underwood, *The king's mother: Lady Margaret Beaufort, countess of Richmond and Derby* (Cambridge, 1992), pp. 220, 228; KCMB, x, 1508/9 and 1509/10 accounts.

67 Bullimong – a mixture of various kinds of grain sown together for feeding cattle: *OED*, ii, p. 643.

68 *St Radegund*, pp. 145–75.

69 Underwood, 'Impact', pp. 175–6.

70 SJC, D106.2, fols. 5–6, 11; D106.10, fol. 19.

71 A. Watkins, 'Landowners and their estates in the Forest of Arden in the fifteenth century', *Agricultural History Review*, 45 (1997), 18–33.

72 CCC, 'Registrum Accounts', fols. 141, 154v–155, 166v, 179v, 189v, 196v.

73 CCC, 'Liber Albus', fol. 68v.

Most rectories, though, like other estates, were leased to a resident 'farmer': often, although not always, this lessee was the vicar, who paid a *firma* or fixed sum every year to the college in return for the right to collect the income. St Radegund's Priory, for example, received £6 13s 4d per annum from John Hixon for the tithes of St Giles' Church, Cambridge, in the 1450s.[74] Particularly during the period of rising cereal prices in the sixteenth century, rectories were sought for the cereals that the tithe and glebe lands could provide. Dr John Tayler, master of St John's College, Cambridge, 1538–46, and dean of Lincoln from 1544, requested the advowson of the parsonage of Washingborough, 'which wolde fynde me well my drynk corne & some parte towarde my bread corne'.[75]

Most colleges relied on cash purchases of food for the majority of their needs, and food was often bought unprocessed. Bakers and brewers proliferated in towns, and were the main source of supply for most urban inhabitants and many country dwellers, but the larger Cambridge colleges, like other aristocratic households, bought only limited quantities of bread and ale, preferring to do their own baking and brewing.[76] In the lists of colleges' employees in the survey of 1546, King's Hall, Trinity Hall and King's College employed a baker, while King's Hall and Peterhouse had bakehouses in the fifteenth century. Only King's Hall listed a brewer as being employed in 1546, although Queens' had built a brewhouse in 1533/4.[77] Other college bakehouses and brewhouses may have relied on casual labour or been leased out, and some colleges may have baked bread in their kitchens. Around 1532, the borough corporation complained that when the assize of bread and ale had been granted to the university in 1382, it had consisted mainly of hostels and halls, which were supplied with bread, ale and other victuals, by the townspeople; whereas at the present, the greater part of the university consisted of colleges which provided their own bakehouses and brewhouses.[78] Some smaller colleges, though, still relied on the town's bakers and brewers. Although Corpus Christi College ordered the construction of a bakehouse in 1456, the building was used successively as a tennis court and for college accommodation, and in 1586 the college still relied on supplies of bread from the town. Gonville and Caius College decided only in 1579 to abandon buying bread from the townspeople and to build a suitable oven in the college kitchen.[79]

The larger Cambridge colleges did not use formal markets to obtain most of their grain and fuel. King's Hall sometimes bought small amounts of wheat, up to 5 quarters, from the market.[80] King's College reduced its purchases in the market place from 17 per cent of the total amount bought between 1450 and 1480, to 12 per cent of the total amount bought between 1545 and 1558.[81] During these years,

---

74 Evans and Faith, 'College estates', pp. 675–6; *St Radegund*, pp. 147, 163.
75 'Notes from the college records', *The Eagle*, 18 (1895), 545.
76 Dyer, *Standards*, pp. 57, 196–8.
77 *Documents*, i, p. 151, 158, 243; Willis and Clark, *Architectural history*, i, p. 26, ii, p. 440; QC, Magnum Journale, ii, fols. 193, 194v–195.
78 CCA, X/69(ii), printed in *Annals*, i, p. 349.
79 Willis and Clark, *Architectural history*, i, pp. 184, 259–60; Siraut, 'Cambridge', p. 211.
80 KH a/c, xix, fol. 199v, xx, fol. 175, xxiv, fol. 64, xxv, fol. 30.
81 KCMB, ii–vii, xii–xiv.

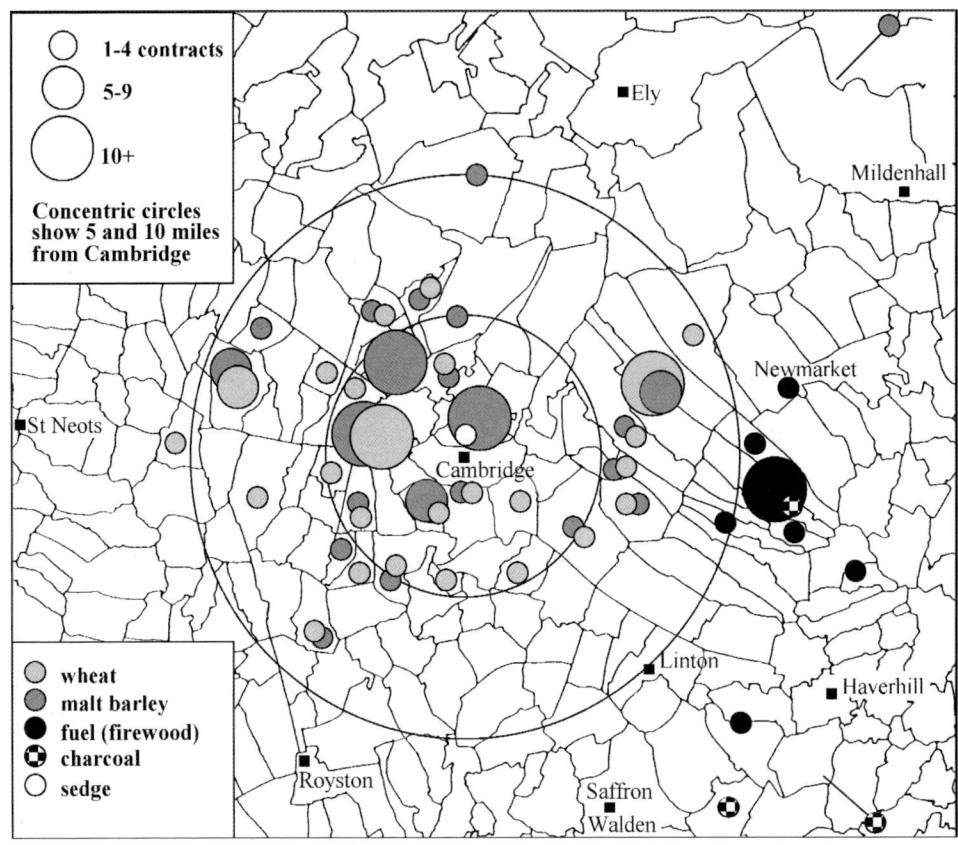

Figure 6.3 King's Hall suppliers, 1451–1500
Source: KH a/c, xi–xix.

the college became increasingly reliant on private contracts with producers. Throughout the medieval and early modern period, much trade in grain occurred outside formal markets. Producers sold their surpluses directly to middlemen, brewers and bakers, neighbouring landlords traded supplies, landless villagers obtained produce from their neighbours, and grain was purveyed directly from sellers to supply royal armies.[82] In the absence of significant supplies from home farms, tenants, or the market place, King's Hall and King's College looked primarily to contracts with local suppliers.

The King's Hall accounts record purchases of wheat, malt barley and various types of fuel as *conventiones* (agreements) between the college and suppliers covering the purchase and delivery of goods, stating the supplier's name and often his residence, the quantity of the commodity, delivery date and the terms of payment. Other purchases recorded as *emptiones* (purchases) seem to have been made and payment

---

82 Britnell, *Commercialisation*, pp. 98–9.

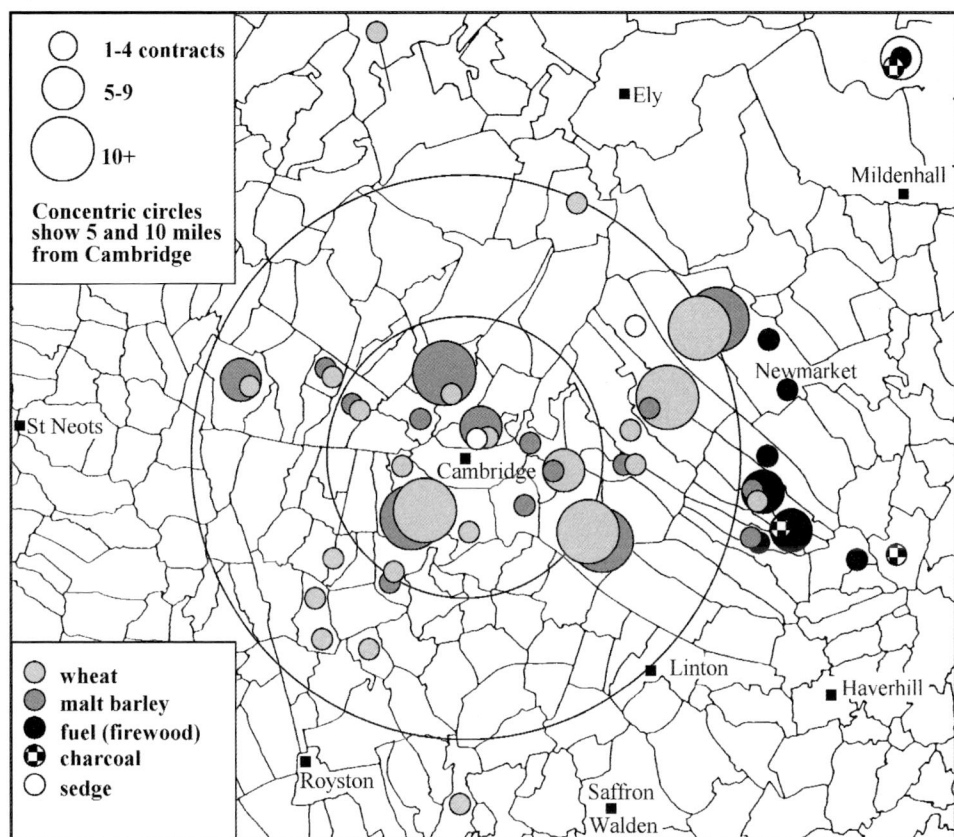

Figure 6.4 King's Hall suppliers, 1501–44
Source: KH a/c, xix–xxvi.

supplied at the same time: some purchases were made *in foro* (in the market place) some were bought from the same suppliers as those who made contracts with the college, but the source of most of these purchases is not recorded. The King's College Mundum Books also record purchases of wheat, malt barley and fuel, many probably made in similar private agreements, as many were paid in instalments.[83] In both series of accounts, the names and residences of the suppliers are often, although not always, given. These details were entered into a relational database and the contracts grouped by suppliers of the same surname unless different recorded forenames or places of residence for that surname were found.

The hinterland for grain supplies upon which King's Hall and King's College relied was not extensive, as Figures 6.3–6.6 reveal. Approximately half the contracts came from within 5 miles of Cambridge, and nearly all the contracts came from within 10 miles. While the area supplying the Cambridge colleges with grain was localised, it

---

83 KH a/c, xi–xxvi; KCMB, ii–vii, xii–xiv.

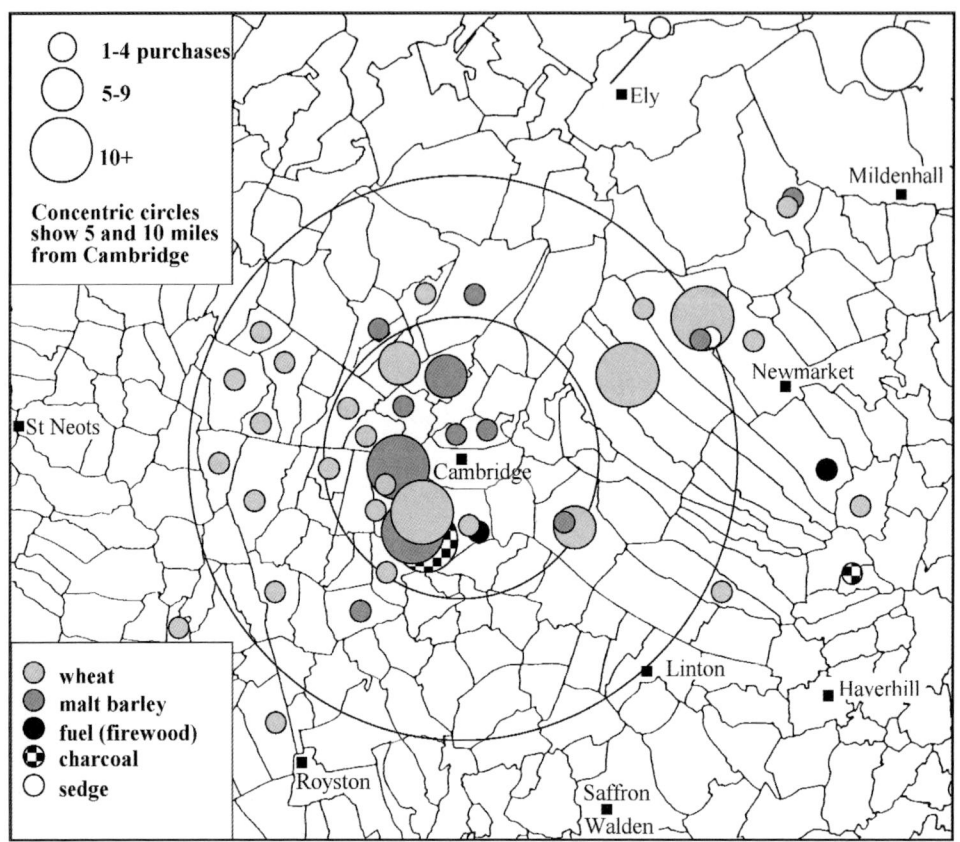

Figure 6.5 King's College purchases, 1450–80
Source: KCMB, ii–vii.

was similar to the hinterlands of other medieval towns of comparable size, such as early fourteenth-century Colchester, which drew foodstuffs from within an 8-mile radius of the town. Even London, where the population may have reached 80,000 or 100,000 inhabitants around 1300, only appears to have drawn grain from up to 20 miles from the city by land, and up to 60 miles by water. A smaller town like Northallerton in Yorkshire, with just over 700 inhabitants in the 1540s, drew its grain and meat supplies from a far more restricted area, extending only 5 to 7 miles from the town.[84] It appears that the suppliers serving King's Hall and King's College generally reflected Cambridge's hinterland for grain, although the large and wealthy colleges may also have been able to draw on supplies from further afield.

Supplies of fuel to Cambridge were more geographically restricted than supplies of grain. Cambridgeshire was sparsely wooded, with woodland concentrated in the east

---

84 Britnell, *Colchester*, pp. 41–7; Campbell et al., *Medieval capital*, pp. 9, 173; C.M. Newman, *Late medieval Northallerton: a small town and its hinterland, c.1470–1540* (Stamford, 1999), pp. 15, 100–9.

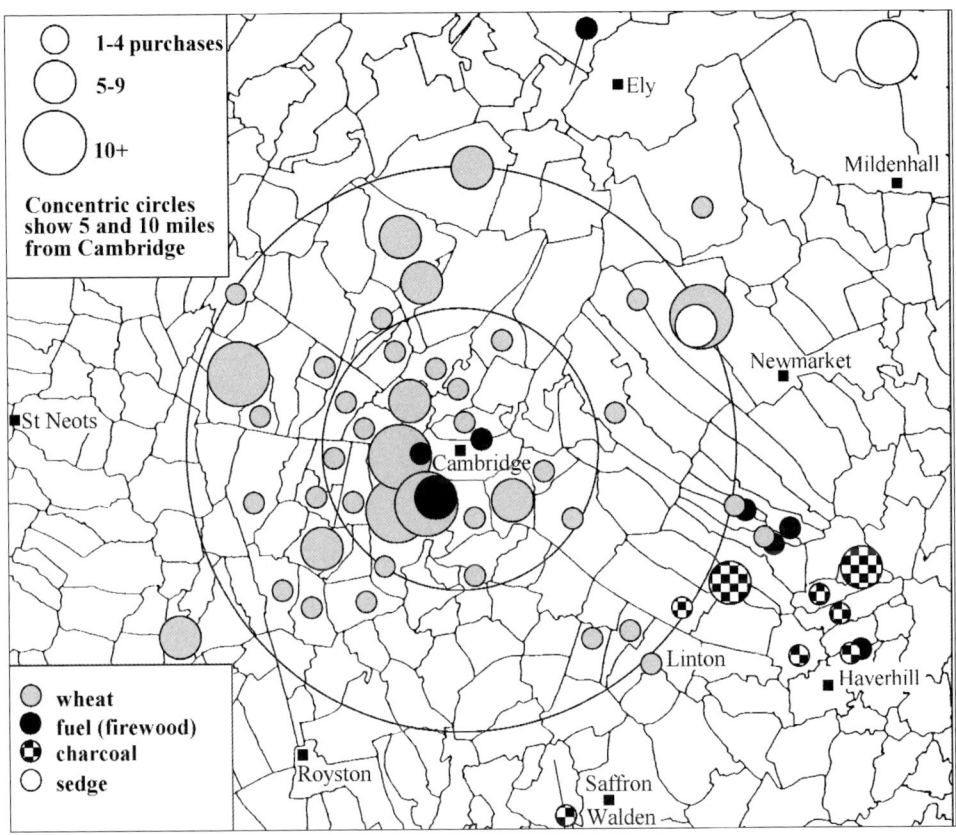

Figure 6.6: King's College purchases, 1545–58
Source: KCMB, xii–xiv.

and west of the county.[85] Reflecting this shortage of woodland, Figures 6.3–6.6 show that King's Hall and King's College drew fuel from further south and east than the areas producing wheat and barley, into the adjoining counties of Essex and Suffolk. Cambridge's hinterland for fuel may have been more extensive than for other medieval towns. Around 1400, London's supply zone for faggots probably extended only 9 to 11 miles overland.[86] The Cambridge colleges, however, relied on supplies from up to 15 miles away. As Figures 6.6 and 6.7 show, by the mid-sixteenth century, the colleges were having to look to even more distant suppliers of firewood and charcoal, implying that resources closer to the town were becoming exhausted. William Harrison commented on this shortage in his description of Cambridge in the 1570s: 'Only wood is the chief want to such as study there, wherefore this kind of

---

85 O. Rackham, *Ancient woodland: its history, vegetation and uses in England* (London, 1980), pp. 122–3.

86 Galloway et al., 'Fuelling the city', pp. 458–9, 466.

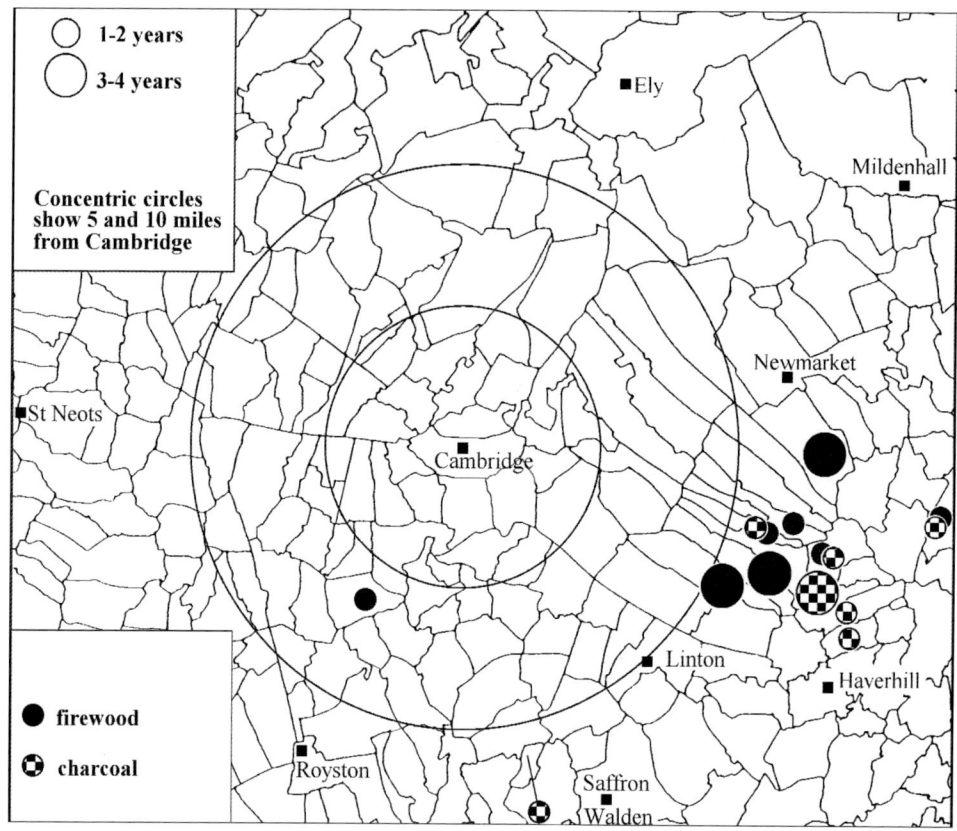

Figure 6.7 Trinity College fuel supplies, 1547–63
Source: TCSB a/c, 1546-7–1562/3; TCJB a/c, 1549/50–1562/3.

provision is brought them either from Essex and other places thereabouts, as is also their coal [charcoal]'.[87]

In addition to contracts with suppliers, there were other means of buying firewood and charcoal. Trinity College once obtained wood from its farmers at Barrington, occasionally bought wood in the market place, and in 1560 bought forfeited charcoal from the university taxors.[88] At least some colleges must have bought firewood while still growing as underwood, as Cambridge Corporation complained that masters of colleges and hostels refused to pay tolls on carts carrying wood and charcoal bought in the country 'at the Stubb or by the hundreth'.[89] Some firewood was also purchased at the town's inns. Around 1491, the king's chief judge expressed dissatisfaction to the

---

[87] J. Hatcher, *The history of the British coal industry*, i: *before 1700, towards the age of coal* (Oxford, 1993), p. 44; Harrison, *Description*, p. 67.

[88] TCSB a/c, i, fols. 96, 97, 220v, 369; TCJB a/c, i, fol. 122.

[89] CCA, X/38. Buying at the stubb meant buying underwood while it was still growing: *OED*, xvi, p. 968.

university about faggots made and sold at inns, and in the later sixteenth century, the university's leet courts fined innholders selling underweight parcels of firewood.[90]

The fenland provided additional sources of fuel. Some colleges occasionally bought turves,[91] but they seem to have preferred to use sedge, another product of the fen, which provided fuel, thatch, and litter.[92] King's Hall and King's College purchased large quantities of sedge from Lakenheath, and also from Chesterton, Reach, Burwell and Littleport (Figures 6.3–6.6). Many parts of the fenland were accessible by water, reducing the cost of carriage, and King's College collected sedge from the Great Bridge and the landing place known as the 'Seggeshith' in Cambridge.[93]

Coal supplies from Newcastle-upon-Tyne to Cambridge via the port of Lynn emerged during the sixteenth century to provide alternative fuel to replace the diminishing reserves of firewood. Evidence of trading links between the two towns emerges during the sixteenth century, when coal shipments between Newcastle and London also became more regular. Lynn was one of the main ports trading with Newcastle, with over 90 ship movements recorded in the accounts between 1508 and 1511.[94] Responding to a legal dispute with Lynn, the mayor and four aldermen of Newcastle sealed an indenture in 1510, testifying to the delivery of coal purchased there by four men from Cambridge, to be delivered at Lynn.[95] Cambridge Corporation twice promised protection to merchants sailing to Newcastle for coal against suits by King's Lynn during the 1540s, and in 1560 the mayor of Lynn stopped the unloading of a cargo of Newcastle coal in a dispute with Cambridge. Two Cambridge burgesses, Thomas Brakyn and John Line, held the post of collector of customs at Newcastle in 1543, although they probably exercised these offices through deputies.[96] William Harrison observed that Cambridge enjoyed a 'great plenty' of coal, carried along the River Cam from Lynn.[97]

Despite the trading links between Cambridge and Newcastle, and occasional examples of deliveries of coal, like those to King's Hall in 1482/3 and to Peterhouse in the early 1500s, the colleges do not appear to have burned coal regularly until the later sixteenth century. Coal burning required particular grates, hearths, chimneys and ventilation, so it was often slow to be adopted for domestic purposes. Coal did not become a significant and regular purchase at King's College until 1580.[98]

Fewer details survive about the supply of other foodstuffs. Fruit and vegetables

---

90 UA, Luard 133; C.U.R. 17, fol. 15.

91 KCMB, i, fols. 67–67v; Peterhouse Computus rolls, 1458/9 a/c.

92 T.A. Rowell, 'Sedge (*Cladium mariscus*) in Cambridgeshire: its use and production since the seventeenth century', *Agricultural History Review*, 34 (1986), 140–3.

93 KCMB, ii, fol. 67, v, fol. 118v.

94 Hatcher, *Coal*, pp. 25–6; *The accounts of the Chamberlains of Newcastle upon Tyne 1508–1511*, ed. C.M. Fraser, Soc. of Antiquities of Newcastle upon Tyne Record Ser., III (Newcastle, 1987), pp. viii, xiii–xiv.

95 CCA, X/7.

96 CCA, Palmer/Barnard vol. 57, fols. 5, 27; W.J. Jones, *The Elizabethan court of Chancery* (Oxford, 1967), p. 368, n. 3; Bindoff, *House of Commons*, i, p. 485, ii, p. 533.

97 *Annals*, ii, pp. 181, 229; Hatcher, *Coal*, p. 44; Harrison, *Description*, p. 67.

98 KH a/c, xvi, fol. 93v; Rogers, *Agriculture and prices*, iii, pp. 265–8; Hatcher, *Coal*, p. 44.

were grown within college and town gardens, and livestock were pastured on the town commons. The townspeople and institutions looked to nearby villages for additional pasture. Cambridge butchers were leasing the commons at Barton, three miles away, in 1512. The fen-edge and fenland to the north in particular, provided additional hay and pasture land.[99] Livestock purchases are not recorded in the King's Hall accounts, but the records from King's College show purchases in the 1450s and 1460s from the college's estates in Essex and Suffolk, and even 150 sheep from Combe in Hampshire in 1457. King's College also purchased some livestock in the market, at Reach and Ely fairs, from the priors of Barnwell and Spalding, and from Cambridgeshire villages where the college did not have any landholdings.[100] Livestock was high in value relative to its bulk and could be led to the point of consumption, reducing transport costs, so livestock products could be brought to towns from greater distances than supplies of grain or fuel. London's demand for meat in the fifteenth century, for example, was partly met by commercial droving routes from Warwickshire, Northamptonshire, Cheshire and north Wales.[101] In the early sixteenth century, King's College sold the by-products from animals it had slaughtered, with sales of wool, sheep and cow skins, pigs' heads, and intestines bringing around £20 in income between 1505/6 and 1507/8. However, by the 1540s this had ceased, and the college was buying meat from one or two butchers, some apparently supplying their meat ready-cooked as 'boyled' or 'rostted'.[102]

Suppliers of corn and fuel

Many of the colleges' suppliers can be traced further using the 1524–5 taxation records and other documents, providing a rare opportunity to examine the types of people who were marketing agricultural produce in this period. Many large landowners abandoned the direct cultivation of their manorial demesnes during the later middle ages, leasing their lands to a variety of tenants, including gentry, yeomen and husbandmen, who have left few records.[103] Postan argued that this created a less market-oriented and more self-sufficient 'natural' economy. Indeed it has been suggested that at the beginning of the sixteenth century, only 20 per cent of farmers were producing food for the market.[104] The evidence from King's Hall and King's College, however, shows that many lessees of demesnes, together with other yeomen and husbandmen, were engaging in some commercial production through marketing their produce to the colleges.

---

99 VCH Cambs., v, p. 168; Lee, 'Food and fuel supplies', 257–8.

100 KCMB, ii–vi; J. Saltmarsh, 'Hand-list of the estates of King's College, Cambridge', *Bulletin of the Institute of Historical Research*, 12 (1934), 32–8.

101 Galloway, 'England, 1300–1570', pp. 115–16.

102 KCMB, x, 1505/6–1507/8 accounts, xiii, 1552/3 accounts.

103 F.R.H. Du Boulay, 'Who were farming the English demesnes at the end of the middle ages?', *EcHR*, 2nd ser., 17 (1965), 443–55; B. Harvey, 'The leasing of the abbot of Westminster's demesnes in the later middle ages', *EcHR*, 2nd ser., 22 (1969), 17–27; J.N. Hare, 'The demesne lessees of fifteenth-century Wiltshire', *Agricultural History Review*, 29 (1981), 1–15.

104 M.M. Postan, 'The fifteenth century', *EcHR*, 9 (1938–9), 162–3; M. Overton, *Agricultural revolution in England: the transformation of the agrarian economy 1500–1850* (Cambridge, 1996), p. 22.

Several suppliers of wheat and barley to the two colleges were among the wealthiest men in their communities, with more than £20 in goods or lands in the 1520s.[105] These wealthy farmers and leading yeomen usually held their lands on a variety of different tenures, often including leases of the lord's manorial lands. They employed local wage-labourers or resident servants and produced a surplus which was marketed.[106] Many had taken up leases of demesnes of other farms, like Thomas Baron of Comberton, who furnished King's Hall with 20 quarters of wheat and barley in 1475, was the farmer of Barnwell Priory's land in 1498, and provided a window with a request for prayers in the parish church. Henry Cook, farmer of Chesterton, sent six consignments of wheat and barley between 1505 and 1529. When Cook died in 1535, he was lessee to Clare College, and probably also held the lease of the Barnwell Priory demesne at Chesterton.[107] Farmers of leases of lands (*firmarii*) at Bourn, Chesterton, Dry Drayton and Malton supplied King's Hall, and farmers at Bourn and Swaffham Prior brought wheat to King's College in the late fifteenth century.[108]

A handful of Cambridgeshire gentry supplied the colleges, most notably John Benet of Burwell, gentleman, assessed at £100 in 1522, who made 16 contracts of wheat and barley with King's Hall between 1517 and 1527. Two other occasional suppliers of wheat were Edward Langley, lord of Lolworth manor, and Richard Childe of Harlton, who was probably lord of Huntingdon or Harlton manor.[109] Many members of the gentry took demesne leases across the country and, in some regions, engaged in specialised farming for the market.[110]

Other suppliers of King's Hall and King's College came from less wealthy groups. Several were husbandmen, assessed at £2 to £4 in goods in the lay subsidies of 1524–5, and perhaps holding tenements of 30–40 acres. They had sufficient surpluses to be able to market their produce, at least in some years, while a few, like the Harris family at Elsworth and the Cakebreds at Fulbourn, regularly filled contracts for King's Hall. These husbandmen usually supplied smaller contracts, of up to 20 quarters of wheat or barley, and most came from villages only 2 or 3 miles outside Cambridge, rather than from the more distant parts of the town's hinterland. A few women sold wheat to King's College, generally in very small quantities of a few bushels.[111] They are likely to have combined retailing grain with baking, brewing, or selling poultry, vegetables and dairy products.[112]

Several clergy also supplied the two colleges. John Petyt, vicar of Shudy Camps

---

105 *LP*, iii (2), no. 2640, pp. 1116–19.
106 Bailey, 'Rural society', p. 151.
107 KH a/c, xv, fol. 25, xx–xxiii, *passim*; *VCH Cambs.*, v, pp. 183, 187, ix, p. 15.
108 KH a/c, xii, fols. 15v, 53, xiii, fol. 144, xxvi, fol. 109v; KCMB, iii, fol. 31, v, fol. 94.
109 KH a/c, xii, fol. 15v, xxi, fol. 113v, xii, *passim*; *VCH Cambs.*, v, p. 217, ix, pp. 158–9.
110 C. Carpenter, 'The fifteenth-century English gentry and their estates', in M. Jones, ed., *Gentry and lesser nobility in late medieval Europe* (Gloucester, 1986), pp. 36–60; C. Dyer, 'A small landowner in the fifteenth century', *Midland History*, 1, part 3 (1972), 1–14; Du Boulay, 'English demesnes', 450.
111 KCMB, iii, fols. 108–108v, xii, 1536/7 accounts, xiii, 1547/8, 1548/9, 1549/50, 1551/2 accounts.
112 Mate, *Women*, pp. 32, 44–6; Kowaleski, 'Grain trade', pp. 46–7.

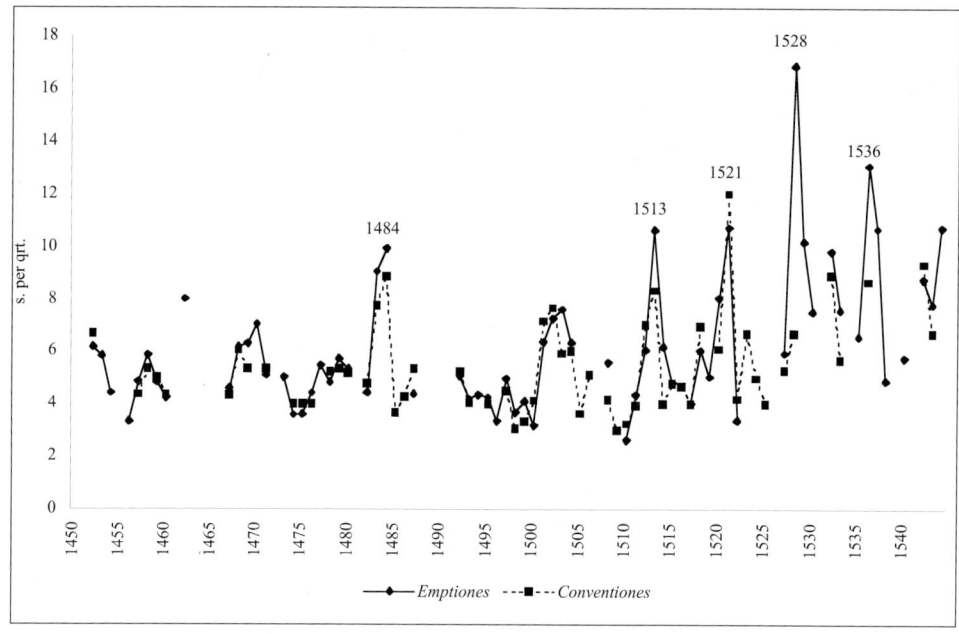

Figure 6.8 King's Hall wheat prices, 1450–1544
Source: KH a/c, xi–xxvi.

provided King's Hall with two consignments of fuel in the 1470s.[113] The vicars of Burwell and Oakington,[114] and the rectors of Chesterton, Dry Drayton, Ditton, Girton and Rampton, also sent wheat and barley to King's Hall.[115] King's College was supplied with wheat by the rectors of Boxworth, Elsworth, Eversden, Grantchester, Knapwell, Willingham and Wimpole, and the vicar of Madingley.[116] Clergy could supply agricultural produce received in tithes from their parishioners, or produce they had grown on their glebe lands. Tithes were frequently farmed (leased) out in the later middle ages, and the farmers of the rectories at Wilbraham, Barton, and Burwell supplied the two colleges. Tithe farmers and clergy were also active in the grain markets at Exeter and York.[117]

Suppliers of fuel tended to be men of lesser wealth, assessed on £2 or less in the 1524–5 subsidies, like Thomas Hithe of Dullingham and Thomas Yeve/Ive of Swavesey. Some suppliers were more prosperous, though, such as John Folkes, who was the farmer of the demesne of Stetchworth manor, John Harvy of Stetchworth, assessed at £8 in goods in 1524, and John Loveday and Thomas Wellis, who owned

---

113 KH a/c, xiv, fols. 45, 129; VCH Cambs., vi, p. 57.
114 KH a/c, xv, fol. 83v, xvii, fols. 93, 116v, xxiv, fols. 95–95v.
115 KH a/c, xii, fol. 145, xiii, fol. 146, xvii, fol. 69, xviii, fol. 20, xxiii, fol. 91v, xxiv, fols. 25, 152.
116 KCMB, v, fol. 31, vi, fol. 112v, xii, 1536/7 accounts, xiii, 1547/8, 1548/9, 1549/50, 1551/2 accounts, xiv, 1553/4, 1554/5 accounts.
117 Kowaleski, 'Grain trade', pp. 35–7; Swanson, Medieval artisans, p. 136.

College consumption

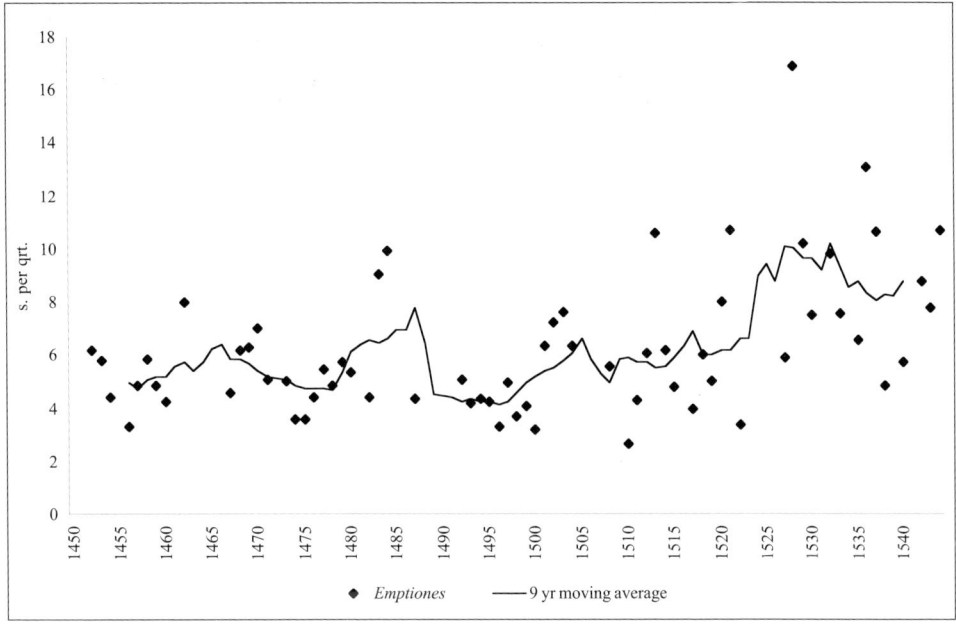

Figure 6.9 Average of King's Hall wheat prices, 1450–1544
Source: KH a/c, xi–xxvi.

£12 and £10 in goods at Burrough Green.[118]

The occupational titles like *carbonarii*, 'turffeman', 'sedgeman' and woodman given to some suppliers may indicate that these men were specialised traders in their commodities.[119] Other traders with particular specialisms who supplied wheat and barley to King's Hall were an innkeeper of Chesterton in 1468, a limeburner from Hinton in 1484 and a maltman in 1485.[120]

Wheat prices and shortages

Figure 6.8 shows the annual average price of wheat calculated from the King's Hall accounts. The price in shillings per quarter for every transaction, irrespective of the quantity bought or sold, has been used to produce the mean price for the year. This assumes that a small purchase was as typical of market prices as a larger entry.[121] Estimates of consumption have not been made, as the King's Hall and King's College accounts show wide fluctuations in the number of entries and total amount of wheat

---

118 TNA: PRO E 179/81/126, E 179/81/134; *Suffolk in 1524*, p. 226.
119 KH a/c, xiii, fol. 63, xvi, fol. 62v, xvii, fol. 91v, xx, fols. 19, 136v, 203v, xxi, fols. 58v, 148, xxiv, fol. 96; *St Radegund*, p. 158.
120 KH a/c, xiii, fol. 114, xvii, fols. 93v, 116.
121 This method of calculating the price was used by Thorold Rogers and Beveridge: Rogers, *Agriculture and prices*, iv, p. 211; Beveridge, *Prices and wages*, p. xliii.

and fuel purchased each year, suggesting that not every transaction may have been recorded.

While King's Hall saw large increases in wheat prices in some years, generally coinciding with years of widespread harvest failure across the country,[122] the college was able to limit these price rises. The maximum recorded prices that King's Hall paid for a quarter of wheat were 18.27s in 1528 and 18.67s in 1536. The worst year of harvest failure for the college was 1528, for even the lowest price in that year was 16s. The dearth of 1527–8 led to disturbances in Norwich and Yarmouth, and Henry VIII's government was so concerned about the shortage that it ordered a country-wide search of all available corn.[123] The advantage that King's Hall gained from the agreements with suppliers was most apparent in these years of scarcity. For example, in 1484, the average price of wheat bought through contracts was 8.83s per quarter, compared to 9.93s per quarter for other purchases made that year.

Grain shortages led to the temporary expansion of an urban hinterland, and in years of particularly high prices, King's Hall sought some grain from more distant suppliers. In 1484, for example, the college bought barley from Joanna Dutton, of Methwold in Norfolk, 29 miles away; in 1512, the college purchased from William Hopper of Chrishall in Essex, 13 miles distant. There was also a tendency at such times to resort to more unusual suppliers. In 1483, the master of St John's Hospital in Cambridge sold 14 quarters of wheat at 8s per quarter and Lord John Filay sold 5 quarters at the same price.[124] In 1501 a baker called Gybson supplied 25 quarters of wheat, and William Syre of Coton sold wheat described as *frumento antiquo*, possibly because the college was unable to secure better quality supplies.[125] If even a large and wealthy institution felt the effects of harvest fluctuations, the average townsman would have suffered much more.

With a fairly steady demand and little grain stored from one year to the next, wheat prices were very sensitive to the harvest, and fluctuated more sharply than those of any other major commodity. It can be difficult to discern long-term trends, but in an attempt to smooth out the annual fluctuations, a 9-year moving average has been calculated in Figure 6.9. While groups of poor harvests in the 1460s, 1480s and 1500s are still reflected in the average, the effects of inflation only began to appear in the mid-1510s and 1520s, when the average price remained above 6s per quarter, and prices rose further in the late 1520s. These trends reflect those found in the national

---

122 W.G. Hoskins, 'Harvest fluctuations and English economic history, 1480–1619', *Agricultural History Review*, 12 (1964), 31–5, 39, 44–5; C.J. Harrison, 'Grain price analysis and harvest qualities', *Agricultural History Review*, 19 (1971), 152–3. Note that Hoskins and Harrison label the period Michaelmas (29 September) 1450 to Michaelmas (29 September) 1451 as the harvest year 1450, whereas this study follows the convention adopted by Titow and Phelps-Brown, and describes the same period as the harvest year 1451: J.Z. Titow, *English rural society, 1200–1350* (London, 1969), pp. 27–9.

123 Hoskins, 'Harvest fluctuations', 34; D. Dymond, 'The famine of 1527 in Essex', *Local Population Studies*, 26 (1981), 29–40.

124 KH a/c, xvi, fols. 94, 120, xxi, fol. 113v.

125 KH a/c, xix, fols. 199v–200.

Table 6.2

King's College wheat prices, 1536–62

Year	Average price (s. per qtr.)
1536	13.86
1537	10.21
1542	9.15
1545	10.74
1546	14.04
1548	4.88
1549	7.55
1550	13.41
1552	23.46
1553	9.88
1554	8.70
1555	17.84
1556	20.85
1557	29.09
1558	10.14
1559	9.93
1561	14.67
1562	13.88

Source: KCMB, xii–xv.

price indices of all agricultural products compiled by Bowden, which show sustained increases during these two decades.[126]

Fuel prices have not been calculated, owing to the range of different and imprecise measures used, and the difficulties of measuring transport costs. Rarely itemised separately, transport costs formed a much larger proportion of the total cost than for the carriage of a relatively lighter and less bulky commodity like grain. Other studies, though, suggest that major price increases, above the rate of inflation, occurred during the mid-sixteenth century. Prices of standing underwood in west Cambridgeshire, which cost between 3½d and 4½d per acre in the last quarter of the fifteenth century, jumped from 8d to 2s 6d during the 1540s, and the retail price of firewood may have risen even more.[127]

Grain supplies faced particular pressures during the decade 1550–60. Epidemic disease followed a succession of bad harvests, severely disrupting supplies, while price inflation, which had begun in the early sixteenth century, intensified during the 1540s and 1550s. Although the King's Hall accounts cease in 1544, shortly before the college became part of the new foundation of Trinity College, the King's College Mundum Books cover more years over the mid-sixteenth century than before. One would expect King's Hall and King's College to have similar wheat prices, as both drew on a similar area for supplies, and the average price differed only slightly between the two colleges in 1536, 1537 and 1542. Prices of wheat purchased by King's College in

---

126 P.J. Bowden, 'Statistical appendix', in Bowden, ed., *Chapters from the Agrarian History of England and Wales*, i: *Economic change: wages, profits and rents 1500–1750* (Cambridge, 1990), pp. 148–9.

127 Rackham, *Ancient woodland*, pp. 166–7; Hatcher, *Coal*, p. 36.

Table 6.3

Cambridge wheat and barley prices, 1556–7

	Prices of wheat and barley sold in the market per quarter			Prices of wheat bought by King's College per quarter
	Wheat	Barley		Wheat
28 Nov	32s	23s 8d –24s		
5 Dec		above 25s		
12 Dec	33s 4d +	26s 8d		
16 Dec		(30s) [a]		
19 Dec	36s 8d +	30s		
21 Dec	(40s +) [b]			
24 Dec		37s 4d		
2 Jan	45s 4d	33s 4d		
9 Jan	fell			
16 Jan	fell	26s 8d		
23 Jan	40s			
			31 Jan	39s 6d
6 Feb	rose		6 Feb	37s 4d; 38s 11½d
			2 Mar	40s
			19 Mar	35s 4d; 40s
			29 Apr	37s 4d
			6 May	40s
15 May	32s			
			10 Jul	30s 8d *in foro*

Source: Price of corn sold in the market: *Collection*, pp. 184–236;
Price obtained by King's College: KCMB, xiv, 1556/7 accounts.
Notes: [a] at Royston
[b] at St Ives

this period are shown in Table 6.2.[128] In addition to the college accounts, John Mere, a university bedell, wrote a detailed account of events in the town and university between November 1556 and May 1557, in which he recorded the prices in Cambridge market place during the dearth and the precautions taken against a concurrent outbreak of epidemic disease.[129]

Four poor harvests led to dramatic increases in the average prices of wheat purchased by King's College in the years 1552, 1555, 1556 and 1557 (Table 6.2). Hoskins recorded the harvests in these four years as bad, average, dearth and dearth.[130] Two widespread epidemics, affecting Cambridge during 1551–2 and 1556–9, compounded the misery: the later was one of the most virulent outbreaks of the sixteenth century.[131]

During 1555, when King's College faced a steep increase in wheat prices, Parliament responded to the difficulties that Cambridge experienced in securing food supplies. 'An Act that the Purveyors shall not take Victuals within v. miles of

---

128 Corn rents (see below, pp. 171–2) are excluded from the prices.
129 *Collection*, pp. 184–236.
130 Hoskins, 'Harvest fluctuations', 45 (for the years 1551, 1554, 1555 and 1556).
131 See Chapter 2, above, pp. 49–50.

Cambridge or Oxford' was passed on 21 October 1555. Recalling how the two university towns had formerly been free by custom from purveyance within a 5-mile circuit of each town, the act stated that purveyors had recently frequented the markets excessively. This made 'the Victuals both more scant & much dearer, to a notorious decay of scholars, which also daily in this great dearth is like to increase'. No purveyance was henceforth to be taken from within the town or the 5 miles adjoining, and the university was given the power to determine offences.[132] Purveyance for the king's army or the royal household had led to previous complaints from the town and university.[133] However, the statute was modified in 1571, as the townspeople had 'converted the benefit of the said Act to their private use and commodity without any profit or commodity to the poor scholars'. Thereafter, the vice-chancellor could license purveyors to take victuals or grain in the markets or within 5 miles adjoining. If any person within the precinct of 5 miles reasonably refused to provide necessary provisions for the universities, they would be liable to the demands of the royal purveyors.[134]

The price of wheat bought by King's College peaked during 1557, and John Mere's account of the prices of cereals on Saturdays in Cambridge market place between November 1556 and May 1557 reveals a peak at the beginning of January 1557 (Table 6.3). On 4 January there was a 'greate wante of breade in the town', but by 23 January, more supplies had arrived, and there was 'a greate markett of people and plenty of grayne and other vytells', although the price of wheat was still 25 per cent higher than at the end of the previous November. King's College bought wheat early in 1557, paying up to 40s per quarter, the same price quoted by Mere, and prices do not appear to have decreased significantly until the middle of May. On 11 May, Mere wrote, 'Butter and chese very myche fallen in Suffolke' and on the next day, 'all kynde of grayne fell at Royston and all other markettes'.[135] Mere attributed some of the price rises in Cambridge to the debasement of the coinage, noting on 19 December 1556 that the fall in the value of testons made 'all things dear'.[136]

In response to the shortages and substantial price rises, Norwich and Yarmouth established a permanent grain stock at this time, with funds administered by officials.[137] Although this did not happen in Cambridge, the authorities made provision for the upheaval caused by the dearth and epidemics. The vice-chancellor and mayor commanded the churchwardens in every parish to assess the number of the poor on 6 December, and subsequently ordered a record of how many had entered the parishes within the last three years. Superintendents visited parishes to assess the state of the poor and to determine appropriate relief: the first recorded assessment for poor relief in the town. On 9 December 1556, all infected with 'the plague' were sent to prison. A watch was appointed for 'strange beggars' on 14 December and by 3 January a

---

132 2 & 3 Philip & Mary, c. 15: *SR*, iv, part 1, pp. 289–90.

133 *Annals*, i, pp. 91, 439, ii, pp. 7, 68–9.

134 13 Elizabeth, c. 21: *SR*, iv, part 1, pp. 556–7.

135 KCMB, xiv, 1556/7 accounts; *Collection*, pp. 197, 208, 230.

136 Ibid., pp. 192, 194. The teston was a coin originally worth a shilling, but being of debased metal it fell in value during the 1540s and 1550s: *OED*, xvii, p. 834.

137 Hoskins, 'Harvest fluctuations', 36.

handful of people had been imprisoned for begging. During December the brewers requested and were granted higher prices for drink, but the bakers were summoned before the vice-chancellor for not baking sufficient brown bread for the poor.[138]

Despite the legislation enacted during the autumn of 1555, on 3 January 1557 the Privy Council ordered the justices of the peace in Cambridgeshire to make a search of all corn stored within 5 miles of the university. If the view of corn appeared insufficient, they were to order the university to be furnished with supplies from other nearby towns, and any person hindering the justices was to appear before the Privy Council. On the same day, the Privy Council asked the vice-chancellor to ensure that corn brought to the town was not conveyed outside it by badgers until the victuallers of the town and university were sufficiently furnished. These orders seem to have been received in Cambridge on 7 January.[139] Searches of grain appear to have been commissioned across the country in 1549–50 and 1556–7 with powers to force those with surpluses to bring their supplies to the market.[140] Commissioners had first been appointed by central government to survey stocks of available grain in 1527, although the mayor of Coventry had compiled a local census of available corn supplies in 1520. Such searches became the established practice at times of dearth during the sixteenth century, and the directions were codified into *Books of Orders*, issued by the Privy Council in 1586/7.[141]

The impact on towns of major shortages of grain has formed another strand of the debate over urban decline. Clark and Slack identified harvest failure as one of several factors, including commercial depression and the burden of poor migrants, which created serious instability within the urban hierarchy during the sixteenth century. The evidence from Cambridge during the 1550s, however, supports Goose's argument that the social discontent generated by shortages of food was sporadic and restricted, as the government and urban authorities worked together to make sure that food supplies to towns were maintained in periods of dearth.[142]

The long-term price rises in foodstuffs, which began in the early sixteenth century, and increased rapidly during the 1550s, were not accompanied by equivalent rises in wages or rents. Historians have discussed the extent to which this price inflation impoverished the wage-labourer,[143] yet it also placed institutions like the colleges in financial difficulties. Saltmarsh estimated that the decennial average expenditure on foodstuffs at King's College rose by 55 per cent between 1501–10 and 1541–50, but the decennial average estate revenue rose by only 18 per cent. To combat this shortfall, the college increasingly collected fines when leases were made, introduced

---

138 *Collection*, pp. 187–8, 190–1, 193, 196–7; Goose, 'Fertility and mortality', pp. 205–8.

139 UA, Collect.Admin.5, fols. 139v–140; *Collection*, p. 198.

140 P. Slack, 'Social policy and the constraints of government, 1547–58', in J. Loach and R. Tittler, eds., *The mid-Tudor polity c.1540–1560* (London, 1980), pp. 105–6.

141 *Coventry Leet Book*, iii, pp. 674–5; Dymond, 'Famine', 29–40; R.B. Outhwaite, *Dearth, public policy and social disturbance in England, 1550–1800* (London, 1991), pp. 39–41.

142 Clark and Slack, *English towns*, pp. 13–16; Goose, 'Urban variable', 167, 180; Dyer, *Decline and growth*, pp. 45–6.

143 See above, pp. 14–15.

Table 6.4

Wheat supplied to King's College in corn rents and other purchases, 1557–62

	Corn rents qrts.	Other purchases qrts.
1557	4.0	108.4
1558	76.0	72.5
1559	91.0	83.5
1561	105.5	1.0
1562	122.5	73.25

Source: KCMB, xiv–xv, 1557–62 accounts.

reversionary leases, and began to look to alternative methods of securing supplies of corn.[144]

King's College began to receive rents partly in wheat, beginning with the lease of Horstead in 1551, to take effect from Michaelmas 1557. From the account of 1557/8 onwards, the Mundum Books record wheat received from college estates including Grantchester, Dunton Waylett (Essex), Fordingbridge (Hampshire), Biggin (Hertfordshire) and Horstead (Norfolk) *ex conventione lesse* (by the agreement of the lessee).[145] The college always paid the lessee 6s 8d per quarter for this wheat, a price which in the years 1557 to 1562 ranged from between 2s to 22s below the average market price. Delivery dates were stipulated in the contracts and staggered over the year to ensure a continuous supply: the wheat from Horstead, for example, had to be delivered between Michaelmas and Christmas, that from Fordingbridge between Christmas and Easter, and that from Great Abington at the feast of St John the Baptist.[146] Between 2 and 10 quarters were collected from each estate, and over the next few years the corn rents provided a growing proportion of the wheat purchased, as shown in Table 6.4.

During the 1550s and 1560s, King's College tenants also began to supply other foodstuffs as part of their rents, for which, unlike the wheat, they were not usually reimbursed. The lessees of Barton manor and Biggin had to provide a boar at Christmas. The lease of Isleham manor made in 1561, to commence in 1568, specified that in addition to the £9 annual rent, 20 wethers were to be supplied, with heads, hearts and livers, every carcass weighing 40 lbs. Wethers were also to be supplied from Cottenham and Grantchester under leases of 1563 and 1567.[147] King's College began to take payments of wheat for entry fines for landholdings from the mid-1550s too. Hartleys brought 5 bushels of wheat for the fine for his customary land

---

144 J. Saltmarsh, 'The employment of the estates of King's College in the fifteenth and sixteenth centuries; with special reference to the origins of beneficial leasing' (unpublished fellowship dissertation, King's College, Cambridge, 1930), pp. 223–30, deposited in King's College Archives, JS 1/36, Copy A.

145 KCMB, xiv–xv, 1558/9–1561/2 accounts; KC Ledger Book, i, fols. 352–352v, 360–1, 365v–366, 366v–367.

146 KC Ledger Book, i, fols. 352–352v, 360–1, 364.

147 KC Ledger Book, i, fols. 361, 366v–7, ii, pp. 59, 85, 139–40.

in Grantchester, Grymstow was charged with 20 quarters of wheat for his entry to the farm of Barton manor, and Stephen of Coton gave 4 quarters for his copyhold fine.[148]

The move towards the payment of rents partly in kind could be found elsewhere, in response to the price inflation. Leases of the estates of Winchester College began to include the provision of fixed amounts of grain, livestock, firewood or fodder as part of their rents from 1551. Eton College collected rents in the form of grain and livestock from 1553.[149] Corn rents were systemised by an act of parliament in 1576, which stated that one-third of the rent in all future college leases was to be received in wheat at 6s 8d and malt barley at 5s per quarter, or in cash, at current market prices for wheat and malt. The corn was to be used only for the commons of the colleges and could not be sold.[150]

By the early 1560s, King's College had reduced its purchases of corn by more than half, which must have had a considerable impact on the local market. At a time of rising prices, and perhaps hastened by the scarcities of the 1550s, the college withdrew from the open market and increasingly relied upon its own estates for cheaper and more reliable supplies. This reversion to rents in kind was similar to the system of food rents that had supplied ecclesiastical and royal estates in the early middle ages.[151]

Conclusion

The expansion of the university and colleges between 1450 and 1560 created significant new demand, leading to the development of specialised trades within the town. However, many higher value goods came from outside the region, and particularly from London. Many provincial towns faced competition from the capital during the later middle ages. The inventory of a York chapman in 1446 contained debts to London merchants and goods including 'London' purses, glasses and a belt.[152] Margaret Paston complained of the 'right febill cheys' in the drapers' shops of Norwich, the largest provincial city in the country, and asked her son John to obtain cloth for her in London.[153] With the presence of the royal household and government, London could sustain specialised markets and services that other English towns struggled to compete against.[154] Consumers, particularly those with large incomes, found that only London could supply the range and quality of goods they required. The foundation of new and wealthier colleges, such as King's and St John's, created institutions that were more likely to look to London for supplies, than smaller colleges like Corpus and Peterhouse, or the poorer institutions of St John's Hospital and St

---

148 KCMB, xiv, 1554/5, 1555/6 accounts, xv, 1558/9 accounts.

149 Beveridge, *Wages and prices*, pp. 9, 101.

150 18 Elizabeth, c. 6: *SR*, iv, part 1, pp. 616–17; G.E. Aylmer, 'The economics and finances of the colleges and university c.1530–1640', in J. McConica, ed., *The history of the university of Oxford*, iii: *the collegiate university* (Oxford, 1986), pp. 535–43.

151 Miller, *Abbey and bishopric*, pp. 41–2.

152 Kermode, *Merchants*, p. 309.

153 *PL*, i, p. 252.

154 Kermode, *Merchants*, p. 253.

Radegund's Priory.

With the establishment of new colleges and the expansion of existing institutions, the university became increasingly independent of the townspeople for the provision of both higher value goods and basic foodstuffs. In the 1530s, the university could even go so far as to declare a total ban on the supply of victuals by freemen, although admittedly it did rely on a prominent section of the townspeople, its privileged persons, for a range of goods and services. Some colleges and religious houses organised the cultivation of their own estates to provide foodstuffs for their households, and drew tithes and rents in kind. Several colleges possessed their own facilities for baking and brewing, rather than relying on tradesmen in the town. When purchasing supplies of corn and fuel, Cambridge market was not used extensively, as only smaller quantities could usually be procured there. Instead, the larger colleges relied heavily on direct contracts with producers in the region around Cambridge. The accounts of King's Hall and King's College show that this hinterland extended to around 10 miles in radius around the town for supplies of wheat and malt barley, and up to 15 miles, sometimes more, for fuel. In contrast to the model of an urban hinterland proposed by Von Thünen, which placed a zone of forestry close to the city and commercial grain production beyond this, firewood was brought to Cambridge over longer distances than grain. Much depended on the availability of natural resources and transport links.[155]

A variety of suppliers sent corn and fuel to King's College and King's Hall during the 1450–1560 period, including a large number of demesne lessees, yeomen and husbandmen. A marked trend can be discerned, however, towards more frequent direct contracts with leading suppliers, and a commensurate decline in purchases in the market place. Some of these Cambridgeshire suppliers appear to have resembled demesne farmers in other areas of the country, like those in the west midlands and the south-east, who consolidated holdings, and oriented their production towards markets, often meeting demand from nearby towns. Such farmers were arguably adopting more 'capitalist' methods of production.[156]

Yet the hinterland from which Cambridge drew its basic food supplies, like those of most medieval towns, was very restricted. Even the largest and wealthiest colleges relied on a relatively small area for their corn, and they faced large price increases in years of scarcity. In response to rising prices, in the late 1550s King's College, and subsequently other colleges, began to rely increasingly on rents received in kind from their own estates. This was not a move towards a more capitalist, market-oriented economy, but to increasing self-sufficiency. Rents paid in food rather than in cash echoed the practices of the early middle ages and, it has been suggested, helped to preserve the medieval pattern of tenure and cultivation in the common fields of Cambridgeshire until the nineteenth century.[157]

---

155 Lee, 'Feeding the colleges', 243-64.

156 C. Dyer, 'Were there any capitalists in fifteenth-century England?', in C. Dyer, ed., *Everyday life in medieval England* (London, 1994), pp. 316–20; Mate, 'Land market', 60–1.

157 W. Cunningham, 'The economic history of Cambridgeshire', in *Ely Diocesan Remembrancer* (1909), 21–2.

Chapter 7

Property and building projects

This chapter examines two inter-related aspects of the economy of Cambridge and its region, which illustrate additional links between the town and hinterland, and provide indications of economic activity in the town. Firstly, the property market in the town is examined through the rental income received by Cambridge Corporation and the arrears owed to Corpus Christi College. Secondly, the many construction projects that took place in the town in this period are explored to reveal the sources of supply for building materials and labour.

Urban land market

The depopulation that most towns experienced in the fourteenth and fifteenth centuries reduced demand for urban property. Although initially after the Black Death, the increased income of many townspeople and the expansion of cloth-making led to buoyant demand in some towns, depression became more general after 1420. The overall extent and density of property was reduced: fewer lands and houses were subdivided, and gardens and waste grounds appeared on the former sites of buildings. The property income of Oseney Abbey in Oxford and the cathedral priory at Canterbury declined during the second half of the fifteenth century, reaching a nadir in Canterbury in the last quarter of the century and at Oxford in the early 1500s. Empty sites and dilapidated properties could be found throughout the smaller town of Wells by the first quarter of the fifteenth century, and the borough's rental income had fallen further by the mid-sixteenth century. Rents in some London suburbs began to recover before the end of the fifteenth century, but property values and settlement densities in many central commercial and residential districts of the capital did not increase substantially until after 1550.[1]

Few published studies have examined the property market in Cambridge, apart from the acquisition of land for sites where colleges were founded.[2] Examination of the property rentals of St John's Hospital has shown that the institution suffered from the difficulties encountered by many urban landlords in the later middle ages: large and long-standing arrears, dilapidation of properties, and a major fall in land values. In 1490, rents in Cambridge comprised 31 per cent of the hospital's total income. St John's College consolidated this estate by acquiring additional properties in the town.[3]

---

1 A.F. Butcher, 'Rent and the urban economy: Oxford and Canterbury in the later middle ages', *Southern History*, 1 (1979), 11–43; D.G. Shaw, *The creation of a community: the city of Wells in the middle ages* (Oxford, 1993), pp. 47–54; D. Keene, 'The property market in English towns A.D. 1100–1600', in J-C. Maire Vigueur, ed., *D'Une Ville à l'autre: Structures, Matérielles et Organisation de L'Espace dans les villes Européenes XIIIe–XVIe Siècle* (Rome, 1989), pp. 214–17; Rosser, *Medieval Westminster*, pp. 74–92, 173–7.

2 Willis and Clark, *Architectural history*, i–iii, *passim*.

3 Rubin, *Charity and community*, pp. 226–35; Underwood, 'Impact', pp. 178–9.

Table 7.1

Property income of the Cambridge colleges, 1546

	Cambridge	Cambridgeshire	Adjacent counties	Elsewhere	Total income
	£	£	£	£	£
King's College	22.08	96.06	224.67	612.24	1,010.65[1]
St John's	54.54	83.17	142.51	256.65	536.87
Christ's	2.62	68.83	102.15	115.90	287.50
Queens'	3.08	106.57	117.03	45.44	272.68
King's Hall	11.50	73.67	75.30	53.55	214.01
Corpus Christi	124.71	46.66	0.00	0.00	171.38
Pembroke	0.80	96.81	33.00	40.53	171.14
Michaelhouse	16.24	106.90	4.35	14.17	141.66
Peterhouse	17.83	104.79	9.18	6.35	138.15
Clare Hall	14.45	79.95	28.97	8.99	132.36
Jesus	41.41	62.34	0.00	26.67	130.42
Gonville Hall	18.40	35.25	66.33	0.00	119.97
Trinity Hall	23.85	6.00	57.71	31.53	119.10
St Catharine's	8.10	34.92	12.90	0.00	55.93
Magdalene	0.84	0.00	20.00	23.06	43.90

Source: Documents, i, pp. 105–294.
Notes: All sources of income are stated, and are net. Cambridgeshire includes the Isle of Ely but excludes the town of Cambridge. Adjacent counties comprise Bedfordshire, Essex, Hertfordshire, Huntingdonshire, Norfolk and Suffolk.
[1] There is a discrepancy between the sum of individual sources of property income and the total income stated in the survey

The survey of the colleges undertaken in 1546 provides a convenient starting point for examining the extent of landholdings in the town and region. The amount of property owned by colleges in Cambridge varied considerably as Table 7.1 reveals. The largest net income from property in the town was received by Corpus Christi College, which had been founded by two town guilds; large property holdings in the town were also held by St John's and Jesus Colleges, which had formerly been religious houses. The older colleges and religious houses had accumulated urban property over several centuries through pious gifts from property holders in the town. Urban rents ranged from substantial incomes, like the 66s 8d yielded from a tenement in Holy Trinity parish for St John's College in 1519–20, to 'quit-rents' of a few pence, representing arbitration payments, pious rent charges, and sums in lieu of personal services.[4]

Many colleges held considerable estates outside Cambridge. The older foundations of Corpus Christi, Peterhouse and Michaelhouse drew the largest proportion of their incomes from within Cambridgeshire, while King's College and St John's received greater revenues from estates in other counties. King's drew income in 15 English counties that stretched from Devon to Suffolk and from Lancashire to Sussex. The range of sources of income was also wide: in the case of King's College it included

---

[4] Underwood, 'Impact', p. 179; C.P. Hall, 'Quit-rents', *Letter of the Corpus Association*, 61 (1982), 49–54.

rents, farms, tithes, perquisites of courts, entry fines, and revenue from mills, woods, pasture and marsh, sales of wood, London houses, and six brick kilns at Ruislip in Middlesex.[5] The distribution of college estates depended largely on the gifts of founders and benefactors, many of whom, until the Reformation, obliged the colleges to offer prayers in return for their gifts. The personal connections of some founders led to concentrations of properties in particular areas, while the high proportion of income derived from estates in Cambridgeshire and neighbouring counties suggests that, as among the Oxford colleges, there was a strong preference for holding properties near the university town.[6]

Many residents of Cambridge also had property interests outside the town.[7] Several Cambridge townsmen who stood as members of parliament for the borough, for example, invested in property in the region; they were men of substantial means, as the wages paid by the borough were insufficient to cover their daily expenses in London. John Leynton acquired Caxton manor in 1488, Thomas Brakyn purchased Chesterton manor in 1540, and Edward Slegge obtained a 21-year lease of lands at Comberton in 1550, and later purchased lands of former chantries in Cambridgeshire, Staffordshire and elsewhere worth £1,539.[8]

Through the landholdings of townspeople and town institutions, Cambridge was linked not only to many parts of the county and neighbouring counties, but also to estates much further afield. The extent of these links varied considerably, but in the case of the colleges might include the appointment of fellows to church livings and the supply of foodstuffs by tenants. Some Oxford colleges recruited scholars and servants from their estates.[9]

Cambridge Corporation was another significant landowner in the town, and the property accounted for by the borough treasurers produced a gross income of about £25 in the 1540s. This was not large compared to some of the colleges, but provides a useful indicator of the pattern of rents over the fifteenth and sixteenth centuries. The corporation's property income consisted of rents from houses, shops, lands and market stalls. In addition, empty or waste grounds were frequently let to the owners of adjoining houses, and rents were charged for encroachments on waste sites, ditches and lanes with, for example, buttresses, chimneys and drains. Cambridge Corporation had requested the right to make its profit from the small lanes and waste places of the town in 1330; no royal licence approving this request is recorded, but the corporation's right was effectively conceded in the fifteenth century when Henry VI and Edward IV purchased waste ground from the corporation for the colleges of King's and Queens'.[10] The treasurers also recorded a handful of other items under the

---

5   *Documents*, i, pp. 246–63; See also Saltmarsh,'Hand-list', 32–8.
6   Evans and Faith,'College estates', pp. 651–6.
7   For other towns, see Kermode, *Merchants*, pp. 276–90; Britnell, *Colchester*, pp. 209–10, 260–1; Thrupp, *Merchant class*, pp. 118–30.
8   Wedgewood, *History of Parliament*, p. 543; Bindoff, *House of Commons*, i, pp. 43, 485, iii, p. 327.
9   For food supplies, see above, Chapter 6; Evans and Faith, 'College estates', pp. 655–6, 687; *Canterbury College, Oxford*, iv, ed. W.A. Pantin, Oxford Historical Soc., new ser., XXX (Oxford, 1985), p. 91.
10 Maitland, *Township*, pp. 83–4, 188–90; *CBD*, pp. xxxvii.

Property and building projects

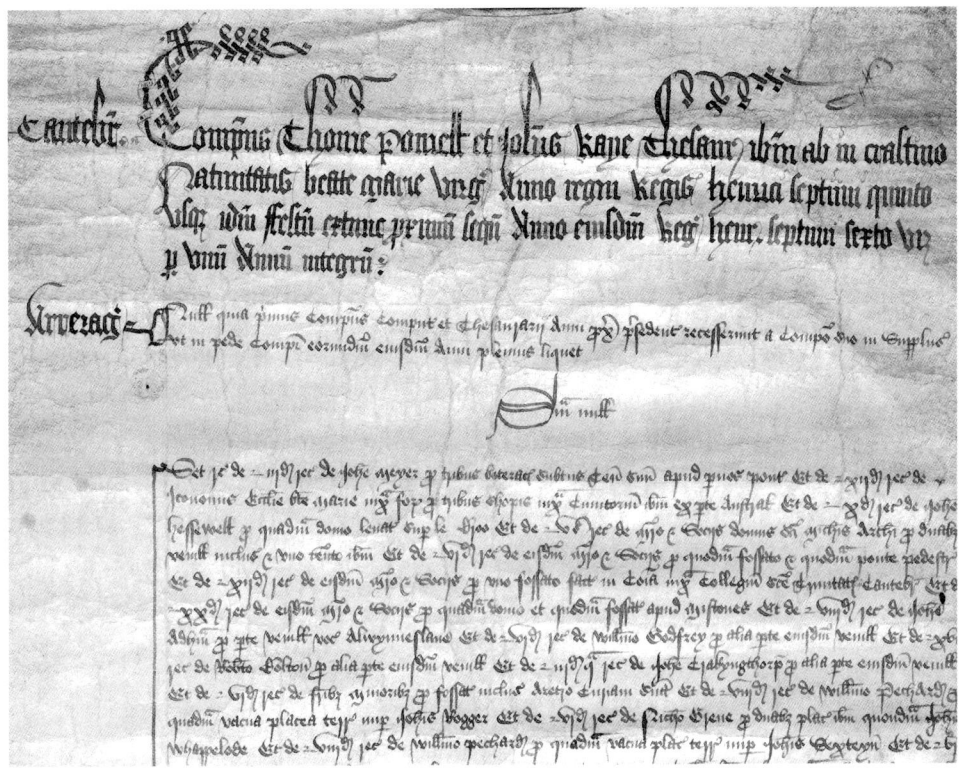

Figure 7.1 Cambridge borough treasurers' accounts of 1488/9, showing list of property rents (CCA, X/71/5: by permission of the County Record Office, Cambridge)

section for property income in their accounts, which have been excluded from the calculations used here.[11]

Figure 7.2 presents the corporation's gross income and the mean average annual rent. The latter series is a rather crude measure, because the range of rents was so large. Like many urban landlords, Cambridge Corporation received many small payments or 'quit-rents'.[12] Nonetheless, the average annual rent provides a useful indicator because the corporation was obtaining an ever-growing number of properties. Property income came from 61 different properties in 1422/3, 81 in 1500/1, and 128 in 1560/1. The treasurers' accounts show a sharp decline in property income and average rents during the 1420s and 1430s. When the surviving accounts resume again in the 1480s both series declined further, and the average rent probably reached its nadir around 1500. By the 1520s, the average rent had almost, but not quite, returned to the levels of the 1420s and 1430s. The former fifteenth-century level of

---

11 Items excluded are the farm of the fish and flesh stalls (see Chapter 4), the farm of the sergeants' maces, leases of the mills (see above, p. 58), rents of booths (see Chapter 5), and profits from the sale of timber.

12 Hall, 'Quit-rents', 49–54.

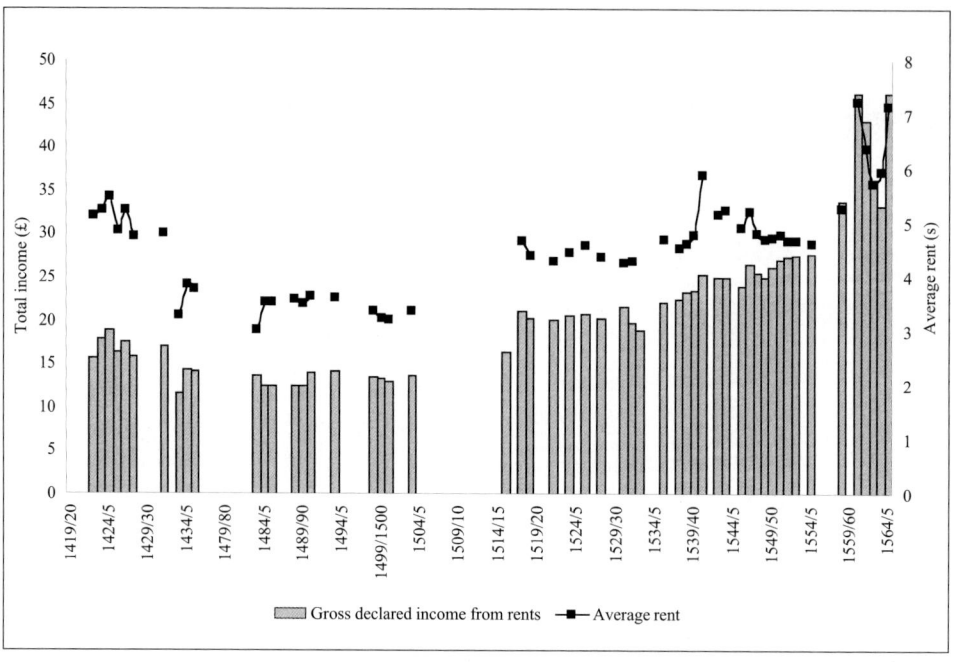

Figure 7.2 Cambridge Corporation's property income
Source: CCA, X/70/1–10, X/71/1–10, X/71A, XVII/24A; CCTA, i–ii.

average rent was not reached again consistently until the 1540s and not exceeded until the 1550s and 1560s. Furthermore, the severe inflation of the mid-sixteenth century meant that money was worth less than in the early fifteenth century: the price index of a shopping basket of consumables prepared by Phelps Brown and Hopkins, with a base of 100 in 1451–75, had risen to 265 by 1560.[13] So in real terms, average rents had still not returned to the level of 130 years before, although there had been a substantial recovery from their nadir at the beginning of the sixteenth century.

Entry fines and leases determined by the corporation, which are recorded from 1544 in the Common Day Book, reinforce the impression given by the movements in property income, that demand for property was still relatively limited in the mid-sixteenth century. In the 1540s and 1550s property was let for fairly long periods of time: terms of between 20 and 40 years were common, while two leases for 99 years were recorded. Fines were generally relatively low, and could be less than the annual rent, although Dr Hatcher paid a fine of £13 6s 8d for a 99-year lease of several houses.[14] However, the rents accruing to other landlords, including many colleges, were slow to increase in the sixteenth century. This time lag was due to the length of leases and the failure of many landowners to distinguish the long-term rise in prices, even after demand for land must have risen with the growth in population.[15]

---

13 Phelps Brown and Hopkins, *Perspectives*, pp. 13–59.
14 CCA, Palmer/Barnard vol. 57, fols. 8–9, 11v, 16, 18v, 22v, 25v, 31v, 64v.
15 Aylmer, 'Economics and finances', pp. 524–5.

Property and building projects

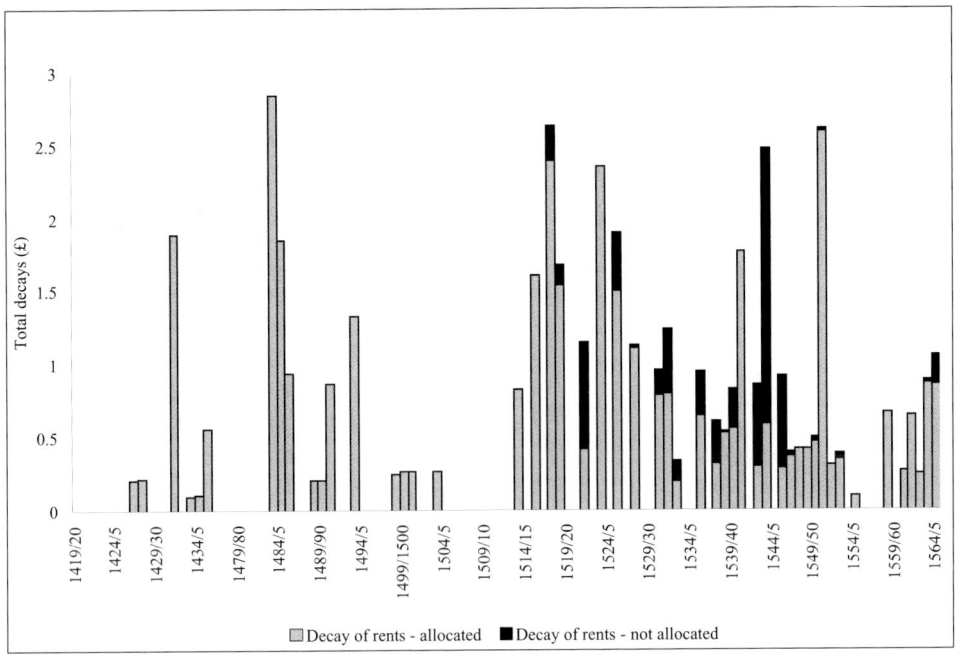

Figure 7.3 Decays of rent from Cambridge Corporation's property
Source: CCA, X/70/1–10, X/71/1–10, X/71A, XVII/24A; CCTA, i–i.

The property income recorded in the accounts of the Cambridge borough treasurers, like those of other institutions, shows only the theoretical amount due. Many of these rents could not in practice be collected, and such rents were usually listed under headings of decays or defaults of rent. A similar picture has emerged in other late medieval towns. Of the rents in Newcastle-upon-Tyne acquired by University College, Oxford, possibly only half the annual declared value reached the college during the 1450s and early 1460s, and in the next 15 years less than a third of the total rent was collected. This absence of payments occurred despite a progressive fall in property values, and the periodic writing-off of arrears. By 1509–10, half of Oseney Abbey's rents in Oxford were in decay. Large amounts of waste and decay from urban property rents were also recorded among the accounts of York Minster and Durham Priory from the mid-fifteenth century.[16] Rural rents, too, were more commonly static or declining than rising in the late medieval period, and many lords faced major problems in drawing their full revenues.[17]

In the Cambridge treasurers' accounts, decays or defaults of rents included cases

---

16   A.F. Butcher, 'Rent, population and economic change in late-medieval Newcastle', *Northern History*, 14 (1978), 67–77; Butcher, 'Oxford and Canterbury', 37; R.B. Dobson, 'Cathedral chapters and cathedral cities: York, Durham and Carlisle in the fifteenth century', *Northern History*, 19 (1983), 36; M. Bonney, *Lordship and the urban community: Durham and its overlords, 1250–1540* (Cambridge, 1990), pp. 123–8.

17   Britnell, *Commercialisation*, pp. 193–4; Evans and Faith, 'College estates', pp. 689–91.

Table 7.2

Cambridge rents of Corpus Christi College, 1536/7–1551

	Total declared value of rents £	Total rents received £	Arrears £	Decay £	Vacant £
1536/7	149.37	102.26	41.43	3.10	0
1537/8	147.33	118.66	22.11	6.60	0
1538/9	143.16	121.64	17.26	4.01	0
1539/40	148.08	112.31	30.80	5.30	0
1540/1	147.81	109.99	28.07	9.20	0
1541/2	144.15	112.22	25.44	6.30	0
1542/3	144.00	111.35	23.29	9.40	0
1543/4	144.25	107.43	25.94	10.38	0
1544/5	138.75	102.99	26.08	9.68	0
1545/6	136.15	104.39	26.15	5.86	0
1546/7	134.77	97.20	28.48	1.61	7.63
1551	131.12				

Source: 1536/7–1546/7: CCC, Accounts, 'Arreragia', 1523–47; 1551: CCC, XXXIX.119.
Note: includes all property in Cambridge and lands in Cambridge fields, but not rents from Grantchester and Barton, which are not recorded consistently in the 'Arreragia'.

where rents had been reduced, or properties were vacant and in the hands of the treasurers.[18] They were recorded under the heading *defectus redditus* and sometimes also after the balance had been calculated at the end of the account. Figure 7.3 relates only to decays from property rents: other items listed in the accounts have been excluded. The corporation's decays of rents were generally fairly small in the fifteenth century, usually totalling less than 3 per cent of the gross income. This suggests that the lists of rents due were revised fairly frequently to reflect changes in rents collected. Only in 1483/4 did defects of rents amount to nearly 21 per cent of the gross income, when rents could not be extracted from a number of shops. When the accounts moved from being compiled on parchment rolls to paper books, which begin to survive from 1515/16, the treasurers recorded both decays of rent allocated and not allocated. Decays of rents increased slightly in total during the sixteenth century, but as the total gross income from rents was also rising, the proportion of the total rental income in decay did not increase.

The continuing problems of managing an urban estate in Cambridge in the mid-sixteenth century are illustrated by a book of rent arrears of tenants of Corpus Christi College, dating from 1523 to 1547.[19] Initially, tenants with arrears were listed for each Cambridge parish. For the last 11 years, though, from 1535/6, a more systematic approach was adopted, with all tenants being recorded, and arrears listed to the left of the names and payments to the right; totals of payments, arrears, and decays of rent – reductions to the stated rent – were calculated for each parish, making comparisons much easier. These rents can also be compared with those listed in a rental of 1551.[20]

---

18 e.g. CCA, X/71/7.
19 CCC, Accounts, 'Arreragia', 1523–47.
20 CCC, XXXIX.119.

Table 7.3

Distribution of reductions by parish in the Cambridge rents of Corpus Christi College, 1536/7–1551

Cambridge parish	1536/7 total declared rent £	1546/7 total declared rent £	1551 total declared rent £	1536/7–1551 change %
St Peter and St Giles	3.28	3.23	3.18	-3.05
St Clement and St Sepulchre	7.78	5.78	4.37	-43.84
Holy Trinity	6.93	6.93	6.08	-12.15
St Edward	14.99	12.89	12.62	-15.79
St Benedict	30.85	29.17	28.63	-7.19
All Saints	14.00	13.03	13.79	-1.52
St Michael	2.33	2.33	1.97	-15.71
Great St Mary	30.13	29.18	26.33	-12.61
St Botolph	17.68	13.03	16.01	-9.43
St Mary the Less	6.19	6.54	5.88	-5.11
St Andrew	6.60	3.57	3.40	-48.42
Jesus	0.53	0.60	0.60	12.50
Cambridge fields	8.08	8.49	8.26	2.19
Total	149.37	134.77	131.12	-12.22

Source: 1536/7–1546/7: CCC, Accounts, 'Arreragia', 1523–47; 1551: CCC, XXXIX.119.

Between 1536/7 and 1551, Corpus Christi College received between 68 per cent and 85 per cent of the total town rents owed every year, and arrears comprised between 12 per cent and 28 per cent of the total rents (Table 7.2). Decays comprised between 2 per cent and 7 per cent of the total, and there were no vacant holdings, apart from in 1546/7. As in other late medieval towns, Corpus faced the inability or reluctance of tenants to pay the full amount of rent. Unlike some landowners, though, the college did not allow notional arrears to accumulate and instead made regular downward revisions to the total rent. In most years, the total rent roll was reduced slightly, by between 1 and 4 per cent. By 1551, the total declared value of the urban rents was £18 lower or 12 per cent less than in 1536/7, a considerable fall over only 15 years. In real terms, the decline had been even more pronounced, as inflation over the same period was reducing the purchasing power of money.[21]

Table 7.3 reveals that while some reductions to the total declared rents were made in most Cambridge parishes, the largest reductions were concentrated in the parishes of St Andrew, to the east of the town centre, and St Clement and St Sepulchre, to the north. Although these parishes partly covered suburban parts of Cambridge, beyond the river and the King's Ditch, other parishes which also had areas outside these boundaries, like St Mary the Less and St Peter and St Giles, experienced fewer reductions.[22] Only in Jesus parish and in the Cambridge fields, did the total rental income actually increase between 1536/7 and 1551, and even in these areas, some arrears of rent were recorded. This suggests that property values had fallen across

---

21   Phelps Brown and Hopkins, *Perspective*, p. 29.

22   The King's Ditch was originally a defensive feature, which became used as a sewer and rubbish tip. Its course is shown on Lyne's map of 1574. For parish boundaries, see Lobel, 'Cambridge', map 6.

much of the town during the fifteenth century, and failed to recover substantially even by the middle of the sixteenth century.

One factor, specific to Cambridge, which may have contributed to the decline in rental income, was the falling demand from members of the university for rented accommodation. Earlier generations of scholars had required rooms for lodgings and teaching, and by 1231, the university had established a regulatory body to maintain a balance between the needs of landlords and scholars as tenants. This provided a structure for setting rents and helped to develop a range of properties customarily used by scholars. Landlords included individuals, ranging from the beneficed clergy to burgesses, and institutions which owned student hostels, such as Barnwell Priory and St Radegund's Priory. Over the later fifteenth and sixteenth centuries, as the university and colleges developed purpose-built accommodation, there were fewer opportunities for urban landlords to let premises to masters and students.[23] As with the supply of foodstuffs, the university was becoming increasingly self-sufficient from the townspeople.

While Cambridge was one of some 80 towns named in the Rebuilding Acts passed by parliament between 1536 and 1544, it is difficult to make any judgement about the state of the urban property market from these statutes.[24] In a standard form, the acts described the danger presented by many dilapidated buildings and vacant sites near the main streets and ordered owners to restore these properties within a set period, and if they neglected to do so, the corporation could rebuild them. Phythian-Adams viewed these statutes as evidence of widespread urban decline, while Bridbury attributed them to a demand for housing in a period of growth. However, in practice, relatively few properties in any town appear to have been affected by these new measures, and most of the known applications of this legislation occurred in the 1570s and subsequent decades.[25] In 1544, only two years after its rebuilding act, Cambridge secured a bill for paving the town streets. This described the town as 'wele inhabyted and replenysshed withe people bothe in the Universitie ... also wyth dyvers and sundry Artyficers & other inhabitauntes', suggesting some recovery of population after the fifteenth-century decline. The bill required owners to pay for the paving outside their houses; lessees could pay and then retain the amount out of their rent.[26] The introduction of these additional expenses might suggest that the urban land market had experienced at least some recovery by the 1540s.

Building projects

The built environment of English towns during the later middle ages reflected the changed balance of population and resources. On the one hand, the contraction in the size of many urban populations led to properties becoming larger and the

---

23   Cobban, *University life*, pp. 183–9.
24   Cambridge is included in 33 Hen VIII, c. 36: *SR*, iii, p. 875.
25   Phythian-Adams, 'Urban decay', p. 178; Bridbury, 'English provincial towns', 23–4; Dyer, *Decline and growth*, pp. 35–7; R. Tittler, 'For the "re-edification of townes": the rebuilding statutes of Henry VIII', *Albion*, 22 (1990), 591–605.
26   35 Hen VIII, c. 15: *SR*, iii, pp. 974–5.

Figure 7.4 King's College Chapel, looking south-west. Construction was undertaken in three main phases, from 1446 to 1461, between 1477 and 1484, and from 1508 to 1515

abandonment of some marginal sites. On the other hand, the increased incomes and standards of living for many after the Black Death were reflected by a general improvement in housing between 1350 and 1520. Spending on houses increased not only because materials and labour had become more expensive, but because houses were being built to higher specifications. Improved standards of carpentry and the appearance of more efficient fireplaces and chimneys were found in many peasant houses, while some wealthier townspeople added tiled roofs and glazed windows, and many purchased large quantities of clothing, bedding and household textiles.[27] There was a notable fashion to build town halls and restyle parish churches in late medieval towns, although such rebuilding is often obscured by the lack of an accurate chronology and uncertainty as to who was actually funding the work: church rebuilding, for example, may indicate individual rather than collective prosperity.[28]

Throughout the late medieval period, Cambridge resounded to the noise of building work. From the mid-fifteenth century onwards, St Catharine's, Queens' and King's Colleges and the university's canon and civil law schools were constructed. In the early sixteenth century the pace of activity intensified, with the construction of

---

27 J. Schofield and G. Stell, 'The built environment 1300–1540', in *CUHB*, i, pp. 384–93; Dyer, *Standards*, pp. 166–7, 204–7.

28 Bridbury, 'English provincial towns', 14; Postan, 'Fifteenth century', 164–5; Dobson, 'Urban decline', pp. 273–5.

Table 7.4

College building projects, 1450–1560

	1450	1460	1470	1480	1490	1500
Peterhouse	1450 kitchen	1460–66 chambers, combination room				
Clare Hall						
Pembroke	1452 library	1463 chapel features				
Gonville Hall				1481 garden walls	1490 east range of Gonville court	
Trinity Hall						
Corpus Christi	1443–74 library, master's lodge	1456 bakehouse begins			1487–1515 new buildings, fittings	
King's College	1441–c.1454 work on inital site	1446–61 chapel building		1477–84 chapel building		
Queens'	1448–9 Front Court				1494–5 cloister work	
St Catharine's				1473 first buildings completed		
Jesus					1495–6 alterations	
King's Hall & Trinity College		1464–85 chapel			1490–2 porter's lodge	
Schools & libraries	1457 Canon law school, library	1457–71 Philosophy & Civil law schools, library	1470–3 library			

	1510	1520	1530	1540	1550	1560
Peterhouse						
Clare Hall		1523–8 rebuilding after fire	1535 chapel			
Pembroke			1534–7 chapel: west window			
Gonville Hall						
Trinity Hall	1513 chapel completed			1545 walls		
Corpus Christi				1544–53 dovehouse, gallery	1557–69 library	
King's College	1508–15 chapel building	1515–31 chapel glazing	1531–5 roodloft	1536 lodge	1544–5 high altar installed	
Queens'		1515–16 cloister roof repairs	1533–4 brewhouse built			
St Catharine's		1517 chambers on south side				
Jesus	1503–7 contributions to buildings west of entrance					
Christ's	1505–11 college buildings erected					
St John's	1511–16 building	1516–19 chapel adapted	1528 small additional court			
Magdalene		1519 hall built				
King's Hall & Trinity College		1518–24 and 1528–35 gateway tower		1547 hall, buttery repairs	1554–67 chambers, kitchen, chapel	

Sources: RCHMC; Willis & Clark, *Architectural history*, i–iii.

buildings for the new colleges of Jesus, Christ's and St John's. As well as the construction of King's College Chapel, one of the last major ecclesiastical building projects in England, many parish churches were extended or altered. The study of this building work relies on documentary and physical evidence; in Cambridge both survive in large quantities, and have been collated by Willis and Clark and the Royal Commission on Historical Monuments.[29]

Cycles of building activity are difficult to identify. A study of the chronology of major church building during the middle ages found a peak between 1210 and 1350, followed by a decline reaching a nadir in the mid-fifteenth century, attributed to the loss in incomes after the Black Death experienced by ecclesiastical and aristocratic patrons.[30] A period of intensive rebuilding across the country, accompanied by an increase in household furnishings and equipment, was identified between 1570 and

---

29   Willis and Clark, *Architectural history*, i–iii; RCHMC.
30   Dyer, *Standards*, pp. 101–2.

1640, but more recently, it has been claimed that more was achieved between 1660 and 1739. A regular cycle of 20-year peaks in building activity has also been detected from the mid-sixteenth century onwards.[31]

Peaks in building activity in Cambridge can be identified more readily from the work produced for the colleges. Building projects tended to occur when student numbers were highest: between the late sixteenth and mid-nineteenth centuries, the largest amount of building occurred when university matriculations peaked between 1610 and 1640 and between 1820 and 1830.[32] In the absence of matriculation figures, such trends cannot be discerned with the same degree of confidence before the late sixteenth century. Nonetheless, it seems likely that the increase in student numbers during the fifteenth century led to a renewed programme of building. Table 7.4, which provides a time line of major college building projects in Cambridge, shows the extensive building work which took place during the late fifteenth and early sixteenth centuries, and the particular concentration of activity which occurred around the 1510s and 1520s.

This flurry of activity was not confined to new buildings. Older colleges extended and improved their accommodation as they increasingly housed more university members. A short account of the history of Corpus Christi College, produced for the use of Archbishop Matthew Parker, relates that there was little glass or panelling in the chambers of the college before Henry VIII's reign, and describes how glazing, plastering, and panelling of the master's lodgings and the fellows' chambers were added between 1509 and the 1560s.[33] This may reflect the increase in standards of living among college fellows which has been identified as occurring after 1500.[34]

Several of the town's churches were extended or rebuilt in this period. Work is most well-documented at Great St Mary's, where the nave, chapels and aisles were rebuilt between 1478 and 1519, and work on the tower continued intermittently until 1608. At St Edward's, north and south chapels and chancel arcades were added between 1446 and 1466, and the nave roof of St Bene't's was renewed in 1452. St Bene't's and St Mary the Less had additional building by the colleges of Corpus Christi and Peterhouse in the later fifteenth century. Fifteenth and early sixteenth-century work can also be found in the churches of St Botolph, St Clement, and Holy Trinity.[35]

Many of the parish churches in the county also had construction works in progress during at least some part of the second half of the fifteenth and early sixteenth centuries, ranging from small additions such as a porch or new window to clerestories and towers. Some rebuilding was essential, as at Great Eversden, where lightning damaged the church in 1466, and at Kingston, where the church burnt down and the bell tower was brought down by the wind. Most work, though, was the result of pious bequests and a desire to increase the light and height of earlier buildings. At many

---

31   W.G. Hoskins, 'The rebuilding of rural England, 1570–1640', *Past and Present*, 4 (1953), 44–59; R. Machin, 'The Great Rebuilding: a reassessment', *Past and Present*, 77 (1977), 33–56; R. Machin, 'The mechanism of the pre-industrial building cycle', *Vernacular Architecture*, 8 (1977), 815–19.

32   *RCHMC*, chart facing p. lxxxiii.

33   Willis and Clark, *Architectural history*, i, pp. 242, 252–5.

34   See Chapter 6, above, p. 149.

35   *RCHMC*, pp. 258, 264, 267, 269, 271, 275, 281.

churches, the sight of activity in a neighbouring parish probably stimulated new work: there was a campaign of tower building in west Cambridgeshire around 1400; rebuilding in a cluster of parishes, possibly inspired by Burwell, in the 1490s, and works at a string of churches between Cambridge and Haverhill in the early sixteenth century.[36]

The lack of extensive landed estates in Cambridgeshire meant that noble households undertook relatively little building work in the county. The bishop of Ely's palaces at Downham and Ely were both rebuilt by Bishop Alcock (1486-1500) and a brick solar tower was constructed at Castle Camps around 1500.[37] Several large houses were built, though, by men with successful careers in royal service: Lord North, son of a London merchant, who became Chancellor of the Court of Augmentations, built Kirtling Tower in 1530 and a funeral chapel in the parish church. Thomas Wendy, physician to Henry VIII, bought property in 1541 to construct Haslingfield Hall. John Hynde commenced Madingley Hall soon after 1543. Sir John Huddleston, vice-chamberlain and privy-councillor by 1554, rebuilt Sawston Hall, probably between 1557 and 1584.[38]

Building materials

Building work in Cambridge relied heavily on materials from outside the town. Cambridgeshire has been described as among the least fortunate of English counties for the availability of local building materials.[39] Although clay was readily available for brickmaking, and the Fens provided reed and sedge for thatch, there was no good stone and even wood was in short supply.

Clunch, a soft limestone, comes from chalk in the southern and eastern parts of the county. The stone is easily carved, making it suitable for sculpture, but weathers quickly, and so was often faced with rendering, imported stone, or brick. The stone was used extensively for many local churches and Cambridge colleges, and in the sixteenth century its use in secular buildings became more widespread, possibly after demand from church building had fallen. Clunch was quarried in several places within 10 miles of Cambridge: in the west at Barrington, the Eversdens, Harlton, Haslingfield and Orwell, towards the fen-edge at Burwell, Swaffham Prior and Reach, and at Hinton, where lime was also obtained.[40] Several of these quarries were used for building projects at King's Hall, Christ's and St John's.[41] Some colleges even secured rights to quarries. St John's extracted stone at Hinton from a quarry owned by its founder, Lady Margaret Beaufort, and Trinity College reserved the stone quarry at

---

36 S. Cotton, 'Perpendicular churches', in C. Hicks, ed., *Cambridgeshire churches* (Stamford, 1997), pp. 95–106.

37 A. Emery, *Greater medieval houses of England and Wales 1300–1500*, ii: *East Anglia, central England and Wales* (Cambridge, 2000), pp. 16, 83, 89, 165.

38 Pevsner, *Buildings*, pp. 404, 419–20, 436, 453; *VCH Cambs.*, vi, pp. 250–1.

39 Pevsner, *Buildings*, p. 289.

40 *RCHMC*, p. xcviii; *RCHMW*, p. xxxi; *RCHMNE*, pp. xxviii–xxix. Hinton is now known as Cherry Hinton.

41 SJC, D106.1, fols. 8v, 10v, 16; C17.23; D107.7, pp. 20, 25, 26; Cobban, *King's Hall*, pp. 216–17.

Barrington in their lease of the rectory in 1575.[42]

For stone of higher quality than clunch, builders in Cambridge and its region had to rely on imports from quarries in the limestone belt which stretched across Northamptonshire and Rutland, and lay about 40 miles from Cambridge. These East Midland quarries supplied building stone to a large number of cathedrals, castles, monasteries and churches across East Anglia.[43] Stone from quarries at Barnack, south-east of Stamford, was used in some Cambridge churches, and by several fenland monasteries, which acquired quarrying rights there. Supplies had been exhausted, though, by the beginning of the sixteenth century.[44] Weldon, north of Kettering, supplied stone for King's College Chapel, for most of Bishop Alcock's work at Jesus College, for part of King's Hall tower in 1520/1, and for Great St Mary's Church in 1522.[45] Other quarries in the East Midlands at King's Cliffe, Clipsham, and Ancaster provided stone for Cambridge colleges and stone slates were brought from Collyweston, near Stamford.[46]

The most distant sources of building stone used in Cambridge in this period were the supplies of magnesium limestone obtained from Yorkshire for King's College Chapel. In 1446, Henry VI granted to the college a quarry in Thefdale, or Thevesdale, near Tadcaster, which had supplied stone to York Minster and other Yorkshire abbeys. The college also obtained the right of carriage from the quarry over Henry Vavasour's estate to the River Wharfe. Three years later, arrangements were made for the college to use the nearby quarry of Huddleston. Stone for the vaults of the porches was brought from Hampole near Doncaster in 1513.[47]

With a lack of good quality building stone in the region, derelict buildings in Cambridge were quickly plundered for their stone. Henry VI permitted King's College to take stone from the Great Hall of Cambridge Castle, and rapid destruction followed in Elizabeth's reign.[48] This practice increased when the dissolution of the monasteries made available a large amount of surplus building materials. Initially, the former friaries in the town were used. Great St Mary's Church brought timber and stone from the Dominican friary, and slate from the Augustinian and Carmelite friaries in 1545–6 and 1552.[49] Trinity College was granted the site of the Franciscan friary in Cambridge, and removed 2,950 loads of stone in 1555/6.[50] Queens' College used slates, tiles and timber from the Carmelite house that adjoined them, and King's College purchased stone from this house in 1536.[51] During the 1560s and 1570s, several Cambridge colleges reused stone from more distant abbeys. In addition to receiving stone from

---

42 SJC, C17.23; Trinity College, Lease Book, 1547–85, fols. 197–198v.

43 J.S. Alexander, 'Building stone from the East Midland quarries: sources, transportation and usage', *Medieval Archaeology*, 39 (1995), 107–35.

44 *VCH Northamptonshire*, ii, pp. 293–5.

45 KH a/c, xxii, fol. 120; *Churchwardens' accounts of St Mary the Great*, p. 46; *RCHMC*, p. xcix.

46 *RCHMC*, p. xcix; KH a/c, xxii, fol. 66v; SJC, C17.23; Alexander, 'Building stone', 113–14.

47 Willis and Clark, *Architectural history*, i, pp. 466, 480; *VCH Yorkshire*, ii, pp. 376–7.

48 Taylor, *Cambridge*, p. 54.

49 *Churchwardens' accounts of St Mary the Great*, pp. 107, 109, 111–12, 125.

50 TCSB a/c, fols. 67v, 143v, 230; Willis and Clark, *Architectural history*, ii, pp. 465, 562, 726.

51 Willis and Clark, *Architectural history*, i, p. 543, n. 1, ii, pp. 4, 35.

Figure 7.5 Queens' College gatehouse, looking east. The gatehouse and Front Court were built in 1448–9

Barnwell Priory, Corpus Christi College obtained supplies from Thorney Abbey, and King's, Trinity, and Gonville and Caius took stone from Ramsey Abbey.[52] Surplus building materials were also occasionally procured from other institutions in the town.[53]

With such a heavy reliance on stone brought from outside the region, brickmaking developed early. In the mid-fourteenth century, bricks were being produced at Ely and

---

52   Ibid., i, pp. 174, 290, 536, ii, pp. 566–7.
53   TCSB a/c, fol. 205; *Churchwardens' accounts of St Mary the Great*, pp. 20, 22; Cobban, *King's Hall*, p. 217, n. 13.

Waldersea, near Wisbech.[54] Queens' was the first Cambridge college to use exposed brickwork extensively in its Front Court of 1448–9, and was followed by Jesus, Christ's and St John's at the turn of the sixteenth century. Brick was also used for many domestic buildings in the county, including Ely and Downham palaces in the late fifteenth century, and Malton Farm at Orwell, Kingswood Farm at Kingston, Kirting Tower and Madingley Hall in the first half of the sixteenth century. Bricks could be produced locally from clay in many parts of the region. King's Hall, for example, obtained bricks for its Great Gate from a supplier in Ely in 1528/9, and Trinity College bought them from Ditton in 1553/4.[55]

St John's College organised the production of its own bricks. By an indenture of 1511, Richard Reculver of East Greenwich, 'brickman', agreed to produce 800,000 bricks of 10 inches by 5 inches by 2½ inches. Reculver agreed to be present at all times when the bricks were being moulded and set, and was to be paid in instalments at the casting, moulding, firing, and delivery. Reculver and his servant spent seven days going to Cambridge to view the ground where bricks could be made.[56] John Fothed, master of Michaelhouse, warned John Fisher that 'Here is very skarys wood to bryne your great kylne of breke, and that will make the breke derer', but wood was secured at Coton,[57] and at 'Haylys Wood'.[58]

As Cambridgeshire lacked extensive woodland, building timber was in short supply, and like charcoal and firewood, tended to come from the wooded parts of East Anglia. During the fifteenth and sixteenth centuries, the colleges made purchases from Worlington and Haverhill in Suffolk, Ashdon, Balsham, Canefield Park, Hadstock, Shalford, Thaxted, Walden, Wethersfield, and Weybridge in Essex, and Winfarthing Park, near Diss in Norfolk.[59] Timber occasionally came from London, such as the 'quarter boards' bought by the churchwardens of Holy Trinity in 1525/6, and the wainscot examined by Nicholas Joiner for Christ's College in 1510.[60] Timber could also be obtained from Lynn and at the Cambridge fairs. Although the records do not state the origin of this timber, it had probably been imported, through Lynn's trading links with the Baltic.[61]

The weight and bulk of many building materials meant that water transport was used where possible to reduce the costs of carriage. Supplies such as slates, thatch, tiles and bricks could be unloaded at the Great Bridge in Cambridge, where there was a staithe, and the churchwardens of Great St Mary's, Queens' College and the

---

54 D. Sherlock, 'Brickmaking accounts for Wisbech, 1333–1356', *PCAS*, 87 (1998), 59–69.
55 KH a/c, xxiv, fol. 34v; TCJB a/c, fol. 133.
56 SJC, D57.173, D57.28.
57 'Notes from the college records', *The Eagle*, 16 (1891), 349, and *The Eagle*, 26 (1905), 300.
58 SJC, C17.23. Presumably this was Hayley Wood, near Gamlingay, owned by the bishop of Ely: Rackham, *Ancient woodland*, pp. 37, 137.
59 SJC, C17.23; TCSB a/c, fol. 70; Willis and Clark, *Architectural history*, i, p. 473, ii, pp. 440, 443.
60 CCRO, P22/5/1, fol. 91v; SJC, D106.1, fol. 14. For the term 'quarter boards', see L.F. Salzman, *Building in England down to 1540: a documentary history* (Oxford, 1952), p. 242.
61 CCA, X/71/3, X/71/5; SJC, D106.1, fol. 9v; *St Radegund*, pp. 153, 170, 171; Rackham, *Ancient woodland*, p. 151.

borough and university authorities used this facility.[62] The quarries at Burwell, Swaffham and Reach were linked to the Cam by navigable canals, called lodes. Stone from Weldon and King's Cliffe was carted to Gunwade on the River Nene and thence shipped to Cambridge, for Trinity College in 1560–1, and for Corpus Christi College and Great St Mary's Church in the late sixteenth century.[63] Moving stone by water rather than land provided significant savings. John Glasse, waterman, carried 3½ tons of freestone for the church walls of Great St Mary's in his keel from Weldon in Northamptonshire to Jesus Green in Cambridge at a cost of 5s in 1522. It cost another 2s to carry the same stone less than a mile to the churchyard.[64] Timber from Winfarthing Park was taken by carts to Brandon Ferry, and then by water and land to St John's College in Cambridge in 1512–14. Major building projects required extensive provision of transport involving many people. Six different carters carried over 700 cartloads of Hinton stone during the building of Christ's College in 1510.[65]

Building craftsmen

In addition to building materials, large numbers of building workers were drawn from Cambridge's region and beyond for the colleges' construction works. In the mid-fifteenth century, for example, Corpus Christi College employed tilers from Stuntney, Ely, and 'Berwey',[66] carpenters from Haslingfield, and a 'thakman' from Swaffham.[67] In contrast, Cambridge Corporation's building and repair work involved relatively few men from outside the town, apart from a few residents from the neighbouring villages of Barnwell, Girton, Hinton, Milton and Trumpington, who provided carrying services or cleaned the King's Ditch.[68]

Many carpenters employed on projects in Cambridge were brought from Essex and Suffolk. Thomas Sturgeon of Elsenham in Essex was appointed chief carpenter at King's College in 1443 and provided carpentry work at Queens' College in 1448–9.[69] William Harward and William Bakon, carpenters of Halstead, agreed to provide the ceilings, floor and roof of the university schools in 1466, and were bound with Thomas Gawge of Dunmow, timberman, and Thomas Bowman of Braintree, pailmaker, to complete the work. William Harward and another carpenter from Halstead also worked at Peterhouse.[70] Cambridge Corporation employed three carpenters from Cressing in Essex to make the roof of the tollbooth in 1509. Thomas Loveday of Sudbury, Suffolk, agreed to produce woodwork at St John's College in 1516, and

---

62 *Churchwardens' accounts of St Mary the Great*, p. 109; QC, Magnum Journale, ii, fol. 27; CCA, X/71/7, X/71/10; CCTA, i, fol. 51v; *Grace Book A*, p. 130.

63 *RCHMC*, p. ciii.

64 *Churchwardens' accounts of St Mary the Great*, pp. 46–7.

65 SJC, C17.23, D106.1, fols. 10v, 16.

66 Possibly Bury St Edmunds.

67 CCC, 'Liber Albus', fols. 97, 98, 108–109v, 110v.

68 CCA, X/71/9; CCTA, i, fols. 18, 27, 98v, 159, 160v.

69 Harvey, *Architects*, p. 289.

70 UA, Luard 128–9; Willis and Clark, *Architectural history*, i, p. 12, n. 4, p. 13, iii, pp. 13, 92–4.

Property and building projects

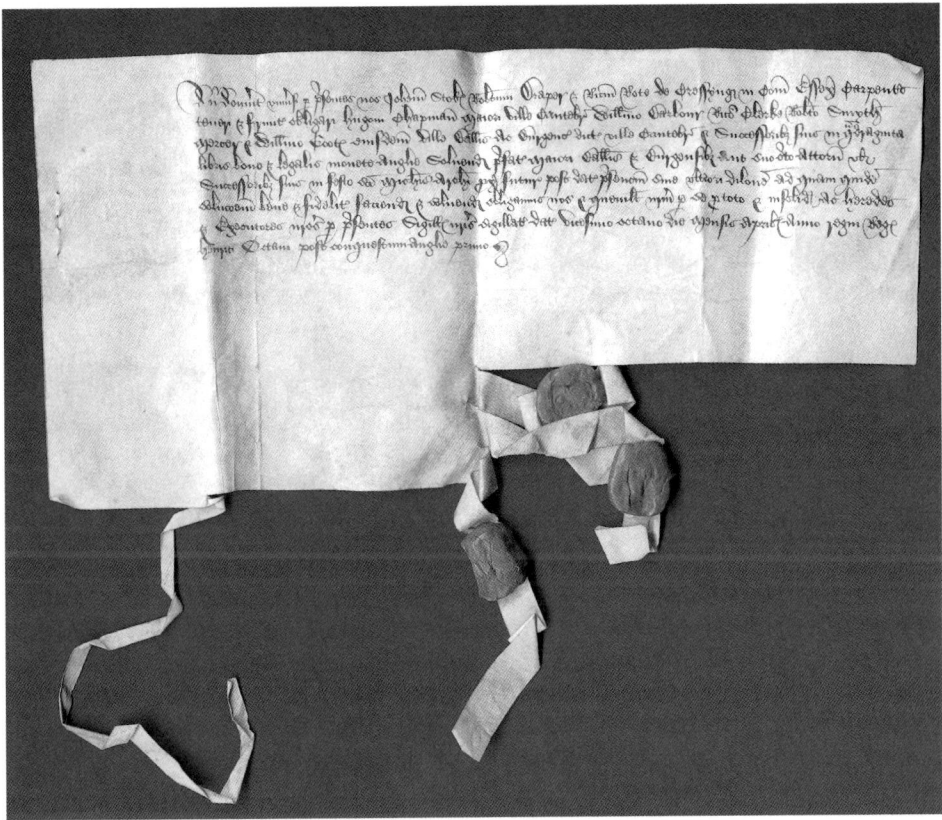

Figure 7.6 Bond sealed by John Stokes, Robert Draper and Richard Rete, carpenters of Cressing, Essex, for Hugh Chapman, mayor of Cambridge, and his bailiffs on 28 April 1509. This was a bond of £40 for performance of a contract for work on the roof of the tollbooth in Cambridge (CCA, VI/4: by permission of the County Record Office, Cambridge)

supplied timber for the gateway at King's Hall in 1528–9.[71] Carvers from Drinkstone and Ashfield in Suffolk contracted to erect the rood loft at Great St Mary's Church in 1520,[72] and two carpenters from Haverhill in Suffolk built walls of a brewhouse at Queens' in 1534.[73] Carpenters were probably recruited from these more wooded counties because they often supplied their own materials. There were, of course, also local carpenters who were employed in college works.[74]

Glaziers and other specialised craftsmen often came from outside the town. A glazier from Walden repaired windows in the choir of Hinton Church, while a London

---

71 CCA, VI/4; Willis and Clark, *Architectural history*, ii, pp. 243–4, 453–4.

72 S. Sanders, *Historical and architectural notes on Great St Mary's Church, Cambridge*, CASOS, X (Cambridge, 1869), pp. 63–7.

73 QC, Magnum Journale, ii, fol. 194v.

74 Harvey, *Architects*, pp. 42–3, 214; Willis and Clark, *Architectural history*, i, p. 12, ii, p. 562.

glazier worked in Great St Mary's.[75] St John's College employed Richard Wright of Bury St Edmunds. Trinity College hired glaziers from London and Thaxted.[76] Not surprisingly when so many building projects were in progress, specialist craftsmen often worked for more than one institution in the town.[77]

The few surviving details of building projects in the region outside Cambridge suggest that similar sources of materials and labour were used. Repairs to college property were often undertaken by craftsmen who had worked at the college. Thomas Sturgeon, chief carpenter of works at King's College, also carried out work on the college's properties at Grantchester Mill, Merton Hall grange, a barn at Felstead, and the Hart Inn at Huntingdon.[78] Bricklayers came to King's Hall in 1452/3 from Felmersham in Bedfordshire, where the parish church had been appropriated to the college.[79] Trinity College employed the glazier of St Bene't's parish to repair windows at Bottisham and Barrington as well as within the college.[80] For repairs to the manor of Malton, Christ's College sent carpenters Colyns, Tompson and Awnger, who had worked at the college, as well as John Nicholson, who provided workmen and supervised the work, but relied on different thatchers, labourers and bricklayers, who were probably local. Bricks for Malton were bought from Raffe Buntynge, just as bricks for the college had been, but for tiles the college went to Hitchin.[81] St John's Hospital used John Algor 'the reeder' to repair St John's barns in the west fields of Cambridge and the chancel at Horningsea Church, and also used William Turner, slater, at both locations.[82]

Cambridge lay within reach of two provincial towns that accommodated significant artistic communities during the fifteenth and early sixteenth centuries. Bury St Edmunds supported at least seven painters and stainers, brass workshops, a local school of illuminators, and the Chirche family's bell foundry. Norwich was the most productive centre for brass engraving outside London, and housed the region's leading group of glaziers. The Cambridge colleges, though, often took their custom to London, which had a concentration of artists and craftsmen found nowhere else in England. The crown's expenditure on art and architecture overshadowed all other patrons, and provided employment, training, experience and influence for craftsmen. London also hosted, particularly in its suburbs, many foreign craftsmen, principally from France and the Low Countries.[83]

Many of the most specialised craftsmen working in Cambridge came from London. Richard Reculver of East Greenwich produced bricks for St John's College in 1511. At least two joiners working at Christ's College in 1510 were from London, and the

---

75 Peterhouse Computus rolls, 1463/4; *Churchwardens' accounts of St Mary the Great*, p. 30.
76 Willis and Clark, *Architectural history*, ii, pp. 347–8; TCSB a/c, fol. 5v, TCJB a/c, fol. 447.
77 TNA: PRO E 101/553/15; Harvey, *Architects*, pp. 94–7, 165, 291–2.
78 Harvey, *Architects*, p. 289.
79 Willis and Clark, *Architectural history*, ii, pp. 449; Cobban, *King's Hall*, p. 205.
80 TCSB a/c, fols. 101, 103, 146v, 192.
81 SJC, D106.1, fols. 14v, 41v.
82 SJC, D102.3, fols. 12, 13.
83 N. Rogers, 'Regional production', in R. Marks and P. Williamson, eds., *Gothic: art for England 1400–1547* (London, 2003), pp. 86–97.

accounts include the cost of carrying their tools to Cambridge.[84] Most of the leading glaziers working at King's College Chapel came from a colony of glass artists who lived in Southwark or in other London suburbs.[85] John Wramp of the parish of Our Lady St Ursula in the Strand in London agreed to glaze five windows with Normandy glass for St John's College. Anthony Trassillion (or Tresylyan) of Westminster, clockmaker, provided a clock for St John's College in 1522, with quarter chimes. He kept a shop in King Street in Westminster and at his death in 1532 his stock included a gilded cuckoo clock valued at £10.[86]

Several craftsmen may have originated from overseas. John Utynam was brought from Flanders to make coloured glass for Eton and King's Colleges in 1449. Barnard Flower, who was probably German, and Galyon Hone, James Nicholson and Francis Williamson, who were born in the Low Countries, all lived in Southwark and carried out glazing in King's College Chapel. The designs of the glass have been attributed to Adrian van den Houte of Mechlin, on the border of Brabant, and Dierick Vellert of Antwerp.[87] Dyrik Harrison of London, possibly a Fleming, worked on the stalls of Christ's College in 1510 and with another Fleming, Giles Fambeler, carved the panelling for the hall of Queens' in 1531–2. The screen and stalls in King's College Chapel may have been carved by foreign craftsmen like Philip the carver, who dined at the college in 1534/5.[88]

Church bells had to be obtained from outside Cambridge as there were no bell foundries in the town.[89] London dominated the supply, producing over half the surviving church bells in the modern county of Cambridgeshire. Thomas Chirche of Bury, bell-founder, was employed by St John's Hospital, Great St Mary's, and King's College.[90] Other Cambridgeshire church bells came from Norwich and probably King's Lynn and Essex, while occasionally, founders with more distant origins were used. The bell at Caldecot Parish Church was cast around 1520 at Reading, and the hall bell of Peterhouse of 1548 bears the inscription of Peeter Vanden Ghein of Mechlin or Malines in the Low Countries.[91]

Monumental brasses were obtained from workshops in London, Norwich and Bury in the fifteenth century, but between c.1506 and 1541 a distinctive series emerged throughout Cambridgeshire, which has been attributed to a Cambridge engraver. Amounting to over half the surviving brasses from this period, these brasses survive in locations stretching from Wilburton in the Isle of Ely to Broxbourne in Hertfordshire,

---

84 SJC, D57.173, D106.1, fol. 11.
85 H. Wayment, *King's College Chapel, Cambridge. The great windows: introduction and guide* (Cambridge, 1982), pp. 6–9.
86 SJC, D56.181, D56.183; Rosser, *Medieval Westminster*, p. 163.
87 RCHMC, p. cxiii; Wayment, *Great windows*, pp. 6–11.
88 Harvey, *Architects*, pp. 105, 130, 232.
89 J.J. Raven, *The church bells of Cambridgeshire*, CASOS, XVIII–XIX (Cambridge, 2nd edn., 1881), pp. 29–35.
90 SJC, D106.2, fols. 4, 7, 12; Raven, *Church bells*, pp. 36–7; J.W. Clark, 'History of the peal of bells belonging to King's College, Cambridge', PCAS, 4 (1876–80), 234.
91 R.W.M. Clouston, 'Cambridgeshire bells', in Hicks, ed., *Cambridgeshire churches*, pp. 364–9; RCHMC, p. 162.

and from Higham Ferrers in Northamptonshire to Stoke by Clare in Suffolk. Cambridge would have provided a favourable location for a workshop, with river access to the east coast ports for latten and pitch and to the area around Stamford and Peterborough for stone. The engraver may have also benefited from the support of patrons such as Lady Margaret Beaufort and John Fisher; his clients included several academics like John Argentine and Robert Hacumlyn of King's.[92]

Some Cambridge craftsmen also found work in the local region. Reginald Ely, first master mason of King's College Chapel, was probably responsible for the substantial rebuilding of Burwell Church between c.1454 and 1477, and influenced the design of the tower with octagonal buttresses at Conington. John Wastell, a subsequent master mason at King's College Chapel, may have designed the lower stages of the towers at Great St Mary's and Soham, and the new clerestory and angel roof at Isleham of 1495.[93] John Bury of Cambridge, mason, and Alewyn Newman of Cambridge, carpenter, worked on contracts at Great Chesterford (Essex) in 1491.[94]

Major royal building projects, however, circumvented the market for labour. Master craftsmen and clerks of works were granted powers to enrol craftsmen and labourers through commissions for impressment, and to threaten those who refused to co-operate with imprisonment. Authority to obtain building materials and carriage could also be granted. In 1444, Reginald Ely, head mason of King's College, with the two clerks of works, received a commission to recruit stonemasons, carpenters, plumbers, tilers, smiths, plasterers, and other workmen, and materials, and horses, carriage and freightage, and to set labourers to work at the king's wages. The previous year, Thomas Sturgeon, the chief carpenter, had been granted a similar commission, and further workmen were impressed in 1450 and 1484.[95] Trinity College was given similar commissions for its construction projects in 1554 and 1560, while Christ's College had commissions for bricklayers and carvers in 1510.[96]

The extent of the demand generated by the building work undertaken by the colleges and other landlords in the town and region cannot be estimated with any certainty. College and church building projects necessitated major capital outlays. Christ's College spent £1,625 on building work between 1505 and 1509; the first court of St John's College cost approximately £5,000 between 1511 and 1516. The rebuilding of Great St Mary's Church cost £1,300 from 1478 to 1519. Almost £15,000 was spent constructing King's College Chapel between the reigns of Henry VI and Henry VIII, and accounts do not survive for all periods of building.[97] Large numbers of workmen were also required. During the final phase of building the stonework of King's College Chapel between 1509 and 1515, between 100 and 150 craftsmen and

---

92 N. Rogers, 'Cambridgeshire brasses', in Hicks, ed., *Cambridgeshire churches*, pp. 303–19; J.R. Greenwood, 'Haine's Cambridge school of brasses', *Transactions of the Monumental Brass Soc.*, 11, part 1 (1969), 2–12.

93 Cotton, 'Perpendicular', pp. 100, 103.

94 Salzman, *Building*, pp. 550–1.

95 RCHMC, p. cvi; CPR, 1441–6, pp. 247, 269; CPR, 1452–61, p. 478; CPR, 1476–85, p. 472.

96 Willis and Clark, *Architectural history*, ii, pp. 198, 469–70, 472.

97 Jones and Underwood, *The king's mother*, p. 224, n. 75; Sanders, *Historical and architectural notes*, p. 16; Willis and Clark, *Architectural history*, i, p. 481.

Property and building projects

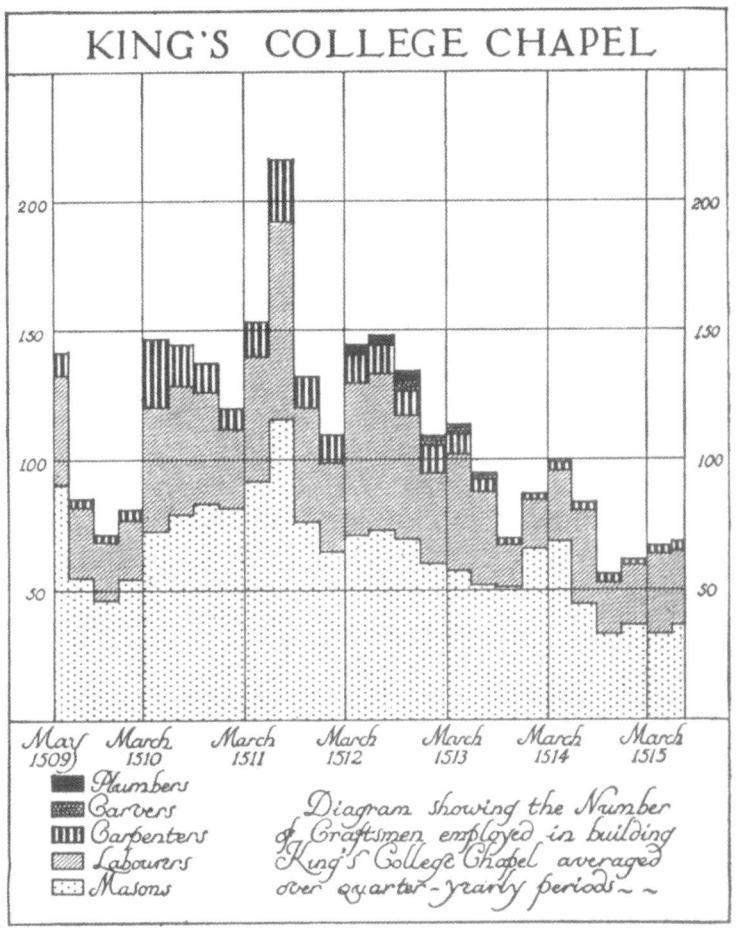

Figure 7.7 Craftsmen employed building King's College Chapel (*RCHMC*, p. 102: Crown copyright, National Monuments Record)

labourers were employed, rising to over 200 during the summer of 1511 (Figure 7.7). For many employees, though, the building work provided by the colleges and other institutions would have been only short term and casual. At Durham Cathedral Priory at the turn of the sixteenth century, just over half of those employed only appeared in a single year of accounts, and only 13 per cent featured in more than 10 years of accounts.[98]

Wage rates

The accounts of building work at the Cambridge colleges also provide valuable wage

---

98   C.M. Newman, 'Employment on the estates of the priory of Durham, 1494–1519: the priory as an employer', *Northern History*, 36 (2000), 43–58.

data for the fifteenth and sixteenth centuries, which has been extracted by several researchers.[99] Information about other workers is very scarce, so labourers and building craftsmen have been generally used as a proxy for other manual workers.[100] Two additional records of wages in Cambridge are examined here – the accounts of Cambridge Corporation and the churchwardens of Holy Trinity. The borough corporation's accounts list a variety of building, repair and maintenance work covering the tollbooth, bridges, houses owned by the town, the King's Ditch, and booths in Stourbridge Fair.[101] At Holy Trinity church, the tasks included construction work and repairs to the church fabric and property owned by the churchwardens.[102]

These accounts record the daily wages paid to building craftsmen and labourers. The craftsmen comprised mainly carpenters, but also tilers, masons, roughmasons and bricklayers. Other craftsmen, such as glaziers, plumbers and goldsmiths, tended to be paid for individual tasks performed.[103] Payment 'by great' or 'in gross' at a set price was occasionally arranged for larger jobs.[104] Labourers performed tasks that did not require specialist skills and were usually hired by the day. Some payments, though, were made in the form of piece rates, such as for ditching, slating and paving, which could be paid by the length of work completed, and the carrying of manure and sand, which was sometimes paid per load.[105] Food and drink payments were rarely recorded: 'mensa' or board was paid at 2d a day to three men repairing a tenement in 1498/9 and to two men in 1517/18, while ale was given to a slater in 1521/2, and these have not been included among the wage rates.[106]

Most studies of wages in other towns between 1450 and 1560 have found stable wage rates up to 1540, and increases thereafter. Phelps Brown and Hopkins' analysis of the wages of building workers in southern England showed a remarkable stability in wages between 1412 and 1532, with craftsmen earning 6d per day and labourers 4d per day. Wages of craftsmen rose to 6d–7d in the period 1532–48, and 7d–8d between 1548 and 1552, and wages of labourers increased to 4d–6d in the period 1545–51. Both groups experienced further rises in the 1550s.[107] Similar increases in wages during the 1540s and 1550s occurred in the wage rates in northern towns examined by Woodward, and among agricultural labourers at Oxford and Cambridge tabulated by Bowden.[108]

As Table 7.5 shows, the majority of recorded wages in the Cambridge accounts were paid to men at the standard rate of 4d per day to labourers, and 6d to craftsmen.

---

99 British Library of Political and Economic Science, London, Beveridge Price History Archive, W5, file 2, Cambridge wages MSS; Thorold Rogers, *Agriculture and prices*, iii, pp. 606–35.
100 D. Woodward, *Men at work: labourers and building craftsmen in the towns of northern England, 1450–1750* (Cambridge, 1995), pp. 3–4, 171–2.
101 CCA, X/71/1–10, X/71A, XVII/24A; CCTA, i.
102 CCRO, P22/5/1.
103 e.g. P22/5/1, fols. 11v, 18v, 91v.
104 CCTA, i, fols. 181v, 256v.
105 CCTA, i, fols. 27v, 160, 182v.
106 CCA, X/71/5, CCTA, i, fols. 28v, 66v.
107 Phelps Brown and Hopkins, *Perspective*, p. 11.
108 Woodward, *Men at work*, pp. 171–2 and appendix 1; Bowden, 'Statistical appendix', p. 166.

Property and building projects

Table 7.5

Cambridge wage rates (accounts of Cambridge Corporation and churchwardens of Holy Trinity)

	Craftsmen d per day	Labourers d per day		Craftsmen d per day	Labourers d per day
1483/4	6		1520/21	6	4
1484/5	6	4	1521/2	6–7	4–6
1485/6			1522/3		
1486/7			1523/4	6	4–6
1487/8			1524/5	6	
1488/9	6		1525/6	6–7	4–5.5
1489/90	6		1526/7	6	4
1490/1	6	4	1527/8	6	4
1491/2			1528/9	6	4
1492/3			1529/30	6	4
1493/4			1530/1	6	
1494/5			1531/2	5–6	
1495/6			1532/3		4
1496/7			1533/4		
1497/8			1534/5		
1498/9	6	4	1535/6	6–7	5
1499/1500	5–6	4	1536/7		
1500/1	6–6.5	4–6	1537/8	7	4
1501/2			1538/9	7	4
1502/3			1539/40	6	4
1503/4		4	1540/1	6	
1504/5			1541/2		
1505/6			1542/3	6	
1506/7	5–6		1543/4	6	4
1507/8	6		1544/5		
1508/9	6		1545/6		6
1509/10		4	1546/7	6.5–7	
1510/11			1547/8	6–7.5	
1511/12	6		1548/9	7	
1512/13			1549/50		
1513/14	6	4			
1514/15					
1515/16	6	4–5			
1516/17					
1517/18	6	4–5			
1518/19	6				
1519/20	6				

Source: CCA, X/71/1–10, X/71A, XVII/24A; CCTA, i; CCRO, P22/5/1.

Some of the wages paid by Cambridge Corporation, though, were higher than the usual rates. Labourers cleaning the King's Ditch were usually paid between 5d and 6d per day, as were men cleaning a stable in 1523/4 and 1525/6.[109] Labourers were also paid 6d a day for claying in 1521/2, and for working on a causeway in 1523/4.[110] There are fewer examples of craftsmen being paid more than 6d, and this may reflect the

---

109 CCA, X/71/1/10; CCTA, i, fols. 19, 27, 65v, 84–5, 98v, 100, 257.
110 CCTA, i, fols. 63v, 86v.

employment of more highly skilled men. A mason and a carpenter received 6½d in 1500/1 and some carpenters received 7d a day in the 1520s and 1530s.[111]

The high wages paid to some labourers in Cambridge may indicate a local building boom. The first three decades of the sixteenth century saw a large amount of building activity by the colleges. When labour was at a premium, unskilled workers rose in status: at the end of the fourteenth century in Stratford-upon-Avon, for example, some labourers were paid the same rates as craftsmen.[112] It is also possible, though, that the labourers working in the King's Ditch were being compensated with higher wages for what must have been extremely unpleasant work in an open sewer. Labourers were occasionally paid extra for very strenuous, difficult, or unpleasant tasks. Thomas Outlawe received an additional ½d from Corpus Christi College in the mid-fifteenth century for cleaning the latrines. Three labourers were paid 20d each for five days for 'haueeing hupe stonnys to ye stepell' of Great St Mary's Church in 1529.[113] The wage rates paid in and around Cambridge for day-to-day agricultural operations, such as hedging and ditching, do not appear to have risen above 4d until the 1540s.[114]

Conclusion

The land market and building sector reveal further examples of the economic links between Cambridge and its region. Colleges and townspeople held estates in the county and beyond. Building projects drew specialist craftsmen from the local area, adjoining counties and from London, while much of the building stone used in the town came from quarries in Northamptonshire and Rutland, and timber from Suffolk and Essex.

The significance of college consumption on the economy of the town and region is again apparent. The colleges held substantial amounts of property in the town and county, and provided employment for servants within their communities. Their building projects must have generated significant, albeit temporary, demand within the local economy, even though many of the specialist craftsmen and the materials they required had to be brought from outside the immediate region.

Evidence from property rentals and building activity within the town suggests a chequered pattern of economic performance in this period. Building work among the colleges peaked in the 1510s and 1520s, and this may have been reflected in evidence of increased wage rates. If localised economic expansion occurred in this period, though, the property market did not share the boom, as Cambridge Corporation's rental income and average rent level reached its nadir around 1500, having fallen from the early fifteenth century. These rents did not recover substantially until the mid-sixteenth century, while evidence from Corpus Christi College shows that high arrears and falling rental income were still being faced at this date.

---

111 X/71/1/10.

112 T.H. Lloyd, *Some aspects of the building industry in medieval Stratford-upon-Avon*, Dugdale Soc. occasional papers, XIV (Oxford, 1961), pp. 14–15.

113 Pearce, 'College accounts', 82; *Churchwardens' accounts of St Mary the Great*, p.67. See also Woodward, *Men at work*, pp. 107–8, for examples elsewhere.

114 Bowden, 'Statistical appendix', p. 166.

Chapter 8

Conclusion

The evidence from the Cambridge region permits a detailed examination of the economic links between the medieval town and its hinterland. Few towns can provide sources like the college accounts that reveal both the geography and duration of trade, so the opportunity to reconstruct this marketing network is particularly valuable. Evidence of both growth and contraction can be identified within the town during the period 1450-1560. Evidence of demographic and economic recovery across the first two-thirds of the sixteenth century in particular, argues against interpretations that characterise these years as an extended period of urban crisis. Cambridge's experience also reveals the impact, albeit limited, of urban demand from a middle-ranking, provincial town on its surrounding region.

Cambridge's economic region in the later middle ages comprised three inter-related spatial areas, with the most local area extending between 10 and 15 miles in radius around the town. The local hinterland incorporated most of Cambridgeshire, the small towns that straddled the county's borders, and the sub-regions of the fen, fen-edge, river valleys, western plateau and south-east uplands. Cambridge market was an important centre for the exchange of produce between these sub-regions, but small towns, village markets, fairs and informal trading sites provided additional locations where basic commodities could be bought and sold. Cambridge drew raw materials and labour from the local region, and in turn supplied it with goods and services. The accounts of King's Hall and King's College reveal that Cambridge's hinterland for basic foodstuffs extended to about 10 miles in radius from the town, while fuel supplies came from up to 15 miles away. The majority of those admitted to the freedom of the borough came from within this area, as did most of those bringing cases to be heard in the borough and university courts. Although the marketing network within the local region changed between 1450 and 1560, with the decline of many village markets, the growth of population in several small towns, and the reliance on more distant sources of fuel, the actual boundaries of this region remained remarkably constant over the period and in subsequent centuries. The ring of small market towns lying between 10 and 15 miles from Cambridge still defined the boundary of the region in which Cambridge provided local goods and services in the later twentieth century.[1]

The local hinterland could not, however, satisfy all the needs of the inhabitants of Cambridge, and some goods and services were brought from a wider region of around 50 miles in radius, with more diverse natural resources, and from several major urban centres, including Bury St Edmunds, Lynn, Northampton, Norwich and London. Cambridgeshire was particularly short of firewood, charcoal and timber, which were supplied from Essex and Suffolk, and building stone, which was taken from quarries in Northamptonshire and Rutland. London dominated regional networks of credit, while

---

1   Gerald Eve and Co., *Report on an assessment of future shopping needs in Cambridge central area* (London, 1965), p. 3.

larger and wealthier institutions, including several Cambridge colleges, purchased bulk commodities as well as luxury goods from the capital. Many of these goods were also bought at Stourbridge Fair, which attracted buyers and sellers from London, East Anglia, the Midlands and more distant towns. Links with this wider region appear to have strengthened in the later middle ages, with the increasing reliance on firewood and charcoal from more distant suppliers, the growing demand for stone and timber for college building projects, and the increasing importance of trading links with London.

In addition, Cambridge had wider links with towns outside these two regions. Coastal and overseas trade, conducted through Lynn, produced further points of contact: Cambridge merchants exported corn from this port to the Low Countries, and imported coal from Newcastle-upon-Tyne. The university recruited heavily from the dioceses of northern and eastern England during the fifteenth century, while the widely scattered land-holding interests of several colleges created additional links. Craftsmen came to work in Cambridge from many parts of the country, particularly from London, and Cambridge also accommodated a number of migrants from overseas.

The local, regional, and wider links which constituted Cambridge's economic region are evident in studies of other late medieval towns, and have been described as comprising local markets and regional trade,[2] or as the *umland*, the immediate market area, where goods were exchanged for basic needs, and the *hinterland*, the wider market area.[3] Concentric regions also underlie the geographical models of central place theory and land use devised by Christaller and Von Thünen. These models, though, give the impression that such regions are static entities, whereas urban regions fluctuated in size and significance over time.[4]

During the course of each year, Cambridge's hinterland was temporarily widened as Stourbridge Fair attracted buyers and sellers from beyond the local region. Cloth from the Stour Valley of Suffolk and fish from the East Anglian coast were brought, while representatives from households like Thetford Priory and Peterborough Abbey, which had little contact with Cambridge during the rest of the year, came to shop at the fair. Traders from other areas of the country, including merchants from London and Coventry, and officials of great households from Nottinghamshire, Oxfordshire and Warwickshire, also attended. Stourbridge Fair extended Cambridge's hinterland over the longer term too: as the fair grew in size and importance during the sixteenth century, it brought traders from further afield, such as Bristol and Yorkshire.[5]

The growth of the university also enlarged the town's hinterland. The building projects of the colleges required large quantities of materials that could not be obtained in the immediate area and brought craftsmen to the town. Scholars migrated to the university from across the country and some from overseas. Specialist academic trades developed to serve the university. Cambridge therefore provided

---

2   Kowaleski, *Exeter*, p. 2.

3   H. Eiden and F. Irsigler, 'Environs and hinterland: Cologne and Nuremberg in the later middle ages', in Galloway, ed., *Trade*, pp. 43–4.

4   Lee, 'Feeding the colleges', 243–64.

5   Chapter 5, above.

Conclusion

some services over a larger hinterland than other towns of similar size. The expansion of the university, though, also reduced its reliance on the town. The status of privileged person created a group of tradesmen who were administered by the university rather than the borough. Several colleges began to build their own private chapels rather than use nearby parish churches. The larger and wealthier colleges which were founded in the fifteenth and sixteenth centuries tended to purchase many of their supplies in bulk from London and other major towns, and at Stourbridge Fair, rather than from tradesmen in Cambridge. These colleges often constructed their own facilities for baking and brewing, and from the 1550s, turned to their own estates to supply their food.

Across the country, marketing during the fifteenth and early sixteenth centuries was becoming more integrated, less reliant on public markets, and increasingly characterised by mercantile rather than casual trade. London's trading links expanded considerably in this period: the capital had always served the consumption needs of the wealthiest aristocratic consumers, but increasingly its mercantile networks were extending to control trade which had previously been handled by provincial merchants.[6] Trends in the Cambridge region reflected these developments. The colleges moved away from using formal markets to making direct contracts with suppliers. Londoners dominated longer-distance networks of credit, and the malt barley and saffron trades expanded to serve the London market.

The fluctuations in the economy of Cambridge and its region between 1450 and 1560 highlight the risks of characterising the whole urban sector, or even individual towns, simply in terms of decline or growth. Identifying the timing of change in Cambridge's economy, as in other towns in this period, is an imprecise exercise that must rely upon the collective evidence of several series of data.[7] The evidence from Cambridge does not support the notion of an urban crisis extending from the fifteenth century through to the 1570s,[8] but suggests many nuances within this period, arguing for a more careful characterisation of the period. The debate over urban fortunes has, however, highlighted a number of features experienced by many late medieval towns, including Cambridge. Like most provincial towns, Cambridge's population probably contracted between 1377 and 1524–5, even if the precise extent of this contraction is uncertain, and the fall was lessened by the expansion of the university. A decline in the corporation's income from property rents and market stalls occurred between the 1420s and 1480s, with some recovery during the sixteenth century. Absolute decline in rents was the experience of almost all towns, and the countryside too, as demand for land fell due to the population loss.[9] Numerous boroughs petitioned for reductions to their fee farms and subsidies, and the burgesses of Cambridge obtained tax remissions in 1433 and 1446 and a fee-farm remission in 1483. The reluctance of leading townsmen to take civic offices is suggested by the multiple terms of office that several Cambridge burgesses had to serve as mayor between the 1450s and early 1500s.

---

6   Britnell, 'Urban demand', pp. 9–21; Kermode, *Merchants*, pp. 308–10.
7   Britnell, *Colchester*, pp. 3–4.
8   As asserted by Phythian-Adams in 'Urban decay', pp. 170–83.
9   Hatcher, *Plague*, pp. 36–44.

Yet there is also evidence of growth in the Cambridge economy, particularly during parts of the sixteenth century. It seems likely from the evidence of taxation records that the population of the town grew between 1524–5 and 1563. Wills also suggest a slight increase in 'replacement' levels during the 1540s and 1550s, and a larger increase after 1560; the latter rise is supported by evidence of natural increase in the parish registers. Cambridge experienced a building boom with a large number of college building projects underway between 1490 and 1530, when admissions of freemen increased, and some wage rates appear to have risen. The building projects and wage rises tended to be concentrated in the 1510s and 1520s, and the corporation's sources of income from property rents, market stalls, and booths at Stourbridge Fair all rose at this time. These were the last decades in which the university faced relative stability before the many religious reforms that affected student numbers, particularly the dissolution of the monasteries in the 1530s. During the 1550s, the corporation's income from stalls in the market rose, while there was also a growth in the numbers of booths transferred, the introduction of fines on leases of booths, and an increase in the admissions of freemen. The corporation's property rents recovered substantially, although not completely in real terms, during the 1540s and 1550s to return to the average levels of the early fifteenth century. Yet the mounting arrears at Corpus Christi College show the continuing difficulties of obtaining income from properties in the town. Despite disruption in the cloth trade, poor harvests and repeated taxation during the 1520s,[10] and epidemics, harvest failure, rapid price inflation and the precarious situation for cloth exports in the 1550s,[11] periods of growth occurred in Cambridge during both decades.

Cambridge probably fared more favourably than many other late medieval towns due to the demand generated by the university. While the number of university members probably doubled between the late fourteenth and mid-fifteenth centuries, even more significant was the creation of seven new colleges between 1420 and 1520. Many of these colleges had incomes and expenditure comparable with the wealthier aristocracy, and had a total net income of £3,500 per annum in 1546. The proportion of scholars grew from less than 20 per cent of the town's total population in 1377 to over 40 per cent by the 1560s. Few other towns experienced a growth in domestic demand on this scale during the later middle ages. In a monastic borough like Wells, clerical consumers only accounted for about 10 to 15 per cent of the total population, and the colleges survived the Reformation while the monasteries did not. Other towns with major institutions that generated significant and continuing demand through the sixteenth century included Oxford, although the university there contracted in size during the later middle ages, and Westminster, which benefited from the growth of the royal household and administration from the 1460s.[12] Yet as the university grew in Cambridge, it also became more self-sufficient, restricting the economic opportunities for those townspeople who were not privileged persons. The local region supplied the university with basic foodstuffs and fuel, but from the 1550s, the larger colleges increasingly turned to provisioning from their own estates. The

---

10 Dymond, 'Famine'; Hoyle, 'Taxation'; Britnell, '1450–1550', pp. 103, 112.
11 Fisher, 'Commercial trends', pp. 89–91; Fisher, 'Influenza and inflation', pp. 163–72.
12 *VCH Oxfordshire*, iv, p. 19; Britnell, 'Economy of British towns', pp. 313–14; Rosser, *Medieval Westminster*, pp. 74–92, 171–3.

colleges also required products such as building stone and certain luxury goods that could not be supplied from the local region.

Although a number of changes occurred in the economy of Cambridge and its region in the 1450–1560 period, it would be difficult to describe any of these developments as revolutionary or transitional. Many of the traditional descriptions of economic transformation attributed to the fifteenth and sixteenth centuries are not appropriate for the town and its region. In an economy where the urban sector was still relatively small, comprising no more than about 10 to 15 per cent of the total population, the opportunities for medieval towns to be agents of modernisation, generating economic development within their hinterlands, were very restricted. There were, however, opportunities for some towns and their regions to specialise in supplying demand for the largest cities, notably London, and overseas markets, particularly through the manufacture of cloth.[13]

Urban demand provided markets for some of the agricultural produce of the Cambridge region, and encouraged the cultivation of particular crops. Malt barley was sent to London, Lynn and other coastal and overseas markets. From the late fifteenth century, many villages in south Cambridgeshire and north Essex began to plant saffron, and the area increasingly specialised in the cultivation of this crop. Saffron was particularly prominent among peasant households, which increased this group's contact with the market. The marketing involved London merchants, and demand from the capital probably stimulated the adoption of the crop, and may have led to the emergence of Walden as a centre for production.

Despite the consumption requirements of towns, the market for foodstuffs in the later middle ages remained poorly developed, with limitations of supply and demand. Some Cambridge institutions relied on home farms to supply at least some of their produce, reducing demand in the market. Formal markets provided limited supplies for large households: King's Hall and King's College bought most of their wheat, malt barley and fuel, with the exception of a few small purchases, outside the market place, through contracts with local suppliers. In years of scarcity, though, even these contracts could be difficult to secure: more distant and infrequent suppliers had to be sought, and price fluctuations were considerable, if less than those charged in the market place. In the 1550s, faced with rising prices and static estate income, King's College, followed by other colleges, increasingly turned to rents of produce from their own estates at guaranteed prices. The close of the period therefore saw a move towards self-sufficiency, rather than market dependence, among Cambridge's largest consumers.

Between 1450 and 1560 Cambridge's economic region consisted of three interconnecting regions linked to the town – a local hinterland extending up to 10–15 miles from the town, a regional hinterland stretching to just over 50 miles away, and more distant ties with other urban centres. During this period the economic region experienced a number of developments: the changing distribution of population and wealth, a reduction in the number of markets, the growth of the malt barley and saffron trades, the expansion of Stourbridge Fair, the enlargement of the university, and an increase in the number of college building projects. These trends did not,

---

13 Yates, 'Rural society', 630–3, 636; Keene, 'Small towns', pp. 234–8; Britnell, '1450–1550', pp. 95–7.

however, lead to major structural changes, nor did they fundamentally transform the relationship between the town and its region. Concepts that stress the role of towns as promoters of economic activity can be useful in identifying areas of growth, and particularly in highlighting the influence of London, but the size of most medieval towns in England restricted their impact on surrounding regions.

Conclusion

Bibliography

Manuscript sources

The National Archives: Public Record Office (TNA: PRO)

C 1 Chancery: Six Clerks' Office: Early Proceedings, Richard II – Philip & Mary

E 101 Exchequer: King's Remembrancer: Accounts Various

Ulnage accounts
E 101/338/3	Particulars of accounts, Cambridge, 18–20 Ric II
E 101/338/9	Particulars of accounts (Cambs. & Hunts.), 5 & 6 Edw IV
E 101/343/1	Accounts of ulnage (Essex, Suffolk & Cambs.), 5 & 6 Edw IV
E 101/343/7	Particulars of accounts, (Norfolk, Suffolk, Essex, Cambs., Hunts.), 9 & 10 Edw IV
E 101/343/9	Particulars of accounts (same counties) 13 & 14 Edw IV

Sheriff's administrative accounts – Cambridge and Huntingdon
E 101/553/10–11	Expenses of repairs of Cambridge castle, 18 Hen VI
E 101/553/15	Expenses of repairs of Cambridge gaol, 15 & 16 Hen VIII

E 179 Exchequer: King's Remembrancer: Particulars of Accounts and other records relating to Lay and Clerical Taxation

Reductions to fifteenths and tenths in Cambridgeshire
E 179/81/80	Schedule of reductions 1433
E 179/81/120	Schedule of reductions 1490–1

Writs of exemption
E 179/81/107	Assessments and writs exempting Merton College, Oxford, King's College, Cambridge, Denney Abbey (Cambs.), Syon Abbey (Middlesex), and Clare Hall, Cambridge, 1453–5
E 179/241/318	Writs exempting abbeys of Syon, Denney, and Cambridge colleges, and Merton College, Oxford, for liability under tax out of their lands in Cambridgeshire, 1512

Cambridgeshire: returns of the first subsidy, granted in 1523 and collected in 1524

E 179/81/126	Chesterton, Northstowe, Papworth hundreds
E 179/81/129	Armingford hundred
E 179/81/130	Wetherley, Thriplow hundreds
E 179/81/132	Whittlesford, Flendish hundreds
E 179/81/133	Cambridge
E 179/81/134	Chilford, Radfield hundreds
E 179/81/136	Ely, Witchford hundreds

E 179/81/137	Staploe hundred
E 179/81/161	Longstowe hundred
E 179/82/220, part 2	Staploe hundred
E 179/82/224, part 2	Cheveley hundred
E 179/81/147	Whittlesford hundred (subsidy collected in 1525)

Alien subsidies

E 179/81/85	Alien poll tax inquest, 1440, for subsidy granted 1440 (Cambridge)
E 179/81/87	Commission and alien poll tax inquests, 1440, for subsidy granted 1440 (10 Cambs. hundreds)
E 179/81/111	Alien poll tax inquest, 1463, for subsidy granted 1453 (Cambs.)
E 179/235/3	Assessments and particulars of accounts, 1441, for subsidy granted 1440 (Cambridge, Cambs. & Hunts.)
E 179/235/4	Assessments, return of writ and writ, 1440, for subsidy granted 1440 (Cambs. & Hunts.)
PROB 11	Records of the Prerogative Court of Canterbury: Will Registers

SC 11 Special Collections, Rentals and Surveys, Rolls

SC 11/90	Schedule of rents from Stourbridge Fair booths for obits

British Library (BL)

Add. MS 5861	Rev. W. Cole, Collections chiefly relating to Cambridge, lx (transcripts and indexes of wills from the diocese of Ely)
Harleian MS 594, fols. 198–200v	Bishop of Ely's certificate of households in the diocese, 20 Aug 1563

British Library of Political and Economic Science, London

Beveridge Price History Archive, W5, file 2, Cambridge wages MSS

Cambridgeshire County Record Office, Cambridge (CCRO)

Cambridge Corporation Archives (CCA)

I/4	Corporation Cross Book
III/10A, part 1	Leases of booths at Stourbridge Fair
VI/4	Covenant bonds, 1464–1557
X/3	Articles concerning usurpation on the part of the university, 1554
X/6	Proceedings in court of Reach Fair, 1508
X/7	Letters and testimonials from the mayor of Newcastle concerning delivery of coals, 1510
X/20	Determination of Lord Cardinal and Chief Justice, 1526
X/38	Town and university of Cambridge disputes, 16th century
X/40	Petition of town v. university, 1493/4
X/42	Navigation award, Cambridge and King's Lynn, 1551

X/50	Accord between Lynn and Cambridge, 1517/18
X/56	Lease of King's Mill, 1496
X/66	Complaint of town v. university, c.1530
X/69 (ii-iii)	Articles of complaint. Town v. university, c.1532
X/70/1-10	Treasurers' accounts, 1422/3–1435/6
X/71/1-10	Treasurers' accounts, 1483/4–1500/1
X/71A	Treasurers' accounts, 1503/4
X/90	Note of misdemeanours done by university, 1534
X/103	Northampton award, 1519
XVII/24A	Treasurers' accounts, 1513/14
XVIII/12, no. 4	Lease of Whittlesford Bridge, 1566

W.M. Palmer and E.A.B. Barnard, 'Cambridge Corporation Archives' (typescript catalogue, 1929)
Palmer/Barnard vol. 1, Cambridge town pleas, 1389–90
Palmer/Barnard vol. 57, Corporation Common Day Book, 1544–82

Parish registers

Cambridge: All Saints, St Benedict, St Edward, St Mary the Less, St Mary the Great; Arrington, Balsham, Cherry Hinton, Croxton, Coton, Dullingham, Elsworth, Fulbourn St Vigor, Hinxton, Horseheath, Madingley, Melbourn, Shudy Camps, Stretham, Sutton in the Isle

Other collections

Archdeaconry Court of Ely wills, Will Register 1
Consistory Court of Ely wills, Will Register 7

L63/17-18	Foxton Chatteris, Shepreth, Barrington and Madingley court rolls, 1492–1507, 1510–43
L64/1-4	Foxton with members, court rolls, 1537–8, 1539–40, 1541–2, 1547–52
P22/5/1	Churchwardens' accounts, Holy Trinity Church, Cambridge, 1504–58
R59/14/11/7A-B	Great and Little Linton with Chilfords and Michaelotts manor court rolls, 1509–47, 1547–53
488/M, Huddleston MSS	Whittlesford manorial records box 5: court rolls, 1461–83, 1513–23, 1554–76; bailiff's accounts, 1463/4, 1477/8; rentals, 1487/8, 1514

Cambridge Group for the History of Population and Social Structure, Department of Geography, University of Cambridge

Data from the parish registers of Elm, Ely Holy Trinity, Fowlmere, Landbeach, Linton, Willingham

Cambridge University Library (CUL)

University Archives (UA)

Collect.Admin.2	Junior Proctor's Book
Collect.Admin.5	
Collect.Admin.9	
C.U.R. 17	Court Leet, 1382–1422, 1568–87
C.U.R. 36.2	Privileged persons and claims of cognisance

C.U.R. 67(1)	Proclamation of Stourbridge Fair by Sir William Cecil
Luard 128	Indenture of covenant for carpenters' work on new schools, 1466
Luard 129	Bond of carpenters and timbermen to chancellor, 1466
Luard 133	Articles embodying privileges and liberties claimed by university, 1491
Luard 143b	List of those who are to enjoy university privilege, 11 Jul 1502
Luard 145a	Indenture of agreement between university and corporation, 1503
Luard 145b	List of those who are to enjoy university privilege, 12 May 1503
V.C.Ct.I.1	Vice-Chancellor's Court, Act book, fair copy, 1552–7
V.C.Ct.I.24	Vice Chancellor's Court, Act books, draft, 1557–65
WILLS I	Vice Chancellor's Court, Register of wills, 1501–58

Ely diocesan records (EDR)
E1/1(3) and E1/1(6)   Plea rolls of the bishop's liberty, 1424–98

Queens' College archives (QC)
Magnum Journale, ii	Queens' College accounts, 1517–35
QC10	Oakington, Dry Drayton and Cottenham, views of accounts, 4 & 7 Hen VIII

Corpus Christi College, Cambridge (CCC)
MS 106	Documents relating to the University of Cambridge
Accounts, 'Arreragia'	Arrears of rent from college property, 1523–47
'Liber Albus'	College accounts, 1457–67
'Registrum Accounts'	College accounts, 1376–1485
XXXIX.119	Rental of college property, 1551

Downing College, Cambridge
Bowtell MS 1–2, 'Liber Rationalis', Cambridge Corporation Treasurers' accounts, vol. i, 1515/16–1560/1, vol. ii, 1561/2–1588/9

King's College, Cambridge (KC)
King's College Ledger Books, i–ii
King's College Mundum Books, i–vii, x–xv

GRA/656–9, 661, 676   Grantchester bailiffs' accounts 1435/6–1445/6

Peterhouse, Cambridge
Peterhouse Computus rolls, 1455/6–1470/1
H1–H3   Indentures of demise of the rectory of Hinton, 1452, 1459, 1476

St John's College, Cambridge (SJC)
C17.23	Account of Oliver Scales, St John's College building works, 1512–14
D56.181	Memo of agreement by John Wramp for John Fisher's chantry, 1528
D56.183	Agreement with Nicholas Metcalfe and Anthony Trassillion for St John's College clock, 1522
D57.28	Richard Reculver's expenses for inspecting brick grounds, 1510–11
D57.173	Bond, Richard Reculver to John Fisher, for making bricks, 1511
D102.3	St John's Hospital, accounts of receipts 1505–8 and expenses 1505–1509/10
D106.1	Account of John Scott, including expenses for Christ's College Chapel and manor of Malton, 1510–11
D106.2	Accounts of repairs by master of St John's Hospital, c.1500

D106.9	St John's Hospital accounts, 1484/5
D106.10	St John's Hospital accounts, 1505–10 (partly duplicated in D102.3)
D107.7	Accounts of Nicholas Metcalfe, mainly for Fisher's chantry, 1527/8
SB3.1	Bursars' accounts, 1526/7

Trinity College, Cambridge
King's Hall accounts, xi–xxvi, 1450–1544
Trinity College Senior Bursars' accounts, i, 1547/8–1563/4
Trinity College Junior Bursars' accounts, i, 1550/1–1563/4
Trinity College Lease Book, 1547–85

Box 21, item 39, Ickleton, rental 1483
Box 21, item 45, Ickleton, bond 1515

Printed primary sources

The accounts of the Chamberlains of Newcastle upon Tyne 1508–1511, ed. C.M. Fraser, Society of Antiquities of Newcastle upon Tyne Record Ser., III (Newcastle, 1987)
Account rolls of the Obedientiaries of Peterborough, ed. J. Greatrex, Northamptonshire Record Soc., XXXIII (Northampton, 1984)
Acts of the court of the Mercers' Company, 1453–1527, ed. L. Lyell and F.D. Watney (Cambridge, 1936)
The alien communities of London in the fifteenth century: the subsidy rolls of 1440 and 1483–4, ed. J.L. Bolton (Stamford, 1998)
Annals of Cambridge, ed. C.H. Cooper, 5 vols. (Cambridge, 1842–1908)
Book of William Morton, Almoner of Peterborough Monastery 1448–1467, ed. P.I. King, Northamptonshire Record Soc., XVI (Northampton, 1954)
Calendar of Close Rolls, HMSO, 46 vols. (London, 1892–1963)
Calendar of Letter-Books preserved among the archives of the Corporation of the City of London, 1275–1498, ed. R.R. Sharpe, 11 vols. (London 1899–1912), vol. 'L'
Calendar of Patent Rolls, HMSO, 54 vols. (London, 1891–1916)
Calendar of Plea and Memoranda Rolls of the City of London, 1437–1457, ed. P.E. Jones (Cambridge, 1954)
Calendar of State Papers, Domestic Series, of the reign of Edward VI, 1547–1553, ed. C.S. Knighton (London, 1992)
Calendar of wills proved and enrolled in the court of Husting, London A.D.1258–A.D.1688, ed. R.R. Sharpe, 2 vols. (London, 1890)
Cambridge Borough Documents, ed. W.M. Palmer (Cambridge, 1931)
'A Cambridge vintner's accounts, c.1511', ed. E.H. Minns, *PCAS*, 34 (1934), 50–8
Cambridgeshire in the sixteenth century, ed. W.M. Palmer (Cambridge, 1935)
Canterbury College, Oxford, iv, ed. W.A. Pantin, Oxford Historical Soc., new ser., XXX (Oxford, 1985)
Cartulary of Oseney Abbey, vi, ed. H.E. Salter, Oxford Historical Soc., CI (Oxford, 1936)
Charters of the borough of Cambridge, ed. F.W. Maitland and M. Bateson (Cambridge, 1901)
Churchwardens' accounts of St Mary the Great, ed. J.E. Foster, CASOS XXXV (Cambridge, 1905)
A collection of charters, letters and other documents from the MS library of Corpus Christi College, ed. J. Lamb (London, 1838)
The Coventry Leet Book, ed. M. Dormer Harris, Early English Text Soc., 4 vols., CXXXIV, CXXXV, CXXXVIII, CXLVI (London, 1907–13)

Documents relating to the university and colleges of Cambridge, HMSO, 3 vols. (London, 1852), i
Domestic accounts of Merton College Oxford, ed. J.M. Fletcher and C.A. Upton, Oxford Historical Soc., new ser., XXXIV (Oxford, 1996)
'Ely episcopal registers', *Ely Diocesan Remembrancer* (1907–11)
The English manor c.1200–c.1500, ed. M. Bailey (Manchester, 2002)
Erasmus and Cambridge: the Cambridge letters of Erasmus translated, ed. D.F.S. Thomson and H.C. Porter (Toronto, 1963)
Farming and gardening in late medieval Norfolk, ed. C. Noble, C. Moreton and P. Rutledge, Norfolk Record Soc., LXI (Norwich, 1997)
A fifteenth century school book from a manuscript in the British Museum (MS Arundel 249), ed. W. Nelson (Oxford, 1956)
Garrett Godfrey's accounts c.1527–33, ed. E. Leedham-Green, D.E. Rhodes and F.H. Stubbings, Cambridge Bibliographical Soc. monograph, XII (Cambridge, 1992)
Grace Book A, containing the proctors' accounts and other records of the University of Cambridge, 1454–88, ed. S.M. Leathes, CASLMS, I (Cambridge, 1897)
Grace Book B...1488–1511, ed. M. Bateson, CASLMS, II–III (Cambridge, 1903–5), parts i–ii
Grace Book C...1501–1542, ed. W.G. Searle (Cambridge, 1908)
The grete herball which gueth parfyt knowlege and understandyng of all maner of herbes... (Southwark, 1526)
Harrison, William, *The description of England*, ed. G. Edelen, Folger Shakespeare Library (Ithaca, New York, 1968)
Household accounts from medieval England, ed. C.M. Woolgar, 2 parts, BARSEH, new ser., XVII–XVIII (Oxford, 1992–3)
The itinerary of John Leland, ed. L. Toulmin Smith, 5 vols. (London, 1907–10), i
The lay subsidy of 1334, ed. R.E. Glasscock, BARSEH, new ser., II (London, 1975)
The ledger of John Smythe 1538–1550, ed. J. Vanes, Bristol Record Soc. Publications, XXVIII (London, 1974)
Letters and papers, foreign and domestic, of the reign of Henry VIII, ed. J.S. Brewer, J. Gairdner and R.H. Brodie, 2nd edn., 23 vols. (London, 1862–1932)
The military survey of 1522 for Babergh hundred, ed. J. Pound, Suffolk Records Soc., XXVIII (Woodbridge, 1986)
'Notes from the college records', *The Eagle* (Magazine of St John's College, Cambridge), 16–26 (1891–1905)
Paston letters and papers of the fifteenth century, ed. N. Davis, 2 vols. (Oxford, 1971)
The priory of St Radegund Cambridge, ed. A. Gray, CASOS, XXXI (Cambridge, 1898)
The poll taxes of 1377, 1379 and 1381, i: Bedfordshire-Leicestershire, ed. C.C. Fenwick, BARSEH, new ser., XXVII (Oxford, 1998)
Records of the borough of Nottingham 1155–1547, ed. W.H. Stevenson, 3 vols. (London, 1882–5), iii
The register of Thetford Priory, ed. D. Dymond, BARSEH, new ser., XXIV–XXV (Oxford, 1995)
Report on the manuscripts of Lord Middleton preserved at Wollaton Hall, Nottinghamshire, ed. W.H. Stevenson, Historical Manuscripts Commission (London, 1911)
Rotuli Parliamentorum, Record Commission, 6 vols. (London, 1783)
Select cases in Chancery 1364–1471, ed. W.P. Baildon, Selden Soc., X (London, 1896)
Statutes of the Realm (1101–1713), Record Commission, 11 vols. (London 1808–28)
Stow, John, *A survey of London*, ed. C.L. Kingsford, 2 vols. (Oxford, 1908)
Suffolk in 1524, ed. S.H.A. Hervey, Suffolk Green Books, X (Woodbridge, 1910)
Tudor economic documents, ed. R.H. Tawney and E. Power, 3 vols. (London, 1924), iii
Turner, William, *A new herball*, part 1 (1551) ed. G.T.L. Chapman and M.N. Tweddle (Cambridge, 1989)

Valor Ecclesiasticus, ed. J. Caley and J. Hunter, Record Commission, 6 vols. (London, 1810–34), iii

The West Fields of Cambridge, ed. C.P. Hall and J.R. Ravensdale, Cambridgeshire Records Soc., III (Cambridge, 1976)

Secondary sources

Abrams, P., 'Towns and economic growth: some theories and problems', in Abrams and Wrigley, eds., *Towns in societies*, pp. 9–33

Abrams, P. and Wrigley, E.A., eds., *Towns in societies* (Cambridge, 1978)

Adams, T.R., 'Aliens, agriculturalists and entrepreneurs: identifying the market-markers in a Norfolk port from the water-bailiffs' accounts, 1400–60', in D.J. Clayton, R.G. Davies, and P. McNiven, eds., *Trade, devotion and governance: papers in later medieval history* (Stroud, 1994), pp. 140–57

Alexander, J.S., 'Building stone from the East Midland quarries: sources, transportation and usage', *Medieval Archaeology*, 39 (1995), 107–35

Allix, A., 'The geography of fairs: illustrated by Old-World examples', *Geographical Rev.*, 12 (1922), 532–69

Aston, T.H., Duncan, G.D. and Evans, T.A.R., 'The medieval alumni of the University of Cambridge', *Past and Present*, 86 (1980), 9–86

Aston, T.H. and Philpin, C.H.E., eds., *The Brenner debate: agrarian class structure and economic development in pre-industrial Europe* (Cambridge, 1985)

Atkinson, T.D., 'On the house of the Veysy family in Cambridge', *PCAS*, 7 (1893), 93–103

Atkinson, T.D. and Clark, J.W., *Cambridge described & illustrated being a short history of the town and university* (London, 1897)

Aylmer, G.E., 'The economics and finances of the colleges and university c.1530–1640', in J. McConica, ed., *The history of the university of Oxford, iii: the collegiate university* (Oxford, 1986), pp. 521–58

Bailey, M., 'Demographic decline in late medieval England: some thoughts on recent research', *EcHR*, 49 (1996), 1–19

  A marginal economy? East Anglian Breckland in the later Middle Ages (Cambridge, 1989)

  'Rural society', in R. Horrox, ed., *Fifteenth-century attitudes: perceptions of society in late medieval England* (Cambridge, 1994), pp. 150–68

  'A tale of two towns: Buntingford and Standon in the later middle ages', *Journal of Medieval History*, 19 (1993), 351–71

Bainbridge, V., *Gilds in the medieval countryside: social and religious change in Cambridgeshire c.1350–1558* (Woodbridge, 1996)

Barron, C.M., 'Centres of conspicuous consumption: the aristocratic town house in London, 1200–1550', *London Journal*, 20 (1995), 1–16

Barry, J., ed., *The Tudor and Stuart Town: a reader in English urban history, 1530–1688* (Harlow, 1990)

Bartlett, J.N., 'The expansion and decline of York in the later middle ages', *EcHR*, 2nd ser., 12 (1959–60), 17–33

Bennett, J.M., *Ale, beer and brewsters in England: women's work in a changing world, 1300–1600* (Oxford, 1996)

Beresford, M., *New towns of the Middle Ages: town plantation in England, Wales and Gascony* (London, 1967)

Beveridge, W., *Prices and wages in England, from the twelfth to the nineteenth century* (London, 1939)

Bindoff, S.T., ed., *The House of Commons 1509–1558*, The History of Parliament, 3 vols. (London, 1982)

Blanchard, I., *International lead production and trade in the "Age of the Saigerprozess"*

1460–1560 (Stuttgart, 1995)
  'Population change, enclosure, and the early Tudor economy', *EcHR*, 2nd ser., 23 (1970), 433–42

Boalch, D.H., *Makers of the harpsichord & clavichord 1440–1840* (Oxford, 3rd edn., 1995)

Bonney, M., *Lordship and the urban community: Durham and its overlords, 1250–1540* (Cambridge, 1990)

Bowden, P.J., 'Statistical appendix', in P.J. Bowden, ed., *Chapters from the Agrarian History of England and Wales*, i: *Economic change: wages, profits and rents 1500–1750* (Cambridge, 1990), pp. 116–72

Braybrooke, Richard Lord, *The history of Audley End* (London, 1836)

Brenner, R., 'Agrarian class structure and economic development in pre-industrial Europe', in Aston and Philpin, eds., *The Brenner debate*, pp. 10–63
  'Agrarian roots of European capitalism', in Aston and Philpin, eds., *The Brenner debate*, pp. 213–328

Bridbury, A.R., 'Dr Rigby's comment: a reply', *EcHR*, 2nd ser., 39 (1986), 417–22
  Economic growth: England in the later middle ages (London, 1962)
  'English provincial towns in the later middle ages', *EcHR*, 2nd ser., 34 (1981), 1–24
  'Sixteenth–century farming', *EcHR*, 2nd ser., 27 (1974), 538–56

Britnell, R.H., *Britain and Ireland 1050–1530: economy and society* (Oxford, 2004)
  The closing of the middle ages? England, 1471–1529 (Oxford, 1997)
  'Commerce and capitalism in late medieval England: problems of description and theory', *Journal of Historical Sociology*, 6 (1993), pp. 359–76
  The commercialisation of English society, 1000–1500 (Manchester, 2nd edn., 1996)
  'The economy of British towns 600–1300', in *CUHB*, i, pp. 105–26
  'The economy of British towns 1300–1540', in *CUHB*, i, pp. 313–33
  'The English economy and the government, 1450–1550', in Watts, ed., *End of the middle ages?*, pp. 89–116
  Growth and decline in Colchester, 1300–1525 (Cambridge, 1986)
  'The proliferation of markets in England, 1200–1349', *EcHR*, 2nd ser., 34 (1981), 209–21
  'Urban demand in the English economy, 1300–1600', in Galloway, ed., *Trade*, pp. 1–21

Britnell, R. and Hatcher, J., eds., *Progress and problems in medieval England: essays in honour of Edward Miller* (Cambridge, 1996)

Brodt, B., 'East Anglia', in *CUHB*, i, pp. 639–56

Brooke, C.N.L., 'The churches of medieval Cambridge', in D. Beales and G. Best, eds., *History, society and the churches: Essays in honour of Owen Chadwick* (Cambridge, 1985), pp. 49–76

Brooke, C., Highfield, R. and Swaan, W., *Oxford and Cambridge* (Cambridge, 1988)

Bryan, P. and Wise, N., 'A reconstruction of the medieval Cambridge market place', *PCAS*, 91 (2002), 73–87.

Bushell, W.D., *The church of St Mary the Great: The university church at Cambridge* (Cambridge, 1948)

Butcher, A.F., 'Rent, population and economic change in late-medieval Newcastle', *Northern History*, 14 (1978), 67–77
  'Rent and the urban economy: Oxford and Canterbury in the later middle ages', *Southern History*, 1 (1979), 11–43

Campbell, B.M.S., 'The population of early Tudor England: a re-evaluation of the 1522 muster returns and 1524 and 1525 lay subsidies', *Journal of Historical Geography*, 7 (1981), 145–54

Campbell, B.M.S., Galloway, J.A., Keene, D. and Murphy, M., *A medieval capital and its grain supply: agrarian production and distribution in the London region c.1300*, Historical Geography Research Ser., XXX (London, 1993)

Campbell, B.M.S. and Overton, M., 'A new perspective of medieval and early modern agriculture: six centuries of Norfolk farming c.1250–c.1850', *Past and Present*, 141 (1993), 38–105

Carpenter, C., 'The fifteenth-century English gentry and their estates', in M. Jones, ed., *Gentry and lesser nobility in late medieval Europe* (Gloucester, 1986), pp. 36–60

Carus-Wilson, E.M., 'The aulnage accounts: a criticism', in E.M. Carus-Wilson, *Medieval merchant venturers* (London, 1954), pp. 279–91

  'The medieval trade of the ports of the Wash', *Medieval Archaeology*, 6–7 (1962–3), 182–201

Carus-Wilson, E.M. and Coleman, O., *England's export trade, 1275–1547* (Oxford, 1963)

Chartres, J.A., 'Markets and fairs in England and Wales, 1500 to 1860', University of Leeds, School of Business and Economic Studies, Discussion paper ser., G93/03 (Leeds, 1993)

Christaller, W., *Central places in southern Germany*, trans. C.W. Baskin (Englewood Cliffs, N.J., 1966)

Clapham, J.H., 'A thirteenth-century market town: Linton, Cambs.', *Cambridge Historical Journal*, 4 (1933), 194–202

Clark, A., 'Saffron and Walden', *Essex Rev.*, 19 (1910), 57–64

Clark, J.W., 'History of the peal of bells belonging to King's College, Cambridge', *PCAS*, 4 (1876–80), 223–43

Clark, J.W. and Gray, A., *Old plans of Cambridge 1574 to 1798*, 2 vols. (Cambridge, 1921)

Clark, P., ed., *The Cambridge Urban History of Britain*, ii: *1540–1840* (Cambridge, 2000)

Clark, P. and Slack, P., *English towns in transition 1500–1700* (Oxford, 1976)

Clouston, R.W.M., 'Cambridgeshire bells', in C. Hicks, ed., *Cambridgeshire churches*, pp. 361–77

Cobban, A.B., 'Commoners in medieval Cambridge colleges', in Zutshi, ed., *Medieval Cambridge*, pp. 47–64

  English university life in the Middle Ages (London, 1999)

  The King's Hall within the University of Cambridge in the later middle ages (Cambridge, 1969)

  The medieval English universities: Oxford and Cambridge to c.1500 (Aldershot, 1988)

Corfield, P.J. and Harte, N.B., eds., *London and the English economy 1500–1700* (London, 1990)

Cornwall, J.C.K., 'English population in the early sixteenth century', *EcHR*, 2nd ser., 23 (1970), 32–44

  Wealth and society in early sixteenth-century England (London, 1988)

Cotton, S., 'Perpendicular churches', in C. Hicks, ed., *Cambridgeshire churches*, pp. 95–106

Cromarty, D., 'Chepying Walden 1381–1420, a study from the court rolls', *Essex Journal*, 2 (1967), 104–13, 122–39, 181–6

Cunningham, W., 'The economic history of Cambridgeshire', in *Ely Diocesan Remembrancer* (1909), 19–24

  The growth of English industry and commerce during the early and middle ages (Cambridge, 5th edn., 1915)

Dale, M.K., 'The London silkwomen of the fifteenth century', *EcHR*, 4 (1932–4), 324–35

Danckwerts, P.V., 'The inheritors of Barnwell Priory', *PCAS*, 70 (1980), 211–34

Darby, H.C., *The medieval Fenland* (Newton Abbot, 2nd edn., 1974)

  Medieval Cambridgeshire (Cambridge, 1977)

Darby, H.C., Glasscock, R.E., Sheail, J. and Versey, G.R., 'The changing geographical distribution of wealth in England: 1086–1334–1525', *Journal of Historical Geography*, 5 (1979), 247–62

Davis, J., 'Baking for the common good: a reassessment of the assize of bread in medieval England', *EcHR*, 57 (2004), 465–502

Deacon, B. and Donald, M., 'In search of a community history', *Family and Community History*, 7 (2004), 13–18
Dickinson, R.E., *City and region: a geographical interpretation* (London, 1964)
Dobb, M., *Studies in the development of capitalism* (London, 1946)
Dobson, M.J., *Contours of death and disease in early modern England* (Cambridge, 1997)
Dobson, R.B., 'Admissions to the freedom of the city of York in the later Middle Ages', *EcHR*, 2nd ser., 26 (1973), 1–22
  'Aliens in the city of York during the fifteenth century', in J. Mitchell, ed., *England and the continent in the middle ages* (Stamford, 2000), pp. 249–66
  'Cathedral chapters and cathedral cities: York, Durham and Carlisle in the fifteenth century', *Northern History*, 19 (1983), 15–44
  'General survey 1300–1540', in *CUHB*, i, pp. 273–90
  'The monastic orders in late medieval Cambridge', in P. Biller and R.B. Dobson, eds., *The medieval church: universities, heresy and the religious life*, Studies in Church History Subsidia, XI (Woodbridge, 1999), pp. 239–69
  The Peasants' Revolt of 1381 (London, 2nd edn., 1983)
  'The religious orders 1370–1540', in J.I. Catto and R. Evans, eds., *The history of the university of Oxford*, ii: *late medieval Oxford* (Oxford, 1992), pp. 539–80
  'Urban decline in late medieval England', in Holt and Rosser, eds., *Medieval town*, pp. 265–86
Doughty, R.A., 'Industrial prices and inflation in southern England, 1401–1640', *Explorations in Economic History*, 12 (1975), 177–92
Du Boulay, F.R.H., 'Who were farming the English demesnes at the end of the middle ages?', *EcHR*, 2nd ser., 17 (1965), 443–55
Dyer, A., 'The bishops' census of 1563: its significance and accuracy', *Local Population Studies*, 49 (1992), 19–37
  The city of Worcester in the sixteenth century (Leicester, 1973)
  Decline and growth in English towns 1400–1640 (Cambridge, 2nd edn., 1995)
  'Growth and decay in English towns 1500–1700', *Urban History Yearbook 1979*, 60–72
  'Ranking lists of English medieval towns', in *CUHB*, i, pp. 747–70
  '"Urban decline" in England, 1377–1525' in T.R. Slater, ed., *Towns in decline AD1000–1600* (Aldershot, 2000), pp. 266–88
Dyer, C., 'The consumer and the market in the later middle ages', *EcHR*, 2nd ser., 42 (1989), 305–27
  'The hidden trade of the Middle Ages: evidence from the West Midlands of England', *Journal of Historical Geography*, 18 (1992), 141–57
  Making a living in the Middle Ages: the people of Britain 850–1520 (London, 2002)
  'Market towns and the countryside in late medieval England', *Canadian Journal of History*, 31 (1996), 17–35
  'A small landowner in the fifteenth century', *Midland History*, 1, part 3 (1972), 1–14
  Standards of living in the later middle ages: social change in England, c.1200–1520 (Cambridge, 1989)
  'Were peasants self-sufficient? English villagers and the market, 900–1300', in E. Mornet, ed., *Campagnes médiévales: l'homme et son espace* (Paris, 1995), pp. 653–66
  'Were there any capitalists in fifteenth-century England?', in C. Dyer, ed., *Everyday life in medieval England* (London, 1994), pp. 305–27
Dymond, D., 'The famine of 1527 in Essex', *Local Population Studies*, 26 (1981), 29–40
Dymond, D. and Virgoe, R., 'The reduced population and wealth of early fifteenth-century Suffolk', *Proceedings of Suffolk Institute of Archaeology*, 36 (1985–8), 73–100
Edwards, P.R., 'The horse trade in Tudor and Stuart England', in F.M.L. Thompson, ed., *Horses in European economic history: a preliminary canter* (Reading, 1983), pp. 113–31

Eiden, H. and Irsigler, F., 'Environs and hinterland: Cologne and Nuremberg in the later middle ages', in Galloway, ed., *Trade*, pp. 43–57

Elton, G.R., *Star Chamber stories* (London, 1958)

Emden, A.B., *A biographical register of the University of Cambridge to 1500* (Cambridge, 1963)

Emery, A., *Greater medieval houses of England and Wales 1300–1500*, ii: *East Anglia, central England and Wales* (Cambridge, 2000)

Epstein, S.R., 'Regional fairs, institutional innovation, and economic growth in late medieval Europe', *EcHR*, 47 (1994), 459–82

Evans, T.A.R. and Faith, R.J., 'College estates and university finances, 1350–1500', in J.I. Catto and R. Evans, eds., *The history of the University of Oxford*, ii: *late medieval Oxford* (Oxford, 1992), pp. 635–707

Everitt, A., 'The English urban inn, 1560–1760' in A. Everitt, ed., *Perspectives in English urban history* (London, 1973), pp. 91–137

   'Introduction', in Everitt, ed., *Perspectives*, pp. 1–15

   'The marketing of agricultural produce, 1500–1640', in J. Chartres, ed., *Chapters from the Agrarian History of England and Wales*, iv: *Agricultural markets and trade, 1500–1750* (Cambridge, 1990), pp. 15–141

Fairclough, K., 'A Tudor canal scheme for the River Lea', *London Journal*, 5 (1979), 218–27

Farmer, D.L., 'Marketing the produce of the countryside, 1200–1500', in E. Miller, ed., *The agrarian history of England and Wales*, iii: *1348–1500* (Cambridge, 1991), pp. 324–430

Fletcher, A., *Tudor rebellions* (Harlow, 3rd edn., 1983)

Fisher, F.J., 'Commercial trends and policy in sixteenth-century England', in Corfield and Harte, eds., *London and the English economy 1500–1700*, pp. 81–103

   'The development of London as a centre of conspicuous consumption in the sixteenth and seventeenth centuries', in Corfield and Harte, eds., *London and the English economy 1500–1700*, pp. 105–18

   'Influenza and inflation in Tudor England', in Corfield and Harte, eds., *London and the English economy 1500–1700*, pp. 163–72

   'London as an "engine of economic growth"', in Corfield and Harte, eds., *London and the English economy 1500–1700*, pp. 185–98

Fudge, J.D., *Cargoes, embargoes and emissaries. The commercial and political interaction of England and the German Hanse 1450–1510* (Toronto, 1995)

Galley, C., *The demography of early modern towns: York in the sixteenth and seventeenth century* (Liverpool, 1998)

Galloway, J.A., 'Driven by drink? Ale consumption and the agrarian economy of the London region c.1300–1400', in M. Carlin and J.T. Rosenthal, eds., *Food and eating in medieval Europe* (London, 1998), pp. 87–100

   'Town and country in England, 1300–1570', in S.R. Epstein, ed., *Town and country in Europe 1300–1800* (Cambridge, 2001), pp. 106–31

   ed., *Trade, urban hinterlands and market integration, c.1300–1600* (London, 2000)

Galloway, J.A., Keene, D. and Murphy, M., 'Fuelling the city: production and distribution of firewood and fuel in London's region, 1290–1400', *EcHR*, 49 (1996), 447–72

Gerald Eve and Co., *Report on an assessment of future shopping needs in Cambridge central area* (London, 1965)

Gibson, J., *Probate jurisdictions: where to look for wills* (Solihull, 3rd edn., 1989)

Glennie, P., 'In search of agrarian capitalism: manorial land markets and the acquisition of land in the Lea Valley c.1450–c.1560', *Continuity and Change*, 3 (1988), 11–40

Goddard, A.R., 'Ickleton church and priory', *PCAS*, 11 (1903–6), 181–95

Goose, N., 'The bishops' census of 1563: a re-examination of its reliability', *Local Population Studies*, 56 (1996), 43–53

'The Dutch in Colchester in the 16th and 17th centuries: opposition and integration', in R. Vigne and C. Littleton, eds., *From strangers to citizens: the integration of immigrant communities in Britain, Ireland and colonial America, 1550–1750* (London, 2001), pp. 88–98

'The ecclesiastical returns of 1563: a cautionary note', *Local Population Studies*, 34 (1985), 46–7

'English pre-industrial urban economies', in Barry, ed., *Tudor and Stuart town*, pp. 63–73

'Fertility and mortality in pre-industrial English towns from probate and parish register evidence' in T. Arkell, N. Evans and N. Goose, eds., *When death do us part: understanding and interpreting the probate records of early modern England* (Oxford, 2000), pp. 189–212

'Household size and structure in early-Stuart Cambridge', in Barry, ed., *Tudor and Stuart town*, pp. 74–120

'In search of the urban variable: towns and the English economy, 1500–1650', *EcHR*, 2nd ser., 39 (1986), 165–85

'People and society in Hertfordshire's early modern towns' (forthcoming)

'Urban demography in pre-industrial England: what is to be done?' *Urban History*, 21 (1994), 273–84

Grantham, G., 'Agricultural supply during the industrial revolution: French evidence and European implications', *Journal of Economic History*, 49 (1989), 43–72

'Privileged spaces: agricultural productivity and urban provisioning zones in pre-industrial Europe' (English summary), *Annales*, 52 (1997), 729

Gras, N.S.B., *The evolution of the English corn market from the twelfth to the eighteenth century* (Cambridge, Mass., 1915)

Gray, G.J., *The earlier Cambridge stationers and bookbinders and the first Cambridge printer*, Oxford Bibliographical Soc. Illustrated Monographs XIII (Oxford, 1904)

Greenwood, J.R., 'Haine's Cambridge school of brasses', *Transactions of the Monumental Brass Soc.*, 11, part 1 (1969), 2–12

Hadwin, J.F., 'The medieval lay subsidies and economic history', *EcHR*, 2nd ser., 36 (1983), 200–17

Hall, C.P., 'The gild of Corpus Christi and the foundation of Corpus Christi College: an investigation of the documents', in Zutshi, ed., *Medieval Cambridge*, pp. 65–91

'Quit-rents', *Letter of the Corpus Association*, 61 (1982), 49–54

Hall, P., ed., *Von Thünen's isolated state* (London, 1966)

Hammer, C.I., 'The mobility of skilled labour in late medieval England: some Oxford evidence', *Vierteljahrschrift für Sozial- und Wirtschaftsgeschichte*, 63 (1976), 194–210

'Oxford town and Oxford University', in J. McConica, ed., *The history of the University of Oxford*, iii: *the collegiate university* (Oxford, 1986), pp. 69–116

Harding, V., 'Reformation and culture 1540–1700', in *CUHB*, ii, pp. 263–88

Hare, J.N., 'The demesne lessees of fifteenth-century Wiltshire', *Agricultural History Rev.*, 29 (1981), 1–15

'Growth and recession in the fifteenth-century economy: the Wiltshire textile industry and the countryside', *EcHR*, 52 (1999), 1–26

Harrison, C.J., 'Grain price analysis and harvest qualities', *Agricultural History Rev.*, 19 (1971), 135–55

Harrison, D.F., 'Bridges and economic development 1300–1800', *EcHR*, 45 (1992), 240–61

Harvey, B., 'The leasing of the abbot of Westminster's demesnes in the later middle ages', *EcHR*, 2nd ser., 22 (1969), 17–27

Living and dying in medieval England, 1100–1540: the monastic experience (Oxford, 1993)

Harvey, J., *English medieval architects: a biographical dictionary down to 1550* (Gloucester, 1984)
Hatcher, J., 'The great slump of the mid-fifteenth century', in Britnell and Hatcher, eds., *Progress and problems*, pp. 237–72
   The history of the British coal industry, i: *before 1700, towards the age of coal* (Oxford, 1993)
   Plague, population and the English economy, 1348–1530 (London, 1977)
Hatcher, J. and Barker, T.C., *A history of British pewter* (London, 1974)
Hatcher, J. and Bailey, M., *Modelling the middle ages: the history and theory of England's economic development* (Oxford, 2001)
Heal, F., 'The Tudors and church lands: economic problems of the bishopric of Ely during the sixteenth century', *EcHR*, 2nd ser., 26 (1973), 198–217
Heaton, H., *The Yorkshire woollen and worsted industries from the earliest times up to the industrial revolution* (Oxford, 2nd edn., 1965)
Hicks, C., ed., *Cambridgeshire churches* (Stamford, 1997)
Hilton, R.H., *English and French towns in feudal society: a comparative study* (Cambridge, 1992)
   'Towns in English medieval society', in Holt and Rosser, eds., *Medieval town*, pp. 19–28
Hodgen, M.T., 'Fairs of Elizabethan England', *Economic Geography*, 18 (1942), 389–400
Holt, R. and Rosser, G., eds., *The medieval town: a reader in English urban history 1200–1540* (Harlow, 1990)
   'Introduction: the English town in the Middle Ages', in Holt and Rosser, eds., *Medieval town*, pp. 1–18
Horrox, R., 'The urban gentry in the fifteenth century', in J.A.F. Thomson, ed., *Towns and townspeople in the fifteenth century* (Gloucester, 1988), pp. 22–44
Hoskins, W.G., *The age of plunder: the England of Henry VIII, 1500–1547* (London, 1976)
   'English provincial towns in the early sixteenth century', *Transactions of the Royal Historical Soc.*, 5th ser., 6 (1956), 1–19
   'Harvest fluctuations and English economic history, 1480–1619', *Agricultural History Rev.*, 12 (1964), 28–46
   'The rebuilding of rural England, 1570–1640', *Past and Present*, 4 (1953), 44–59
Hoyle, R.W., 'Tenure and the land market in early modern England: or a late contribution to the Brenner debate', *EcHR*, 2nd ser., 43 (1990), 1–20
   Tudor taxation records: a guide for users (London, 1994)
Hulbert, N.F., 'A survey of Somerset fairs', *Proceedings of the Somersetshire Archaeological and Natural History Soc.*, 82 (1936), 83–159
Jones, B.C., 'Westmorland pack-horse men in Southampton', *Transactions of the Cumberland and Westmorland Antiquarian and Archaeological Soc.*, new ser., 59 (1959), 65–84
Jones, M.K. and Underwood, M.G., *The king's mother: Lady Margaret Beaufort, countess of Richmond and Derby* (Cambridge, 1992)
Jones, W.J., *The Elizabethan court of Chancery* (Oxford, 1967)
Jurkowski, M., Smith, C.L. and Crook, D., *Lay taxes in England and Wales 1188–1688* (Kew, 1998)
Keene, D., 'Changes in London's economic hinterland as indicated by debt cases in the Court of Common Pleas', in Galloway, ed., *Trade*, pp. 59–81
   'Medieval London and its region', *London Journal*, 14 (1989), 99–111
   'The property market in English towns A.D. 1100–1600', in J-C. Maire Vigueur, ed., *D'Une Ville à l'autre: Structures, Matérielles et Organisation de L'Espace dans les villes Européenes XIIIe–XVIe Siècle* (Rome, 1989), pp. 201–26

'Small towns and the metropolis: the experience of medieval England', in J-M. Duvosquel and E. Thoen, eds., *Peasants and townsmen in medieval Europe* (Ghent, 1995), pp. 223–38

Kerling, N.J.M., 'Aliens in the county of Norfolk, 1436–1485', *Norfolk Archaeology*, 33 (1965), 200–15

Kermode, J.I., 'The greater towns 1300–1540', in *CUHB*, i, pp. 441–65
  Medieval merchants: York, Beverley and Hull in the later middle ages (Cambridge, 1998)
  'Money and credit in the fifteenth century: some lessons from Yorkshire', *Business History Rev.*, 45 (1991), 475–501
  'The trade of late medieval Chester', in Britnell and Hatcher, eds., *Progress and problems*, pp. 286–307
  'Urban decline? The flight from office in late medieval York', *EcHR*, 2nd ser., 35 (1982), 179–98

Kerridge, E., 'The movement of rent, 1540–1640', *EcHR*, 2nd ser., 6 (1953–4), 16–34

Kowaleski, M., 'The expansion of the south-western fisheries in late medieval England', *EcHR*, 53 (2000), 429–54
  'The grain trade in fourteenth-century Exeter', in E.B. DeWindt, ed., *The salt of common life: individuality and choice in the medieval town, countryside, and church* (Kalamazoo, 1995), pp. 1–52
  Local markets and regional trade in medieval Exeter (Cambridge, 1995)
  'Port towns: England and Wales 1300–1540', in *CUHB*, i, pp. 467–94

Knowles, D. and Hadcock, R.N., *Medieval religious houses: England and Wales* (London, 2nd edn., 1971)

Knowles, R. and Wareing, J., *Economic and social geography made simple* (London, 4th edn., 1981)

Langton, J. and Hoppe, G., *Town and country in the development of early modern western Europe*, Historical Geography Research Ser., XI (Norwich, 1983)

Laughton, J., Jones, E. and Dyer, C., 'The urban hierarchy in the later middle ages: a study of the East Midlands', *Urban History*, 28 (2001), 331–57

Leader, D.R., *A history of the University of Cambridge*, i: *the university to 1546* (Cambridge, 1988)

Lee, J.S., 'Feeding the colleges: Cambridge's food and fuel supplies, 1450–1560' *EcHR*, 56 (2003), 243–64
  'Tracing regional and local changes in population and wealth during the later middle ages using taxation records: Cambridgeshire, 1334–1563', *Local Population Studies*, 69 (2002), 32–50
  'The trade of fifteenth-century Cambridge and its region', in M. Hicks, ed., *The fifteenth century*, ii: *Revolution and consumption in late medieval England* (Woodbridge, 2001), pp. 127–39

Leedham-Green, E., *A concise history of the University of Cambridge* (Cambridge, 1996)
  'The University Archives (what are they, anyway?)', in P. Fox, ed., *Cambridge University Library: the great collections* (Cambridge, 1998), pp. 197–210

Leedham-Green, E. and Rodd, R., eds., *Index of the probate records of the Consistory Court of Ely, 1449–1858*, British Record Soc., CIV, CVI–CVII (London, 1994–6)

Letters, S., with others, *Gazetteer of Markets and Fairs in England and Wales to 1516*, 2 vols. (London, 2003), available online at the Centre for Metropolitan History website http://www.ihr.sas.ac.uk/cmh/gaz/gazweb2.html

Lewis, J.P., *A study of the Cambridge sub-region* (London, 1974)

Lloyd, T.H., *Some aspects of the building industry in medieval Stratford-upon-Avon*, Dugdale Soc. occasional papers, XIV (Oxford, 1961)

Lobel, M.D., 'Cambridge', in M.D. Lobel, ed., *The atlas of historic towns*, ii: *Bristol, Cambridge, Coventry, Norwich* (London, 1975)

Lomas, R.A., 'A northern farm at the end of the middle ages: Elvethall manor, Durham, 1443/4–1513/14', *Northern History*, 18 (1982), 26–53

Lovatt, R., 'Two collegiate loan chests in late medieval Cambridge', in Zutshi, ed., *Medieval Cambridge*, pp. 129–65

Lovatt, R. and M., 'The religious life of the townsmen of medieval Cambridge', in N. Rogers, ed., *Catholics in Cambridge* (Leominster, 2003), pp. 4–21

MacCulloch, D., 'Kett's rebellion in context', *Past and Present*, 84 (1979), 36–59

Machin, R., 'The Great Rebuilding: a reassessment', *Past and Present*, 77 (1977), 33–56

'The mechanism of the pre-industrial building cycle', *Vernacular Architecture*, 8 (1977), 815–19

Maitland, F.W., 'The history of a Cambridgeshire manor', *English Historical Rev.*, 35 (1894), 417–39

Township and borough (Cambridge, 1898)

Marx, K., *Capital*, trans. E. and C. Paul, 2 vols. (London, 1930)

Masschaele, J., 'The multiplicity of medieval markets reconsidered', *Journal of Historical Geography*, 20 (1994), 255–71

Peasants, merchants, and markets: inland trade in medieval England, 1150–1350 (Basingstoke, 1997)

'The public space of the market place in medieval England', *Speculum*, 77 (2002), 383–421

Mate, M., 'The East Sussex land market and agrarian class structure in the late middle ages', *Past and Present*, 139 (1993), 46–65

'The rise and fall of markets in southeast England', *Canadian Journal of History*, 31 (1996), 59–86

Women in medieval English society (Cambridge, 1999)

May, P., 'Newmarket and its market court, 1399–1413', *Proceedings of Suffolk Institute of Archaeology*, 35 (1981), 31–9

Newmarket – medieval and Tudor (Newmarket, 1982)

Mayhew, N.J., 'Population, money supply, and the velocity of circulation in England, 1300–1700', *EcHR*, 48 (1995), 238–57

McCutcheon, K.L., *Yorkshire fairs and markets to the end of the eighteenth century*, Thoresby Soc., XXXIX (Leeds, 1940)

McIntosh, M.K., 'Money lending on the periphery of London 1300–1600', *Albion*, 20 (1988), 557–71

McIntosh, T., *The decline of Stourbridge Fair, 1770–1934*, Friends of the Department of English Local History, University of Leicester, No. 2 (Leicester, 1998)

McKitterick, D., *A history of Cambridge University Press*, i: *printing and the book trade in Cambridge 1534–1698* (Cambridge, 1992)

Miller, E., *The abbey and bishopric of Ely* (Cambridge, 1951)

'Fishponds close and its pondyards', *The Eagle* (Magazine of St John's College), 59 (1963), 353–62

Mills, D., 'Defining community: a critical review of "community" in Family and Community History', *Family and Community History*, 7 (2004), 5–12

Mills, M.H., 'The medieval shire house' in J. Conway Davies, ed., *Studies presented to Sir Hilary Jenkinson* (London, 1957), pp. 254–71

Milner Gray, J., *Biographical notes on the mayors of Cambridge* (Cambridge, 1921)

Morgan, V. and Brooke, C., *A history of the University of Cambridge*, ii: *1546–1750* (Cambridge, 2004)

Moore, E.W., *The fairs of medieval England: an introductory study* (Toronto, 1985)

Moore, J.S., 'Jack Fisher's "flu": a visitation revisited', *EcHR*, 2nd ser., 46 (1993), 280–307

Moorman, J.R.H., *The Grey Friars in Cambridge 1225–1538* (Cambridge, 1952)

Newman, C.M., 'Employment on the estates of the priory of Durham, 1494–1519: the priory as an employer', *Northern History*, 36 (2000), 43–58
  Late medieval Northallerton: a small town and its hinterland, c.1470–1540 (Stamford, 1999)
Newton, K.C., *Thaxted in the fourteenth century* (Chelmsford, 1960)
Nichols, J., *The history and antiquities of Barnwell Abbey, and of Sturbridge Fair*, Bibliotheca Topographica Britannica, no. XXXVIII (London, 1786)
Nightingale, P., 'The lay subsidies and the distribution of wealth in medieval England, 1275–1334', *EcHR*, 57 (2004), 1–32
  A medieval mercantile community: the Grocers' Company and the politics and trade of London, 1000–1485 (New Haven, 1995)
  'Monetary contraction and mercantile credit in later medieval England', *EcHR*, 2nd ser., 43 (1990), 560–75
Outhwaite, R.B., *Dearth, public policy and social disturbance in England, 1550–1800* (London, 1991)
  Inflation in Tudor and early Stuart England (London, 2nd edn., 1982)
Overton, M., *Agricultural revolution in England: the transformation of the agrarian economy 1500–1850* (Cambridge, 1996)
Owen, D.M., *Cambridge University archives: a classified list* (Cambridge, 1988)
The Oxford English Dictionary, 20 vols. (Oxford, 2nd edn., 1989)
Palliser, D.M., 'A regional capital as magnet: immigrants to York, 1477–1566', *Yorkshire Archaeological Journal*, 57 (1985), 111–23
  Tudor York (Oxford, 1979)
  'York under the Tudors: the trading life of the northern capital', in A. Everitt, ed., *Perspectives in English urban history* (London, 1973), pp. 39–59
  ed., *The Cambridge Urban History of Britain*, i: *600–1540* (Cambridge, 2000)
Pam, D.O., *Tudor Enfield: the maltmen and the Lea navigation*, Edmonton Hundred Historical Soc., Occasional Papers, new ser. XVIII (not dated)
Page, F.M., *The estates of Crowland Abbey* (Cambridge, 1934)
Parker, R., *Town and gown: the 700 years war in Cambridge* (Cambridge, 1983)
Patten, J., 'Village and town: an occupational study', *Agricultural History Review*, 20 (1972), 1–16
Pearce, E.C., 'College accounts of John Botwright, master of Corpus Christi, 1443–74', *PCAS*, 22 (1917–20), 76–90
Peek, H.E. and Hall, C., *The archives of the University of Cambridge: an historical introduction* (Cambridge, 1962)
Pevsner, N., *The buildings of England: Cambridgeshire* (London, 2nd edn., 1970)
Phelps Brown, E.H. and Hopkins, S.V., *A perspective of wages and prices* (London, 1981)
Phythian-Adams, C., 'Local history and societal history', *Local Population Studies*, 51 (1993), 30–45
  'Urban decay in late medieval England', in Abrams and Wrigley, eds., *Towns in societies*, pp. 159–85
Pirenne, H., *Medieval cities: their origins and the revival of trade* (Princeton, N.J., 1952)
Poos, L.R., *A rural society after the Black Death: Essex, 1350–1525* (Cambridge, 1991)
Postan, M.M., 'The fifteenth century', *EcHR*, 9 (1938–9), 160–7
Powell, E., *The rising in East Anglia in 1381* (Cambridge, 1896)
Rackham, O., *Ancient woodland: its history, vegetation and uses in England* (London, 1980)
  'Why Corpus Christi?' in M.E. Bury and E.J. Winter, eds., *Corpus within living memory: life in a Cambridge college* (London, 2003), pp. 9–17
Raftis, J.A., *Early Tudor Godmanchester: survivals and new arrivals* (Toronto, 1990)

The estates of Ramsey Abbey: a study in economic growth and organisation (Toronto, 1957)

Ramsay, G.D., 'The distribution of the cloth industry in 1561–2', *English Historical Rev.*, 57 (1942), 361–9

Raven, J.J., *The church bells of Cambridgeshire*, CASOS, XVIII–XIX (Cambridge, 2nd edn., 1881)

Ravensdale, J.R., 'Landbeach in 1549: Kett's rebellion in miniature', in L.M. Munby, ed., *East Anglian studies* (Cambridge, 1968), pp. 94–116

Liable to floods: village landscape on the edge of the Fens, A.D. 450–1850 (Cambridge, 1974)

Reaney, P.H., ed., *The place-names of Cambridgeshire and the Isle of Ely*, English Place-Name Soc., XIX (Cambridge, 1943)

Riden, P., *Record sources for local history* (London, 1987)

Ridout, H., 'Markets and fairs', in T. Kirby and S. Oosthuizen, eds., *An atlas of Cambridgeshire and Huntingdonshire history* (Cambridge, 2000), chapter 44

Rigby, S.H., 'Late medieval urban prosperity: the evidence of the lay subsidies', *EcHR*, 2nd ser., 39 (1986), 411–16

'"Sore decay" and "fair dwellings": Boston and urban decline in the later Middle Ages', *Midland History*, 10 (1985), 47–61

'Urban decline in the later middle ages: some problems in interpreting the statistical data', *Urban History Yearbook* (1979), 46–60

Rodgers, H.B., 'The market area of Preston in the sixteenth and seventeenth centuries', *Geographical Studies*, 3 (1956), 46–55

Rogers, N., 'Cambridgeshire brasses', in Hicks, ed., *Cambridgeshire churches*, pp. 303–19

'Regional production', in R. Marks and P. Williamson, eds., *Gothic: art for England 1400–1547* (London, 2003), pp. 86–97

Rogers, J.E.T., *A history of agriculture and prices in England*, 7 vols. (Oxford, 1866–1902)

Rosser, G., 'London and Westminster: the suburb in the urban economy in the later Middle Ages', in J.A.F. Thomson, ed., *Towns and townspeople in the fifteenth century* (Gloucester, 1988), pp. 45–61

Medieval Westminster, 1200–1540 (Oxford, 1989)

Rowell, T.A., 'Sedge (*Cladium mariscus*) in Cambridgeshire: its use and production since the seventeenth century', *Agricultural History Rev.*, 34 (1986), 140–8

Royal Commission on Historical Monuments, *An inventory of the historical monuments in the city of Cambridge*, 2 vols. (London, 1959)

An inventory of the historical monuments in the county of Cambridge, i: *West Cambridgeshire* (London, 1968), ii: *North-East Cambridgeshire* (London, 1972)

Rubin, M., *Charity and community in medieval Cambridge* (Cambridge, 1987)

Saffron Walden Museum, *Saffron Walden local history activity guide* (Saffron Walden, rev. edn., 1997)

Saltmarsh, J., 'A college home-farm in the fifteenth century', *Economic History*, 3 (1936), 155–72

'Hand-list of the estates of King's College, Cambridge', *Bulletin of the Institute of Historical Research*, 12 (1934), 32–8

Salzman, L.F., *Building in England down to 1540: a documentary history* (Oxford, 1952)

English trade in the middle ages (Oxford, 1931)

Sanders, S., *Historical and architectural notes on Great St Mary's Church, Cambridge*, CASOS, X (Cambridge, 1869)

Scammell, G.V., 'English merchant shipping at the end of the middle ages: some East Coast evidence', *EcHR*, 2nd ser., 13 (1961), 327–41

Schofield, J. and Stell, G., 'The built environment 1300–1540', in *CUHB*, i, pp. 371–93

Schofield, R.S., 'The geographical distribution of wealth in England, 1334–1649', *EcHR*, 2nd ser., 18 (1965), 483–510
 Parish register aggregate analyses: the population history of England database and introductory guide, Local Population Studies Supplement (Colchester, 1998)
Shaw, D.G., *The creation of a community: the city of Wells in the middle ages* (Oxford, 1993)
Sheail, J., *The regional distribution of wealth in England as indicated in the 1524/5 lay subsidy returns*, ed. R.W. Hoyle, List and Index Soc., special ser., XXVIII, 2 vols. (Kew, 1998)
Shepard, A., 'Contesting communities? "Town" and "gown" in Cambridge, c.1560–1640', in A. Shepard and P. Withington, eds., *Communities in early modern England: networks, place, rhetoric* (Manchester, 2000), pp. 216–34
 'Litigation and locality: the Cambridge university courts, 1560–1640', *Urban History*, 31 (2004), 5–28
Sherlock, D., 'Brickmaking accounts for Wisbech, 1333–1356', *PCAS*, 87 (1998), 59–69
Siraut, M.C., 'Accounts of Saint Katherine's Guild at Holy Trinity Church, Cambridge: 1514–37', *PCAS*, 67 (1977), 111–21
 'Physical mobility in Elizabethan Cambridge', *Local Population Studies*, 27 (1981), 65–70
Slack, P., 'Mortality crises and epidemic disease in England, 1485–1610', in C. Webster, ed., *Health, medicine and mortality in the sixteenth century* (Cambridge, 1979), pp. 9–59
 'Social policy and the constraints of government, 1547–58', in J. Loach and R. Tittler, eds., *The mid-Tudor polity c.1540–1560* (London, 1980), pp. 94–115
Smailes, A., *The geography of towns* (London, 1953)
Smith, A., *An inquiry into the nature and causes of the wealth of nations*, ed. R.H. Campbell, A.S. Skinner and W.B. Todd, 2 vols. (Oxford, 1976)
Smith, C.T., 'Cambridge in its regional setting', in J.A. Steers, ed., *The Cambridge region 1965*, British Association for the Advancement of Science (London, 1965), pp. 133–92
Smith, R.M., 'A periodic market and its impact on a manorial community: Botesdale, Suffolk, and the manor of Redgrave, 1280–1300', in Z. Razi and R. Smith, eds., *Medieval society and the manor court* (Oxford, 1996), pp. 450–81
Spufford, M., *Contrasting communities: English villagers in the sixteenth and seventeenth centuries* (Cambridge, 1974)
 'General view of the rural economy of the county of Cambridge', *PCAS*, 89 (2000), 69–85
 The great reclothing of rural England: petty chapmen and their wares in the seventeenth century (London, 1984)
Stone, D., 'The productivity of hired and customary labour: evidence from Wisbech Barton in the fourteenth century', *EcHR*, 50 (1997), 640–56
Swanson, H., *Medieval artisans: an urban class in late medieval England* (Oxford, 1989)
 Medieval British towns (Basingstoke, 1999)
Sweezy, P., 'A critique', in R. Hilton, ed., *The transition from feudalism to capitalism* (London, 1976), pp. 33–56
Talbot, C.H. and Hammond, E.A., *Medical practitioners in medieval England: a biographical register*, Publications of the Wellcome Historical Medical Library, new ser., VIII (London, 1965)
Tawney, R.H., *The agrarian problem in the sixteenth century* (London, 1912)
 Religion and the rise of capitalism (London, 1922)
Taylor, A., *Archaeology of Cambridgeshire*, 2 vols. (March, 1997–8)
 Cambridge. The hidden history (Stroud, 1999)
Taylor, C.C., *The Cambridgeshire landscape* (London, 1973)
 'Medieval market grants and village morphology', *Landscape History*, 4 (1982), 21–8

'Whittlesford: the study of a river-edge village', in M. Aston, D. Austin and C. Dyer, eds., *Rural settlements of medieval England* (Oxford, 1989), pp. 207–27

Teversham, T.F., *A history of the village of Sawston*, 2 parts (Sawston, 1942–7)

Thirsk, J., *Alternative agriculture: a history from the Black Death to the present day* (Oxford, 1997)

Economic policy and projects (Oxford, 1978)

England's agricultural regions and agrarian history 1500–1750 (Basingstoke, 1987)

Thomson, J.A.F., 'Scots in England in the fifteenth century', *Scottish Historical Rev.*, 79 (2000), 1–16

Thornton, G.A., *A history of Clare, Suffolk* (Cambridge, 1928)

Thurley, C. and Thurley, D., eds., *Index of the probate records of the archdeaconry of Ely, 1513–1857*, British Record Soc., 88 (London, 1970)

Thrupp, S.L., 'Aliens in and around London in the fifteenth century', in A.E.J. Hollaender and W. Kellaway, eds., *Studies in London history presented to Philip Edmund Jones* (London, 1969), pp. 251–72

'A survey of the alien population of England in 1440', *Speculum*, 32 (1957), 262–73

The merchant class of medieval London (Chicago, 1948)

Tittler, R., 'For the "re-edification of townes": the rebuilding statutes of Henry VIII', *Albion*, 22 (1990), 591–605

Titow, J.Z., 'The decline of the fair of St Giles, Winchester, in the thirteenth and fourteenth centuries', *Nottingham Medieval Studies*, 31 (1987), 58–75

English rural society, 1200–1350 (London, 1969)

Underwood, M., 'The impact of St John's College as landowner in the west fields of Cambridge in the early sixteenth century', in Zutshi, ed., *Medieval Cambridge*, pp. 167–88

'Religion and the university to 1535', in N. Rogers, ed., *Catholics in Cambridge* (Leominster, 2003), pp. 22–37

Unwin, P.T.H., 'Towns and trade 1066–1500', in Dodgshon and Butlin, eds., *Historical geography*, pp. 123–49

Venn, J.A., *Oxford and Cambridge matriculations 1544–1906, with a graphic chart illustrating the varying fortunes of the two universities* (Cambridge, 1908)

A statistical chart to illustrate the entries at the various colleges in the university of Cambridge, 1504–1907 (Cambridge, 1908)

Verlinden, O., 'Markets and fairs', in M.M. Postan, E.E. Rich and E. Miller, eds., *Cambridge economic history of Europe*, iii: *Economic organisation and policies in the middle ages* (Cambridge, 1963), pp. 119–53

The Victoria County History of the counties of England (London, 1900– in progress)

Virgoe, R., 'The Cambridgeshire election of 1439', *Bulletin of the Institute of Historical Research*, 46 (1973), 95–101

Walford, C., *Fairs, past and present: a chapter in the history of commerce* (London, 1883)

Watkins, A., 'Landowners and their estates in the Forest of Arden in the fifteenth century', *Agricultural History Rev.*, 45 (1997), 18–33

Watts, J.L., ed., *The end of the middle ages? England in the fifteenth and sixteenth centuries* (Stroud, 1998)

'Introduction: history, the fifteenth century and the Renaissance', in Watts, ed., *End of the middle ages?*, pp. 1–22

Wayment, H., *King's College Chapel, Cambridge. The great windows: introduction and guide* (Cambridge, 1982)

Weatherill, L., *Consumer behaviour and material culture in Britain, 1660–1760* (London, 1988)

Webb, J., *Great Tooley of Ipswich: portrait of an early Tudor merchant*, Suffolk Records Soc., V (1962)

Wedgewood, J.C., *The History of Parliament: biographies of the members of the Commons House, 1439–1509* (London, 1936)
Whittle, J., *The development of agrarian capitalism: land and labour in Norfolk, 1440–1580* (Oxford, 2000)
Williams, G., 'Ecclesiastical vestments, books and furniture in the collegiate church of King's College, Cambridge, in the fifteenth century', *Ecclesiologist*, 20 (1859), 304–15
Williams, N.J., *The maritime trade of the East Anglian ports, 1550–1590* (Oxford, 1988)
Willis, R. and Clark, J.W., *The architectural history of the University of Cambridge and of the colleges of Cambridge and Eton*, 4 vols. (Cambridge, 1886, vols. 1–3 reprinted, 1988)
Woodward, D., *Men at work: labourers and building craftsmen in the towns of northern England, 1450–1750* (Cambridge, 1995)
  'Wage rates and living standards in pre-industrial England', *Past and Present*, 91 (1981), 28–46
Wrightson, K., *Earthly necessities: economic lives in early modern Britain* (New Haven, 2000)
Wrightson, K. and Levine, D., *Poverty and piety in an English village, Terling 1525–1700* (London, 1979)
Wrigley, E.A., 'City and country in the past: a sharp divide or a continuum?', *Historical Research*, 64 (1991), 107–20
  'Parasite or stimulus: the town in a pre-industrial economy', in Abrams and Wrigley, eds., *Towns in societies*, pp. 295–309
  'A simple model of London's importance in changing English society and economy, 1650–1750', in Abrams and Wrigley, eds., *Towns in societies*, pp. 215–43
Wrigley, E.A. and Schofield, R.S., *The population history of England, 1541–1871: a reconstruction* (London, 1981)
Yates, M., 'Change and continuities in rural society from the later middle ages to the sixteenth century: the contribution of west Berkshire', *EcHR*, 52 (1999), 617–37
Zutshi, P., 'John Botwright, master of the college, 1443–1474', *Letter of the Corpus Association*, 77 (1998), 13–19
  ed., *Medieval Cambridge: essays on the pre-Reformation university* (Woodbridge, 1993)

Unpublished dissertations

Davis, J., 'The representation, regulation and behaviour of petty traders in late medieval England' (unpublished PhD thesis, University of Cambridge, 2001)
Goose, N., 'Economic and social aspects of provincial towns: a comparative study of Cambridge, Colchester and Reading c.1500–1700' (unpublished PhD thesis, University of Cambridge, 1984)
Hamid, R., 'A service centre hierarchy in Cambridgeshire' (unpublished dissertation, Department of Geography, University of Durham, 1965) (deposited in the Cambridgeshire Collection, Cambridge Central Library)
Koren, A., 'Ely in the late middle ages' (unpublished PhD thesis, Indiana University, 1977)
Lee, J.S., 'Cambridge and its economic region, 1450–1560' (unpublished PhD thesis, University of Cambridge, 2001)
Ridout, H., 'Sturbridge Fair in the eighteenth century' (unpublished Certificate of Local History dissertation, Board of Continuing Education, University of Cambridge, 1992) (deposited in the Cambridgeshire Collection, Cambridge Central Library)
Saltmarsh, J., 'The employment of the estates of King's College in the fifteenth and sixteenth centuries; with special reference to the origins of beneficial leasing' (unpublished fellowship dissertation, King's College, Cambridge, 1930) (deposited in King's College Archives, JS 1/36, Copy A)

Schofield, R.S., 'Parliamentary land taxation 1485–1547' (unpublished PhD thesis, University of Cambridge, 1963)

Siraut, M.C., 'Some aspects of the economic and social history of Cambridge under Elizabeth I' (unpublished M.Litt. thesis, University of Cambridge, 1978)

Threlfall-Holmes, M., 'Monks and markets: Durham Cathedral Priory, 1460–1520' (unpublished PhD thesis, University of Durham, 2000)

Yates, M., 'Continuity and change in rural society c.1400–1600: West Hanney and Shaw (Berkshire) and their region' (unpublished D.Phil. thesis, University of Oxford, 1997)

Index

Note: University institutions are indexed under Cambridge; colleges are indexed separately. Page numbers in italics refer to Tables and Figures.

Adams, William 75
Agriculture 8–15, 86, 173
  enclosure 12, 43, 82
  production for towns 4–7, 10, 102, 152–65
  sub-regions 6, 36, 37–41, *45*, 48, 199
Alcock, John, bishop of Ely 63, 71, 73, 186, 187
Aldreth (Cambs.) 129
Aleyn, William, of Hadleigh 125
Algor, John 192
Aliens 7, 76–81
Alington, William 79
Ancaster (Lincs.) 187
Anglesey Priory (Cambs.) 62
Antwerp 16, 105, 141, 193
Archer, John 74
Argentein family 34
Argentine, John 194
Arrington (Cambs.) *48*
Ashdon (Essex) 189
Ashfield (Suff.) 191
Ashley cum Silverley (Cambs.) 106
Ashwell (Herts.) *33*
Awnger, carpenter 192

Babraham (Cambs.) 108
Bakers and baking 94–6, 112, 155, 163, 166
  Cambridge 55, 92, 95, 105, 170
  in colleges 155, 201
Bakon, William, of Halstead 190
Baldock (Herts.) 102
Balsham (Cambs.) *48*, 82, 88, 90, *117*, 148
Balsham, Hugh, bishop of Ely 63
Baltic, trade with 104, 189
Bankes, Mistress, of London 128
Banwell, Thomas, of Coventry 127
Banwell, William, of Coventry 127
Barker, Robert 58
Barley *see* malt barley
Barnack (Northants.) 187
Barneby, Thomas, of London 128
Barnwell (Cambs.) 61, 92, 99, 109, 130, 190
Barnwell Fair *see* Midsummer Fair
Barnwell Priory 73, 75, 81, 99, 118, 138
  site of 76, 188

Baron, Thomas, of Comberton 163
Barrington (Cambs.)
  fair *117*
  quarry 186, 187
  rectory 67, 108, 187
  repairs at 192
  saffron cultivation 108
  vicar 66–7
  wealth 40
  wood from 160
Barton (Cambs.) 41, 92–3, 162, 164, 171, 172
Bassingbourn (Cambs.) 78, 86, *117*
Bath and Wells, diocese of *65*
Battisford, John, of Chesterton 62
Bayseley, Robert, of Bury 124
Beaufort, Lady Margaret 19, 63, 71, 82, 187, 194
  arms of *64*
Bedford 100, 128
Bell, John 59, 60
Bellfounders 192, 193
Belton, John 60
Benet, John, of Burwell 163
Berkshire *see* West Berkshire
Beton, William, of Shepreth 96
Beverley (Yorks., E.R.) 116
Bicardyke, Ralph, of Cambridge 76
Biggin (Herts.) 171
Billingford, Richard, master of Corpus Christi College 69, *70*
Birmingham 115
Blande, William, of London 59
Blankpayn, John, MP for Cambridge 82
Bodevyle, William 107
Bookbinders and booksellers *78*, 80, 133, 150–1
Boston (Lincs.) 104, 114
Botesdale (Suff.) 96
Bottisham (Cambs.) 62, 82, 93, 130, 192
Botwright, John, master of Corpus Christi College *57*, 143
Bourn (Cambs.) 61, 163
Bowman, Thomas, of Braintree 190
Bowtell, James 21
Boxworth (Cambs.) 74, 164
Bracton 87
Braddeway, Richard, of Stowe 125
Bradford (Yorks., W.R.) 115
Braintree (Essex) 190
Brakyn, Thomas, of Cambridge 161, 176
Brandon (Suff.) 34, 190
Brandon, Charles 49

Brandon, Henry, duke of Somerset 49
Breckland (Norf. and Suff.) 6, 95
Brewers and brewing 7, 92, 94–6, 104, 163
  Cambridge 55, 59, 80, 170, 124
  in colleges 155, 191, 201
  London 106–7
Brickmaking 189, 192
Bridgham (Norf.) 99
Bridgwater (Som.) 124
Brinkley (Cambs.) 88, *177*
Bristol
  fair 116, 199, 124, 140
  population and wealth 2
  Redcliffe 140
  traders 128, 136, 200
Bromehill (Suff.) 134
Brown, Robert 79
Browne, John, of Cambridge 95
Browne, Thomas, of Cambridge 151
Broxbourne (Herts.) 62, 193
Bryket, Patrick 125
Bucer, Martin 80
Buckingham College 63, 75, *see also* Magdalene College
Bucknall (Lincs.) 66
Building
  craftsmen 60, 123, 189–98
  projects
    at churches 69–70, 185–6, 187, 190–8
    at colleges 123, 183–5, 187–98, 202
    for borough corporation 190, *191*, 196–8
  stone 186, 187, 199–200
  timber 189, 198–200
Bull, Master, of Jesus College 71
Buntingford (Herts.) 97, 102
Buntynge, Raff 192
Burcester Priory (Oxon.) 133
Burett, John, of Ickleton 130
Burrough Green (Cambs.) 40, 165
Burwell (Cambs.)
  aliens in 78
  attacks in 82
  church 186, 194
  fair *117*
  grain from 133, 163, 164
  market 86
  quarry 186, 190
  sedge from 161
  wealth 40
Bury, John, of Cambridge 60, 194
Bury St Edmunds (Suff.)
  artists and craftsmen 192
  debt cases 100, 102
  disturbances at 82, 84
  executor from 59
  goods and services from 199
  monks 66

monumental brasses from 193
population and wealth 30, *31–2*, 35
traders 92, 124, 128, 129, 130
trade with 127
Butchers 90, 92, 94–6, 149, 162

Caistor (Lincs.) 102
Cakebred family of Fulbourn 163
Calais 115
Caldecot (Cambs.) 193
Cam, River 18, 58, 139–40, 161, 189–90
Cambridge community
  admissions of freemen 60–2, 80, 199
  borough corporation
    archives 21–2, 60, 85, 178
    building work 190, *191*, 196–8
    courts of law 67, 98–100, 121, 199
    fee farm 43, 50
    income 43, 60, 96, 174, 176–80, 198, 201, 202
    properties 76, 176–80
    purchases at fairs 132
    treasurers' accounts 21–2, 60–2, 89–90, 121–5, 136, 176–80, 196–7
  disputes
    with other towns 91, 161, 201
    with university 52, 81–4, 89, 91–2, 138–9, 151–2
  enclosures 43 n 68, 82
  guilds 71–2
  high steward 62
  market 7, 37, 85, 88, 89, 199
  mayors 19, 52, 59–60, 71, 83, 119, 169, 201
  members of parliament 52, 62, 82, 105, 176
  merchants 7, 52, 105
  occupations 1, 56
  paving act 18, 182
  population and wealth 28–9, *31–2*, 44, 201
  saffron cultivation in 109
  social structure 44
Cambridge churches and parishes
  All Saints by the Castle 69, 74
  All Saints by the Hospital (Jewry) 47, 69, 74, 75, 150, *181*
  appropriation of 71
  Great St Mary's 19, 59, 63
    almshouses 75
    baptisms and burials 47
    building craftsmen at 191–4, 198
    building work at 71, 185, 187, 190, 194
    churchwardens 132
    property 147
    rents in *181*
    university and borough links 71
    university chests in 81
  Holy Sepulchre 69, *181*
  Holy Trinity Church 59, 66, 69, 151, 189

building work 185
churchwardens 132
churchwardens' accounts 196–7
rents in *181*
Jesus parish, rents in 181
Little St Mary's 69, 71
  building work 185
  rents in 181
Our Lady of the Assumption and the English Martyrs 74 n 114
St Andrew the Great 69, 181
St Andrew the Less 69, 181
St Bene't 69, *70*, 71, 80, 192
  building work 185
  parish registers 47, 75
  rents in *181*
St Botolph 63, *181*, 185
St Clement 74, 69, 181, 185
St Edward King and Martyr 47, 69, 70, 71, *181*, 185
St Giles 69, 74, 155, 181
St John Zachary 69, 70
St Michael 66, 69, 71, *181*
St Peter by the Castle 69, 74, 181
see also Cambridge topography, friaries
Cambridge topography
  almshouses 75
  Barnwell Pool 59
  Bridge Street 69
  Butchery 1, 57
  Butter Row 57
  castle 18, 56, 187
  Cordwainer Row 1, 57
  fairs *see* Stourbridge Fair; Midsummer Fair; Garlic Fair
  fields 109, 154, 181, 192
  friaries 74, 75, 145
    Augustinian (Austin) Friars 73, 76, 187
    Carmelite (White) Friars 73, 76, 81, 187, 188
    Dominican (Black) Friars 73, 74, 76, 150, 187
    Franciscan (Grey) Friars 70, 73, 74, 76, 80, *146*, 187
  Gilbertine House of St Edmund's 75, 76
  Great Bridge 18, 56, 58, 59, 80, 161, 189
  hermitages 76
  High Street 19, 56, 58, 69
  hithes 58, 161
  hospitals
    St Anthony and Eligius 73, 75
    St Mary Magdalene 73, 118, 138
    St John's *see* St John's Hospital
  inns 56, 148, 160
  Jesus Green 190
  King's Ditch 181 n 22, 190, 196–8
  market place 56–8, 59, 90, 93, 155
  Merton Hall grange 192
  Midsummer Common 118, 140

mills 58, 59
Milne Street 56, 58, 69
Newmarket Road *118*
paper mill 151
Perse Grammar School 76
Petty Cury 57, 82
Stourbridge Common 118
tollbooth 59, 190, *191*
see also Barnwell Priory; St Radegund's Priory; St John's Hospital; individual colleges
Cambridge University
  academic trades 150–1
  archives 22, 85
  attack on 81
  buildings 19, 183, *184*, 190
  chancellor 67, 107, 137
  commoners 66
  courts of law 67, 91–2, 109, 199
  disputes with town 52, 81–4, 89, 91–2, 138–9, 151–2
  exemption from tax and civic dues 28, 43, 68
  hostels 19, 65, 66, 142, 182
  libraries 19, *184*
  market regulation 89, 91–2
  matriculations 29, 49
  members 52, 149–52, 200
    from overseas *78*, 80
  privileged persons 54, 60, 67–8, 150–2, 201, 202
  self-sufficiency 182
  size 19, 28, 50, 65
  tutorial system 65
  vice-chancellor 19, 28, 54, 67, 83, *90–1*, 169, 170
  see also colleges; individual colleges
Cambridgeshire
  aliens in 76
  landowners 20, 38, 42, 175–6
  parish registers 27, 47–50
  population and wealth 35–6, 44–5
  sub-regions 6, 36, 37–41, *45*, 48, 87, 161, 162, 199
Canefield Park (Essex) 189
Canterbury
  cathedral priory 142, 174
  diocese of *65*
Capell, John, of Stebbing 129–30
Capon, John, of London 110
Carlisle, diocese of *65*
Carver, Philip the 193
Cary, Richard, of Bristol 136
Castle Camps (Cambs.) 38, 186
Catby, John, of London 110
Caxton (Cambs.) 88, 176
Cecil, William, Lord Burghley 137
Chaderton, Hugh 66
Chancery, court of 23, 103–5, 121, 128

Chapman, Hugh, of Cambridge 58, *191*
Chapman, John 59
Chapman, Robert 59
Chapmen 136, 172, *see also* pedlars
Chatteris (Cambs.) 35
Cherry Hinton (Cambs.) 79, 148, 191
  labourers from 190
  limeburner 165
  parish registers *48*
  quarry 186, 187, 190
  rectory 153
Chester 103
Chesterton (Cambs.) 62, 99, 176
  ferry 139
  grain from 153, 163
  innkeeper 165
  rector of 164
  sedge from 161
  traders 92, 93, 124
Chichester, diocese of 65
Childe, Richard, of Harlton 163
Childerely (Cambs.) 42
Chippenham (Cambs.) 20, 82, *117*
Chirche, Thomas, of Bury St Edmunds 192, 193
Chollerton, Edmond 70
Chrishall (Essex) 166
Christ's College 49, 147, 151
  building craftsmen at 192–4
  building work *184*, 187, 189–90, 194
  foundation of 63
  great gate *64*
  Malton manor house 154, 192
  size and income 144, 175
Christaller, Walter 3, 4, 200
Clare Hall or College 56, 70, 71, 119, 133, 163
  building work *184*
  size and income *144, 175*
Clipsham (Rut.) 187
Clopton (Cambs.) 41, 42
Cloth industry 5, 6, 12, 15, 17
  exports 5, 15, 16, 202, 203
  in Cambridge *56*
  in Suffolk 6, 16, 32, 124–7, 132, 140
  wealth from 32, 35–6, 44
Clyfton, Robert 66
Coal 7, 161, 200
Cokkes, William, of London 105
Colchester (Essex) 76, 129, 131, 151
  admissions of freemen 60
  brewing in 95
  cloth industry 16
  hinterland 5–6, 11, 152, 158
  mortality in 49
  occupations in 55
  population and wealth 30, *31*–2, 44
Cole, Richard 79
Coleson, John, of Bury 124

Colleges
  appointments to church livings 176
  building work 123, 183–5, 187–98, 202
  farms 153–4
  fellows, standards of living 149, 185
  food and fuel supplies 152–73
  loan chests 149
  property 175, 180–2, 201, 202
  servants 67–8, 81, 149–50
  size and income 143–5, 175, 202
  tenants 28
  see also Cambridge University; individual colleges
Collyweston (Rut.) 187
Colman, John, of Cornard Magna 125
Colyer, Thomas 75
Colyns, carpenter 192
Combe (Hants.) 162
Comberton (Cambs.) 103, 163, 176
Conington (Cambs.) 194
Cook, Henry, of Chesterton 163
Coope, Robert 60
Corn *see* malt barley; prices, wheat; rents, corn rents
Cornard Magna (Suff.) 125
Corpus Christi College *57*, 78
  accounts 143, 154
  arrears of rent 174, 180, 198, 202
  attack and fear of 81, 82
  bakehouse 155
  building craftsmen at 190, 198
  building work *184*, 185, 188, 190
  Chapel 76
  foundation of 72
  links with parish churches 69–71, 185
  Old Court 19, 63, *147*
  purchases 148, 154, 172
  size and income *144*, 175
  staff employed 81
Cosyn, Thomas 69
Coton (Cambs.) *48*, 154, 166, 189
Coton, Stephen of 172
Cotswolds, cloth industry 16
Cottenham (Cambs.) 15, 82, *117*, 131, 171
Cottered (Herts.) 110
Cotton, Clement 62–3
Coventry (Warw.) 30, 55, 76, 170
  cloth industry 16, 140
  merchants 127, 130, 132, 136, 200
  fairs 115, 116, 134
Coventry and Lichfield, diocese of 65
Credit *see* debt cases
Cressing (Essex) 190, *191*
Crisis mortality 49
Cromwell, Thomas, earl of Essex 82, 119
Crowland Abbey (Lincs.) 63, 66, 75, 131, 151
Croxton (Cambs.) *48*

Cumrew (Cumb.) 130
Dacre, Lord, of Gisland 130
Dale, John, of Cambridge 95
Debt cases 85, 98–103, 136
Deeping (Lincs.) 134
Denny Abbey (Cambs.) 59, 74
Depden (Suff.) 124
Derby 6
Deserted medieval villages 43
Devon, cloth industry 16
Ditton
  bricks from 189
  rector of 164
  see also Fen Ditton; Wood Ditton
Doket, Andrew, president of Queens' College 63, 75
Dorne, John, of Oxford 133
Dover (Kent) 105
Downham Market (Norf.) 82
Downham, palace of bishop of Ely 186, 189
Downing College 21, 22
Draper, Robert, of Cressing *191*
Drinkstone (Suff.) 191
Droitwich (Worcs.) 6
Dry Drayton (Cambs.) 93, 131, 163, 164
Ducheman, Elie 79
Ducheman, Giles 79
Dullingham (Cambs.) *48*, 90, 133, 164
Dunmow (Essex) 190
Dunmow, prior of 133
Dunton Waylett (Essex) 171
Durham
  cathedral priory 142, 153, 179, 195
  diocese of *65*
Dutton, Joanna, of Methwold 166
Dylcock, Henry, of Christ's College 49

Earith (Hunts.) 59
East Hatley (Cambs.) 42
Economic transformation, theories of 13, 203
Edward IV, king of England 176
Elm (Cambs.) *48*, 49
Elsenham (Essex) 190
Elsworth (Cambs.) *48*, 79, 163, 164
Ely (Cambs.) 99
  aliens in 78
  building craftsmen from 190
  cathedral priory 32, 38, 66, 74, 151
  church courts 54
  diocese of *65*
  debt cases *101*
  fairs 116, *117*, 119
    access to 139, 140
    cattle sold at 130
    cloth sold at 125–7
    embroiders at 129
    fish sold at 130, 131

    livestock from 162
    purchases at 134, 148
  parish registers *48*
  population and wealth *31–2*
  market 88, 148
  market place 58
Ely, bishop of 38, 42, 58, 73, 119, 130, 189 n 58, *see also* Alcock, John
  palace of 186, 189
Ely, Reginald, 194
Elyott, William, of Cottered 110
Emmanuel College 74 n 114, 76
Enfield (Midd.) 105
Epidemic disease 14, 15, 17, 61, 202
  in Cambridge 49, 153, 154, 167–70
Erasmus, Desiderius 80, 149
Essewell, John and Ann 59
Essex 35–6, 46, 190–1, 193
Eton College 63, 65, 145, 172, 193
Exeter
  debt cases 101
  diocese of *65*
  economic fortunes 5
  fairs 115, 116
  food supplies 152, 164
Exning (Suff.) 34

Fagius, Paul 80
Fairs
  charters 116
  international 114, 118
  pie-powder courts 137
  purchases at 128–41
  timing of 116–18, 140
  see also individual fairs
Fambeler, Giles, 193
Felmersham (Beds.) 192
Felstead (Essex) 192
Fen Ditton (Cambs.) 78, 140, *see also* Ditton
Fenland *see* Cambridgeshire sub-regions
Fenstanton (Hunts.) *117*
Fermour, John, of Elsworth 79
Filay, Lord John 166
Fish 7, 59, 89, 104, 145–8
  bought at fairs 115–16, 127, 130, 131, 134, 148
Fisher, John 19, 189, 194
Flanders 193
Fletcher, James, of Cambridge 105
Flower, Barnard, of Southwark 193
Folkes, John, of Stetchworth 164
Food supplies
  to Cambridge 4, 7, 107, 152–8, 161–73
  to London 4, 35–6, 46, 105–8, 112, 152, 158, 162
Fordham (Cambs.) *117*, 130
Fordingbridge (Hants.) 171

Index

Forest of Arden 154
Fothed, John, master of Michaelhouse 189
Fowlmere (Cambs.) *48*, 95, *117*
Foxton (Cambs.) 88, 93–6, 113, *117*
Foyster, George, of Cambridge 59, 121
Francis, Nicholas 70
Fraternities *see* Guilds
Frensshman, Janyn 81
Fulbourn (Cambs.) *48*, 78, *101*, 110, 148, 163
Fuel supplies
  to Cambridge 4, 7, 158–61, 164–5, 167, 173, *200*
  to London 4, 112, 159

Gamlingay (Cambs.) 33–4, 189 n 5
Garlic Fair *117*, 119, 124
Gawge, Thomas, of Dunmow 190
Ghein, Peeter Vanden of Mechlin 193
Gildrigg, Thomas, of London 106
Gill, of Cambridge 95
Gilson, William, of Stapleford 109
Girlinge, John, of Stradbroke 130
Girton (Cambs.) 61, 62, 90, 93, 164, 190
Glasse, John, 190
Glastonbury Abbey 142
Glaswright, Robert, of Waldingfield Magna 125
Glaziers 191–3
Gloucester 100
Godfrey, Garrett, of Cambridge 80, 133, 151
Godmanchester (Hunts.) *33*, 100, 103, 109
Godshouse (later Christ's College) 63
Godyn, John, of London 98
Goldwyn, Robert 110
Gonville Hall (Gonville and Caius College) 58, 69, 70, 155, 188
  building work *184*
  size and income *144*, *175*
Goodwyn, Matthew, of Ipswich 136
Grain, searches of 170
Grantchester (Cambs.) 66, 79, 93, 110, 172
  King's College Farm 106, 153–4
  mill 192
  produce from 106, 153–4, 164, 171
Great Abington (Cambs.) 86, 88, *117*, 171
Great Chesterford (Essex) 194
Great Eversden and Little Eversden (Cambs.) 164, 185, 186
Great Shelford (Cambs.) 95, 103, *see also* Shelford
Great Waldingfield (Suff.) 125
Great Wilbraham (Cambs.) 86, *117*
Great Yarmouth (Norf.) 5, 78, 116, 166, 169
Grene, Edward 127
Gryme, Margaret, of Cambridge 121
Grymstow, tenant of King's College 172
Guilden Morden (Cambs.) 40, 74, 81
Guilds 52, 71–2, 84, *93*, *112*, *147*

Gunwade (Northants.) 190
Gybson, baker 166
Gyll, Henry, of Cumrew 130

Hacumlyn, Robert, of King's College 194
Haddenham (Cambs.) 40, 102, 129
Hadleigh (Suff.) 6, 30, *31–2*, 102, 125, 136
Hadstock (Essex) 95, 189
Halifax (Yorks., W.R.) 115
Halstead (Essex) 190
Hamond, John *54*, 55
Hampole (Yorks., W.R.) 187
Hanseatic traders 104, 145
Harleston, Roger, MP, of Cambridge 82
Harlton (Cambs.) 163, 186
Harris family of Elsworth 163
Harrison, Dyrik, of London 193
Harrison, William 16, 34, 116, 119, 159
Harrowden (Northants.) 133
Harston (Cambs.) 106
Hartley, Matthew, of York 136
Hartleys, tenant of King's College 171
Harvest failure 17, 166, 170, 202
Harvy, John, of Stetchworth 164
Harward, William, of Halstead 190
Haselden, Thomas 81
Haslingfield (Cambs.) 76, 186, 190
Hatcher, Dr 178
Hauxton (Cambs.) 108
Haverhill (Suff.) *33*, 95, *117*, 189, 191
Hayrman, Thomas 60
Henry VI, king of England 56, 63, 176
Henry VIII, king of England 63, 143
Hereford, diocese of *65*
Hertford 91
Hertfordshire 35–6
Hessewell, John 60
Higham (Suff.) 126
Higham Ferrers (Northants.) 194
High Wycombe (Bucks.) 112
Hildersham (Cambs.) 86, 88, *117*
Hinderclay (Suff.) 11
Hinton *see* Cherry Hinton
Hinxton (Cambs.) *48*, 92, 108
Histon (Cambs.) 93, 105
Hitchin (Herts.) 102, 192
Hithe, Thomas, of Dullingham 164
Hixon, John 155
Hoddesson, Christopher 123
Hodylston, Thomas, of London 110
Holton, Thomas, of Nayland 125
Hone, Galyon, of Southwark 193
Hopper, William, of Chrishall 166
Horne, Francis van 80
Horneby, Henry 69
Horningsea (Cambs.) 140, 192
Horseheath (Cambs.) *48*, 79

231

Horstead (Norf.) 171
Houte, Adrian van den, glass designer of Mechlin 193
Howden (Yorks., E.R.) 116
Howsden, John, of Grantchester 110
Huddleston (Yorks., W.R.) 187
Huddleston, Sir John, vice-chamberlain 186
Hulme, near Horning (Norf.) 66
Humphrey, duke of Gloucester 145
Hunt, Richard, of London 127
Huntingdon 30, 34, 35, 91
  aliens in 78
  fair *117*
  Hart Inn 192
  market 88
  population and wealth *31–2*
  purchases at 146
  traders 128
Huntingdonshire, 35–6
Hynde, Francis, esquire 123
Hynde, John, of Madingley 62, 186

Ickleton (Cambs.) 40, 74, 82, 92
  fairs *117*, 119, 130
  saffron cultivation 108, 110
Immigration into Cambridge
  from abroad 7, 76–81
  from elsewhere in England 7, 60–2, 65–7
Impington (Cambs.) 86, *117*
Inns 32, 34, 56, 137, 148, 160
Ipswich (Suff.) 30, 82, 127, 136, 146, 151
  population and wealth *31–2*
  purchases from 148
Isle of Ely 35, 37, 38, 45
Isleham (Cambs.) 30, 153, 171, 194

Jacob, William, of Sudbury 125
Jakenett, Thomas 75
Jeffrey, Friar 151
Jesus College 71, 73, 75, 109, 145
  building work *184*, 187, 189
  foundation of 63
  size and income *144*, 175
Johnson, David, of Cambridge 105
Johnson, William 80
Joiner, Nicholas 189

Kendal (Westm.) 125, 146
Kett, Robert 82, 109
King, Thomas, of London 105
King's Cliffe (Northants.) 187, 190
King's College 62, 176
  accounts *see* King's College, Mundum Books
  baker 155
  building craftsmen at 190, 192, 193
  building work 44, 183, 184, 188
  Chapel 70, 141, *183*, 187

  building craftsmen at 193, 194, *195*
  building work *184*, 194
  complaints against 82
  estates 30, 153
  food supplies 153, 162–6, 203
  foundation of 19, 63
  fuel supplies 159–161
  London houses 145, 176
  members 65, 66, 149, 194
  Mundum Books 21, 143, 152, 154, 157, 167, 173, 199
  purchases 145, 146, 147, 172
  at fairs 131, 134
  rents 170–1
  servants 150
  size and income 144, 175
  site 18, 43, 56, 63, 69
  wheat prices 167–9, 170–1
  wills 54, 149
  see also Grantchester, King's College Farm
King's Hall 64
  accounts 21, 143, 152, 156, 167, 173, 199
  building craftsmen at 191, 192
  building work *184*, 187, 189,
  entertainments 150
  estates 153
  feasts 72
  food supplies 155–7, 162–3, 165–6, 203
  fuel supplies 159–161, 164–5
  Great Gate *146*, 189
  links with parish churches 71
  oratory 70
  purchases 147
  purchases at fairs 131, 132, 139
  servants 150, 155
  size and income 144, *175*
King's Lynn (Norf.) 18, 58, 130, 139, 146, 203
  aliens in 78
  bells cast at 193
  debt cases 100, 102
  disputes with Cambridge borough 91, 161, 201
  fair 119, 130
  friaries 74
  guild of Holy Trinity 59
  links of Cambridge burgess with 59
  merchants 126, 129
  population and wealth 30, *31–2*
  trade 104–5, 107, 146, 148, 161, 189, 199, 200
Kingshurst (Warw.) 133
Kingston (Cambs.) *117*, 186, 189
Kirby, Richard, of Landbeach 82
Kirtling (Cambs.) 106, 186, 189
Knapwell (Cambs.) 164

Lake District 16, 125
Lakenheath (Suff.) 161

Index

Lancaster, Duchy of 142
Lancaster, Thomas, of, duke of Clarence 133
Landbeach (Cambs.) 20, *48*, 49, 154
  enclosures at 43 n 68, 82
Landwade (Cambs.) 63
Lane, Thomas 69
Langley, Edward, of Lolworth 163
Lavenham (Suff.) 6, 32
Lea, River 105
Leather trades, in Cambridge 7, *56*, *78*
Leedes, John 69
Leicester 55, 127, 142
Leland, John 105, 115
Leonard, of Christ's College 151
Leynton, John, MP for Cambridge 176
Lime 186
Lincoln 10, 66
  dean of 155
  diocese of *65*
Line, John, of Cambridge 161
Linton (Cambs.) 34, 88, 93, 113
  debt cases at 98
  fairs *117*, 119
  markets 93–6
  parish registers *48*
  population and wealth *33*, 34, 40
  saffron cultivation 108, 109
  social structure 95–6
Little Abington (Cambs.) 40
Littleport (Cambs.) 161
Livestock trade 115, 129–30, 134, 162
Living standards *see* Standards of living
Lolworth (Cambs.) 41, 163
London 10, 16, 30, 61
  aliens in 77, 79–80
  artists and craftsmen 192
  Baynard Castle 145
  Blackwell Hall 136
  bookseller 133
  brewers 106–7
  building craftsmen 192, 200
  courts 98, 100
  diocese of *65*
  exports 16
  Gray's Inn 62
  Greenwich 133, 189
  merchants and tradesmen 5, 6, 18, 86, 104–13, 145
    birthplaces of 83
    companies 128
    debt cases 98–103, 172, 201
    fairs, trading at 116, 120, 127–9, 130, 132, 135–6, 200
    freemen of Cambridge 61
    grocers 59, 105, 110–11, 128, 136
    mercer 103, 137
    pewterers 145
  population and wealth 2, 5, 9
  purchases from 134, 143, 147,149, 152, 172, 201
  rents 174
  St Bartholomew's Fair 119, 137
  Southwark 147, 193
  Steelyard 145
  Strand, parish of Our Lady St Ursula 193
  Stratford-le-Bow 92
  timber from 189
  trading links 4, 7, 104–13, 140, 141, 201, 203
  Westminster 55, 114, 128, 145, 193, 202
Long Melford (Suff.) 6, 32
Loveday, John, of Burrough Green 165
Loveday, Thomas, carpenter of Sudbury 190–1
Low Countries, corn exports to 200
Lowestoft (Suff.) 146
Lyne, Richard *53*, 55, 76, 181 n 22
Lynn *see* King's Lynn

Madingley (Cambs.) *48*, 61, 62, 164
Madingley Hall 186, 189
Magdalene College 76
  building work *184*
  size and income *144*, *175*
  see also Buckingham College
Malaria 48
Malt barley 23, 33, 51, 86, 104–7, 113, 201, 203
Malton (Cambs.) 154, 163, 192
Manfeld, John, of Cambridge 121
Mannyng, Walter, of Stowe 125
March (Cambs.) 48, 129
Margaret, Queen, of Anjou 63
Markets
  charters 86, 88
  contraction of 18
  formal 85
  informal 85
  networks 3, 85, 17, 113, 116
  regulation 89–97
  timing of 88
Mark, John 106
Mechlin 193
Melbourn (Cambs.) *48*
Mepal (Cambs.) 37
Mercantile networks 18
Mere, John, of Cambridge 168
Methwold (Norf.) 166
Michaelhouse 64, 66, 67, 69, 71, 75
  master of 189
  size and income *144*, *175*
Middleburg 105
Midlands, trade with Cambridge 7
Midsummer Fair 92, *117*, 118, 130, 131, 132, 138
Mildenhall (Suff.) *33*, *117*
Mills 7, 58, 59, 96, 151, 192

Milton (Cambs.) 40, 41, 86, *117*, 190
Monks Eleigh (Suff.) 125
Monumental brasses 193
Morehouse, Robert 60
Morley, John 60
Morton, William, of Peterborough Abbey 134
Mountford, Sir William, of Kingshurst 133, 139

Nayland (Suff.) 125, 126
Nede, John 66
Needham Market (Suff.) 127
Nethermyll, Julian, of Coventry 127, 136
Newbury (Berks.) 6
Newcastle-upon-Tyne 161, 179, 200
Newman, Alewyn, of Cambridge 194
Newmarket (Suff.) *33*, 34, 106
  debt cases 100, 103
  fairs *117*
  saffron cultivation 109
  Swan Inn 110
Newport (Essex), Cold Fair 110, 119, 134
Newport Pagnell (Bucks.) 100
Newton by Leverington (Cambs.) *101*
Nicholson, James, of Southwark 193
Nicholson, John 192
Nicholson, Sygar 80
Norfolk 15, 35–6, 46, 78, 92, *101*
North, Lord Edward 106, 186
Northallerton (Yorks., N.R.) 158
Northampton 30, *31–2*, 55, 91, 100, 199
Northumberland, duke of 58
Northumberland, earl of 130
Norwich 66, 82, 102, 146, 169, 172
  aliens in 78
  artists and craftsmen 192, 193
  diocese of 65
  disturbances in 166
  Dominican Friary 76
  economic fortunes 5
  goods and services from 199
  impact on region 10
  population and wealth 2, 30
  monks from 66
  saffron cultivation 109
Nottingham, Lenton Fair 116, 120

Oakington (Cambs.) 15, 131, 164
Ogbourn, prior of 145
Orwell (Cambs.) *117*, 186, 189
Oundle (Northants.), fair 134
Outlawe, Thomas 198
Over (Cambs.) 61, 74
Owellyng, Grafton, of Coventry 127
Oxford 30, 44, 55, 168, 202
  colleges 69, 153, 176, 179
  fairs 116, 129, 133, 135
  Magdalen School 135–6

Merton College 69
Oseney Abbey 134, 174, 179
religious houses 72
St Scholastica's day riot at 83
University 19, 67, 151
University College 179
Oxford, earl of 38

Papworth Everard (Cambs.) 40, 41
Parker, Matthew, archbishop of Canterbury 71, 185
Paston family 137, 143
Paston, John 105, 172
Paston, Margaret 172
Payton, Dame Elizabeth, of Isleham 30
Peasants' Revolt 18, 22, 43, 81, 84, 89, 138
Pedlars 123–4, *see also* chapmen
Pembroke College 70
  building work *184*
  size and income 144, 175
Peterborough (Northants.) 151
  Abbey 131–3, 139 137, 200
  fair 134
Peterhouse
  accounts 143
  brewhouse 155
  building work at *184*, 190
  estates 153
  foundation of 63
  fuel supplies 161
  hall bell 193
  links with parish churches 69, 71, 185
  purchases 131, 148, 172
  servants 150
  size and income *144*, 175
Petrisburgh, Richard, of Colchester 129
Petyt, John, of Shudy Camps 164
Physwick Hostel 64
Pilgrim, Nicholas 80
Plague *see* epidemic disease
Pope, Francis 123
Portsmouth (Hants.) 66
Potton (Beds.) 33, 124
Prices 12, 14, 16, 173
  at Cambridge *168*, 169
  control of 89, 92
  fuel 167
  wheat 11, 14, 167–9, 170–1
Privy Council 18, 106, 170
Puckeridge (Herts.) 74
Pykegrome, Joyce, of London 133

Quarries 186–7, 190, 198
Queens' College 56, 176
  brewhouse 155, 191
  building craftsmen at 190, 193
  building work 183, *184*, 187–8, 189, 190

Index

complaints against 82
foundation of 19, 63
Front Court 188, 189
size and income of 144, *175*
president of 72, 75
purchases 131, 147
servants 150

Rampton (Cambs.) 93, *117*, 119, 164
Ramsey (Hunts.) *33*
Ramsey Abbey 79, 188
Rangyll, Thomas, of Harston 106
Rankyn, Hugh 74
Raynbald, William, of Ipswich 127
Rayner family of Foxton 96
Reach (Cambs.) 82, 133
  fair *117*, 119, 124, 130, 134, 140, 162
  quarry 186, 190
  sedge from 161
Reading (Berks.) 44, 49, 55, 193
Rebuilding Acts 182
Recession 14, 15, 16
Reculver, Richard, of East Greenwich 189, 192
Rede, Roger of Hinton 148
Rents 12, 15–18, 109
  corn rents 153, 171–2, 203
  in Cambridge 174–82, 201–2
  in Cambridge market 89–90, 113
  in Stourbridge Fair 122–3, 202
Rete, Richard, of Cressing *191*
Richard III, king of England 71
Richardson, William, of Cambridge 105
Richardson, William, of Wakefield 136
Ripon (Yorks., W.R.) 115
Roads 34, 42, 94
Robinson, John, of Westminster 128
Robynson, Richard, of London 128
Rochester, diocese of *65*
Rogger, William, of Cambridge 149
Romford (Essex) 103
Rotherham, Thomas, archbishop 71
Royston (Herts.) 33, 34, 105–6
  fairs *117*, 134
  prices at *168*, 169
  prior of 130
Ruislip (Midd.) 176
Rutland 46
Ryley, John, of Coventry *126*
Ryley, Thomas, of Coventry *126*, 127

Saddeler, Robert, of Whittlesford 96
Saffron 6, 23, 32, 51, 108–13, 201, 203
  traded at fairs 110, 131, 136
Saffron Walden (Essex) 6, 34, 76, 95–6, 136
  building craftsmen from 191
  church of St Mary the Virgin 110–1
  debt cases 100, 102

disputes with Cambridge borough 91
fairs *117*, 136
guild of Holy Trinity *112*
market 88
population and wealth 30, *31–2*, 35
saffron cultivation 108–13, 203
timber from 189
traders 97, 113, 124, 128
St Albans (Herts.) *31–2*, 84
St Benet of Hulme (Norf.) 66
St Catharine's College 63
  building work 183, *184*
  size and income *144*, *175*
St Etheldreda 119
St Ives (Hunts.) *33*, 148
  fairs 114, *117*, 130
  prices at *168*, 169
St Ivo 34
St John's College
  building craftsmen at 191–3
  building work *184*, 187, 189, 190–4
  estates 174
  foundation of 63, 73, 75
  master 155
  purchases 147, 172
  servants 150
  size and income *144*, 175
St John's Fair *see* Midsummer Fair
St John's Hospital 192
  building craftsmen at 193
  estates 154
  fishponds 59
  influence of 73–5
  master 166
  purchases 134, 148, 172
  rents 174
  saffron cultivation 109
  site of 63
  size and income 144, 145
  tradesmen at 151
St Neots (Hunts.) *33*, 100, 106, *117*
St Osyth (Essex) 66, 74
St Radegund's Priory 99, 145, 155
  buildings *73*
  dissolution 63, 75
  estates 154
  hostel of 182
  purchases 131, 132, 148, 172
  servants 150
  tithes 74, 109
  see also Garlic Fair
St Rohesia 34
Salisbury 10
  bishop of 143
  cloth 146, 147
  diocese of *65*
  fairs 116, 129

235

Sanders, John, of Coventry 127
Sands, Doctor 71
Sawbridgeworth (Herts.) 109
Sawston (Cambs.) 95, 148
Sawston Hall 186
Saxton, Christopher *36*
Say, Sir John, of Broxbourne 62
Scarlett, John 66
Scote, John, of Whittlesford 96
Sedge 161
Sereman, John, of Boxworth 74
Serle, Henry, of Histon 105
Seymour, Edward, Protector and duke of Somerset 82
Shalford (Essex) 189
Shaw (Berks.) 6
Shelford (Cambs.) 66, 93, *see also* Great Shelford
Shepreth (Cambs.) 92, 93, 96
Shingay (Cambs.) 42
Shouldham (Norf.) 59
Shudy Camps (Cambs.) *48*, 164
Siberch, John, of Cambridge 80, 151
Sidney Sussex College 76
Slegge, Edward, MP for Cambridge 176
Small towns 2–3, 6, 33–4, 100, 112, 199
Smyth, Richard, of Cambridge 146
Smythe, John, of Bristol 136
Soham (Cambs.) 40, 194
Somer, Henry, chancellor of the exchequer 79, 106
Somersham (Hunts.) 66
Southampton 125
Southwold (Suff.) 127
Sowode, William 71
Spalding (Lincs.) 66
Spalding, prior of 162
Speryng, Nicholas 80
Spices 7, 131, 136, 147, 148, *see also* saffron
Stablehill, John 128
Stafford (Staffs.) 128
Stamford (Lincs.) 30, *31–2*, 134
Standards of living, 15, 17, 18, 85–6, 113, 183
Standon (Herts.) 105
Stanton, Hervey de 69
Stapleford (Cambs.) 92, 109
Stationers *see* bookbinders and booksellers
Stebbing (Essex) 129
Steeple Bumpstead (Essex) 130, 148
Steeple Morden (Cambs.) 81
Stetchworth (Cambs.) 164
Stoke by Clare (Suff.) 194
Stokes, John, of Cressing *191*
Stone *see* building stone
Stone, John, of London 106
Stour Valley (Suff.) 35
Stourbridge Chapel *118*, 138
Stourbridge Fair 74, 92, 114, 116–41, 200, 201
  access to 139
  booths 22, 58, 62, 120, 196
  cloth sold at 125–9, 131–2
  college purchases at 131
  fish sold at 130
  grant 118
  importance of 119
  income from 202
  proclamation 137–8
  saffron sold at 110
Stow Bardolph (Norf.) 102
Stow-cum-Quy (Cambs.) 92
Stowe (Suff.) 125
Stowmarket (Suff.) 82, 127
Stow-on-the-Wold (Glos.) 128
Stradbroke (Suff.) 130
Stratford (Essex) 126
Stratford-upon-Avon (Warw.) 198
Stretham (Cambs.) *48*
Stuntney (Cambs.) 190
Sturbridge Fair *see* Stourbridge Fair
Sturgeon, Thomas 190, 192, 194
Sudbury (Suff.) 74, 82, 125, 191
Suffolk 7, 35–6, *101*, 190–1
  cloth industry 6, 16, 32, 124–7, 132, 140
Sutton in the Isle (Cambs.) 37, *48*, 129
Swaffham Bulbeck and Swaffham Prior (Cambs.) *117*, 163, 186, 190
Swavesey (Cambs.) 88, 99, *117*, 119, 164
Symond, Nicholas 79–80
Sympson, William, of London 61
Symton family of Foxton 96
Syre, William, of Coton 166

Tayler, Dr John, master of St John's College 155
Taylor, Thomas, of London 61
Teversham (Cambs.) 40
Textiles *see* cloth industry
Thaxted (Essex) 6, 35, 100, 112, 189, 192
Thefdale (near Tadcaster, Yorks., W.R.) 187
Thetford (Norf.) 34, 127
Thetford Priory 130, 131, 132–4, 139, 200
Thevesdale *see* Thefdale
Thomas, Lord Audley, of Walden 76
Thorney (Cambs.) 66
Thorney Abbey 188
Thriplow (Cambs.) 92, 93, 98, 108
Thünen, Johann von 4, 173, 200
Tithes 74, 108–9, 154–5, 164
Tolls 17, 90–1, 97
Tompson, carpenter 192
Tooley, Henry, of Ipswich 127, 136
Towns
  agents of modernisation 8, 9
  civic government finances 17
  definition of 1
  economies 17

encouraging specialised production 9
hierarchies 1–2, 3, 30–4
hinterlands 3, 4, 6
in feudal society 8–9
role in consumer behaviour 10
see also small towns; urban decline debate
Trassillion, Anthony, of Westminster 193
Tresylyan *see* Trassillion
Trinity College
  accounts 167
  building craftsmen at 192, 194
  building work *184,* 187–90
  complaints against 82
  estates of 110, 187
  foundation of 63–4
  fuel supplies 160
  Great Court *146*
  purchases 131, 132, 139, 147
Trinity Hall 56, 70, 81
  baker 155
  building work *184*
  links with parish churches 71
  size and income *144, 175*
Trumpington (Cambs.) 66, 93, 99, *117,* 190
Trussell, Thomas, of Coventry 127
Tunstead (Norf.) 66
Turner, William 192
Turnour, Agnes, of Depden 124
Turnour, William, of Hadleigh 125
Turves 161

Upminster (Essex) 103
Upwell (Norf.) 100
Urban decline debate 16–18, 24, 43, 50, 174, 182–3, 201
Utynam, John 193

Vaux, Sir Thomas 133
Vavasour, Henry 187
Vellert, Dierick, of Antwerp 193
Ventris, Thomas, of Cambridge 105
Vere, John de 139
Verley, Robert, of Foxton 96
Vessey, Henry 59

Wages and wage-earners 14–15, 45–6, 51, 68, 123, 195–8, 201
Wake, Gerard 80
Wakefield (Yorks., W.R.) 115, 136
Walden *see* Saffron Walden
Waldersea (Cambs.) 189
Walles, William, of Fowlmere 95
Walsingham (Norf.) 66, 136
Waltham Cross (Herts.) 103
Ware (Herts.) 74, 105
Waren, Christopher, of Coventry 127
Warkworth, John 69

Warner, Mr 127
Wars of the Roses 82
Washingborough (Lincs.) 155
Wastell, John 194
Waterbeach (Cambs.) 59, 61, 90
Weldon (Northants.) 187, 190
Welles, Thomas, of Foxton 96
Wellis, Thomas, of Burrough Green 165
Wells (Som.) 174, 202
Wells-next-the-Sea (Norf.) 146 n. 18
Wendy, Thomas, of Haslingfield 76, 186
Wentworth (Cambs.) 37
West Berkshire 41, 46
West Raynham (Norf.) 66
West Riding of Yorkshire, cloth industry 16, 115
West Wratting (Cambs.) 82
Westley Waterless (Cambs.) 40
Westminster *see* London, Westminster
Weston Colville (Cambs.) 74
Wethersfield (Essex) 130, 189
Weybridge (Essex) 189
Whiteby, John, of Whittlesford 96
Whittlesford (Cambs.) 88, 92, 93, 95–6, 98, 113, *117*
Whittlesford Bridge (Cambs.) 95, 96–7, 98, 113
Wicken (Cambs.) 86, *117,* 129
Wiggenhall (Norf.) 100
Wigmore, William, of Cambridge 81
Wilbraham (Cambs.) 90, 92, 164
Wilburton (Cambs.) 15, 40, 42, 92, 193
Williamson, Francis, of Southwark 193
Williamson, Nicholas 79
Willingham (Cambs.) *48,* 102, 164
Willoughby family, of Wollaton 133, 134
Wiltshire 15, 77
Wimpole (Cambs.) 164
Winchester (Hants.) 114, 146, 147
  diocese of *65*
Winchester College 172
Winfarthing Park (Norf.) 189, 190
Wisbech (Cambs.) 30, *31–2,* 78, 101–2, 126, 134
Witcham (Cambs.) 37
Wodecock, Richard, of Cambridge 149
Wodelarke, Robert, provost of King's 63
Wolford, Adam 125
Wollaton (Notts.) 133
Wolleman, John, of Cambridge 154
Wolsey, Thomas, cardinal 82
Women
  brewing and selling ale 95, 124
  college servants 150
  supplying colleges 163
Wood Ditton (Cambs.) 133, *see also* Ditton
Wood, John 62
Woodville, Elizabeth, Queen 63
Woolpit (Suff.) 130
Worcester 83

diocese of *65*
Worlington (Suff.) 189
Wramp, John, of London 193
Wright, Richard, of Bury St Edmunds 192
Wycliffe, John 19
Wye (Kent), fair 115
Wymondham (Norf.) 30, *31–2*, 82

Yardlay, Andrew, of London 136
Yeve, Thomas, of Swavesey 164

Yole, Thomas, of London 106
York 2, 10
   admissions of freemen 60–1, 83
   aliens in 78
   diocese of *65*
   economic fortunes 5, 16
   fairs 116
   food supplies 164
   rents 179
   traders 132, 136, 172